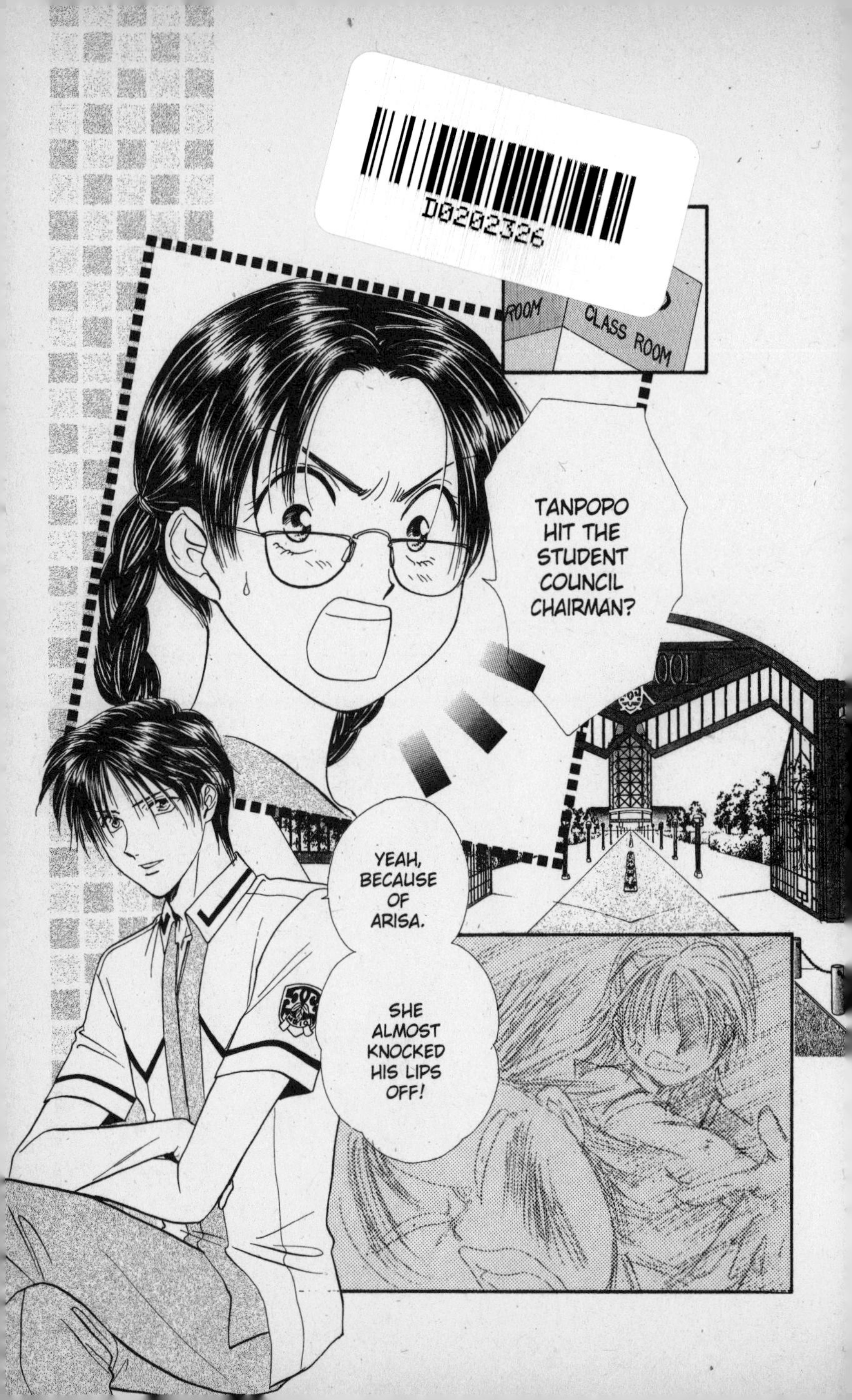
CLASS ROOM
ROOM
TANPOPO HIT THE STUDENT COUNCIL CHAIRMAN?
YEAH, BECAUSE OF ARISA.
SHE ALMOST KNOCKED HIS LIPS OFF!

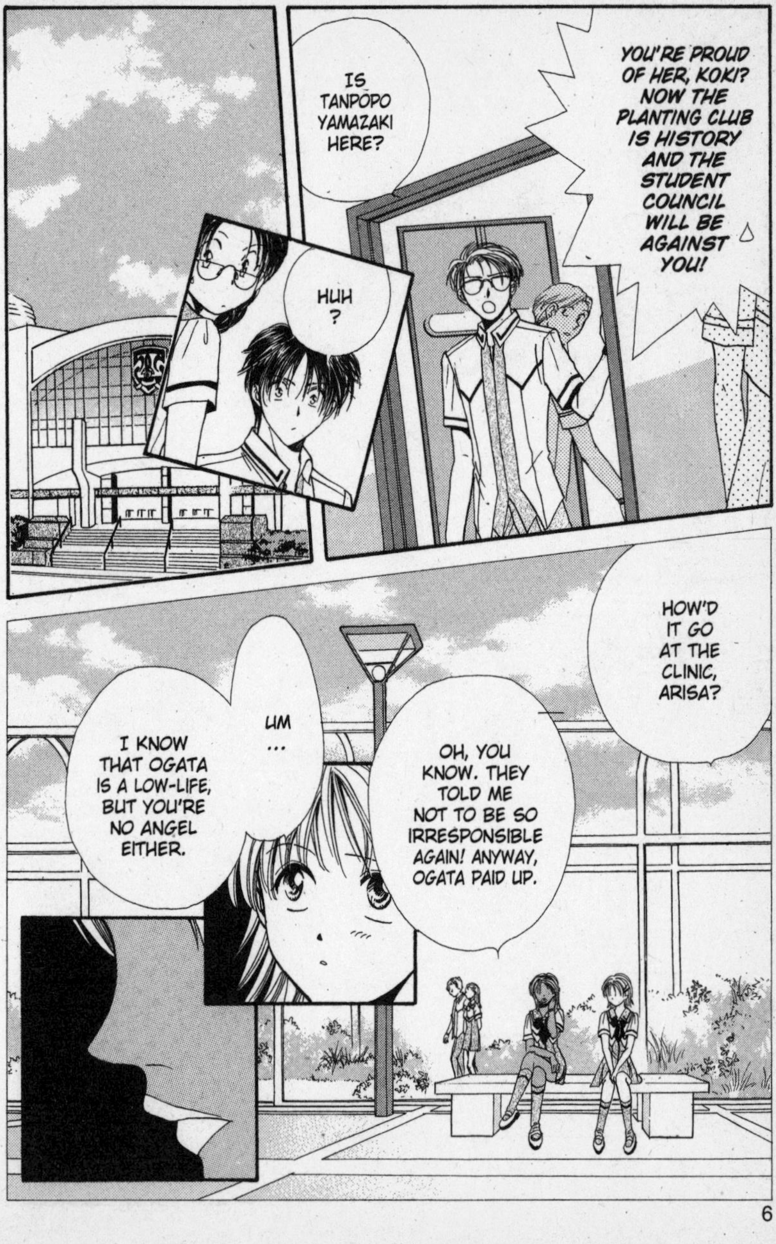
YOU'RE PROUD OF HER, KOKI? NOW THE PLANTING CLUB IS HISTORY AND THE STUDENT COUNCIL WILL BE AGAINST YOU!
IS TANPOPO YAMAZAKI HERE?
HUH ?
HOW'D IT GO AT THE CLINIC, ARISA?
OH, YOU KNOW. THEY TOLD ME NOT TO BE SO IRRESPONSIBLE AGAIN! ANYWAY, OGATA PAID UP.
UM ...
I KNOW THAT OGATA IS A LOW-LIFE, BUT YOU'RE NO ANGEL EITHER.

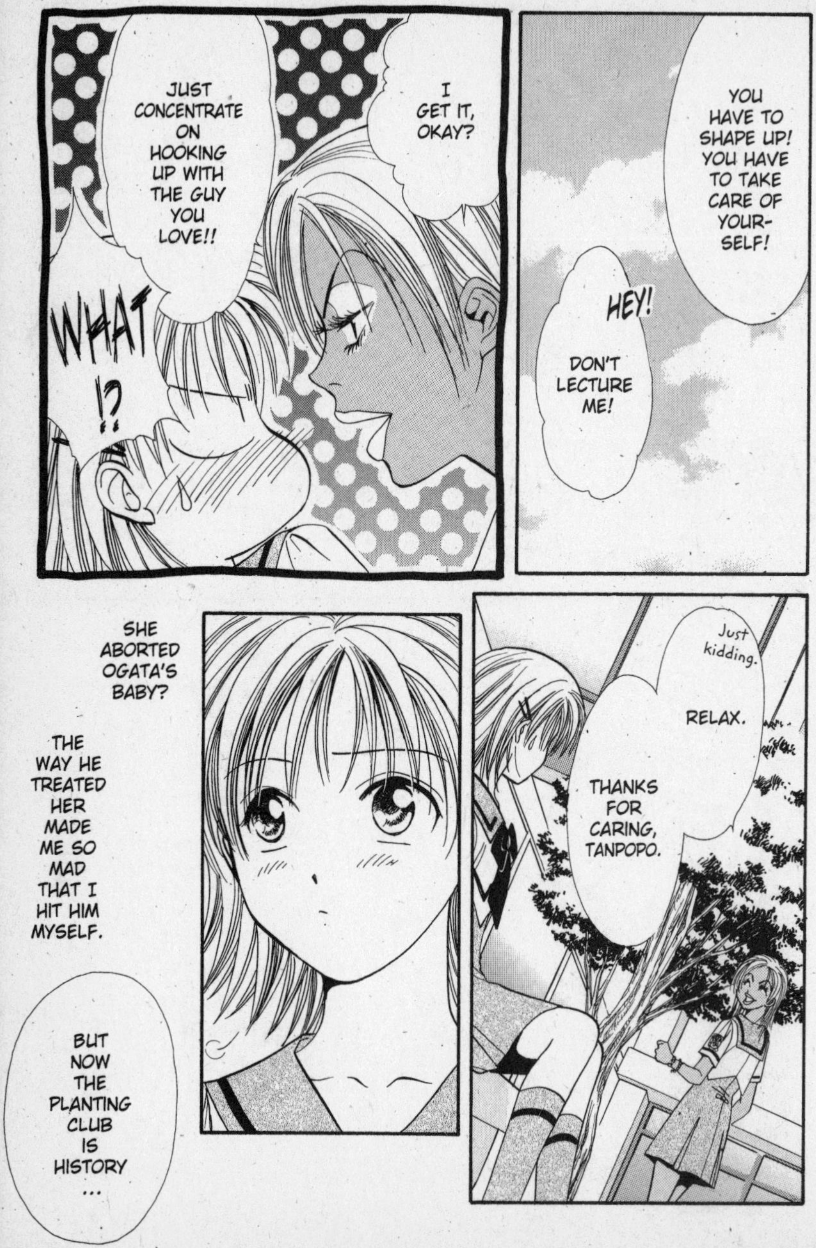
YOU HAVE TO SHAPE UP! YOU HAVE TO TAKE CARE OF YOUR-SELF!
HEY!
DON'T LECTURE ME!
I GET IT, OKAY?
JUST CONCENTRATE ON HOOKING UP WITH THE GUY YOU LOVE!!
WHAT!?
Just kidding.
RELAX.
THANKS FOR CARING, TANPOPO.
SHE ABORTED OGATA'S BABY?
THE WAY HE TREATED HER MADE ME SO MAD THAT I HIT HIM MYSELF.
BUT NOW THE PLANTING CLUB IS HISTORY...

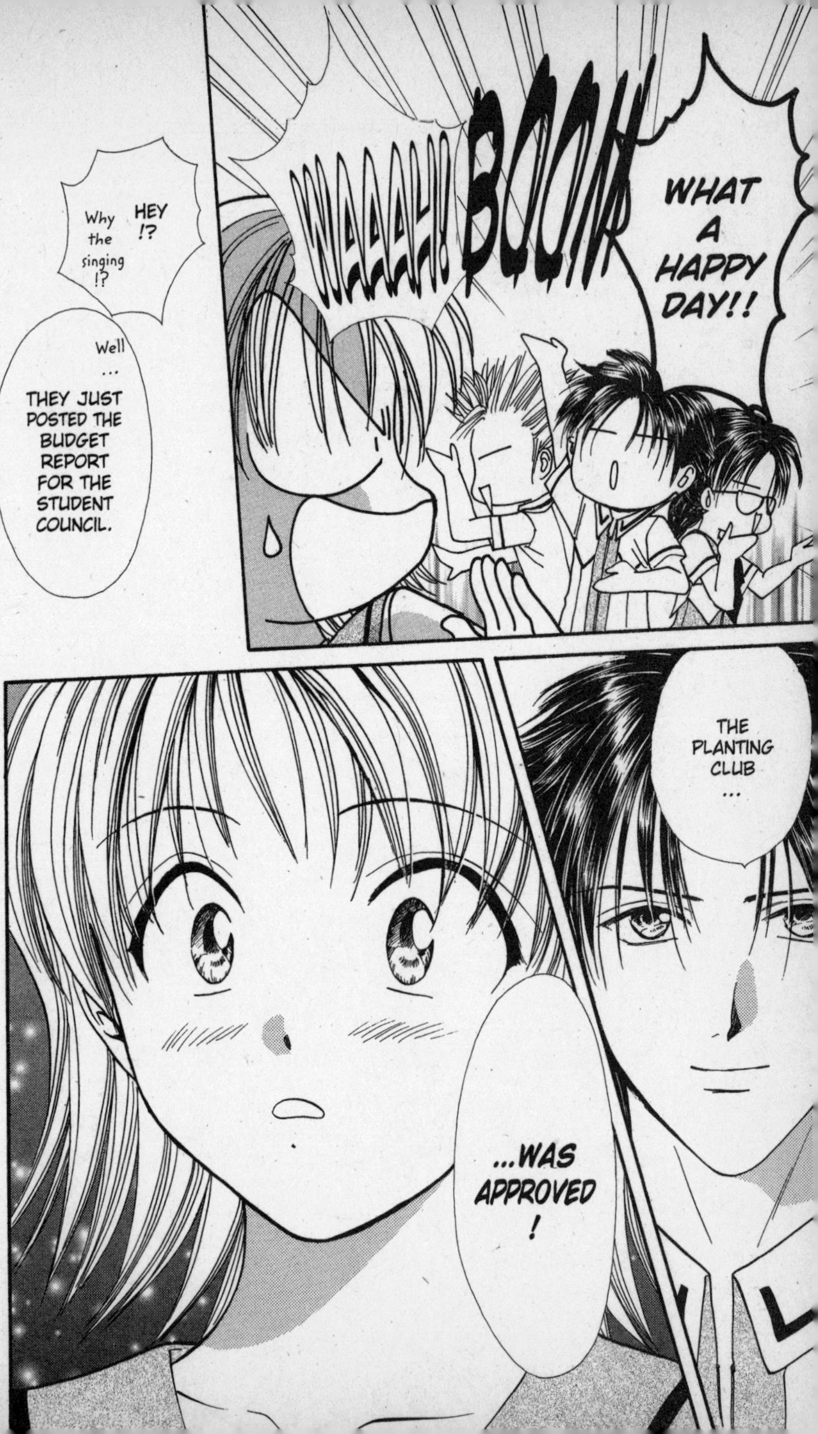
WHAT A HAPPY DAY!!
BOOM
WAAAAH!
HEY !?
Why the singing !?
Well ...
THEY JUST POSTED THE BUDGET REPORT FOR THE STUDENT COUNCIL.
THE PLANTING CLUB ...
...WAS APPROVED !

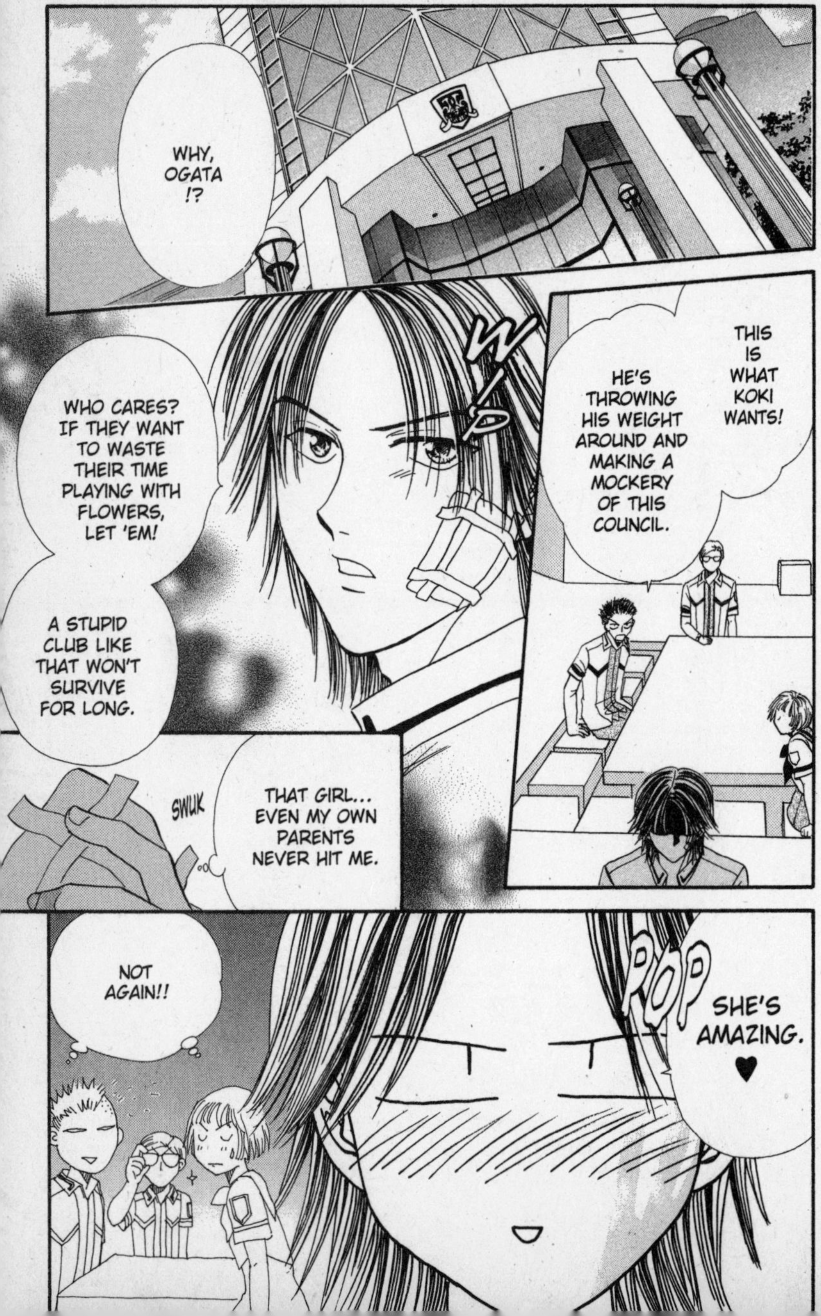
WHY, OGATA !?
THIS IS WHAT KOKI WANTS!
HE'S THROWING HIS WEIGHT AROUND AND MAKING A MOCKERY OF THIS COUNCIL.
WHIP
WHO CARES? IF THEY WANT TO WASTE THEIR TIME PLAYING WITH FLOWERS, LET 'EM!
A STUPID CLUB LIKE THAT WON'T SURVIVE FOR LONG.
THAT GIRL... EVEN MY OWN PARENTS NEVER HIT ME.
SWUK
POP
SHE'S AMAZING. ♥
NOT AGAIN!!

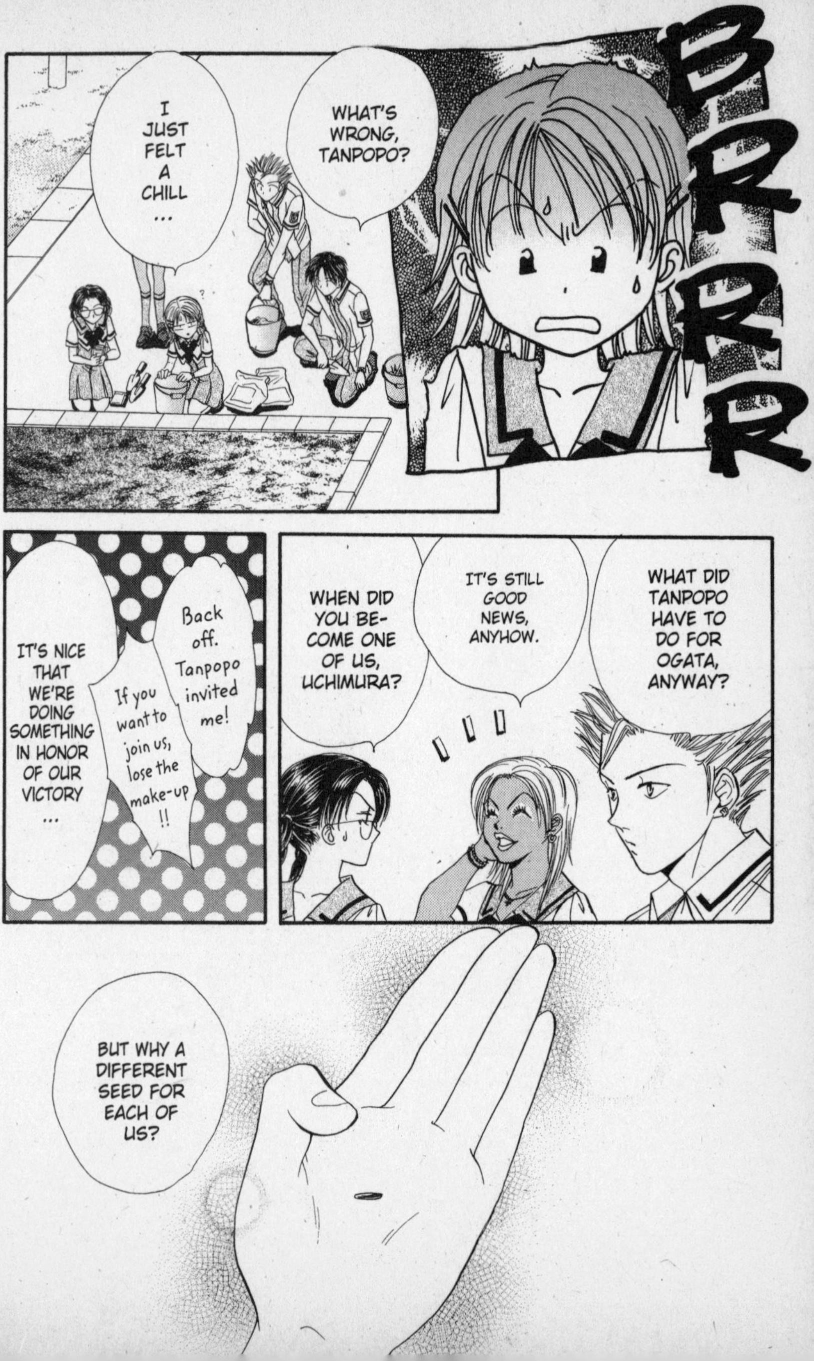
BRRRR
WHAT'S WRONG, TANPOPO?
I JUST FELT A CHILL ...
WHAT DID TANPOPO HAVE TO DO FOR OGATA, ANYWAY?
IT'S STILL GOOD NEWS, ANYHOW.
WHEN DID YOU BE-COME ONE OF US, UCHIMURA?
Back off. Tanpopo invited me!
If you want to join us, lose the make-up!!
IT'S NICE THAT WE'RE DOING SOMETHING IN HONOR OF OUR VICTORY ...
BUT WHY A DIFFERENT SEED FOR EACH OF US?

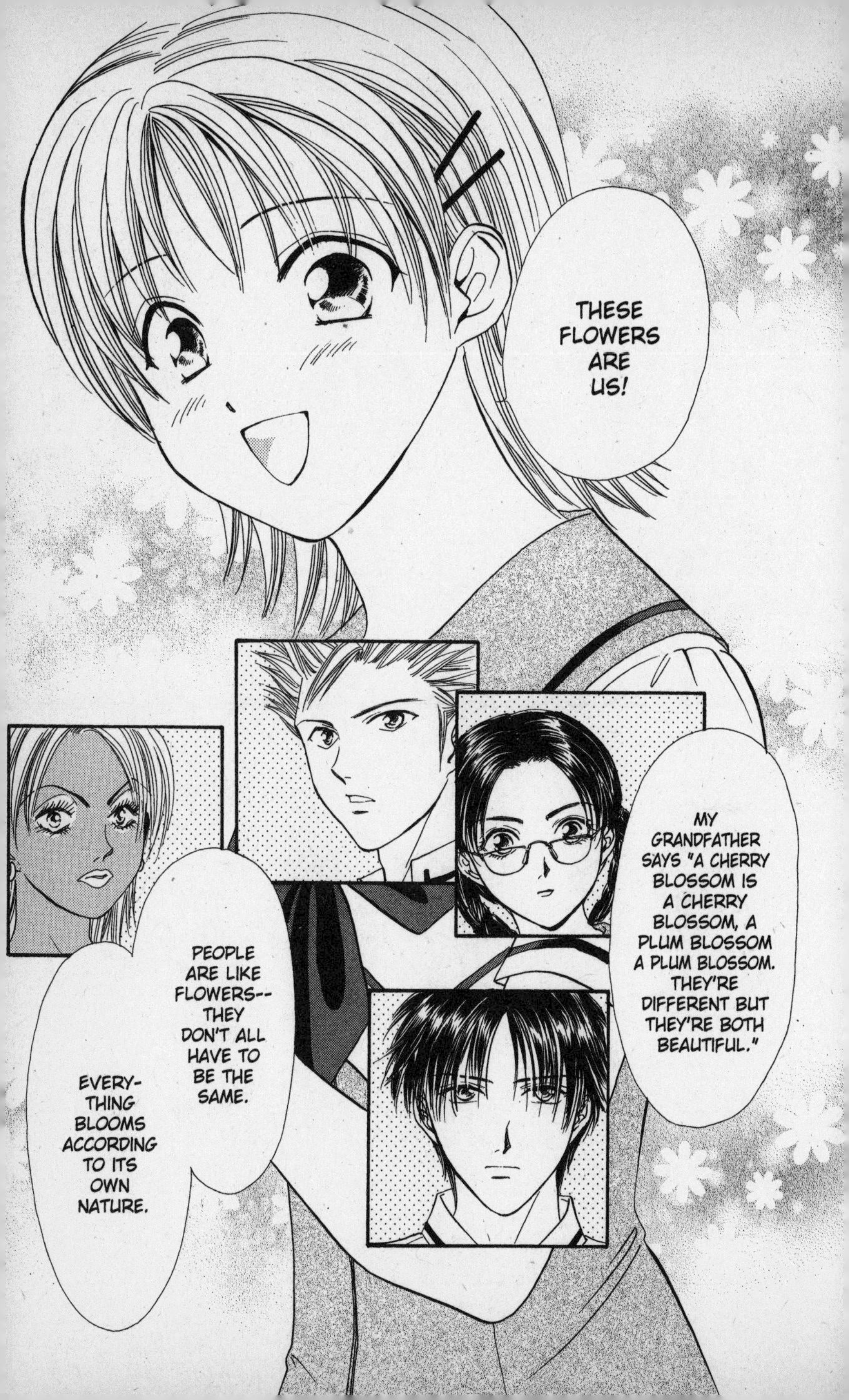
THESE FLOWERS ARE US!
MY GRANDFATHER SAYS "A CHERRY BLOSSOM IS A CHERRY BLOSSOM, A PLUM BLOSSOM A PLUM BLOSSOM. THEY'RE DIFFERENT BUT THEY'RE BOTH BEAUTIFUL."
PEOPLE ARE LIKE FLOWERS-- THEY DON'T ALL HAVE TO BE THE SAME.
EVERY-THING BLOOMS ACCORDING TO ITS OWN NATURE.

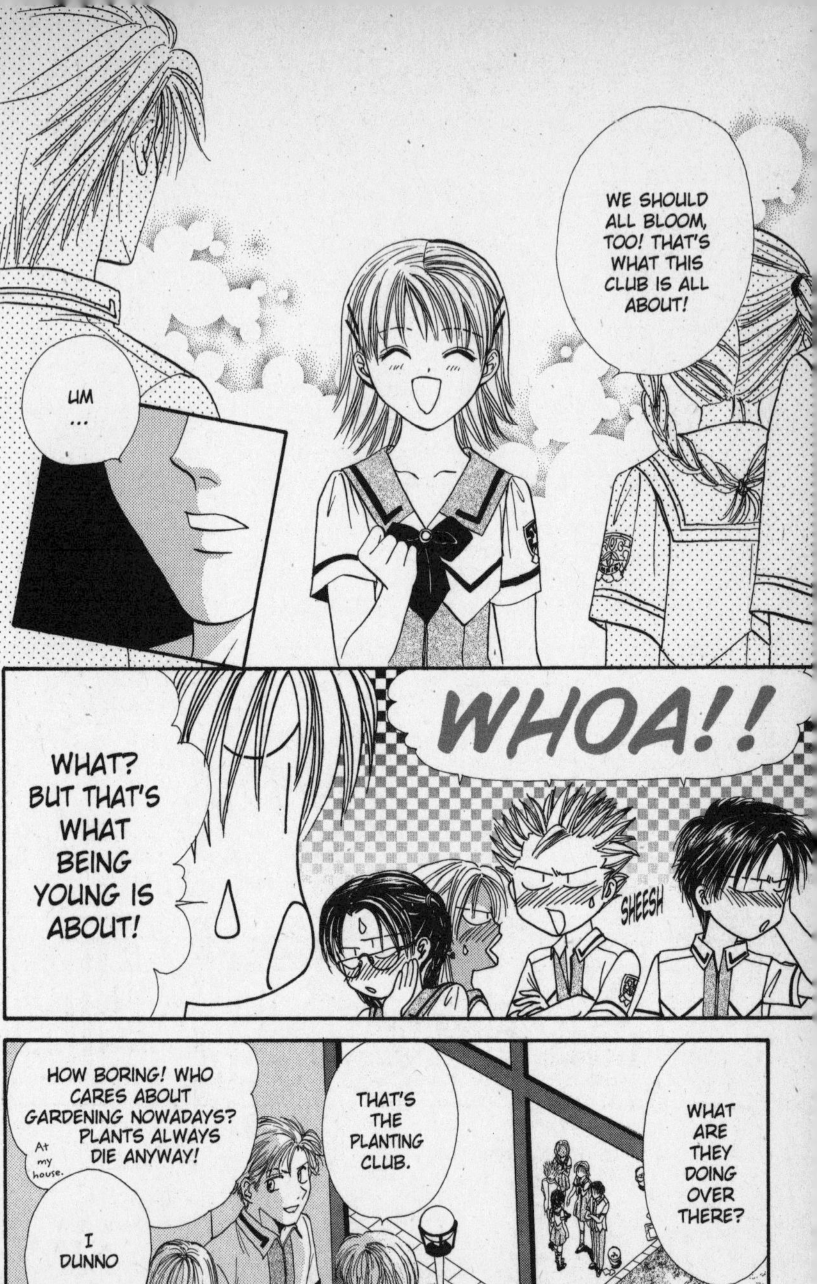
WE SHOULD ALL BLOOM, TOO! THAT'S WHAT THIS CLUB IS ALL ABOUT!
UM ...
WHOA!!
SHEESH
WHAT? BUT THAT'S WHAT BEING YOUNG IS ABOUT!
WHAT ARE THEY DOING OVER THERE?
THAT'S THE PLANTING CLUB.
HOW BORING! WHO CARES ABOUT GARDENING NOWADAYS? PLANTS ALWAYS DIE ANYWAY!
At my house.
I DUNNO ...

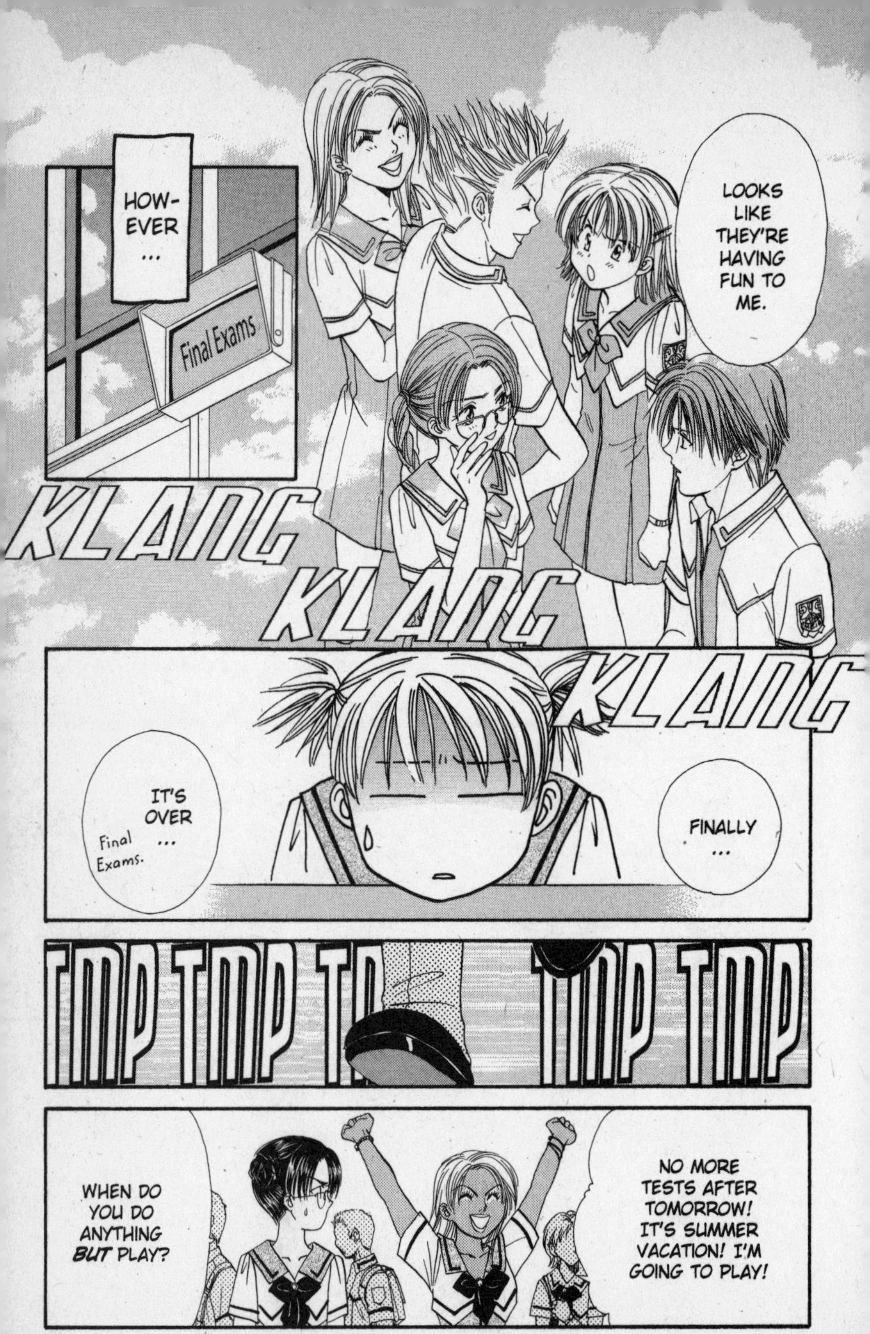

LOOKS LIKE THEY'RE HAVING FUN TO ME.
HOW-EVER ...
Final Exams
KLANG
KLANG
KLANG
FINALLY ...
IT'S OVER ...
Final Exams.
TMP TMP TP TMP TMP
NO MORE TESTS AFTER TOMORROW! IT'S SUMMER VACATION! I'M GOING TO PLAY!
WHEN DO YOU DO ANYTHING *BUT* PLAY?

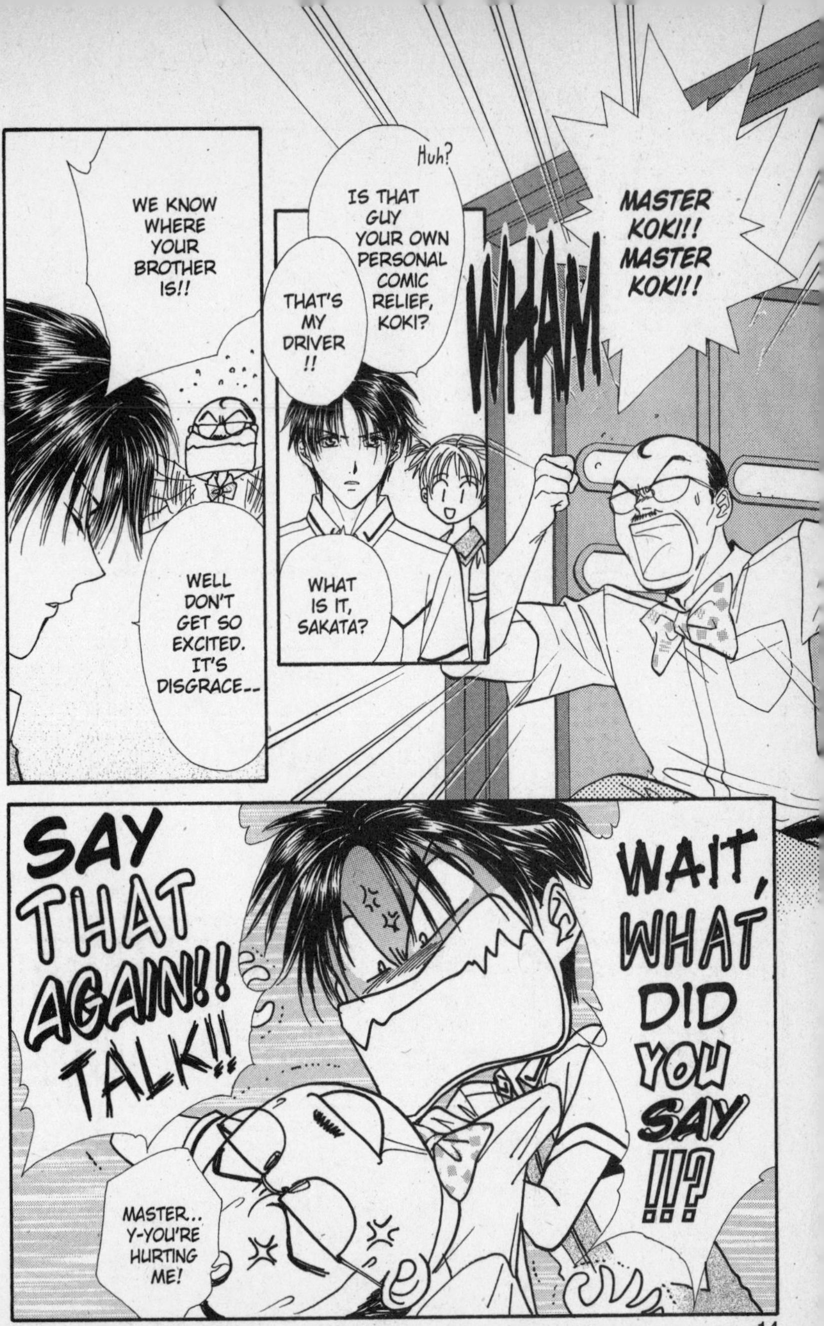
MASTER KOKI!! MASTER KOKI!!
WHAM
Huh?
IS THAT GUY YOUR OWN PERSONAL COMIC RELIEF, KOKI?
THAT'S MY DRIVER!!
WHAT IS IT, SAKATA?
WE KNOW WHERE YOUR BROTHER IS!!
WELL DON'T GET SO EXCITED. IT'S DISGRACE--
WAIT, WHAT DID YOU SAY!!?
SAY THAT AGAIN!! TALK!!
MASTER... Y-YOU'RE HURTING ME!

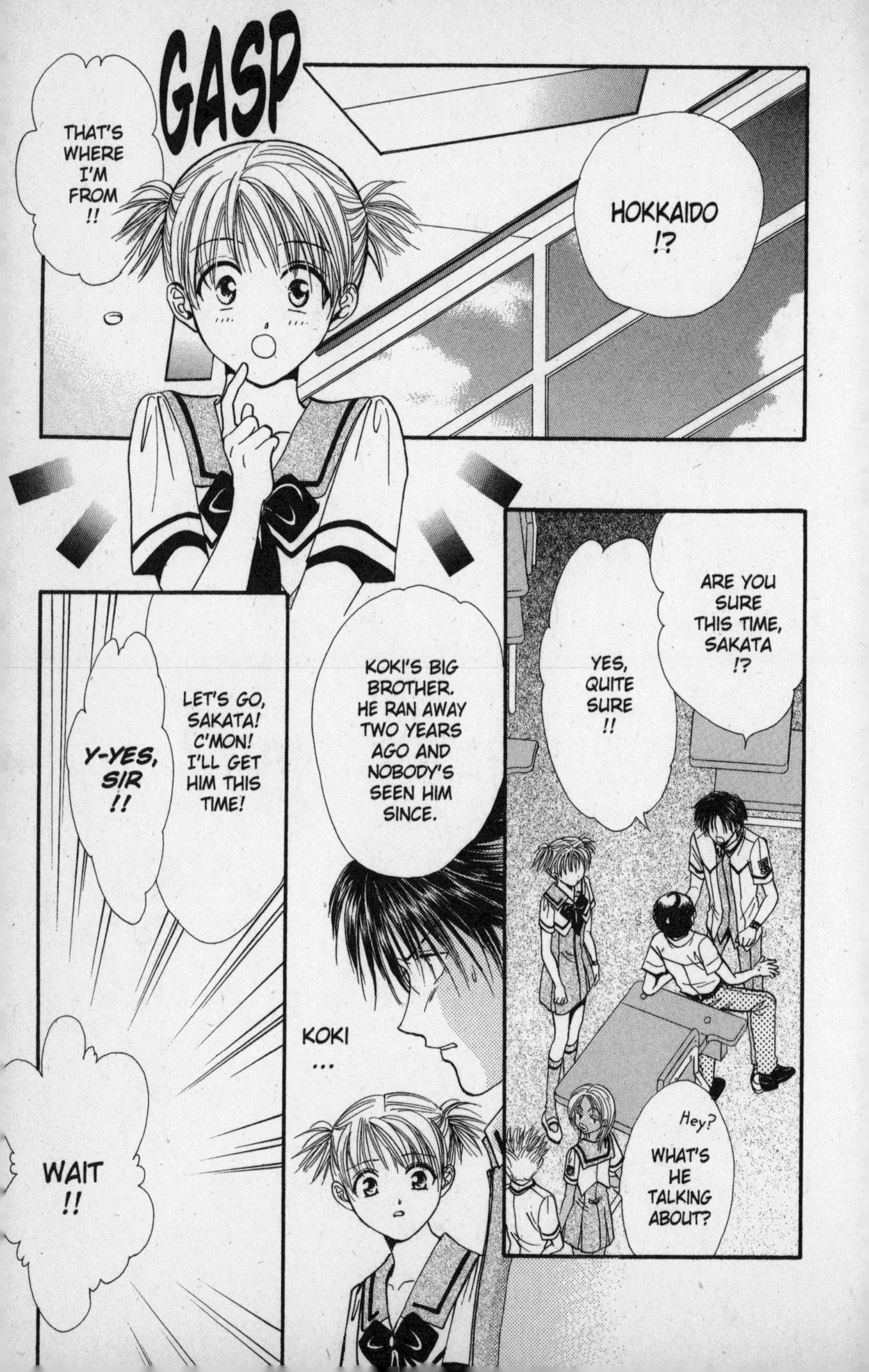
HOKKAIDO !?
GASP
THAT'S WHERE I'M FROM !!
ARE YOU SURE THIS TIME, SAKATA !?
YES, QUITE SURE !!
Hey?
WHAT'S HE TALKING ABOUT?
KOKI'S BIG BROTHER. HE RAN AWAY TWO YEARS AGO AND NOBODY'S SEEN HIM SINCE.
KOKI ...
LET'S GO, SAKATA! C'MON! I'LL GET HIM THIS TIME!
Y-YES, SIR !!
WAIT !!

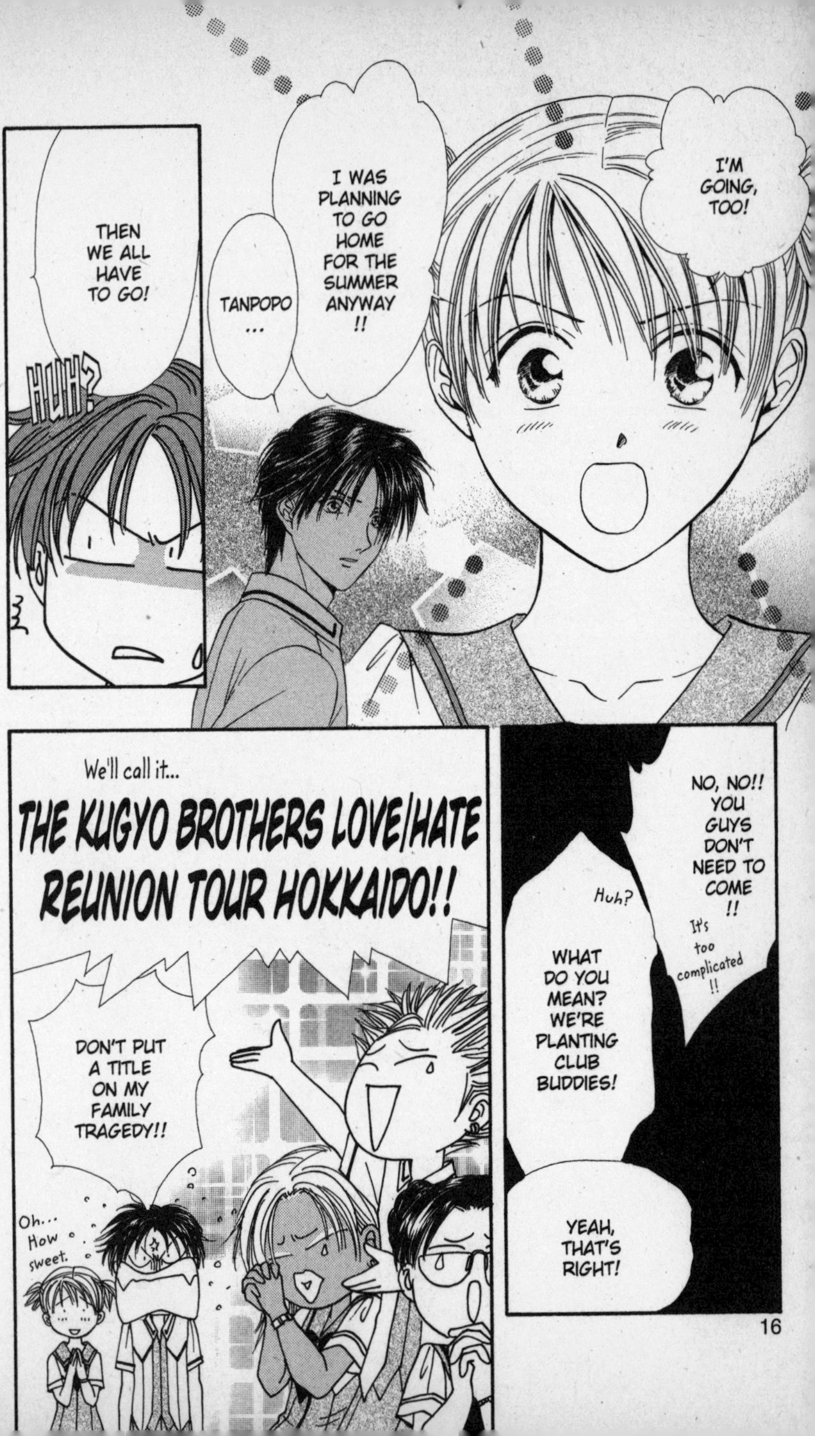
I'M GOING, TOO!
I WAS PLANNING TO GO HOME FOR THE SUMMER ANYWAY!!
TANPOPO...
THEN WE ALL HAVE TO GO!
HUH?
NO, NO!! YOU GUYS DON'T NEED TO COME!!
Huh?
It's too complicated!!
WHAT DO YOU MEAN? WE'RE PLANTING CLUB BUDDIES!
YEAH, THAT'S RIGHT!
We'll call it...
THE KUGYO BROTHERS LOVE/HATE REUNION TOUR HOKKAIDO!!
DON'T PUT A TITLE ON MY FAMILY TRAGEDY!!
Oh... How sweet.

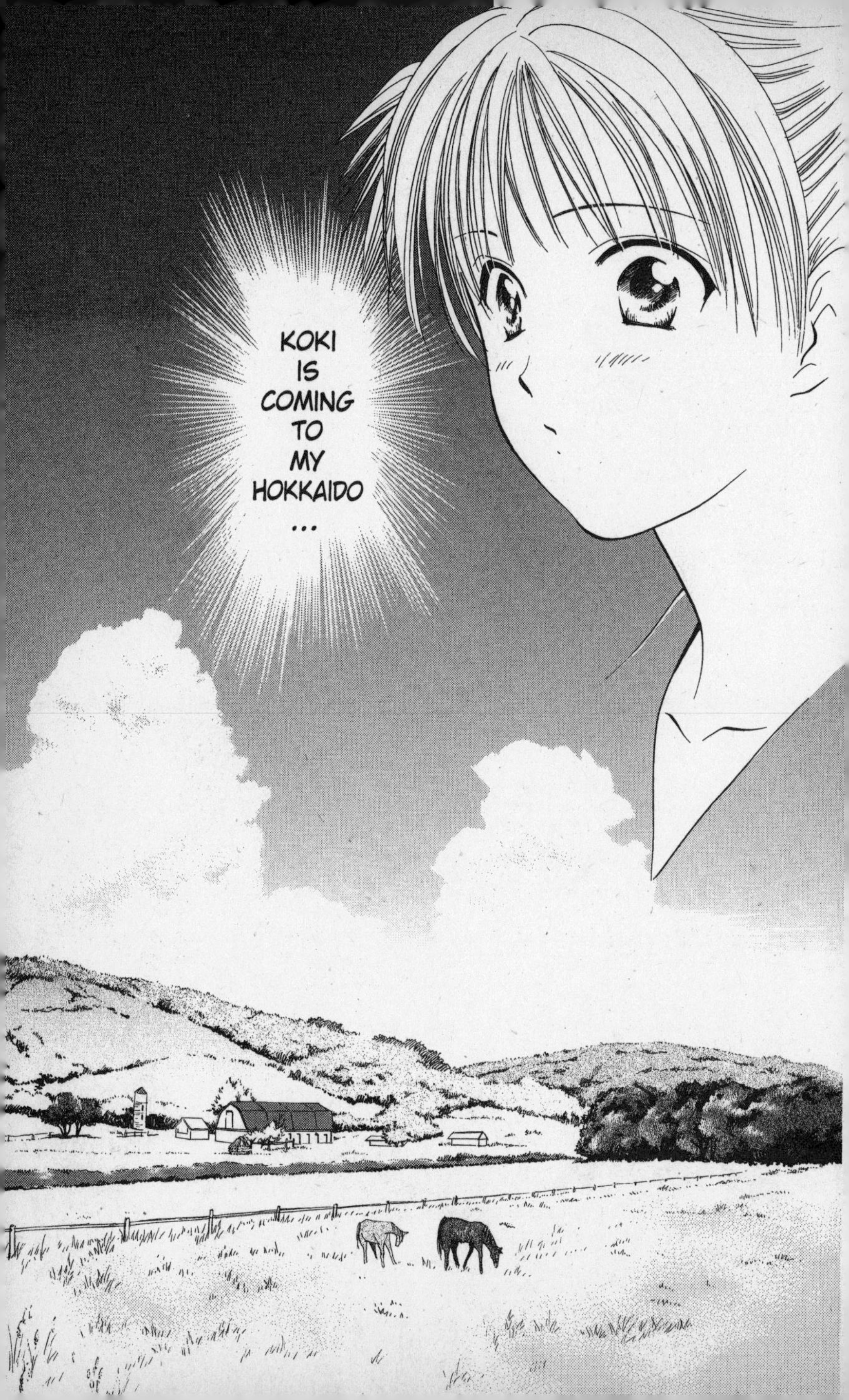
KOKI IS COMING TO MY HOKKAIDO ...

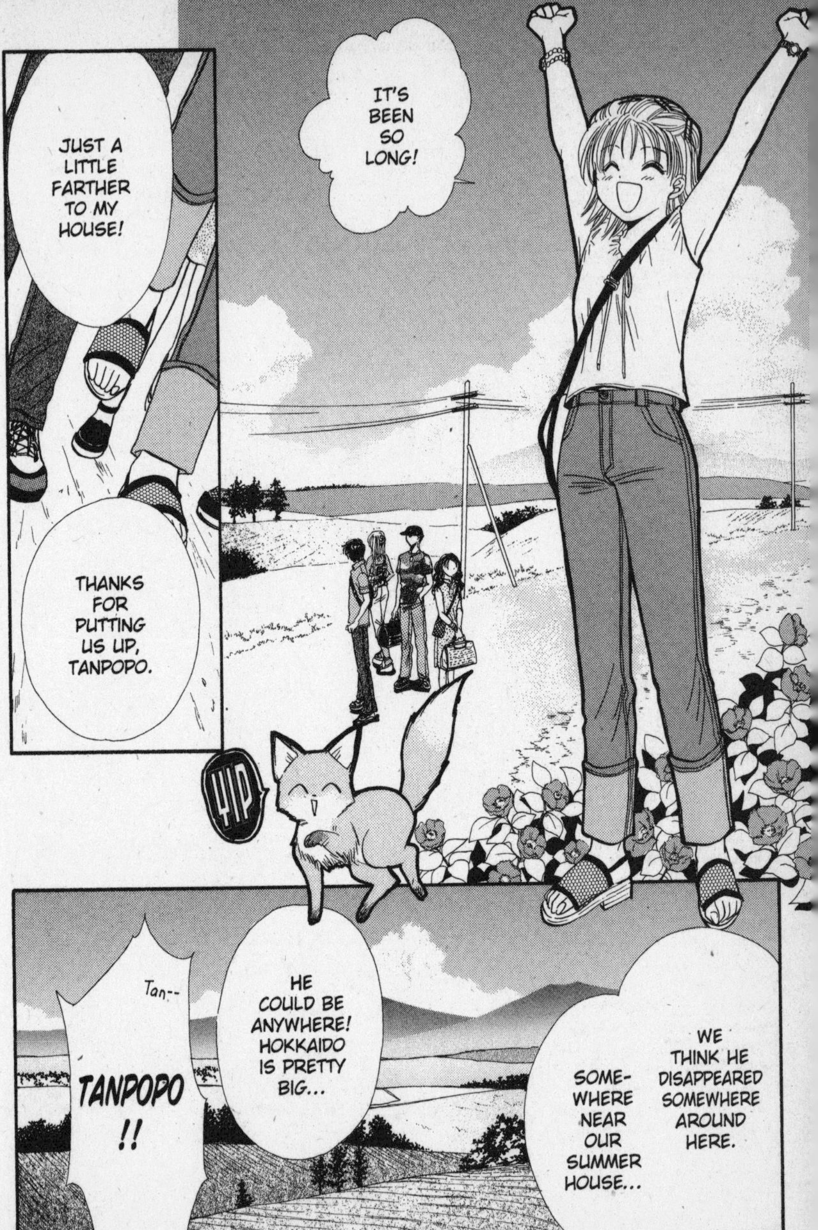

IT'S BEEN SO LONG!
YIP
JUST A LITTLE FARTHER TO MY HOUSE!
THANKS FOR PUTTING US UP, TANPOPO.
WE THINK HE DISAPPEARED SOMEWHERE AROUND HERE.
SOME-WHERE NEAR OUR SUMMER HOUSE...
HE COULD BE ANYWHERE! HOKKAIDO IS PRETTY BIG...
Tan--
TANPOPO!!

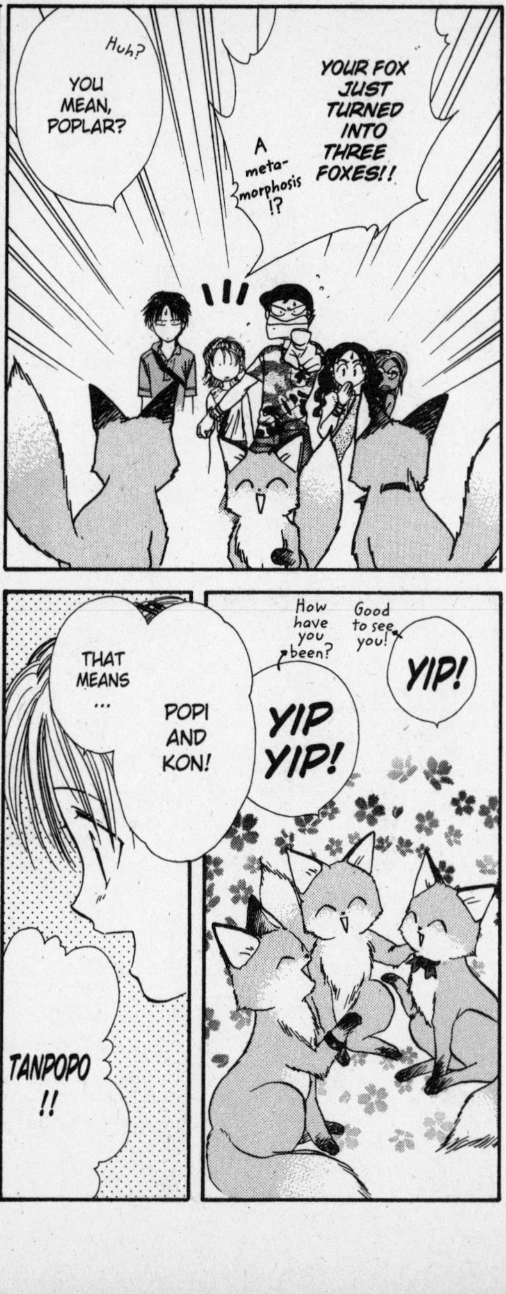
YOUR FOX JUST TURNED INTO THREE FOXES!!
A meta-morphosis !?
Huh?
YOU MEAN, POPLAR?
YIP!
Good to see you!
YIP YIP!
How have you been?
THAT MEANS ...
POPI AND KON!
TANPOPO !!

Hello, hello, this is Watase.

I'm two months late, but Happy New Century! I've been very busy since the first of the year. It's a new century and I just hope someone tells me something deep like, "Hey, you've grown." (Just kidding).

Writing them one by one took me over four days. If I had over a hundred... Oh, I forgot to tell you the subject. I'm talking about my New Year's cards. I caught a cold at the end of the year, so I couldn't do my New Year's cards or any house-cleaning.

I did my big cleaning on January 3. Fool. Then I did this and that, and now I'm writing this. I haven't been able to rest at all! I guess I should be happy that this promises to be a busy year for me.

At the end of 2000, I went to a concert by Junko Iwao who plays Ceres in **Ayashi no Ceres**. It was really good! Ms. Iwao is a good singer and her performance was excellent. It was a very feminine and gentle stage performance. I recommend it!!

Ms. Iwao possesses such grace, you'd never know that she and I were the same age. Even the savages...I mean, men...were taken with her performance. (But, I think they were coerced.) Female fans of **Ceres** are increasing, so I was glad to see women there! ^^ Of course, when she sang the theme song of **Ceres** vol. 2 "Scarlet" (which I asked to have played at the end of the final episode), the room went dead silent. I know it's a little late to say this, but that's a good song!! There are other good songs. On the new album, the song "Canary" is my kiniiri ("favorite"; the Japanese equivalent sounds like "canary"—Ed.)... Was that a pun? Is that the best you can do for the new century, Watase!?

Sorry. I apologize for my assistant's bad joke.

"You're such a panda!!" "You're such a foolish panda" is okay, too. Try using this phrase in your daily conversation. Are you serious!?

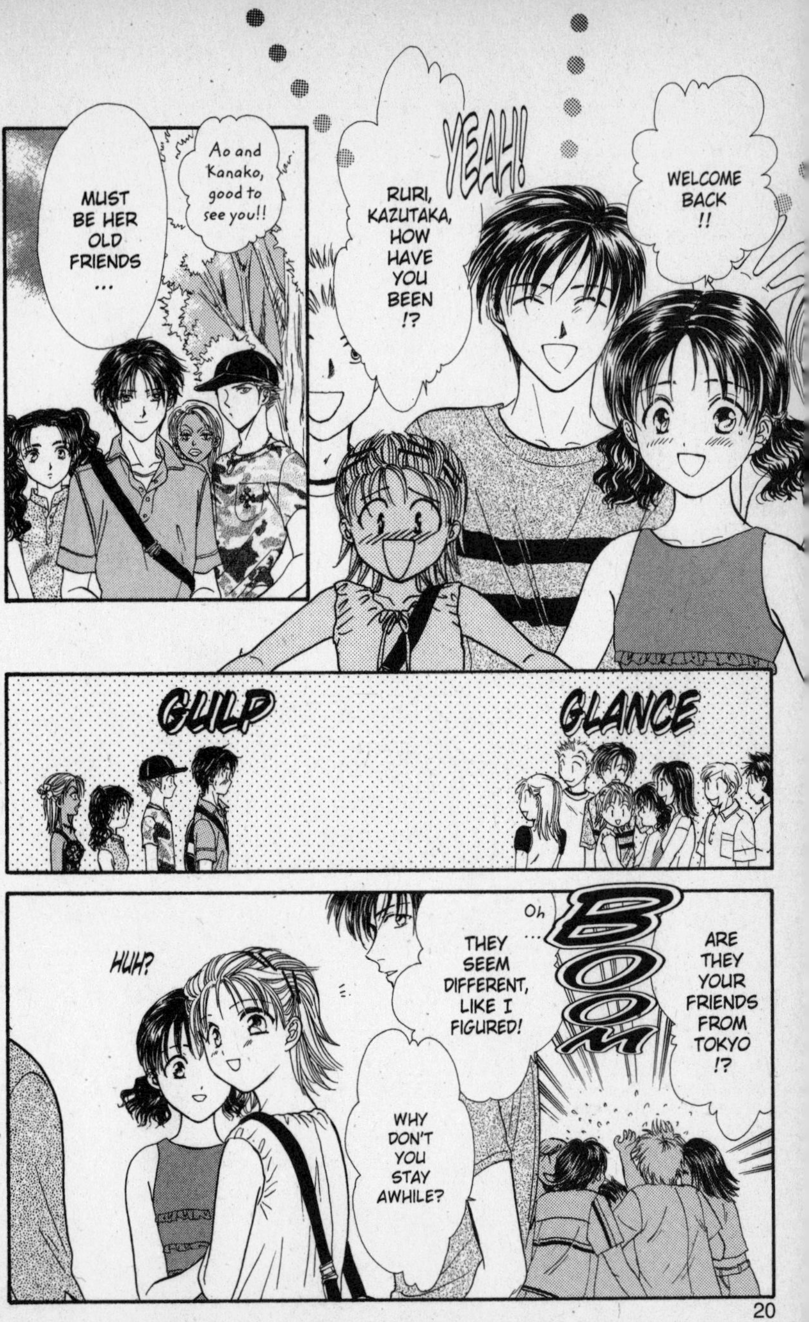
WELCOME BACK !!
YEAH!
RURI, KAZUTAKA, HOW HAVE YOU BEEN !?
Ao and Kanako, good to see you!!
MUST BE HER OLD FRIENDS ...
GLANCE
GULP
ARE THEY YOUR FRIENDS FROM TOKYO !?
BOOM
Oh ...
THEY SEEM DIFFERENT, LIKE I FIGURED!
WHY DON'T YOU STAY AWHILE?
HUH?

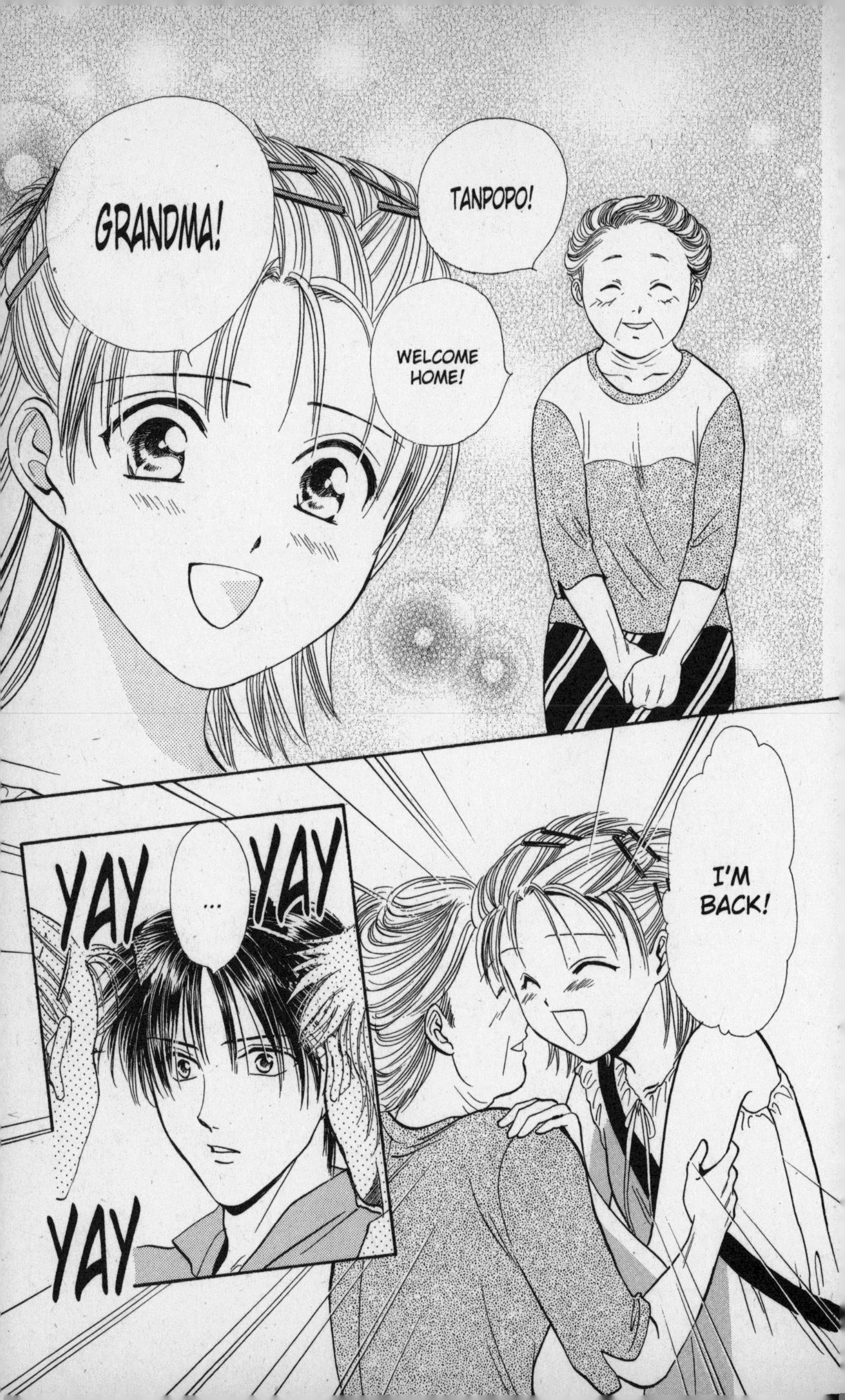
TANPOPO!
WELCOME HOME!
GRANDMA!
I'M BACK!
YAY
YAY
...
YAY

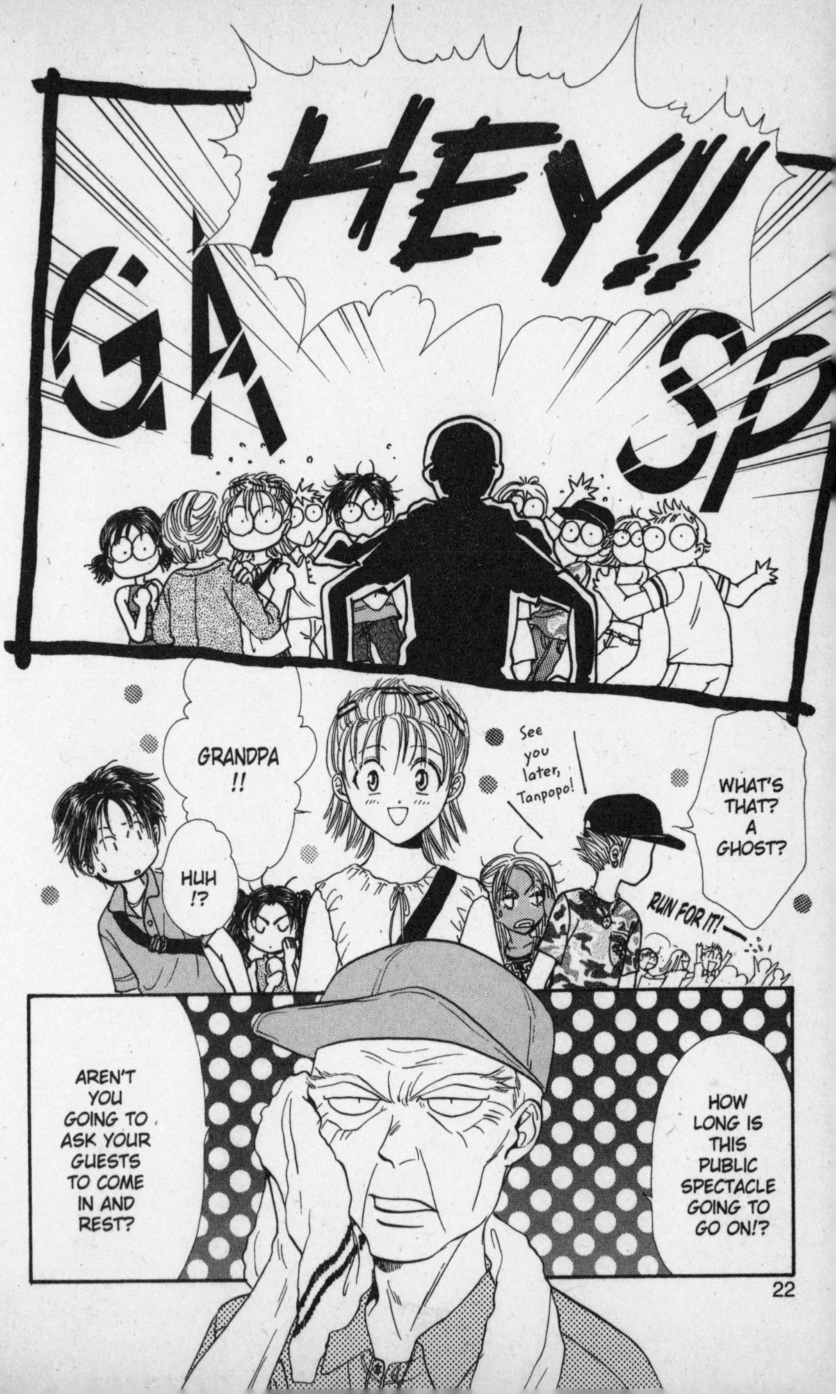
HEY!!
GASP
WHAT'S THAT? A GHOST?
See you later, Tanpopo!
RUN FOR IT!
GRANDPA!!
HUH!?
HOW LONG IS THIS PUBLIC SPECTACLE GOING TO GO ON!?
AREN'T YOU GOING TO ASK YOUR GUESTS TO COME IN AND REST?

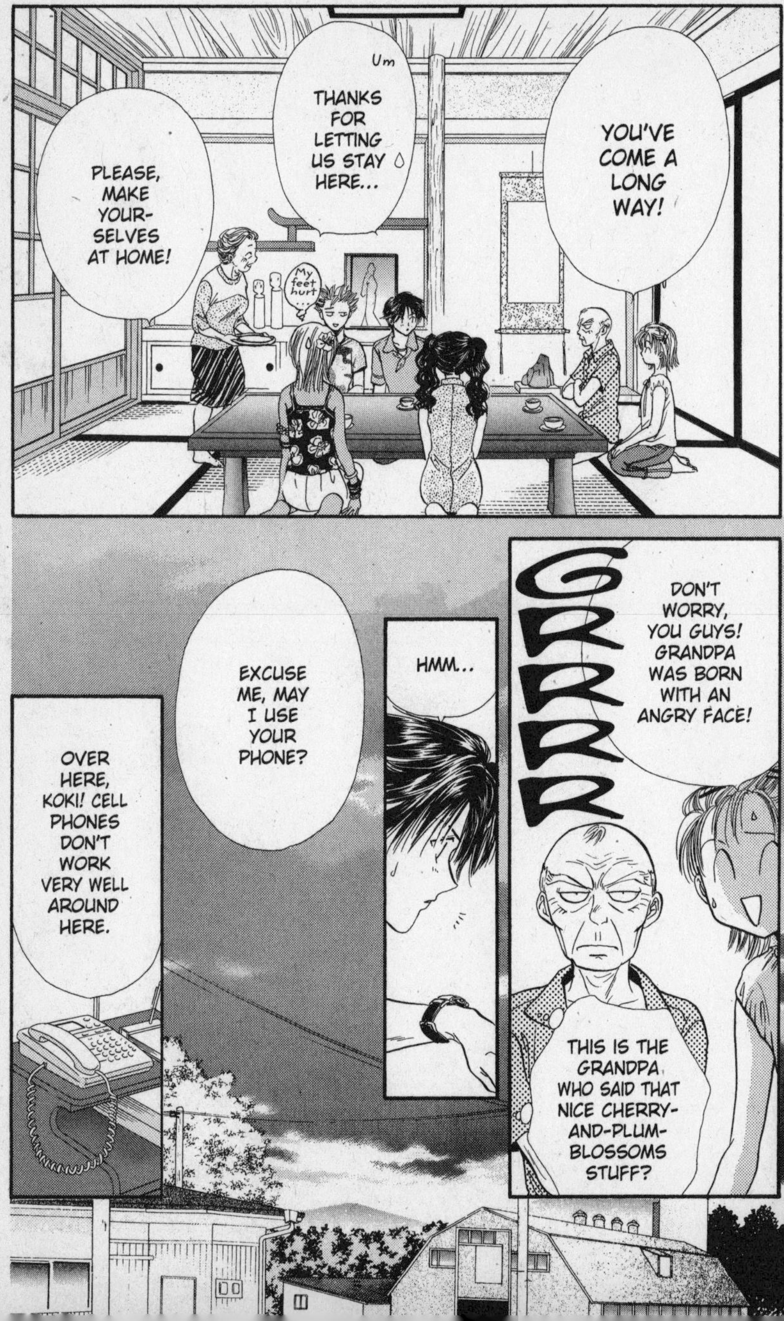
YOU'VE COME A LONG WAY!
Um
THANKS FOR LETTING US STAY HERE...
My feet hurt...
PLEASE, MAKE YOUR-SELVES AT HOME!
GRRRR
DON'T WORRY, YOU GUYS! GRANDPA WAS BORN WITH AN ANGRY FACE!
THIS IS THE GRANDPA WHO SAID THAT NICE CHERRY-AND-PLUM-BLOSSOMS STUFF?
HMM...
EXCUSE ME, MAY I USE YOUR PHONE?
OVER HERE, KOKI! CELL PHONES DON'T WORK VERY WELL AROUND HERE.

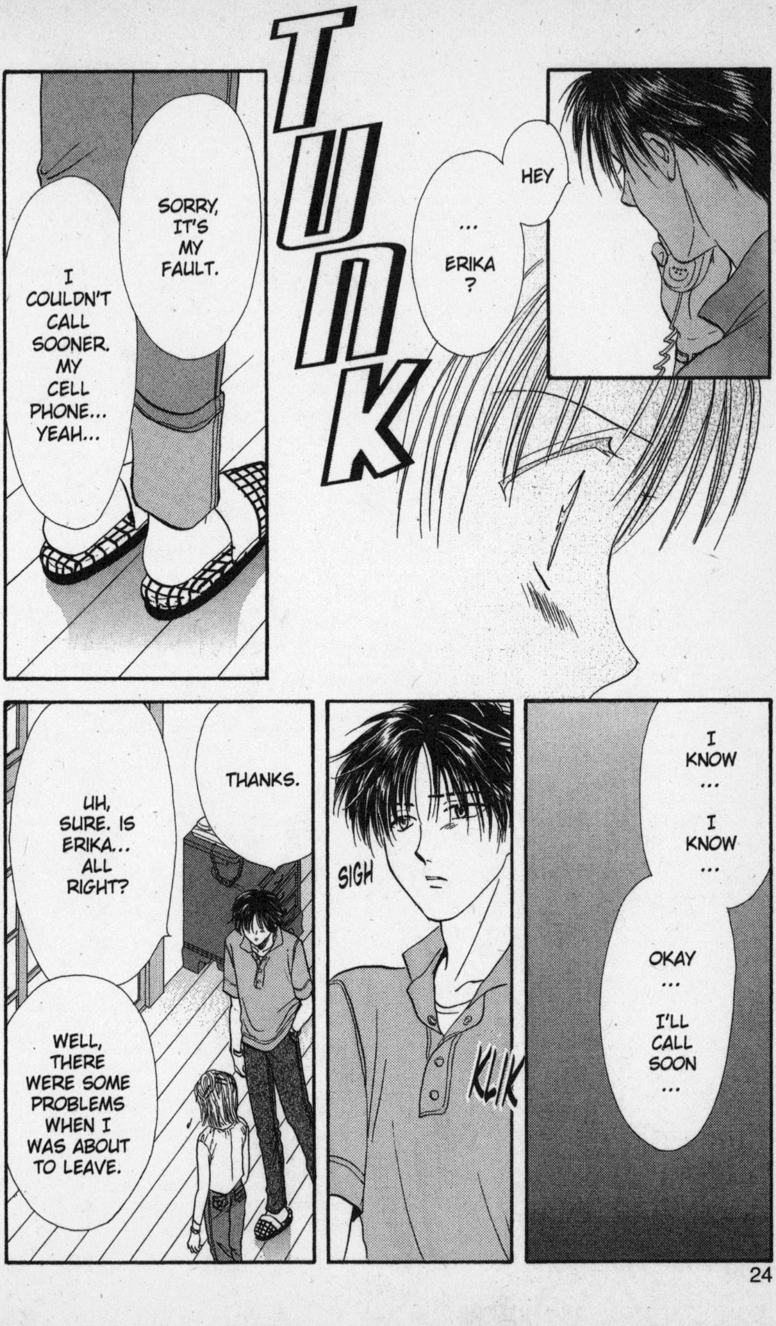
HEY
... ERIKA ?
TUNK
SORRY, IT'S MY FAULT.
I COULDN'T CALL SOONER. MY CELL PHONE... YEAH...
I KNOW ... I KNOW ...
OKAY ... I'LL CALL SOON ...
SIGH
KLIK
THANKS.
UH, SURE. IS ERIKA... ALL RIGHT?
WELL, THERE WERE SOME PROBLEMS WHEN I WAS ABOUT TO LEAVE.

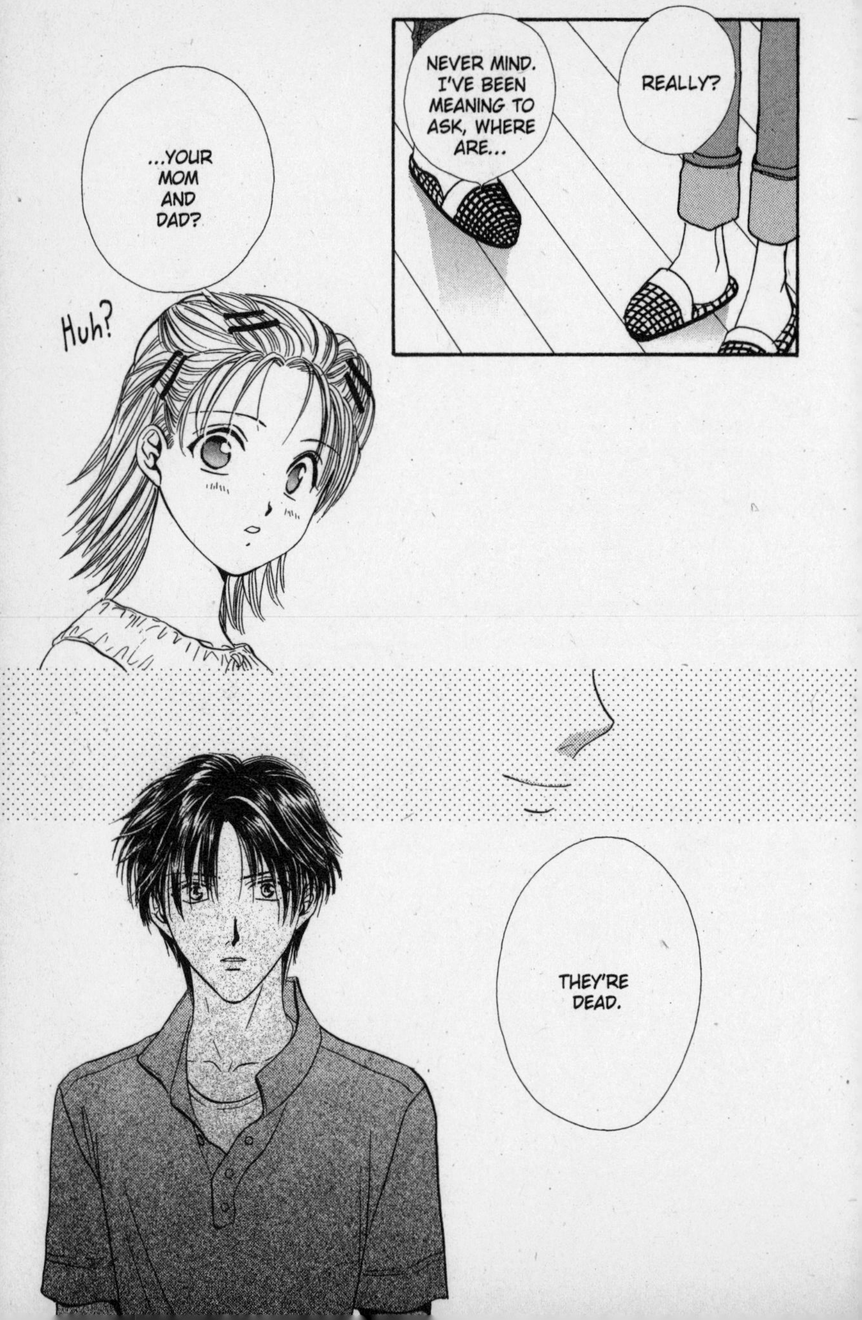
REALLY?
NEVER MIND. I'VE BEEN MEANING TO ASK, WHERE ARE...
...YOUR MOM AND DAD?
Huh?
THEY'RE DEAD.

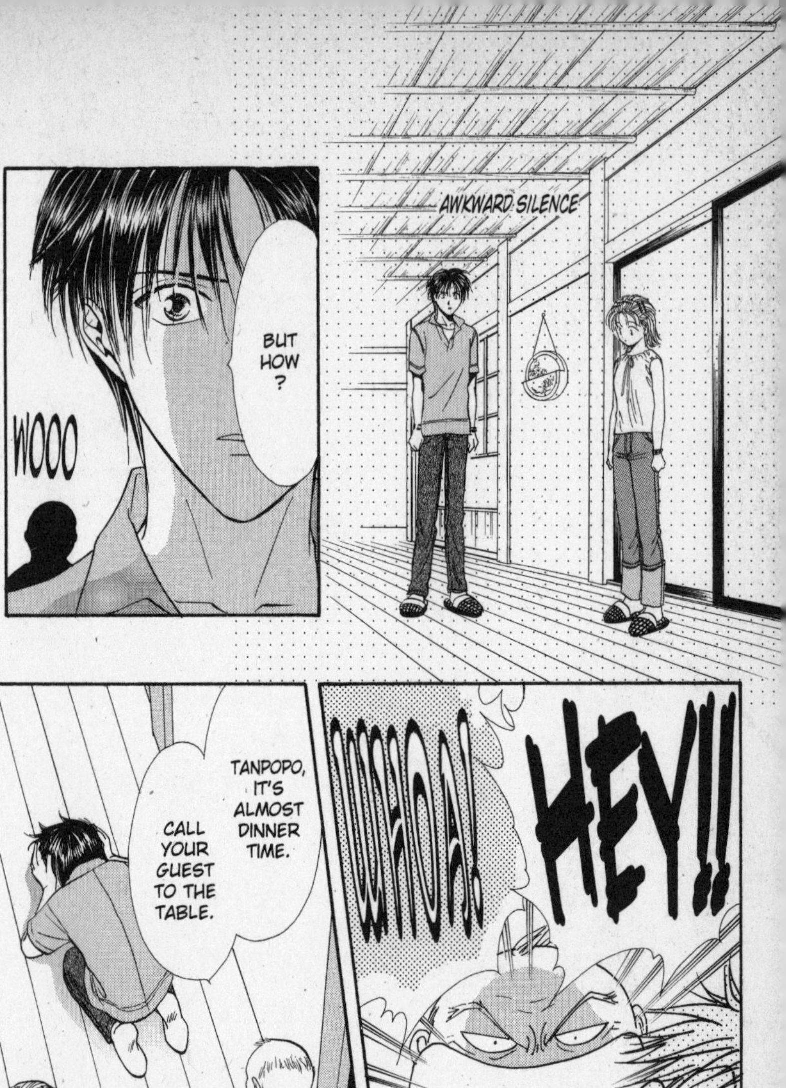
AWKWARD SILENCE
BUT HOW?
WOOO
HEY!!
WHOA!
TANPOPO, IT'S ALMOST DINNER TIME.
CALL YOUR GUEST TO THE TABLE.
SORRY, KOKI. YOU'LL GET USED TO IT.

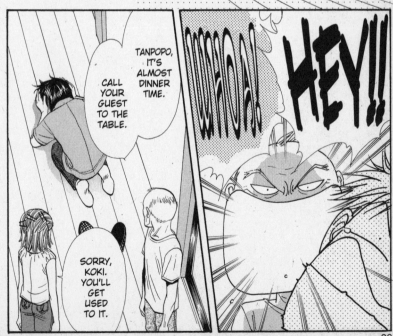

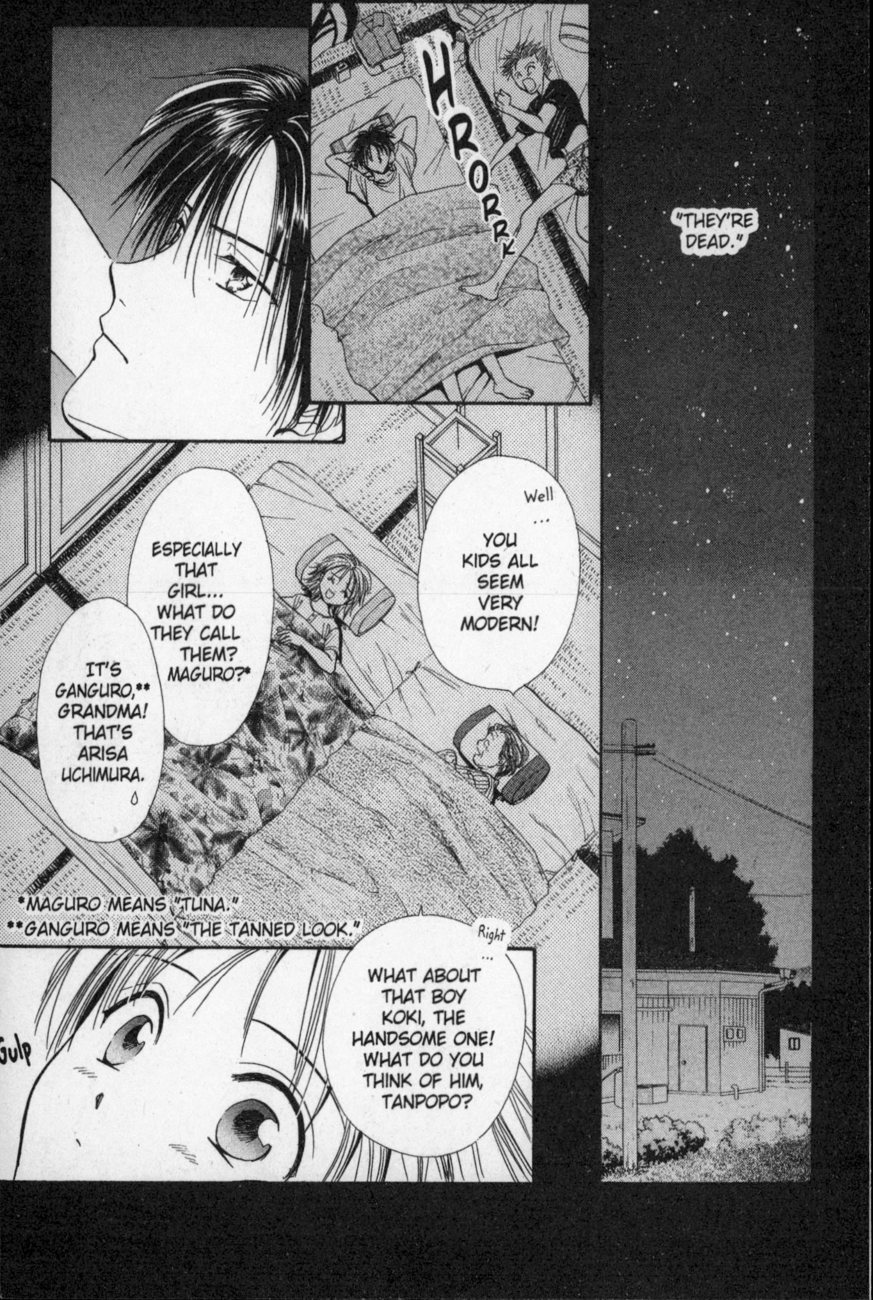
"THEY'RE DEAD."
HRORRK
Well... YOU KIDS ALL SEEM VERY MODERN!
ESPECIALLY THAT GIRL... WHAT DO THEY CALL THEM? MAGURO?*
IT'S GANGURO,** GRANDMA! THAT'S ARISA UCHIMURA.
*MAGURO MEANS "TUNA."
**GANGURO MEANS "THE TANNED LOOK."
Right... WHAT ABOUT THAT BOY KOKI, THE HANDSOME ONE! WHAT DO YOU THINK OF HIM, TANPOPO?
Gulp

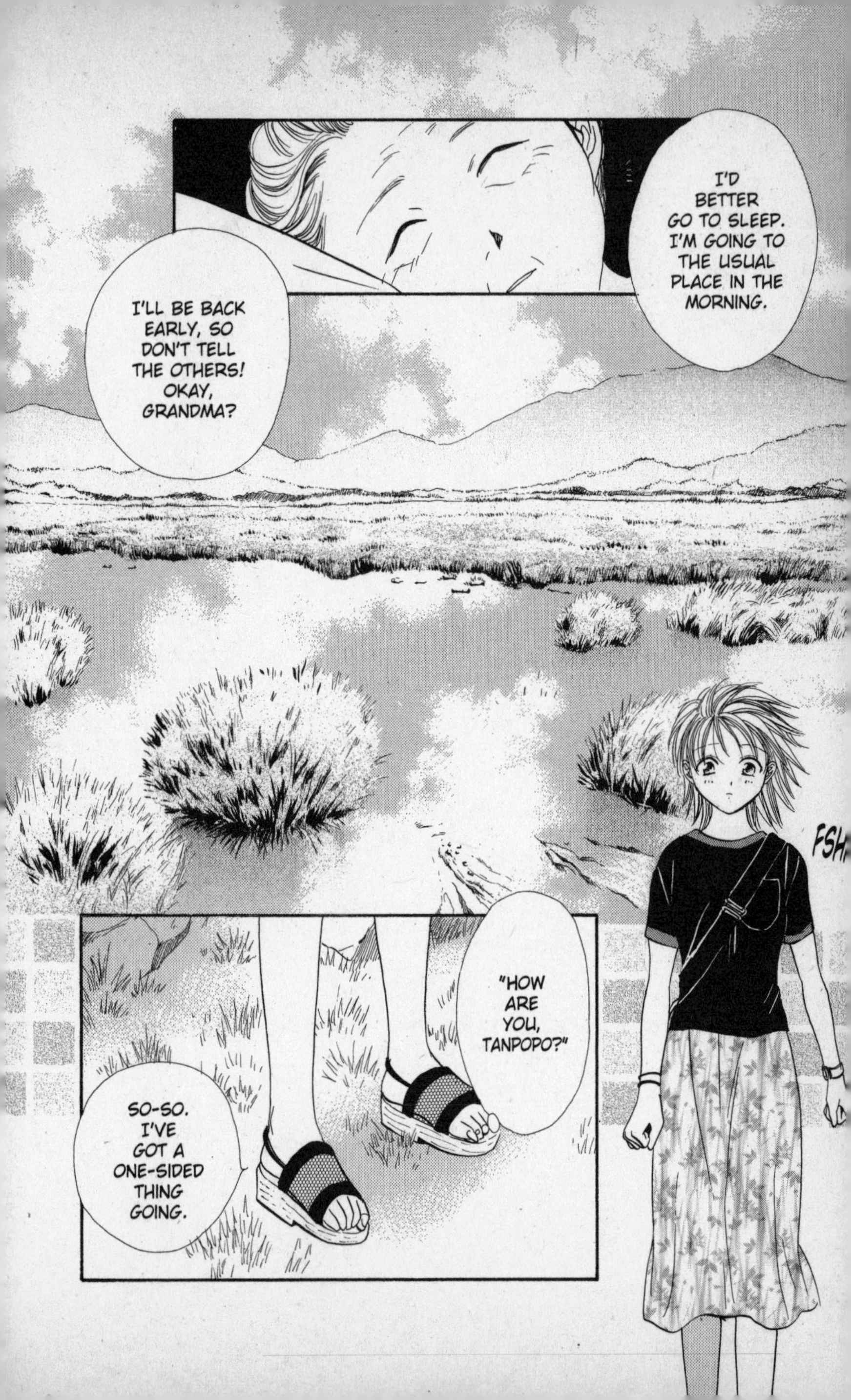
I'D BETTER GO TO SLEEP. I'M GOING TO THE USUAL PLACE IN THE MORNING.
I'LL BE BACK EARLY, SO DON'T TELL THE OTHERS! OKAY, GRANDMA?
FSH
"HOW ARE YOU, TANPOPO?"
SO-SO. I'VE GOT A ONE-SIDED THING GOING.

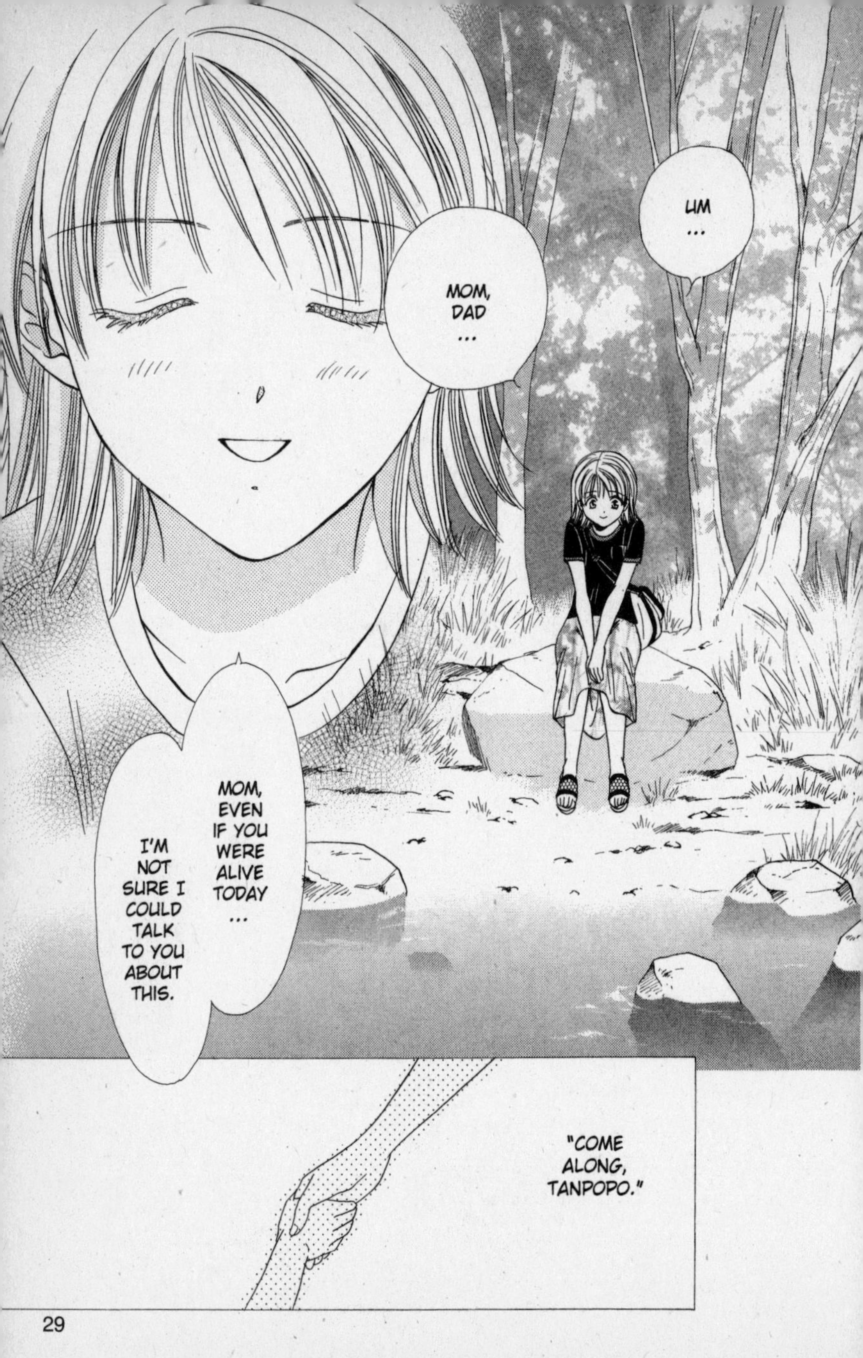
UM ...
MOM, DAD ...
MOM, EVEN IF YOU WERE ALIVE TODAY ...
I'M NOT SURE I COULD TALK TO YOU ABOUT THIS.
"COME ALONG, TANPOPO."

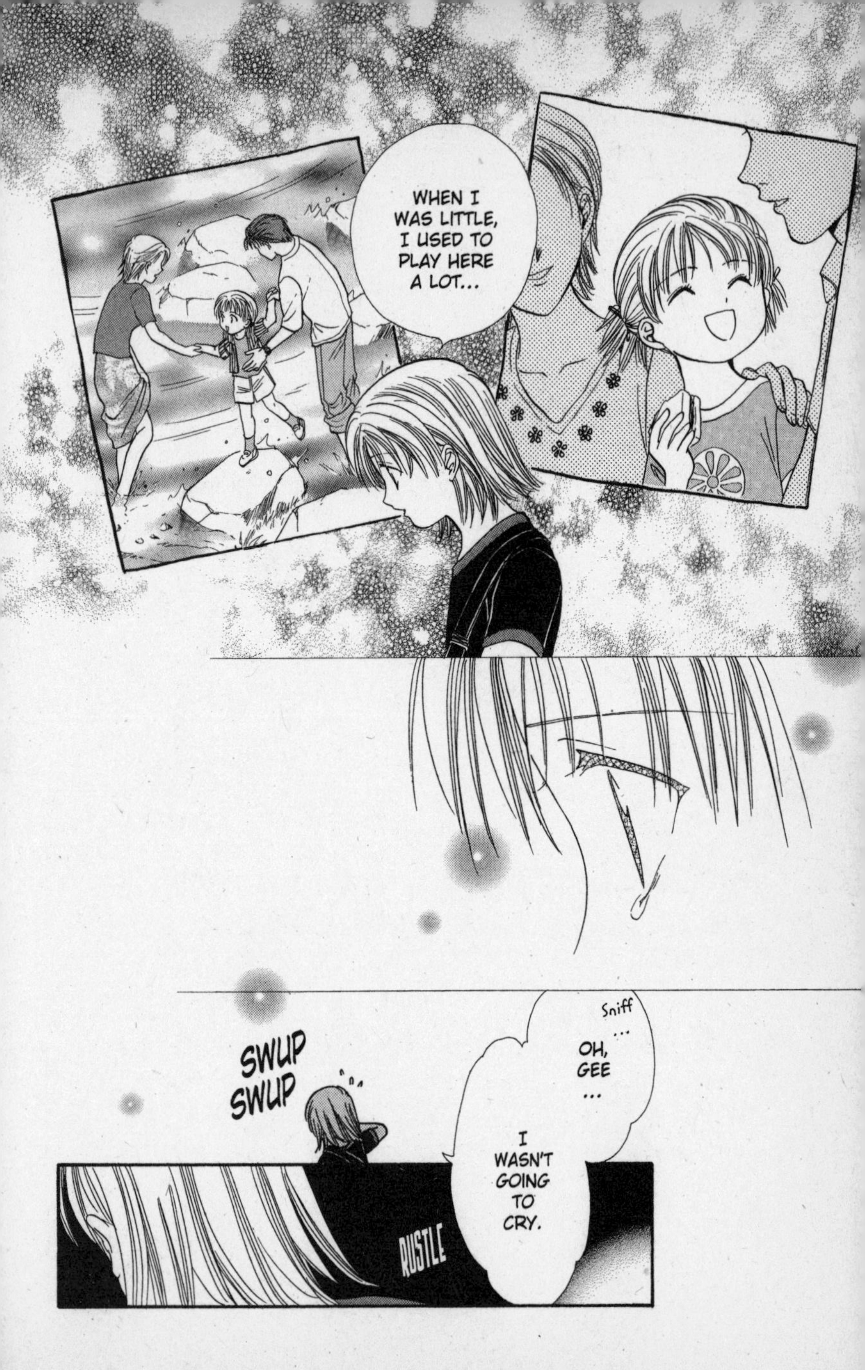
WHEN I WAS LITTLE, I USED TO PLAY HERE A LOT...
Sniff ... OH, GEE ...
I WASN'T GOING TO CRY.
SWUP SWUP
RUSTLE

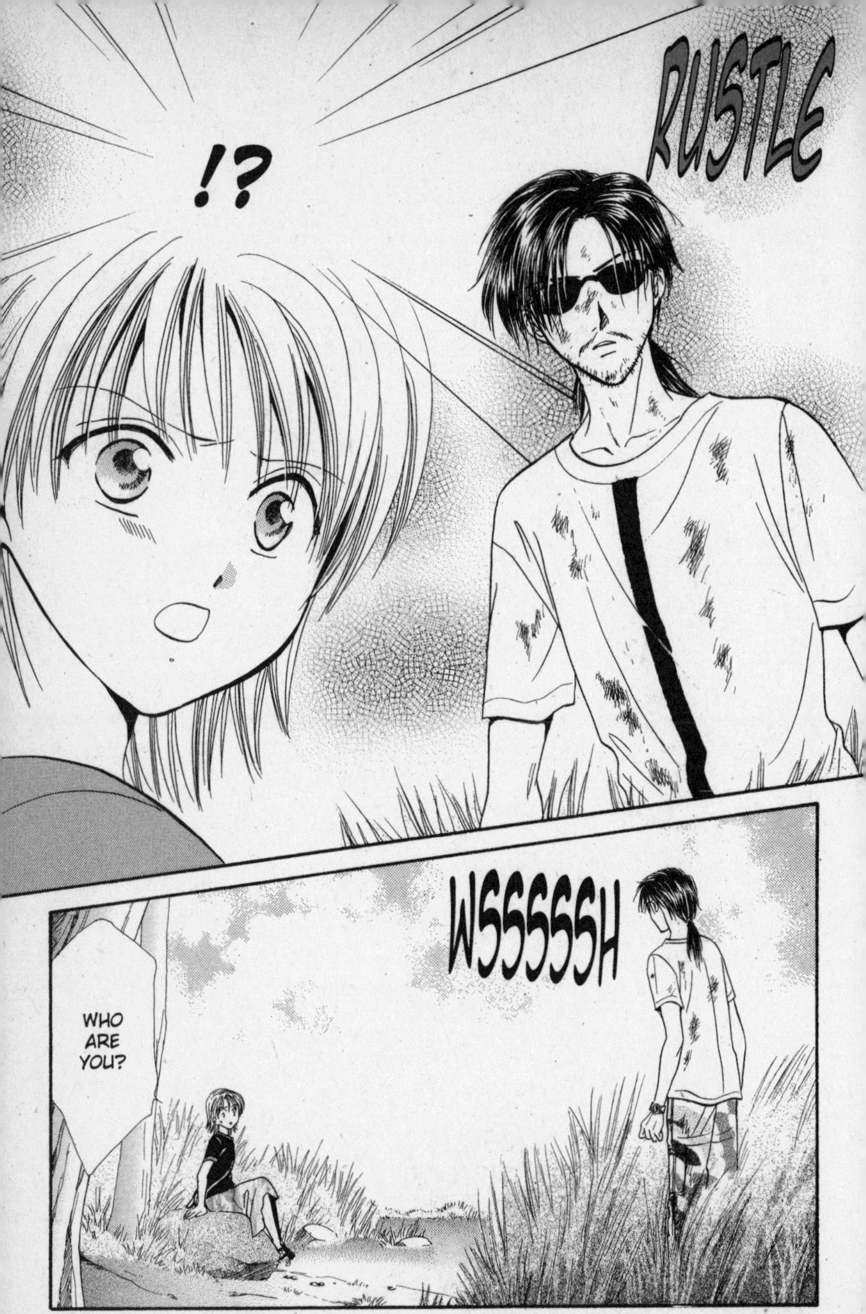
RUSTLE
!?
WSSSSH
WHO ARE YOU?

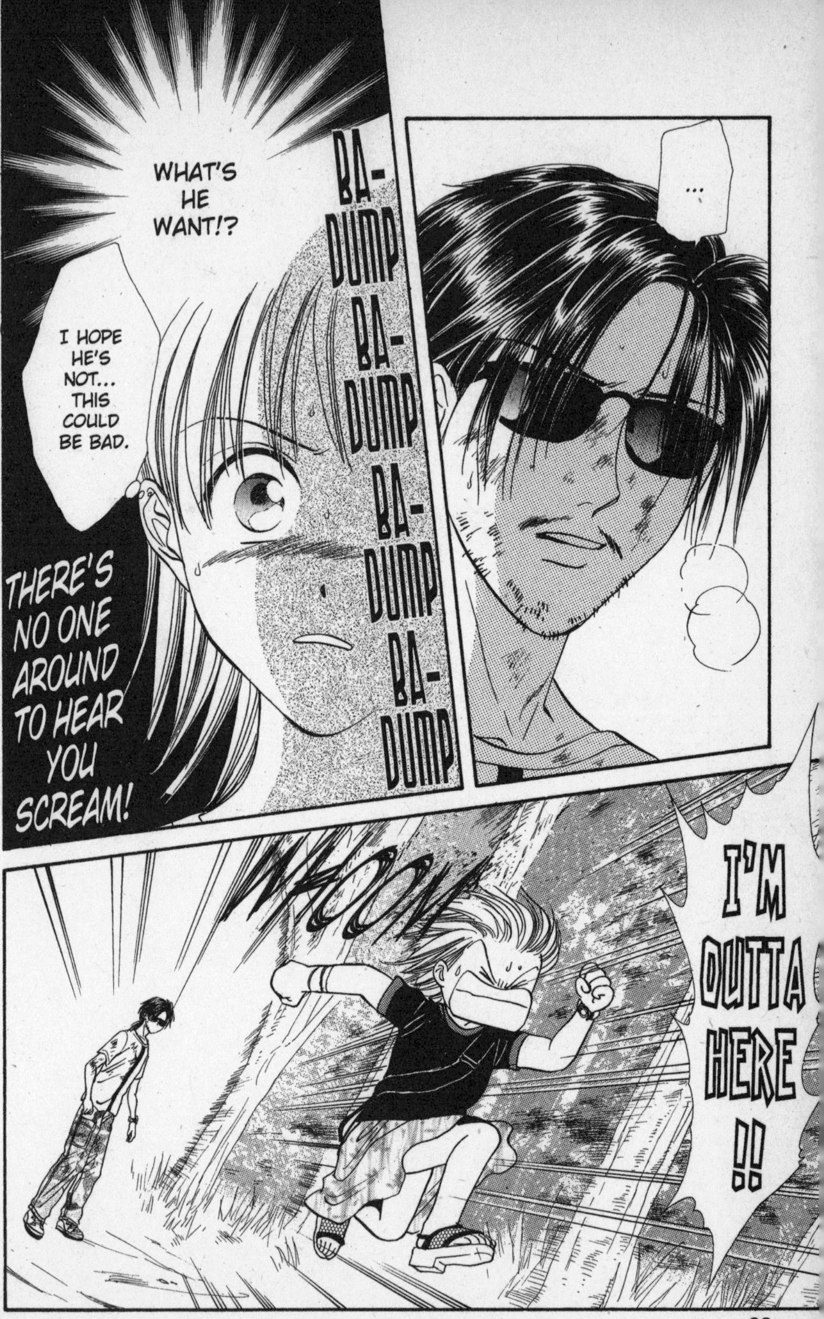
...
BA-DUMP BA-DUMP BA-DUMP BA-DUMP
WHAT'S HE WANT!?
I HOPE HE'S NOT... THIS COULD BE BAD.
THERE'S NO ONE AROUND TO HEAR YOU SCREAM!
I'M OUTTA HERE!!
WHOOOM

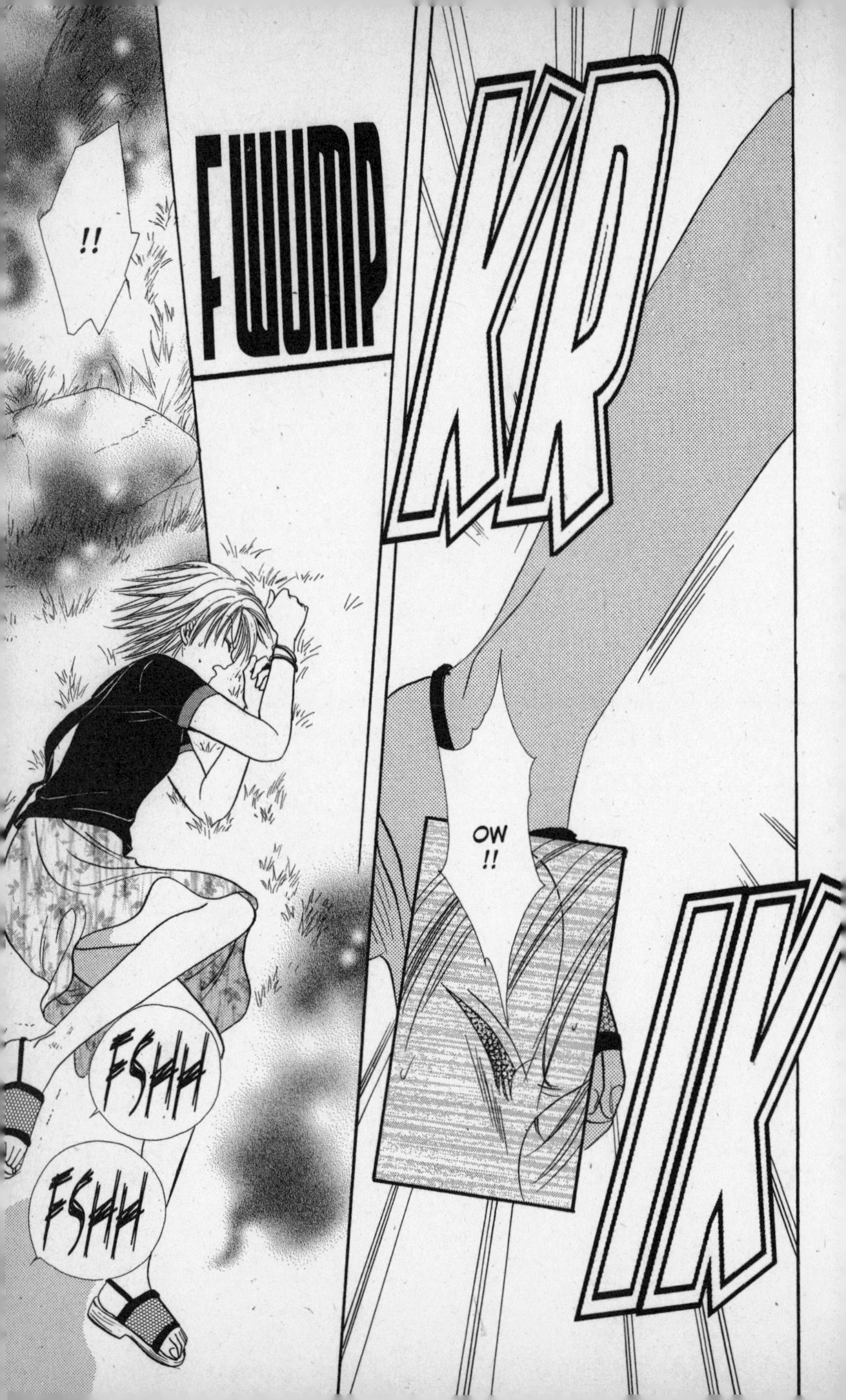
KR
OW !!
IK
FWUMP
!!
FSHH
FSHH

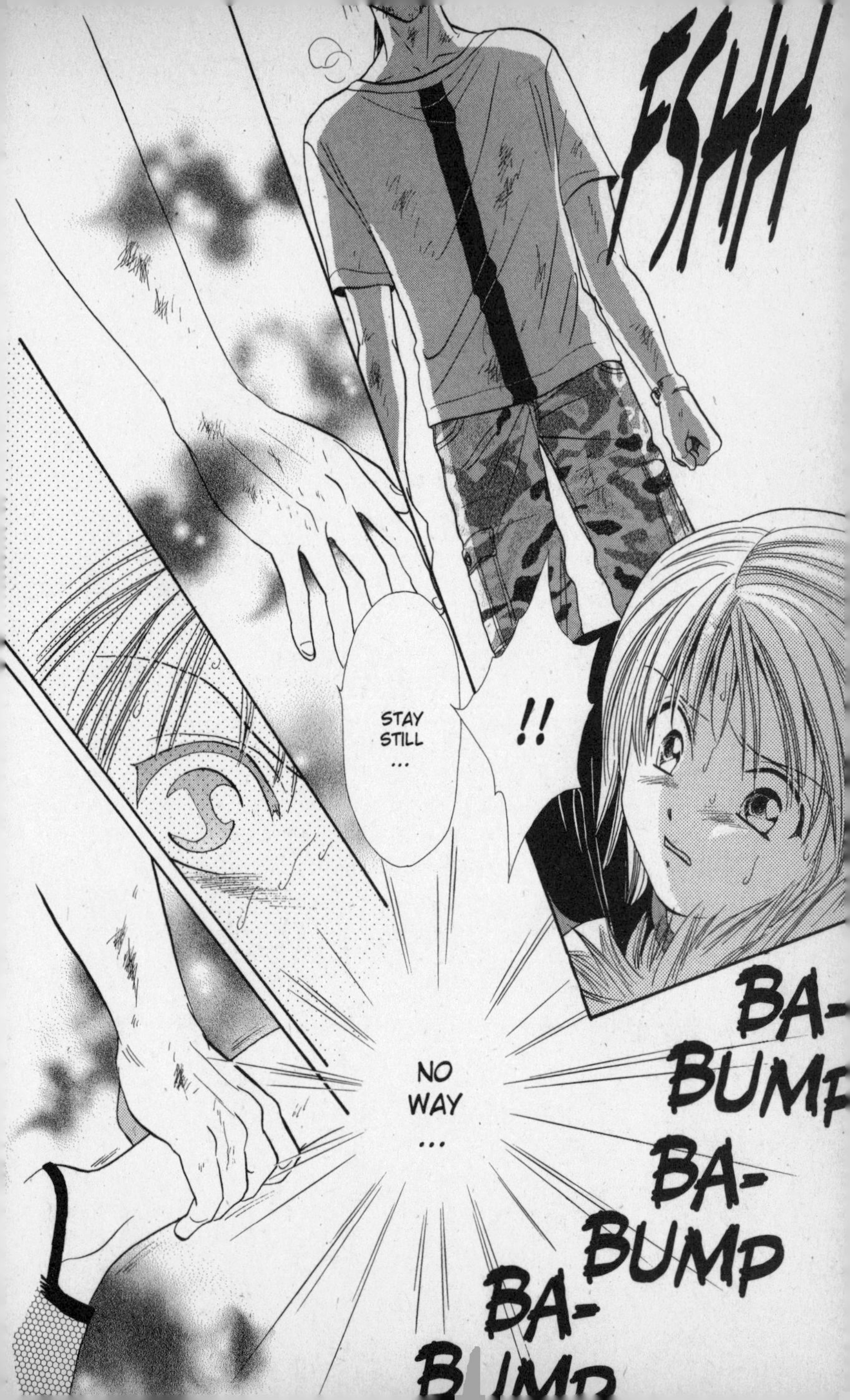
FSHH
STAY STILL ...
!!
BA-BUMP
NO WAY ...
BA-BUMP
BA-

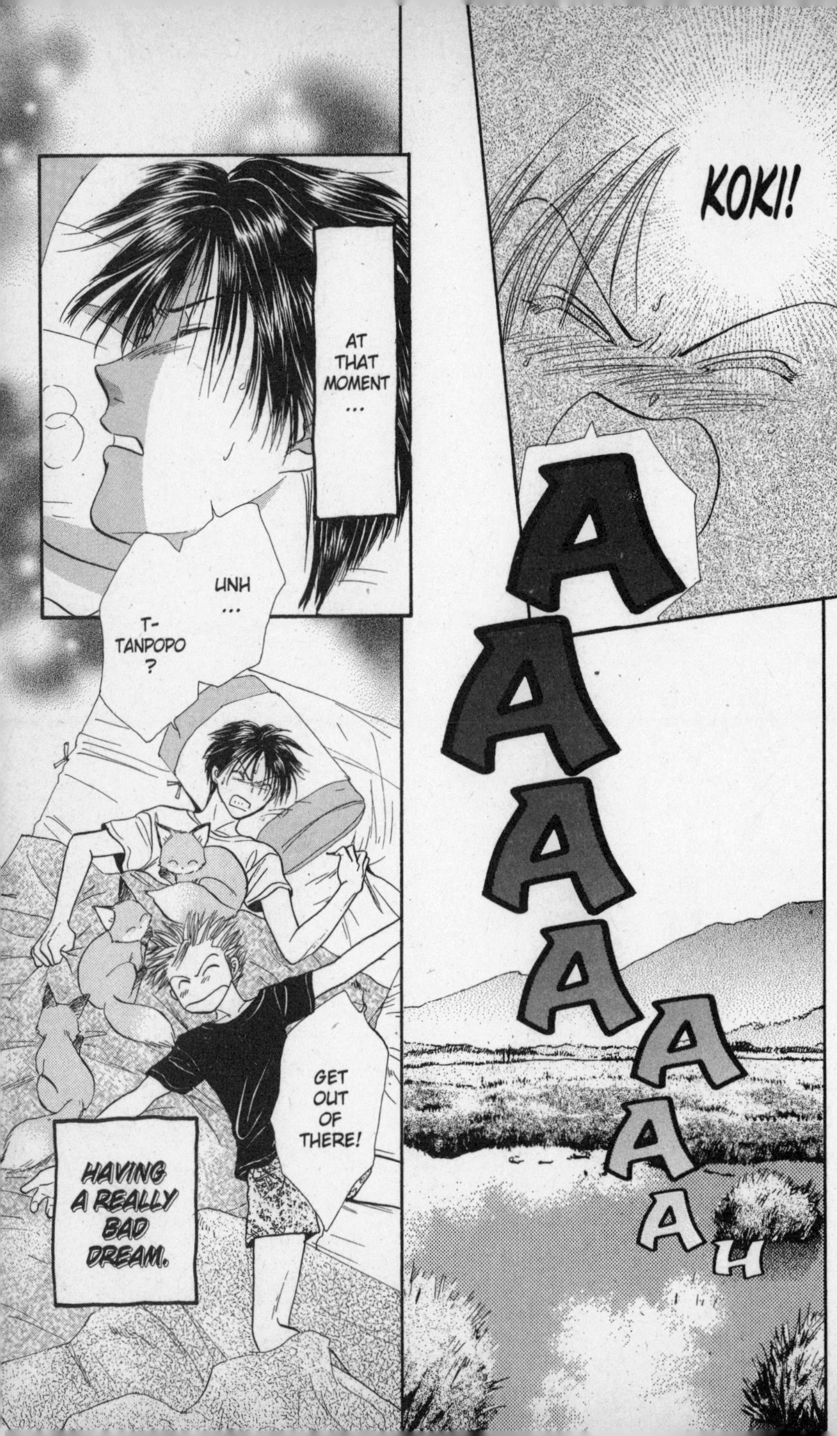
KOKI!
AAAAAAAH
AT THAT MOMENT ...
UNH ...
T-TANPOPO ?
GET OUT OF THERE!
HAVING A REALLY BAD DREAM.

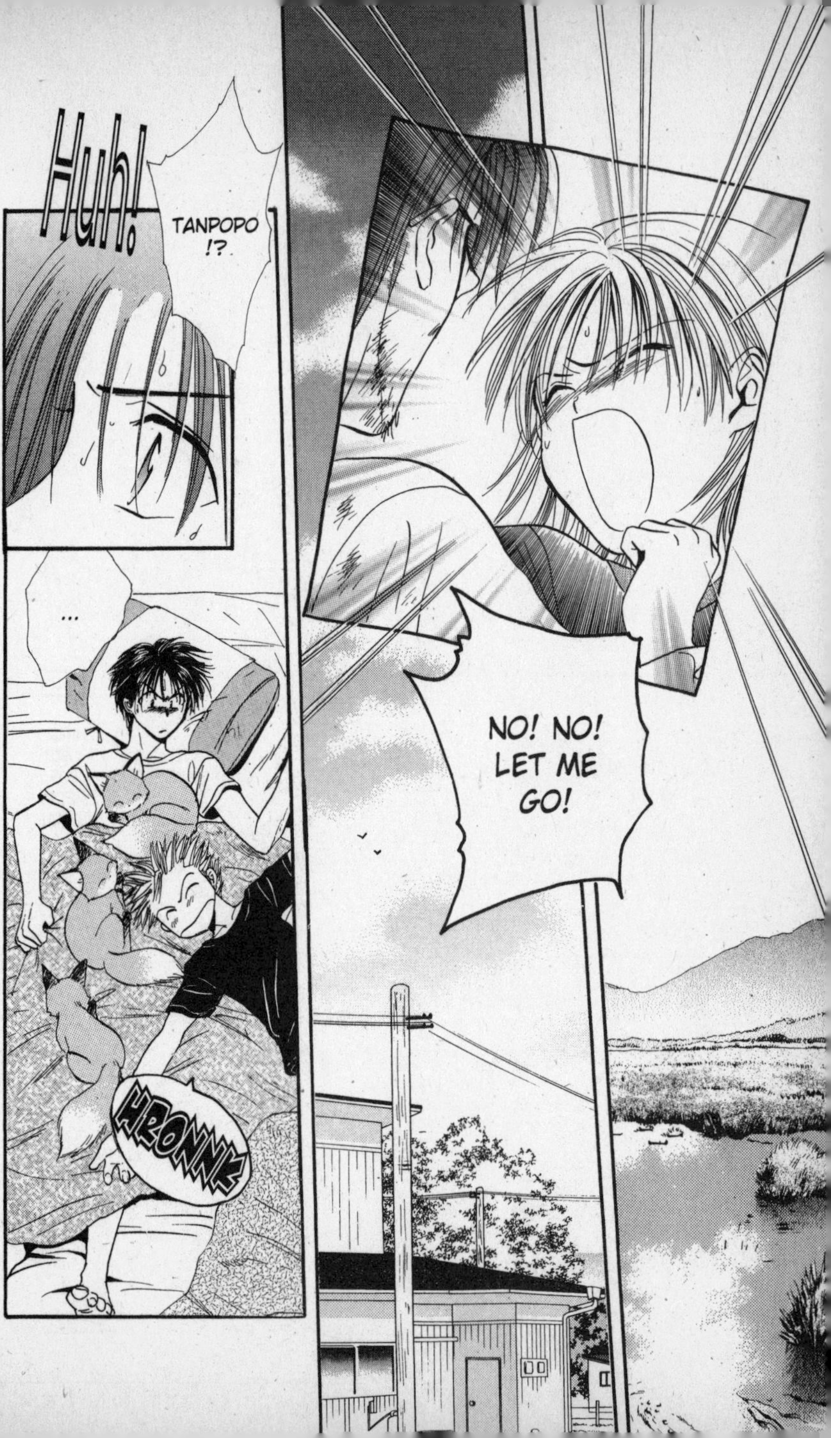
NO! NO! LET ME GO!
Huh!
TANPOPO !?
...
HRONNK

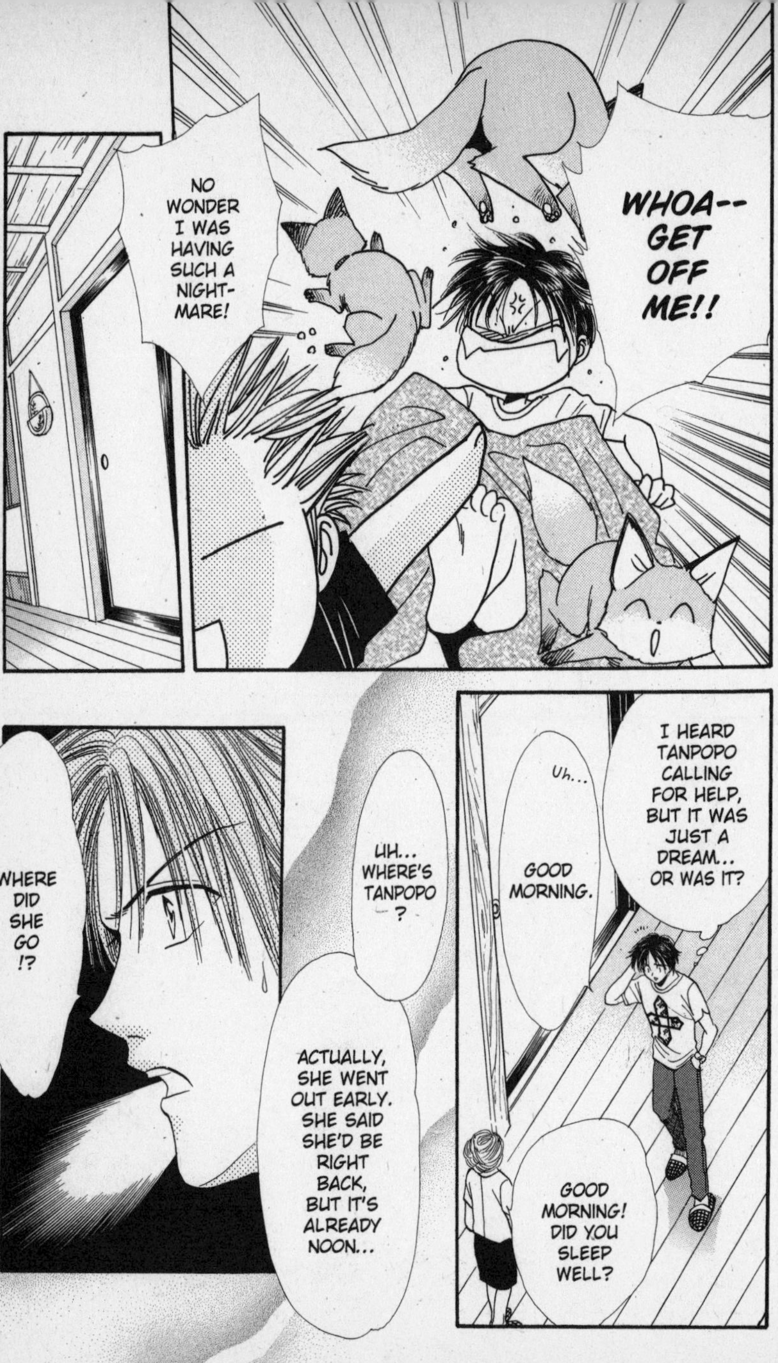
WHOA-- GET OFF ME!!
NO WONDER I WAS HAVING SUCH A NIGHTMARE!
I HEARD TANPOPO CALLING FOR HELP, BUT IT WAS JUST A DREAM... OR WAS IT?
Uh...
GOOD MORNING.
GOOD MORNING! DID YOU SLEEP WELL?
UH... WHERE'S TANPOPO?
ACTUALLY, SHE WENT OUT EARLY. SHE SAID SHE'D BE RIGHT BACK, BUT IT'S ALREADY NOON...
WHERE DID SHE GO!?

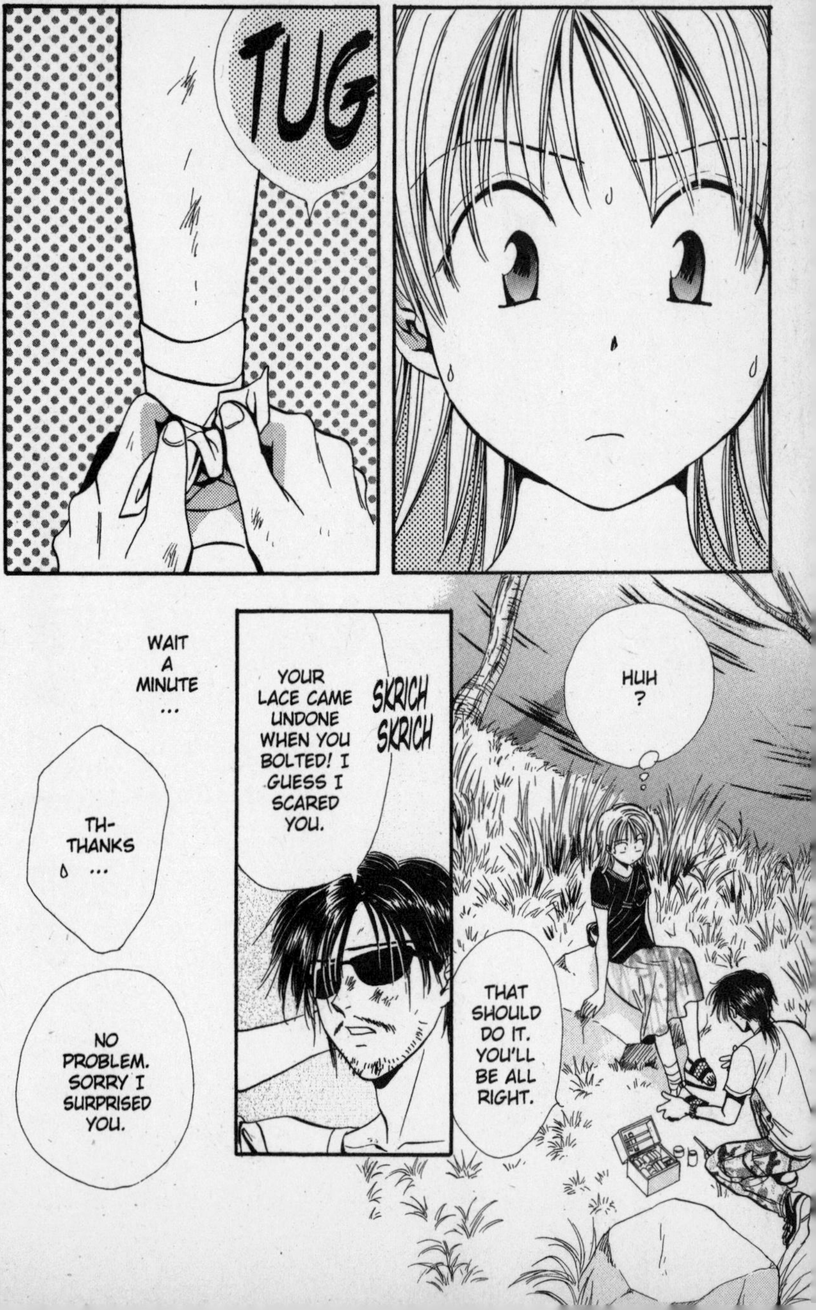
TUG
HUH?
THAT SHOULD DO IT. YOU'LL BE ALL RIGHT.
SKRICH SKRICH
YOUR LACE CAME UNDONE WHEN YOU BOLTED! I GUESS I SCARED YOU.
WAIT A MINUTE...
TH-THANKS...
NO PROBLEM. SORRY I SURPRISED YOU.

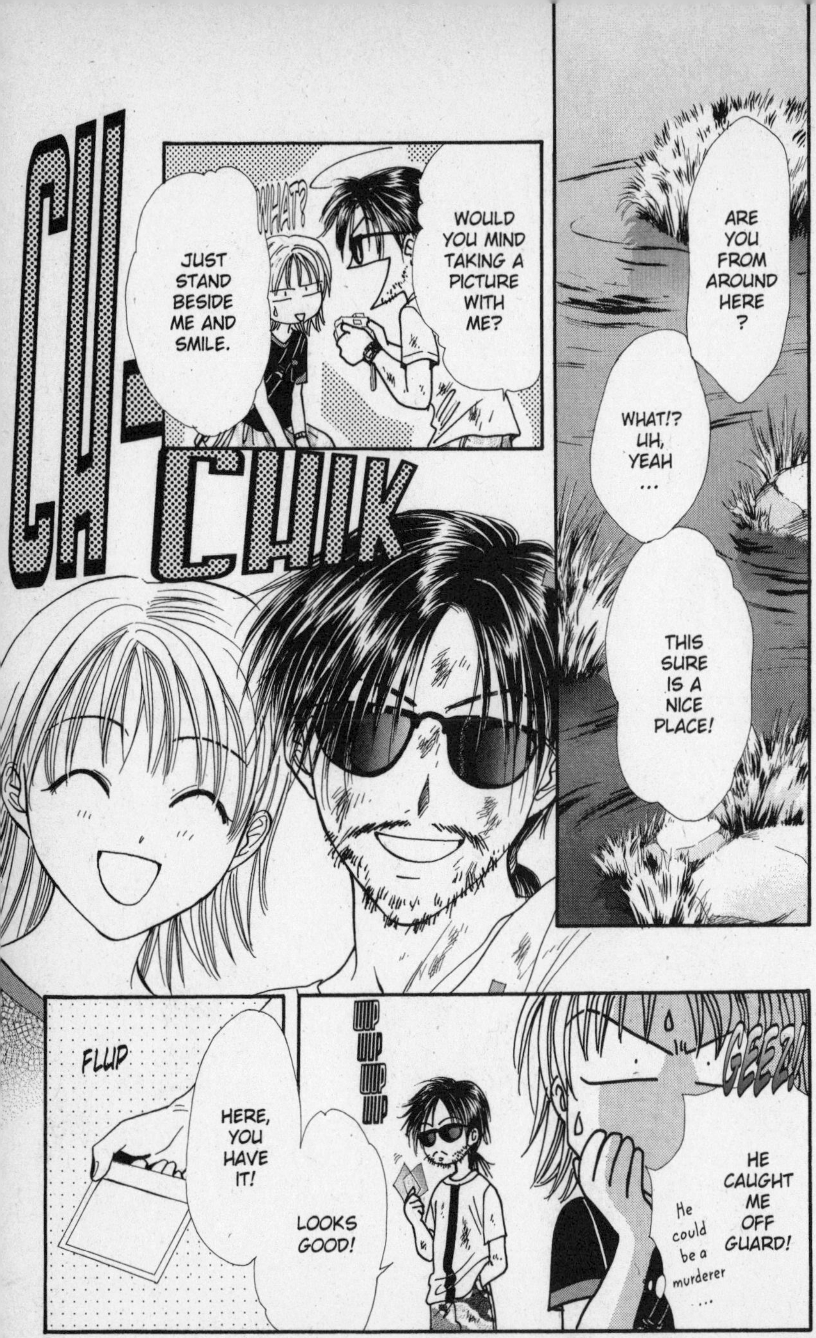
ARE YOU FROM AROUND HERE?
WHAT!? UH, YEAH...
THIS SURE IS A NICE PLACE!
WOULD YOU MIND TAKING A PICTURE WITH ME?
WHAT?
JUST STAND BESIDE ME AND SMILE.
CHI-
CHIK
GEEZ!
HE CAUGHT ME OFF GUARD!
He could be a murderer...
WUP WUP WUP WUP
LOOKS GOOD!
HERE, YOU HAVE IT!
FLUP

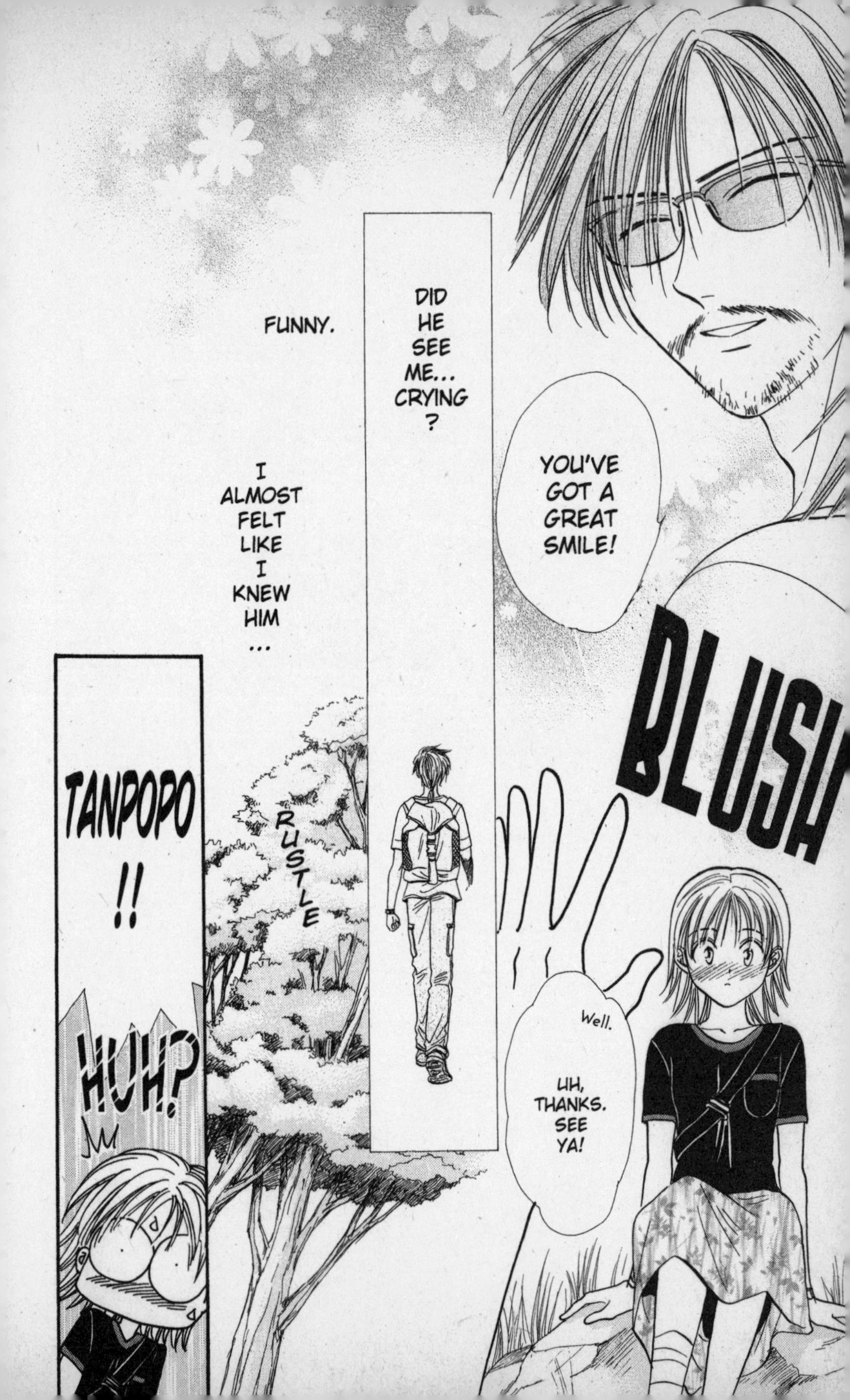
YOU'VE GOT A GREAT SMILE!
BLUSH
Well.
UH, THANKS. SEE YA!
DID HE SEE ME... CRYING?
FUNNY.
I ALMOST FELT LIKE I KNEW HIM...
RUSTLE
TANPOPO!!
HUH?

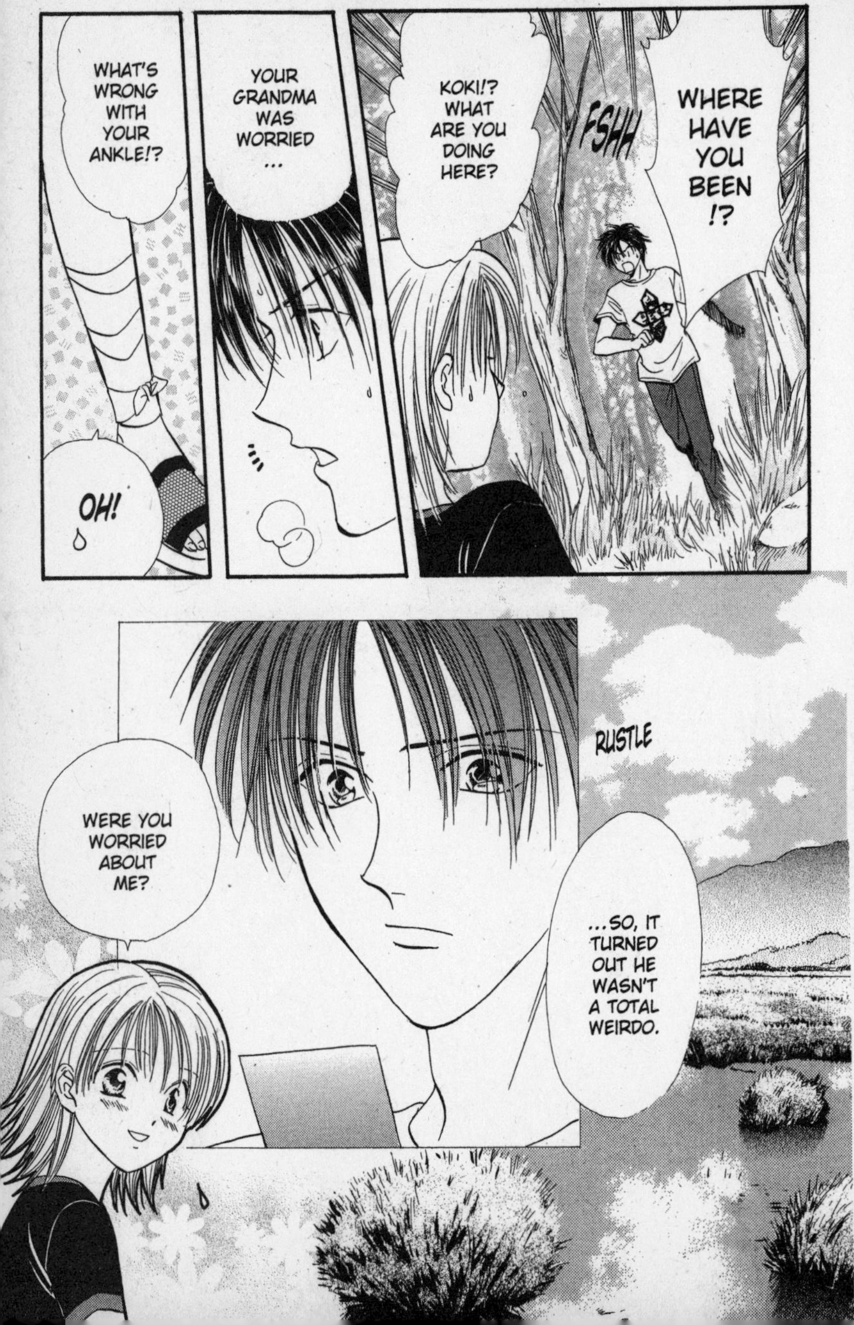
WHERE HAVE YOU BEEN!?
FSHH
KOKI!? WHAT ARE YOU DOING HERE?
YOUR GRANDMA WAS WORRIED...
WHAT'S WRONG WITH YOUR ANKLE!?
OH!
RUSTLE
...SO, IT TURNED OUT HE WASN'T A TOTAL WEIRDO.
WERE YOU WORRIED ABOUT ME?

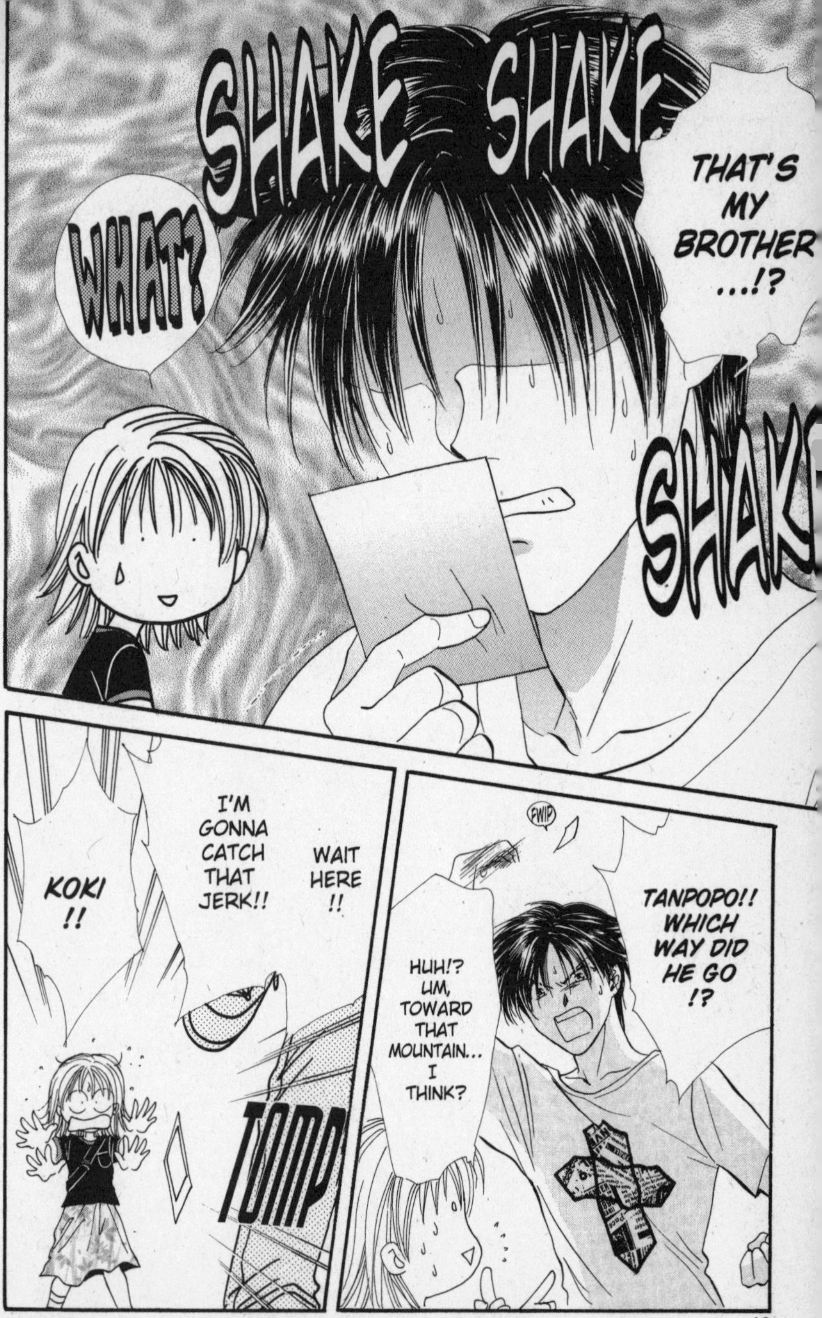
SHAKE SHAKE
THAT'S MY BROTHER ...!?
WHAT?
SHAK
FWIP
TANPOPO!! WHICH WAY DID HE GO!?
HUH!? UM, TOWARD THAT MOUNTAIN... I THINK?
WAIT HERE!!
I'M GONNA CATCH THAT JERK!!
KOKI!!
TOMP

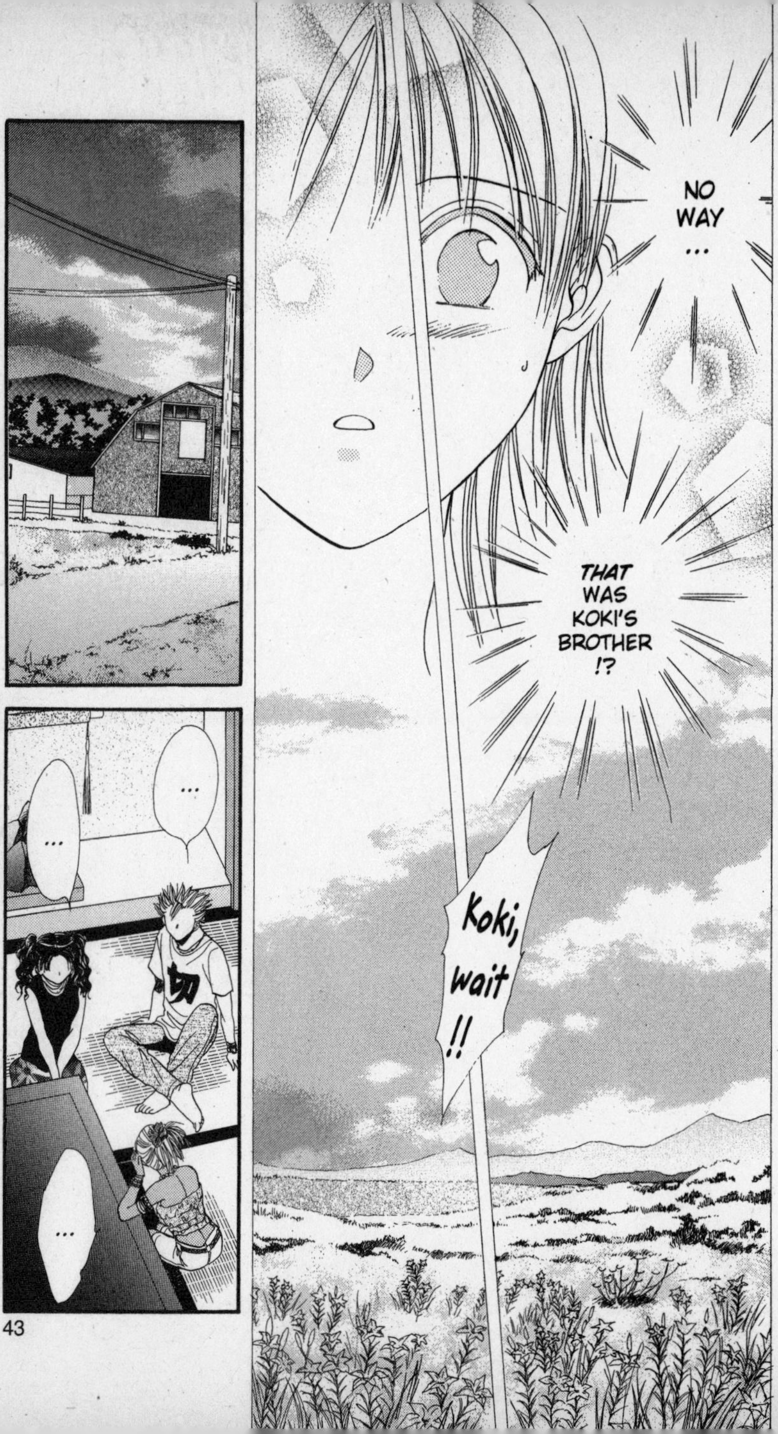
NO WAY ...
THAT WAS KOKI'S BROTHER !?
Koki, wait !!
...
...
...

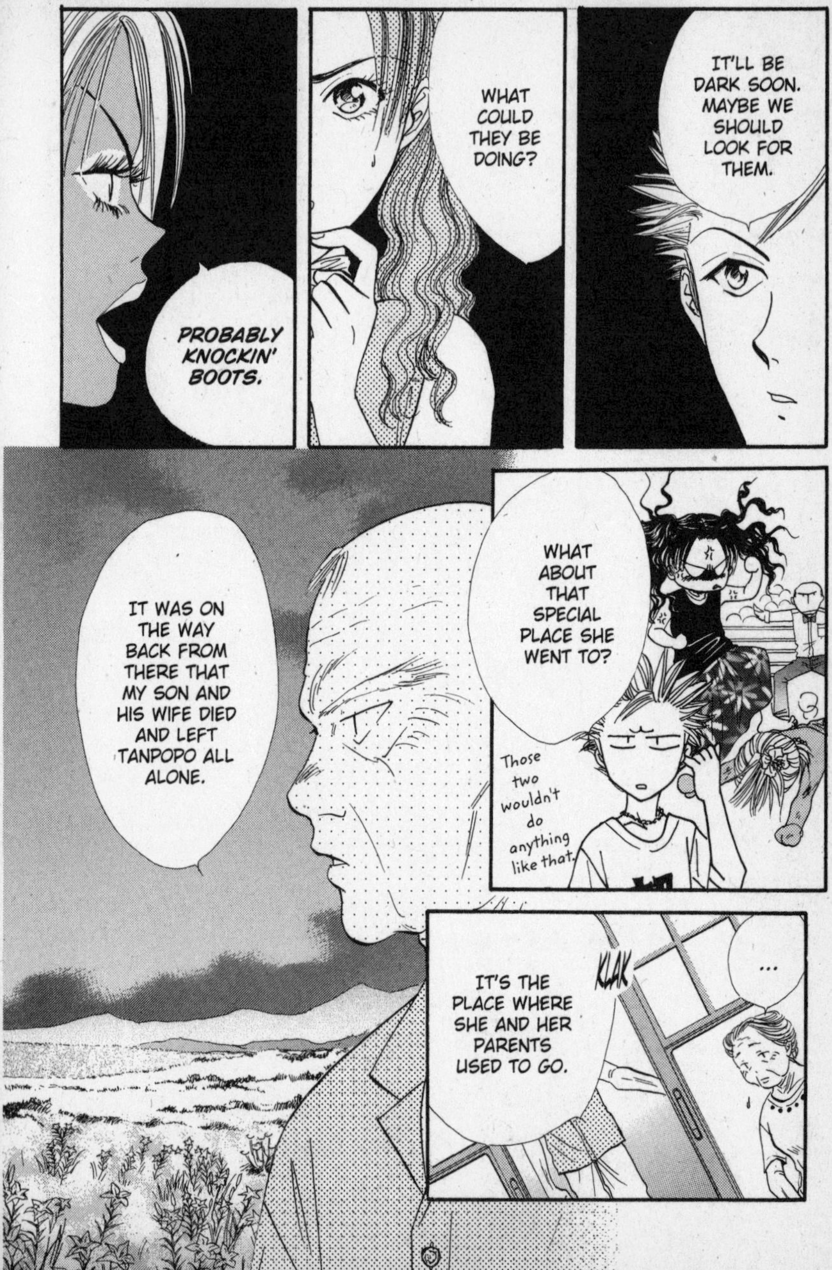
IT'LL BE DARK SOON. MAYBE WE SHOULD LOOK FOR THEM.
WHAT COULD THEY BE DOING?
PROBABLY KNOCKIN' BOOTS.
WHAT ABOUT THAT SPECIAL PLACE SHE WENT TO?
Those two wouldn't do anything like that.
...
KLAK
IT'S THE PLACE WHERE SHE AND HER PARENTS USED TO GO.
IT WAS ON THE WAY BACK FROM THERE THAT MY SON AND HIS WIFE DIED AND LEFT TANPOPO ALL ALONE.

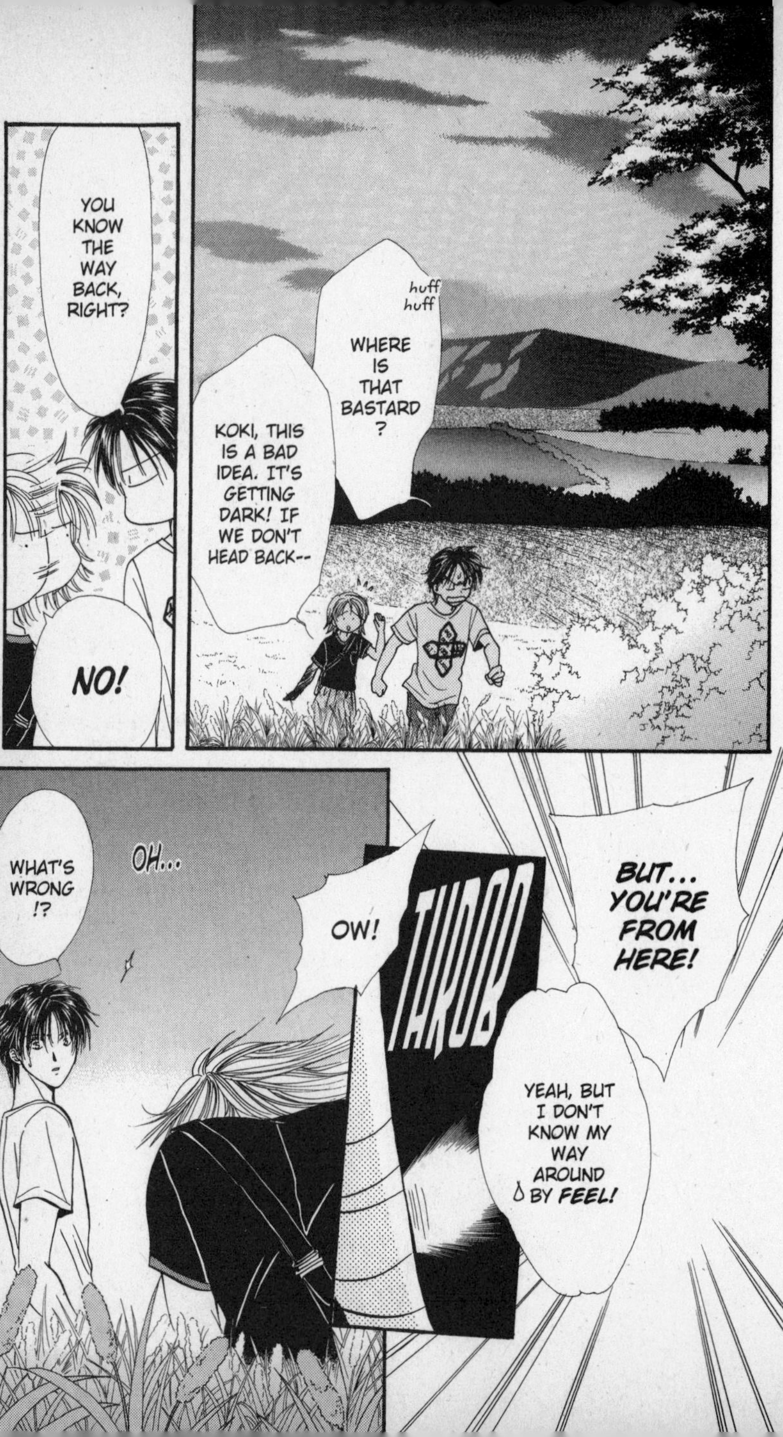
huff huff
WHERE IS THAT BASTARD?
KOKI, THIS IS A BAD IDEA. IT'S GETTING DARK! IF WE DON'T HEAD BACK--
YOU KNOW THE WAY BACK, RIGHT?
NO!
BUT... YOU'RE FROM HERE!
YEAH, BUT I DON'T KNOW MY WAY AROUND BY FEEL!
THROB
OW!
OH...
WHAT'S WRONG!?

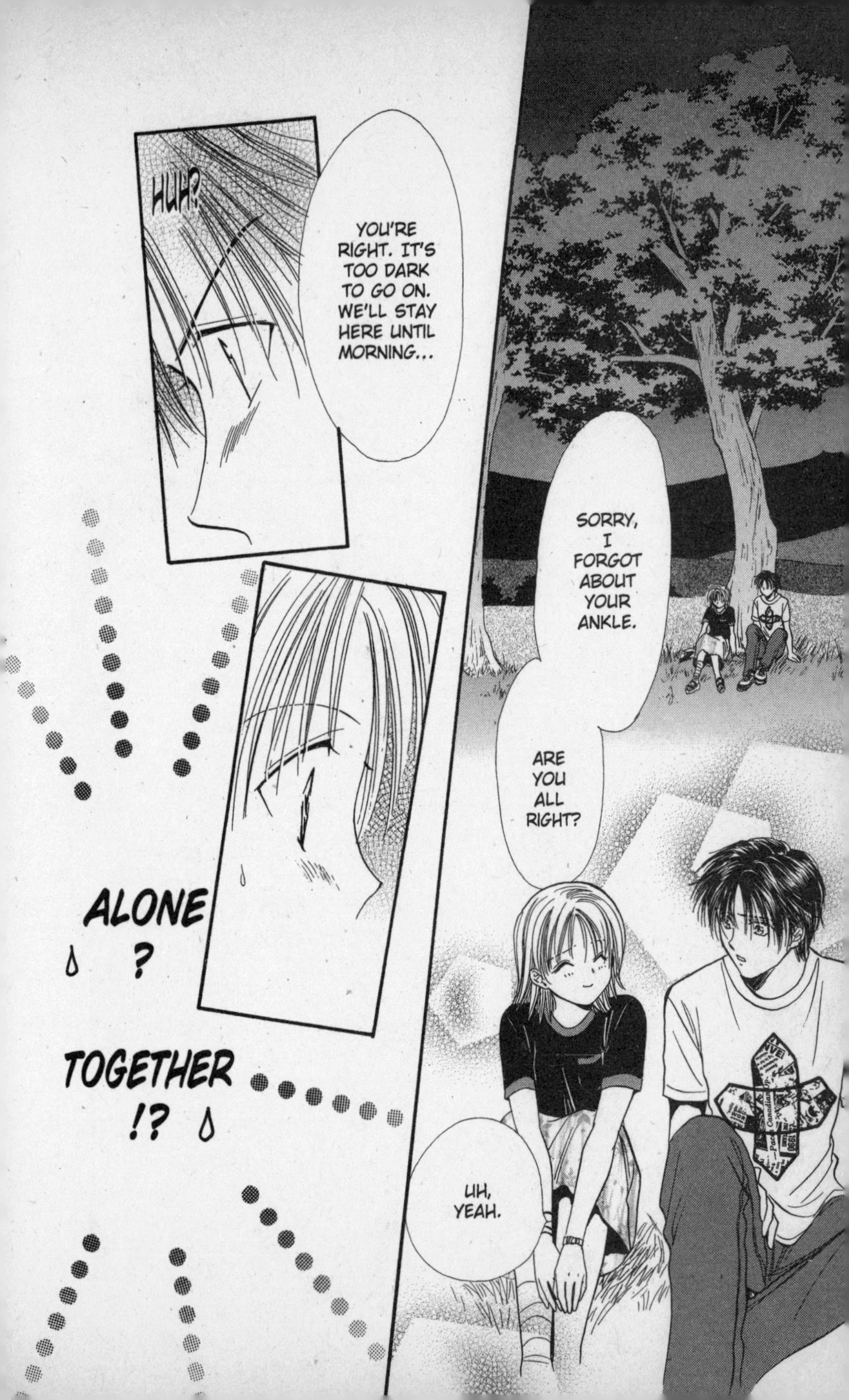
SORRY, I FORGOT ABOUT YOUR ANKLE.
ARE YOU ALL RIGHT?
UH, YEAH.
YOU'RE RIGHT. IT'S TOO DARK TO GO ON. WE'LL STAY HERE UNTIL MORNING...
HUH?
ALONE ?
TOGETHER !?

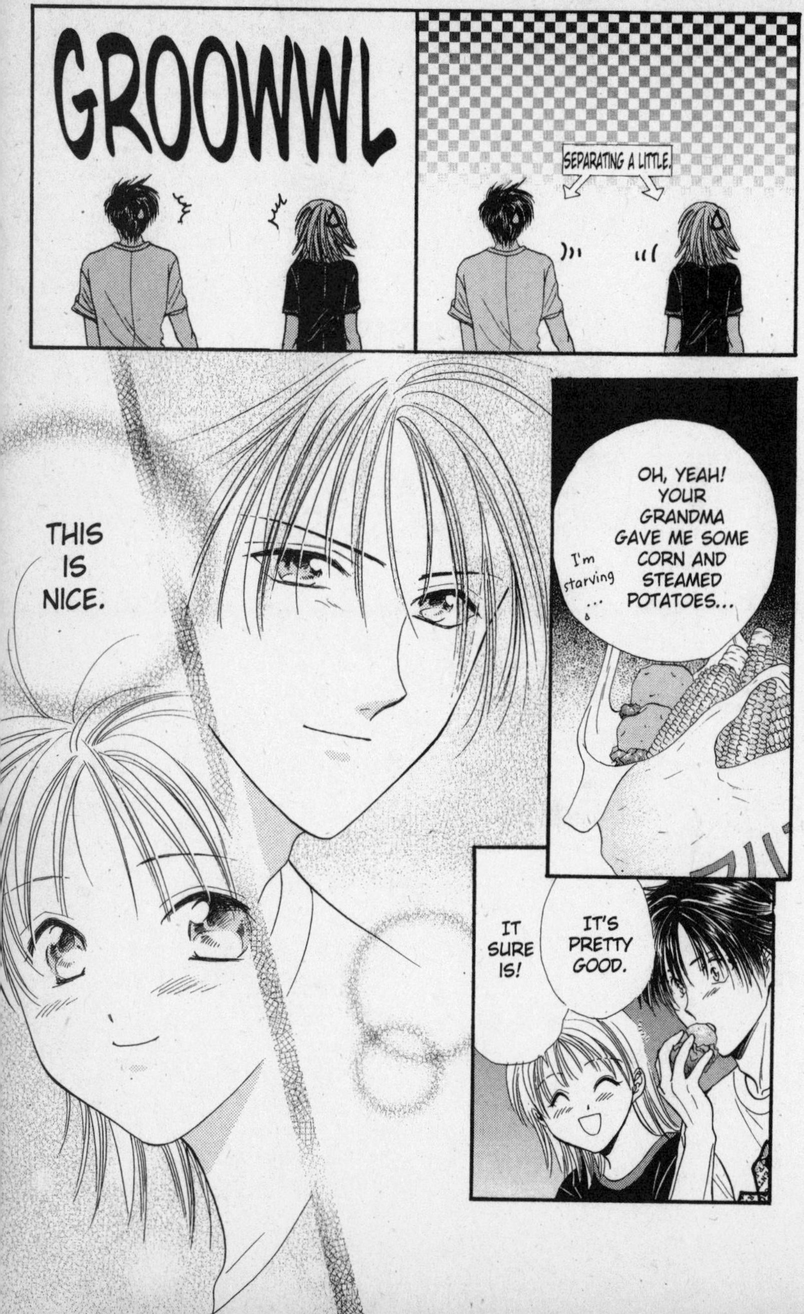
SEPARATING A LITTLE.
GROOWWL
OH, YEAH! YOUR GRANDMA GAVE ME SOME CORN AND STEAMED POTATOES...
I'm starving...
IT'S PRETTY GOOD.
IT SURE IS!
THIS IS NICE.

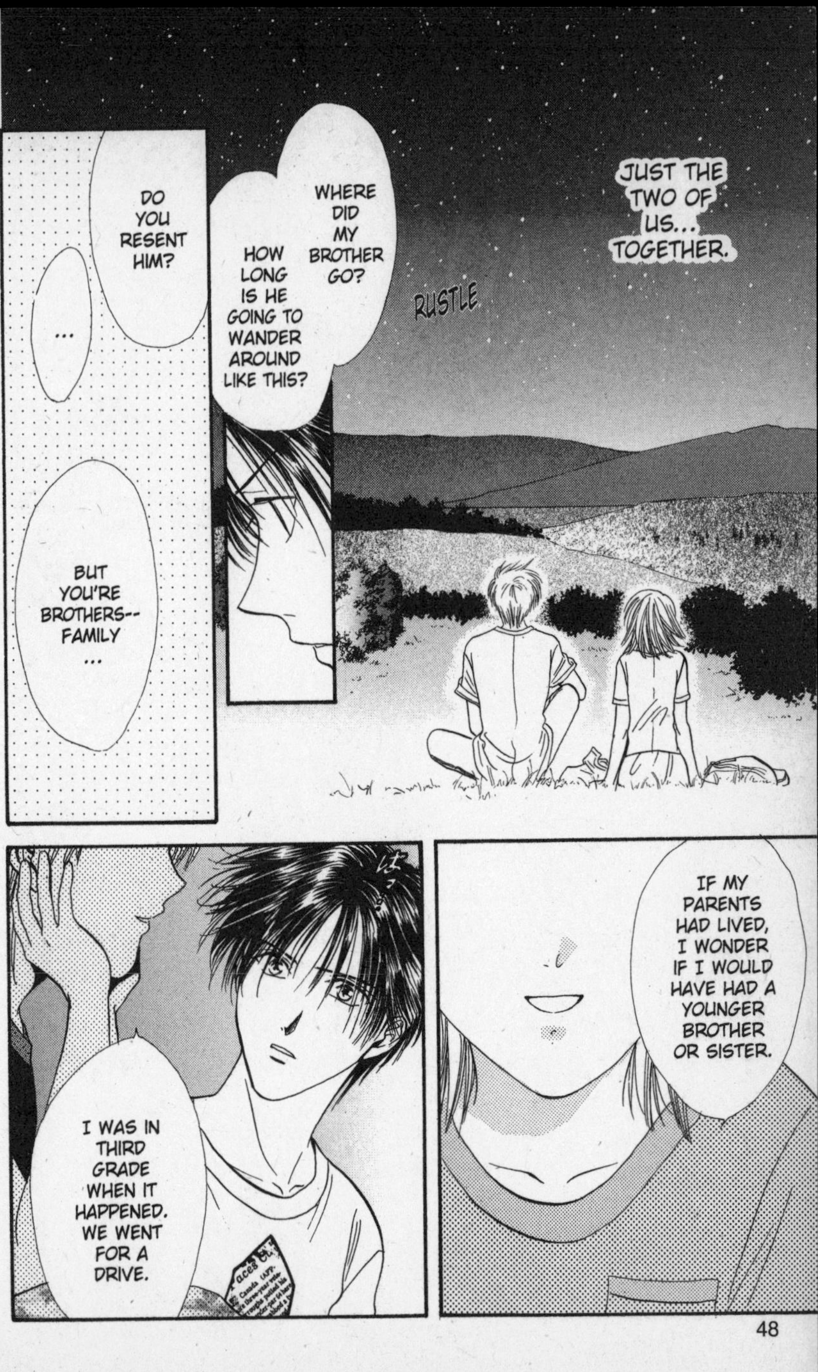
JUST THE TWO OF US... TOGETHER.
RUSTLE
WHERE DID MY BROTHER GO?
HOW LONG IS HE GOING TO WANDER AROUND LIKE THIS?
DO YOU RESENT HIM?
...
BUT YOU'RE BROTHERS--FAMILY ...
IF MY PARENTS HAD LIVED, I WONDER IF I WOULD HAVE HAD A YOUNGER BROTHER OR SISTER.
I WAS IN THIRD GRADE WHEN IT HAPPENED. WE WENT FOR A DRIVE.

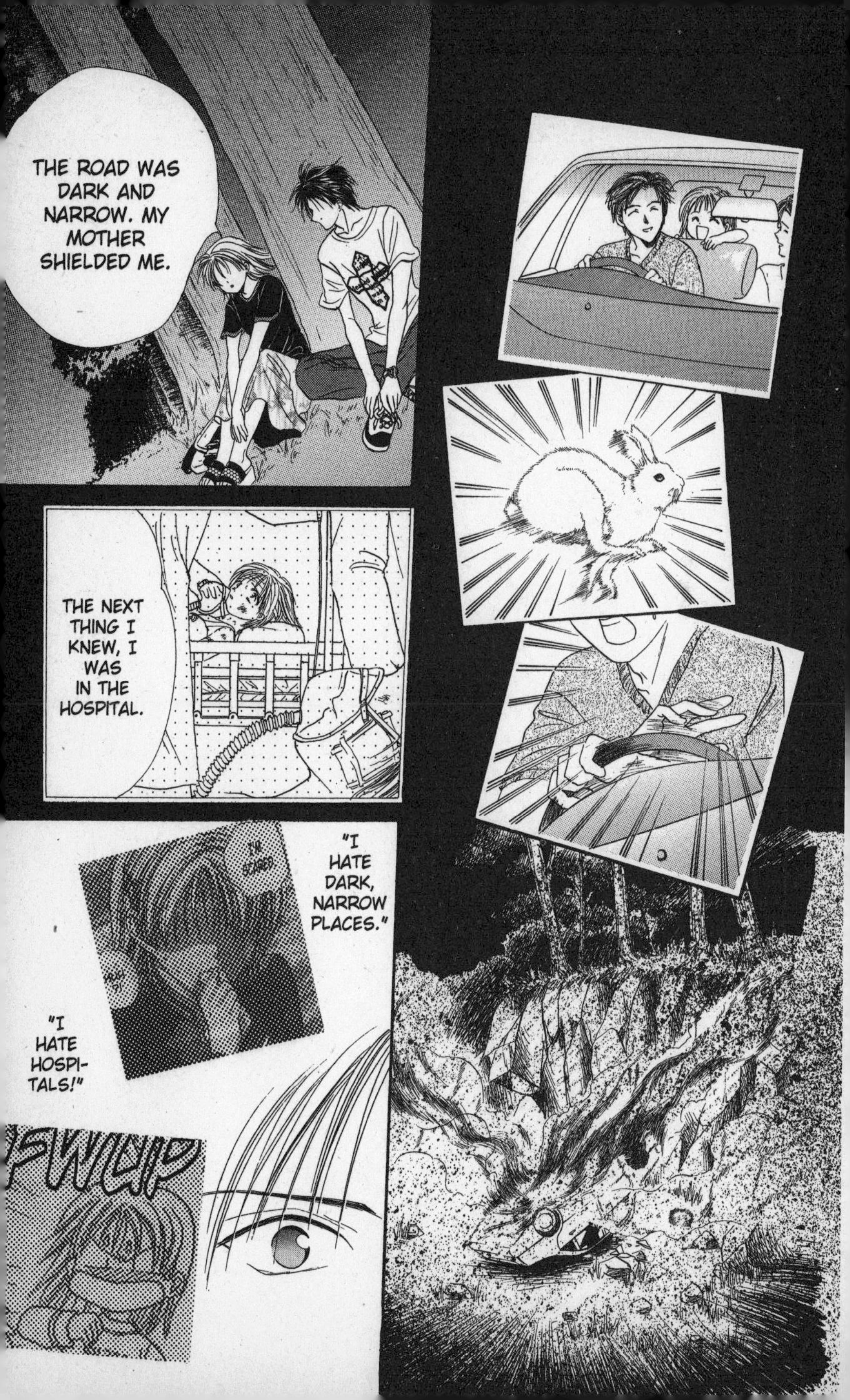
THE ROAD WAS DARK AND NARROW. MY MOTHER SHIELDED ME.
THE NEXT THING I KNEW, I WAS IN THE HOSPITAL.
"I HATE DARK, NARROW PLACES."
I'M SCARED
"I HATE HOSPI-TALS!"
FWUP

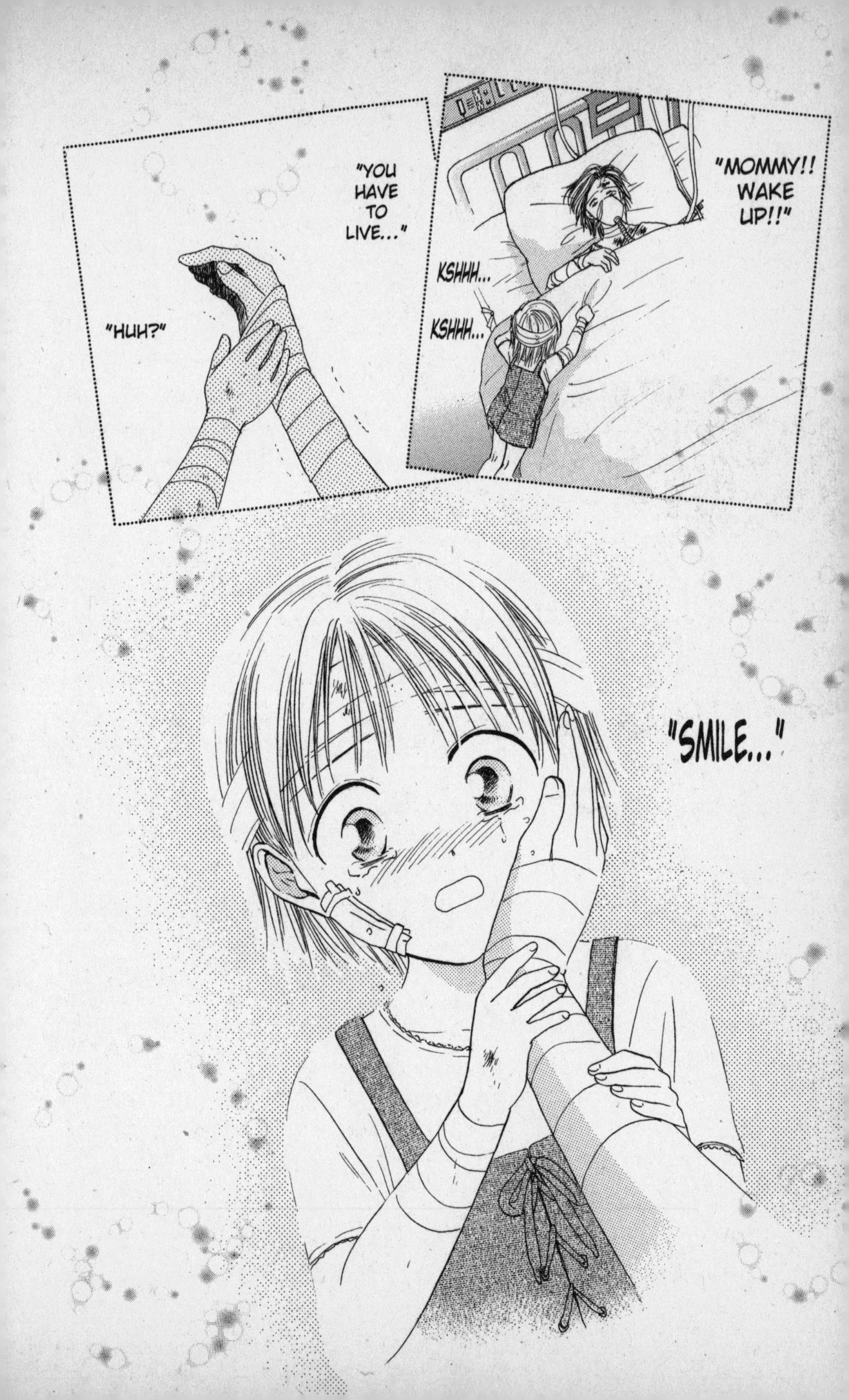
"MOMMY!! WAKE UP!!"
KSHHH...
KSHHH...
"YOU HAVE TO LIVE..."
"HUH?"
"SMILE..."

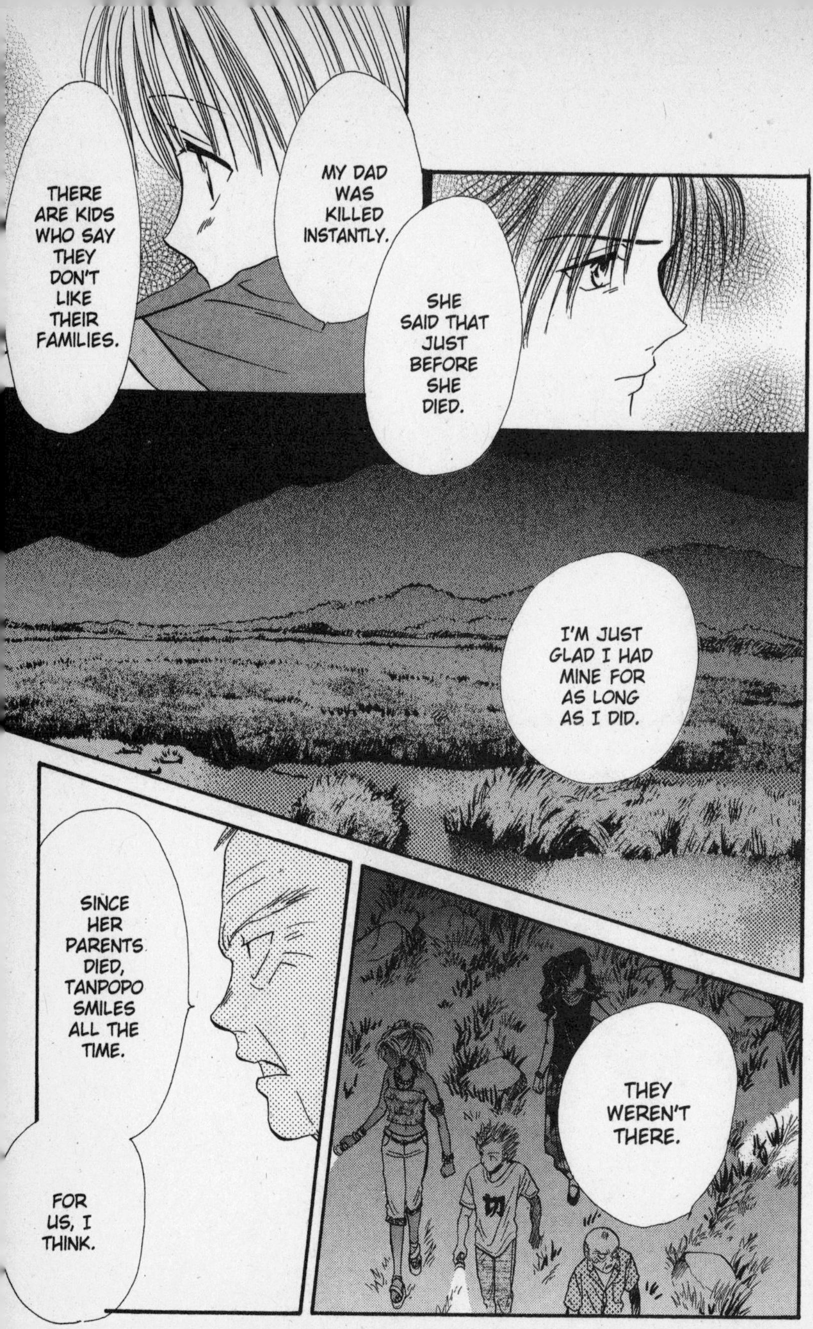

MY DAD WAS KILLED INSTANTLY.
SHE SAID THAT JUST BEFORE SHE DIED.
THERE ARE KIDS WHO SAY THEY DON'T LIKE THEIR FAMILIES.
I'M JUST GLAD I HAD MINE FOR AS LONG AS I DID.
THEY WEREN'T THERE.
SINCE HER PARENTS DIED, TANPOPO SMILES ALL THE TIME.
FOR US, I THINK.

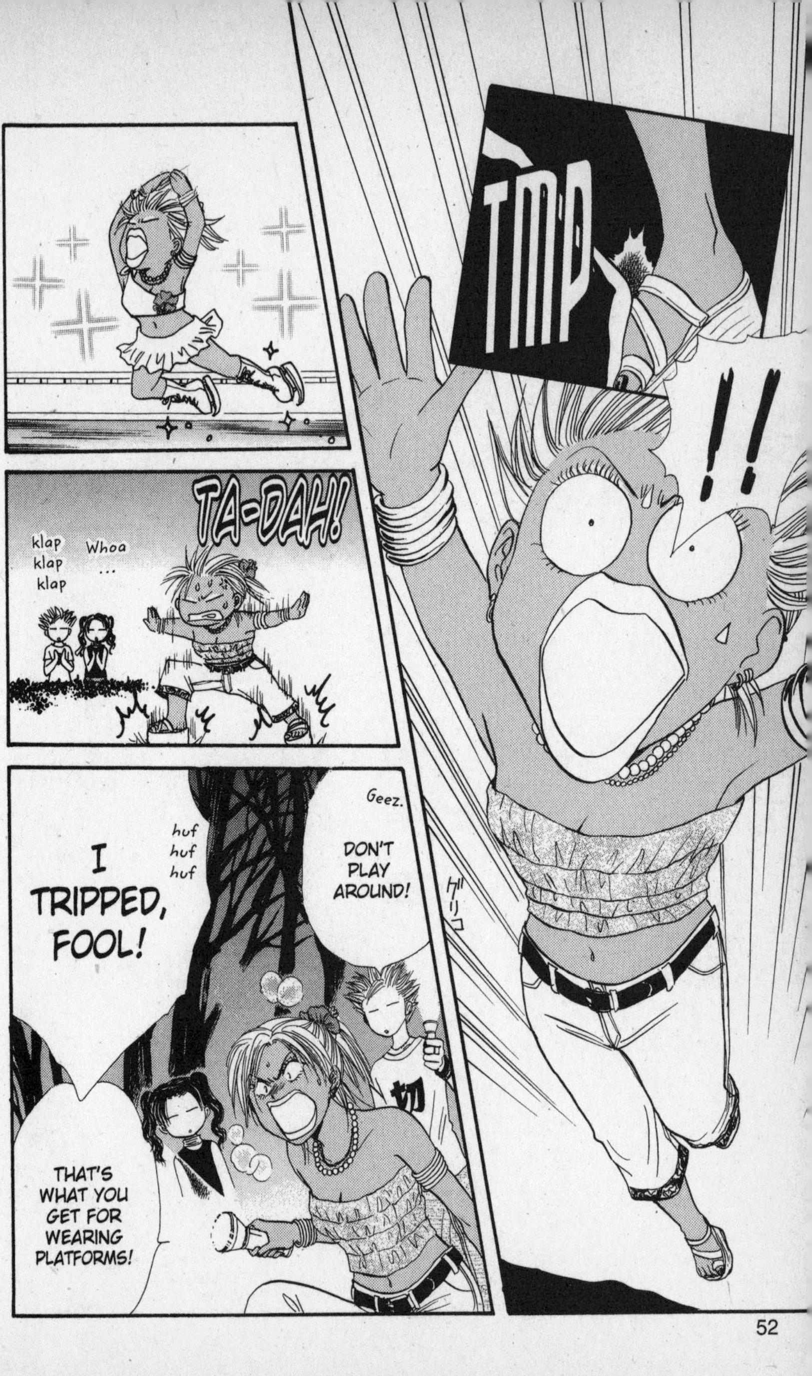
TMP
!!
グリコ
TA-DAH!
Whoa ...
klap klap klap
Geez.
DON'T PLAY AROUND!
huf huf huf
I TRIPPED, FOOL!
THAT'S WHAT YOU GET FOR WEARING PLATFORMS!

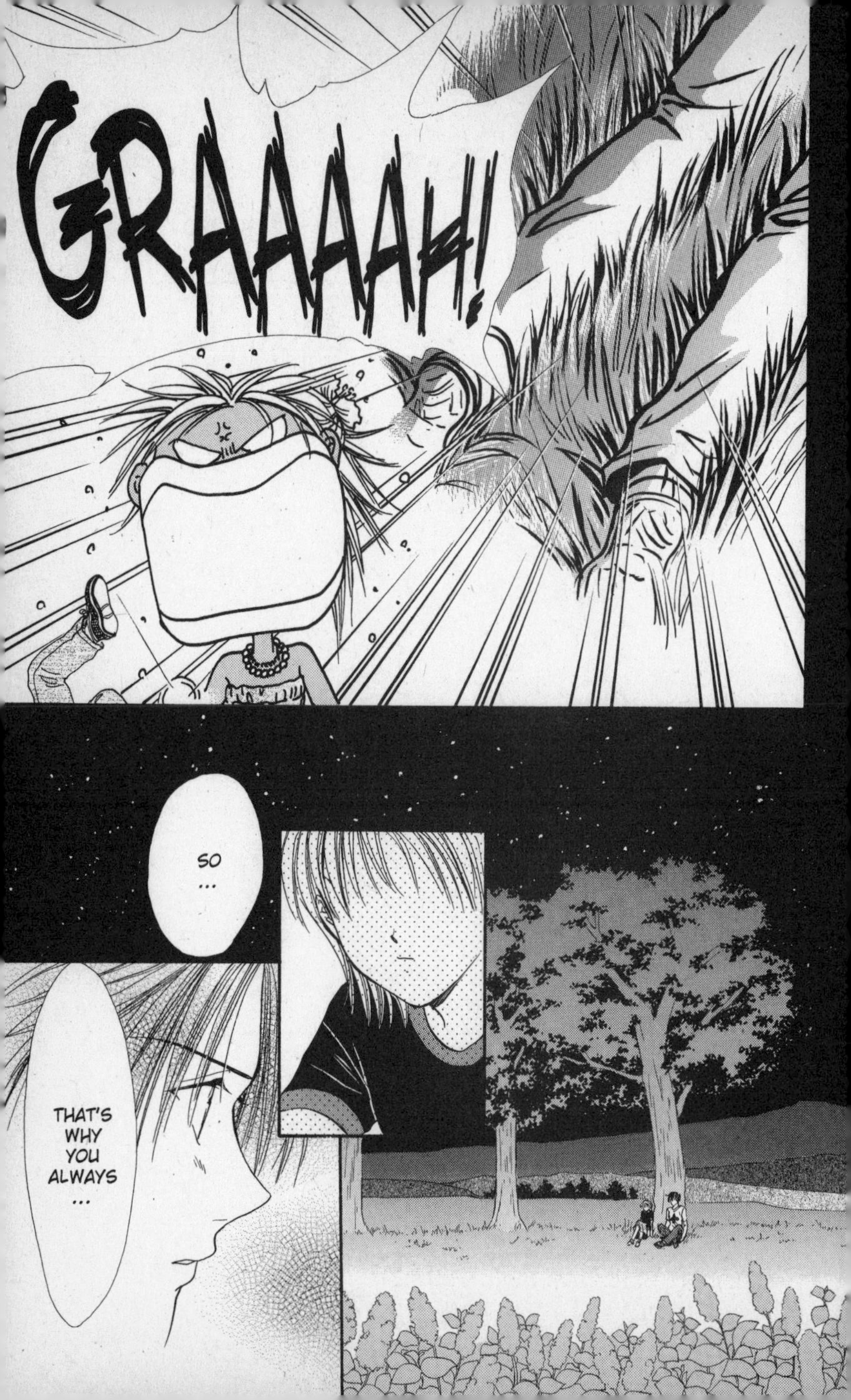
GRAAAAH!
SO ...
THAT'S WHY YOU ALWAYS ...

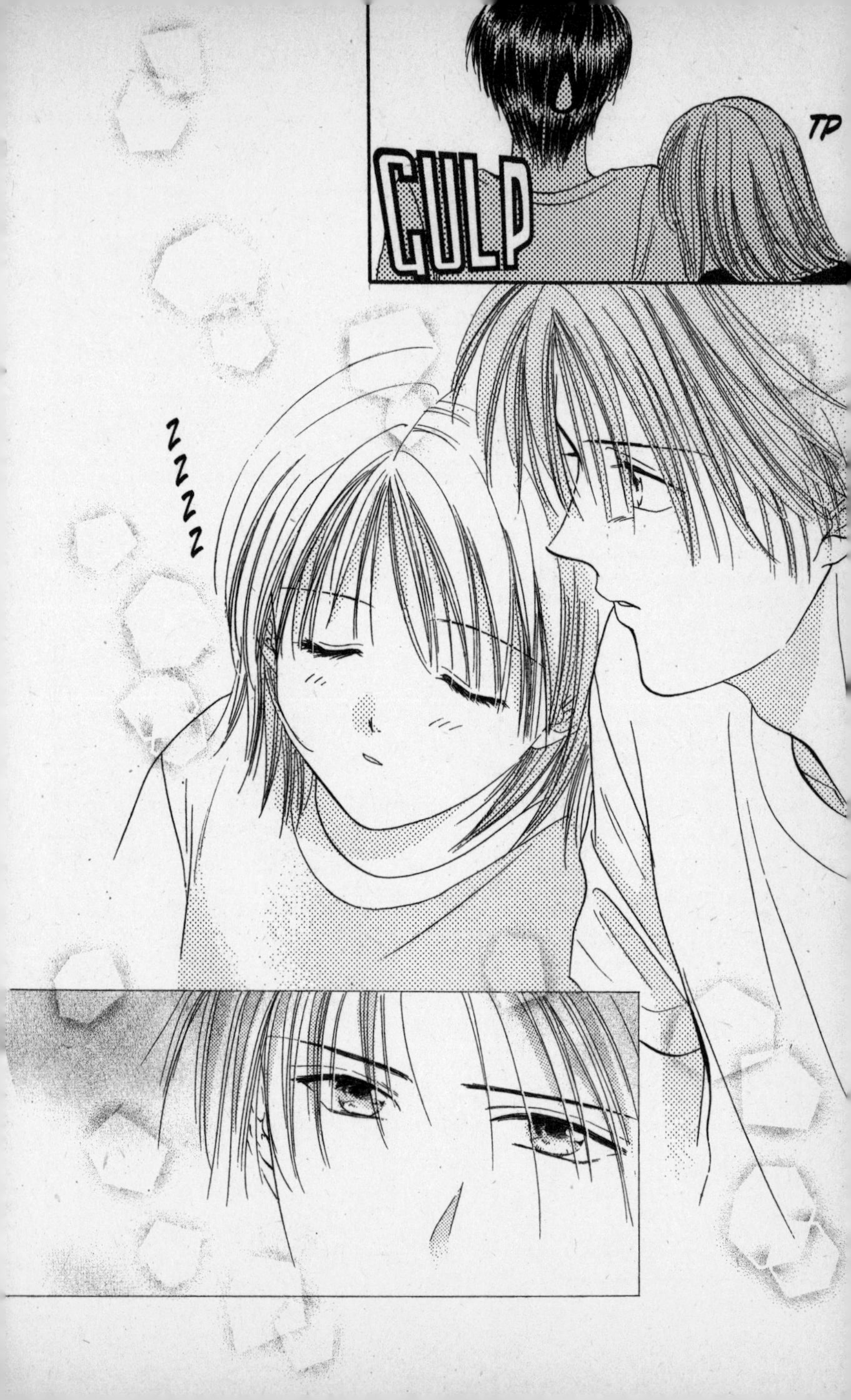
TP
GULP
ZZZZ

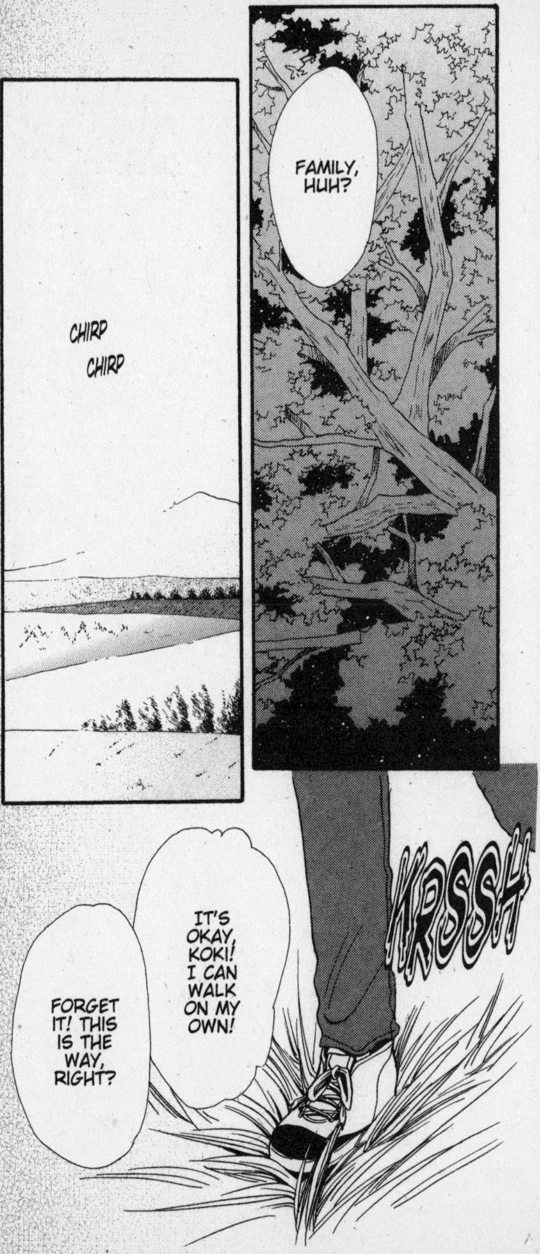
FAMILY, HUH?
CHIRP
CHIRP
KRSSH
IT'S OKAY, KOKI! I CAN WALK ON MY OWN!
FORGET IT! THIS IS THE WAY, RIGHT?

Moving on.

Hokkaido appears in this story, but I haven't been there since a signing event several years ago. Actually, I was supposed go there for research, but we had enough info, so we were able to get by without my going.

I just remembered that a writer acquaintance of mine and her assistant stayed at a hotel once, and they had a close encounter with a ghost! ☺ I mean, in Hokkaido. They told me the name of the hotel and even the room number, but I've forgotten. I'm not going there! It seems you can do a lot there. It's a little scary...that kind of thing doesn't happen in the summer, does it?

Anyway, I just remembered that I saw "The Exorcist: Special Edition." I saw the original a long time ago, so I knew the plot. But it's more than scary, it's a deep movie that can be interpreted many ways. It's very convincing, unlike most splatter flicks or other mindless horror films. This is an "occult" film.

The Devil is quite foul-mouthed, don't you think? Personally, I hate profanity.

But I can handle well-done intelligent profanity. ☺ I mean, who can laugh when they use foul language or just toss around toilet humor. We're not kids. (Kids can't help liking that stuff.) It's okay if that's part of the storyline, but I personally don't like it. When you hear an adult saying such things you think, "Oh well." And, when someone talks dirty, you want to ask, "Are you an animal?" I've never known anyone like that, though.

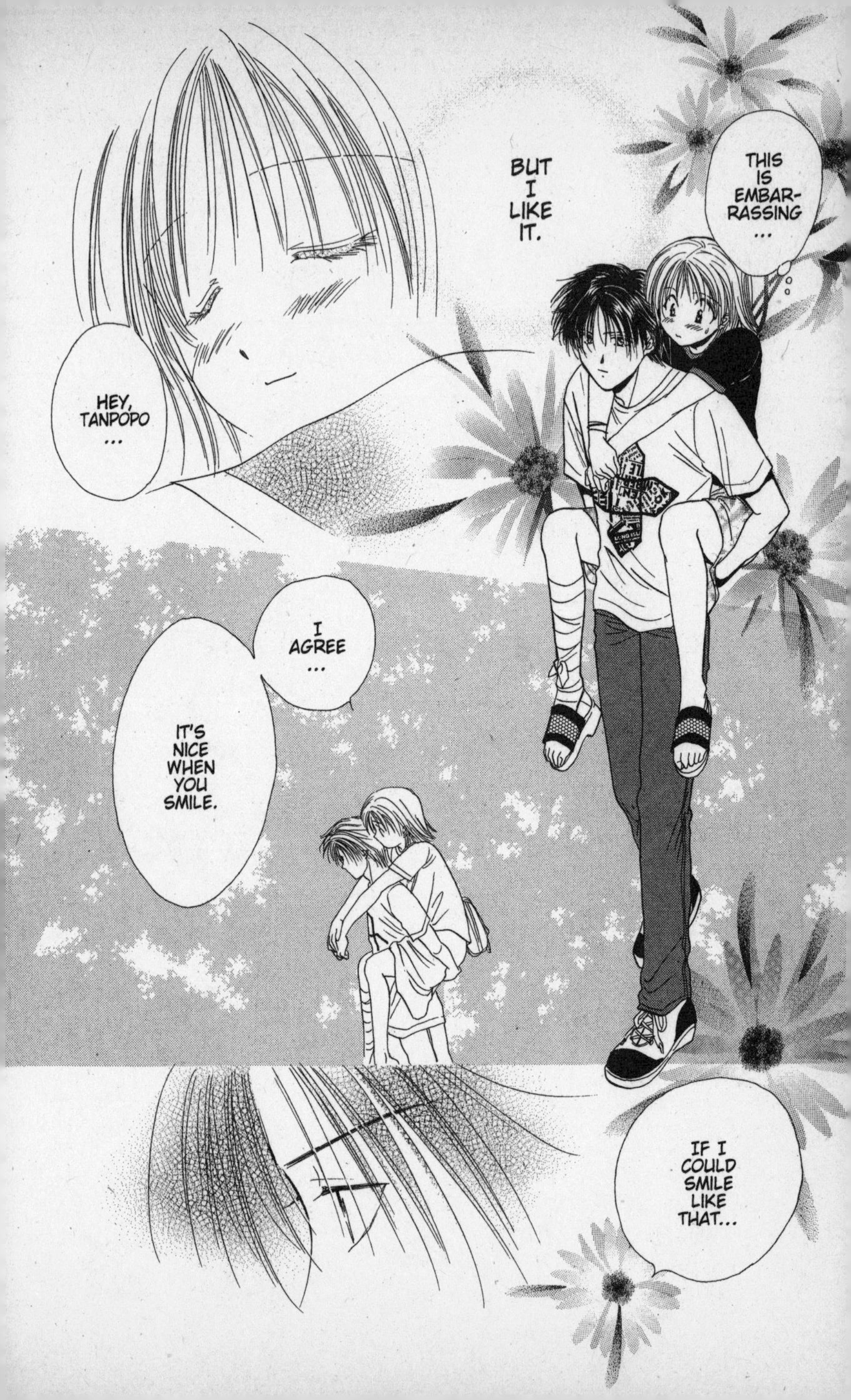
THIS IS EMBARRASSING...
BUT I LIKE IT.
HEY, TANPOPO...
I AGREE...
IT'S NICE WHEN YOU SMILE.
IF I COULD SMILE LIKE THAT...

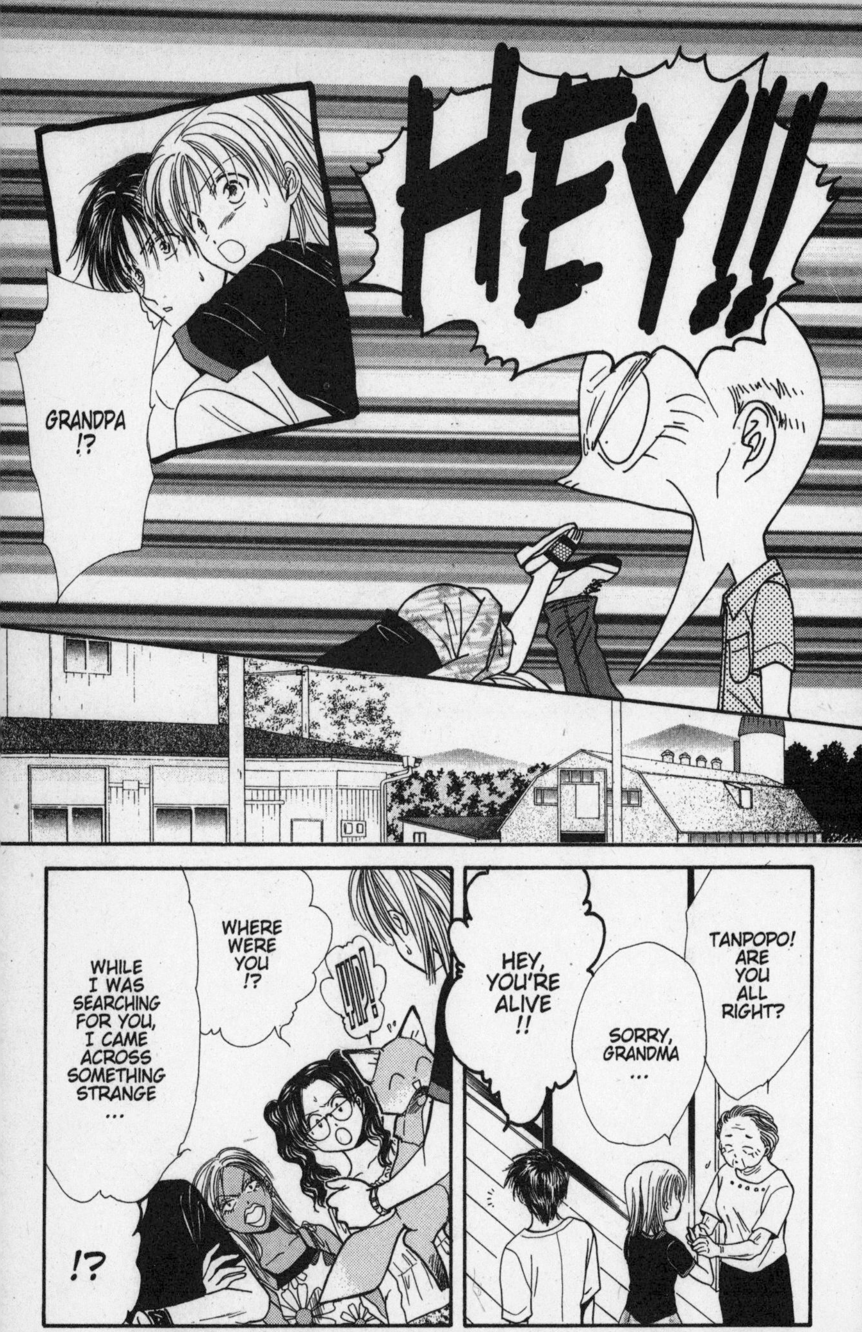
HEY!!
GRANDPA !?
TANPOPO! ARE YOU ALL RIGHT?
SORRY, GRANDMA ...
HEY, YOU'RE ALIVE !!
WHERE WERE YOU !?
YIP!
WHILE I WAS SEARCHING FOR YOU, I CAME ACROSS SOMETHING STRANGE ...
!?

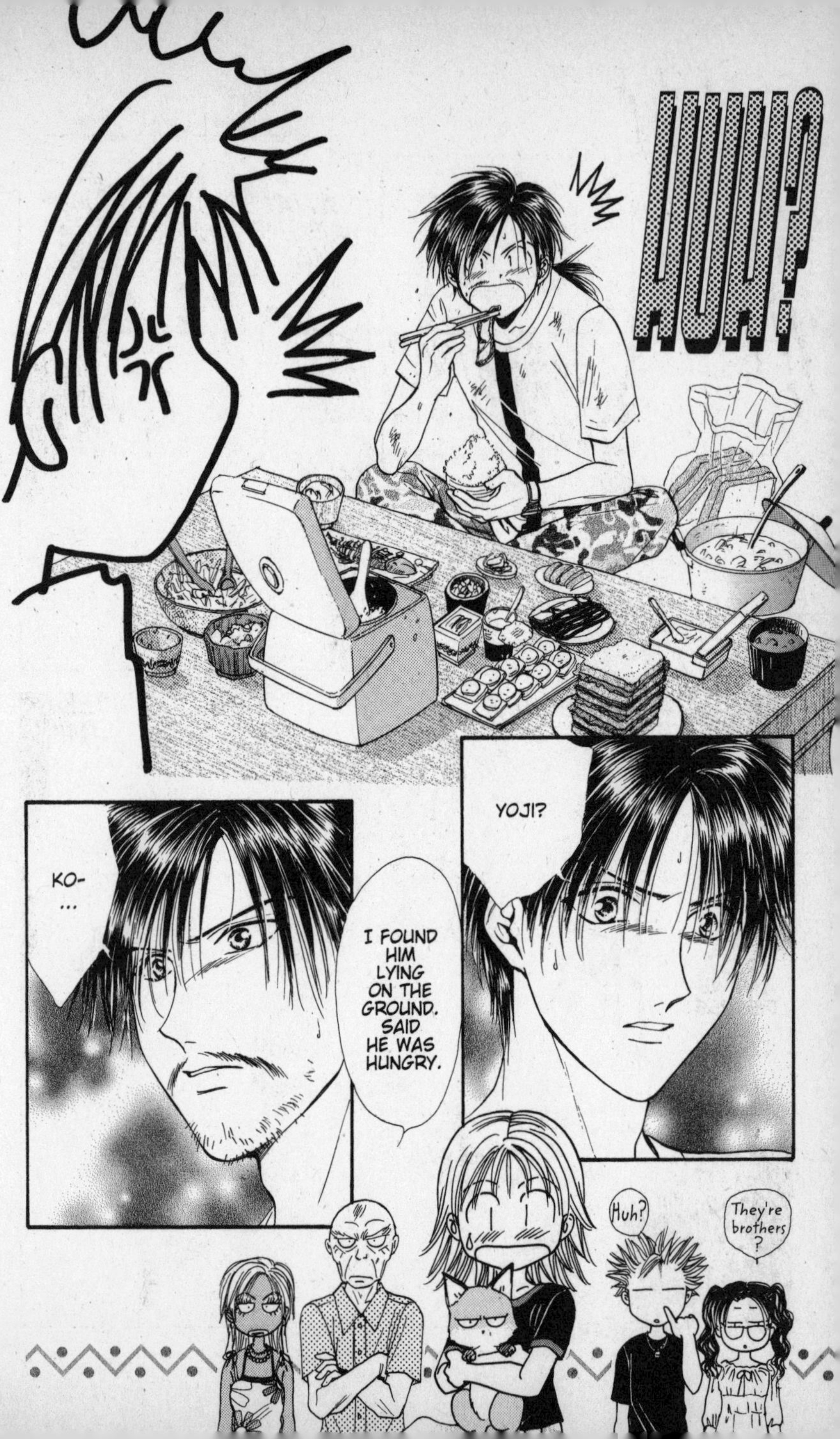
HUH!?
YOJI?
KO-
...
I FOUND HIM LYING ON THE GROUND. SAID HE WAS HUNGRY.
They're brothers?
Huh?

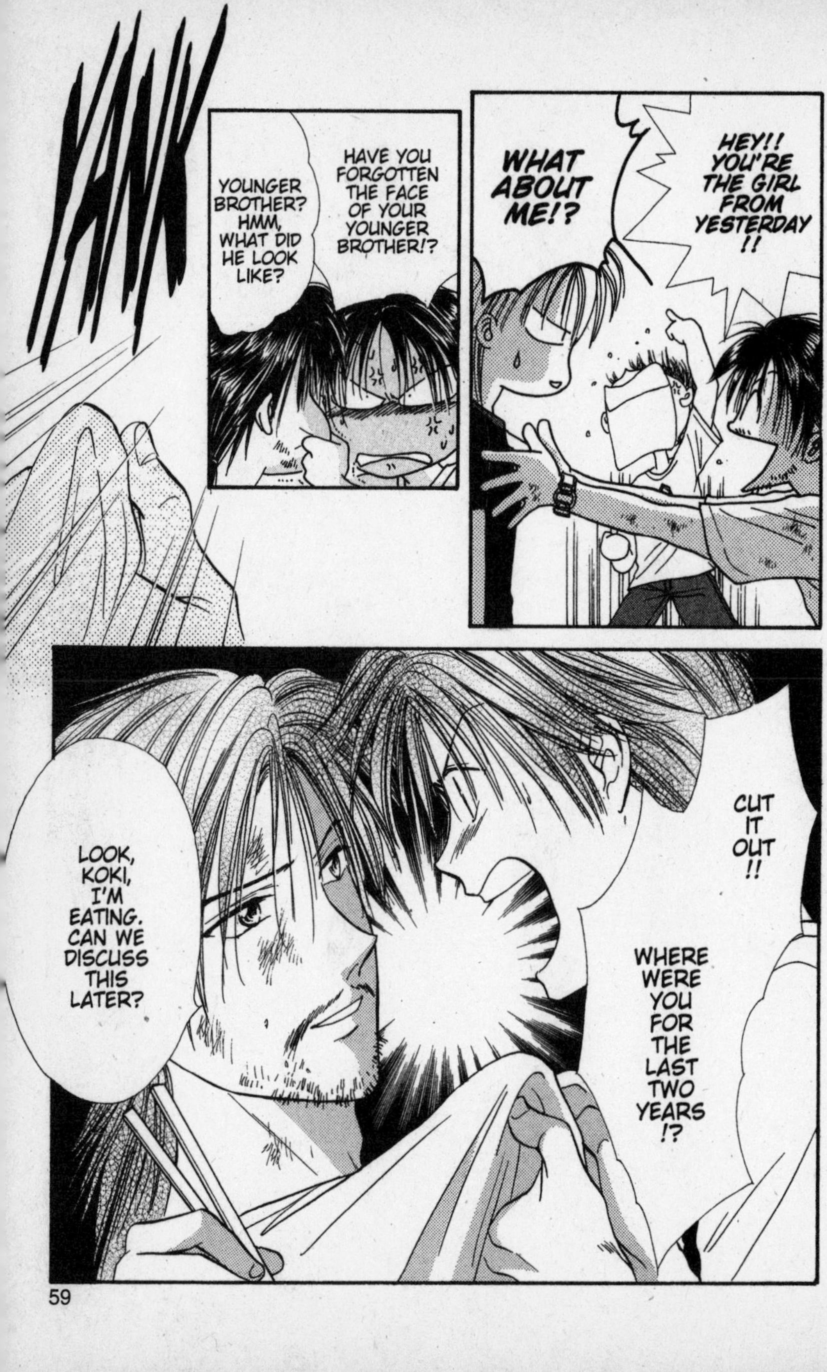
HEY!! YOU'RE THE GIRL FROM YESTERDAY!!
WHAT ABOUT ME!?
HAVE YOU FORGOTTEN THE FACE OF YOUR YOUNGER BROTHER!?
YOUNGER BROTHER? HMM, WHAT DID HE LOOK LIKE?
YANK
CUT IT OUT!!
WHERE WERE YOU FOR THE LAST TWO YEARS!?
LOOK, KOKI, I'M EATING. CAN WE DISCUSS THIS LATER?

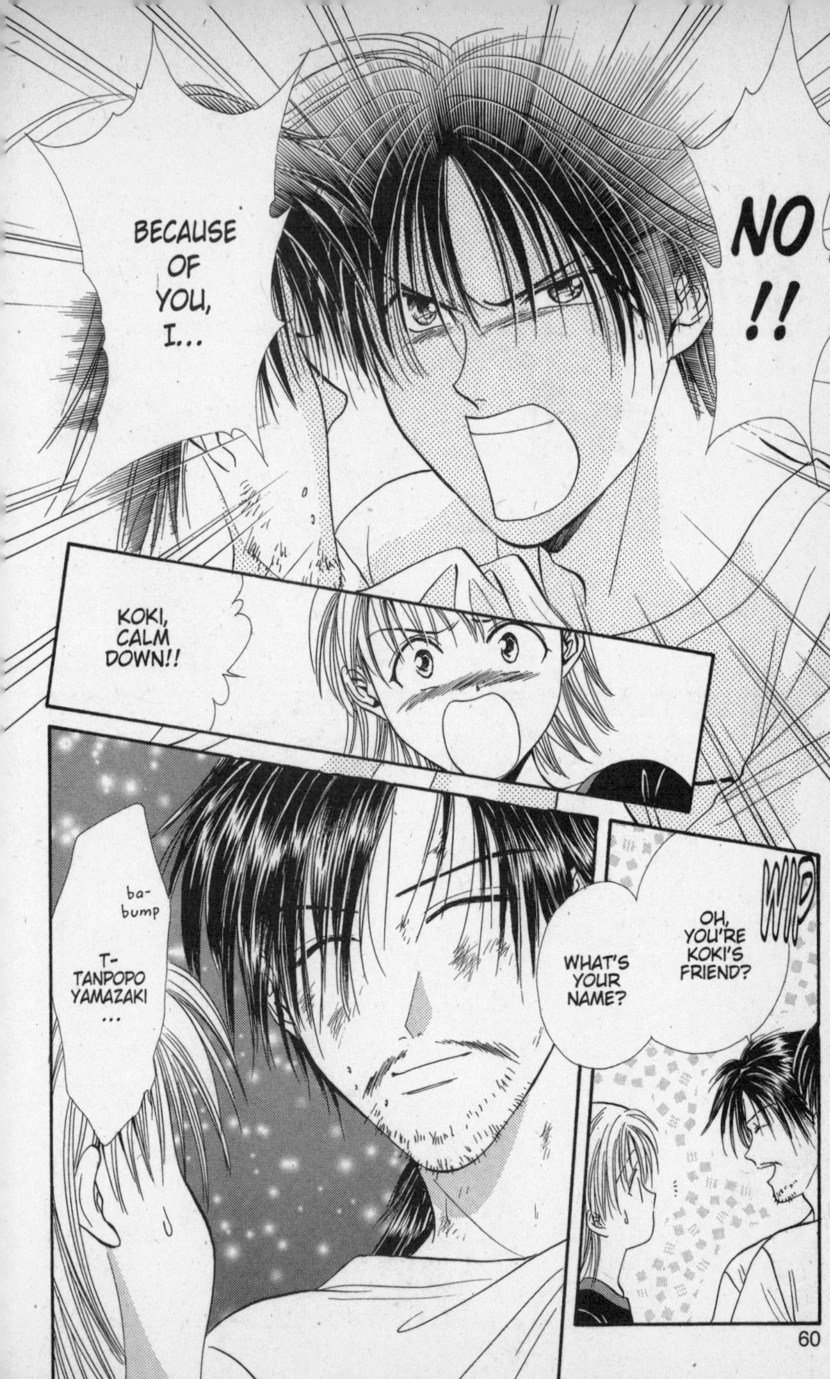
NO!!
BECAUSE OF YOU, I...
KOKI, CALM DOWN!!
WHIP
OH, YOU'RE KOKI'S FRIEND?
WHAT'S YOUR NAME?
ba-bump
T-TANPOPO YAMAZAKI ...

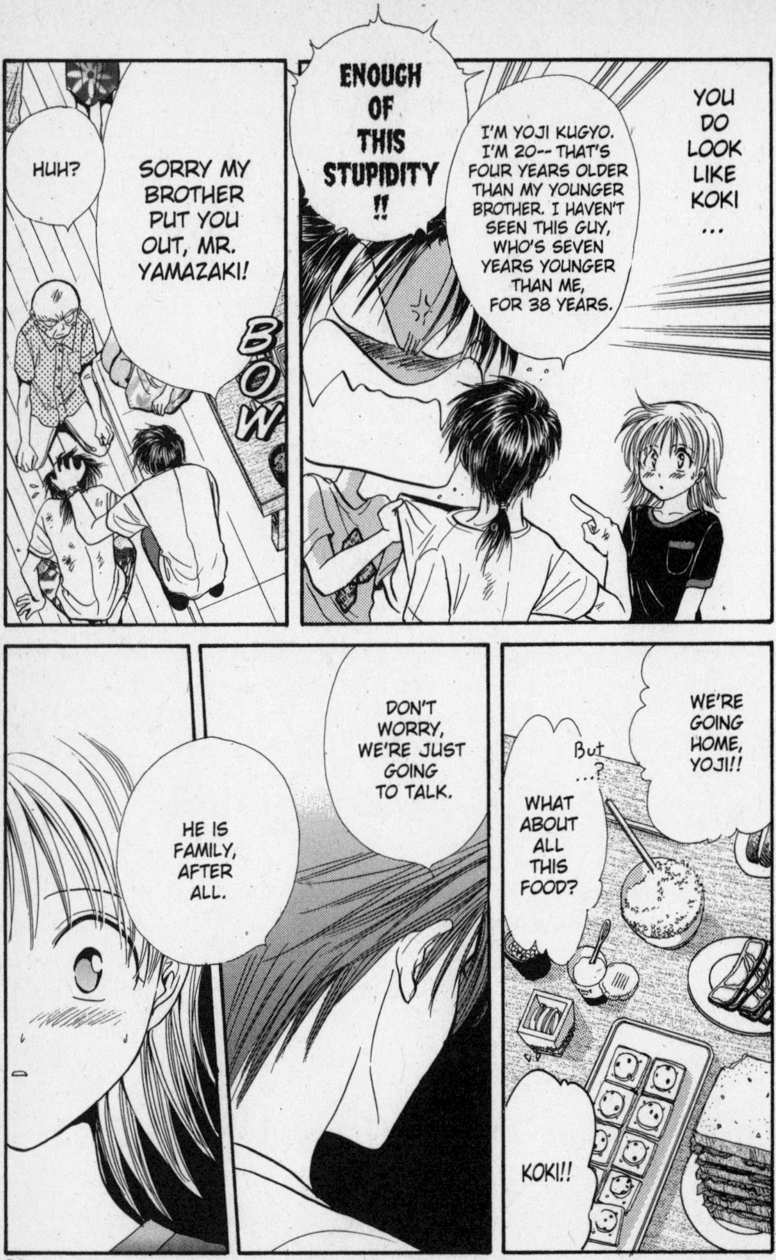
YOU DO LOOK LIKE KOKI...
I'M YOJI KUGYO. I'M 20-- THAT'S FOUR YEARS OLDER THAN MY YOUNGER BROTHER. I HAVEN'T SEEN THIS GUY, WHO'S SEVEN YEARS YOUNGER THAN ME, FOR 38 YEARS.
ENOUGH OF THIS STUPIDITY!!
SORRY MY BROTHER PUT YOU OUT, MR. YAMAZAKI!
HUH?
BOW
WE'RE GOING HOME, YOJI!!
But...?
WHAT ABOUT ALL THIS FOOD?
KOKI!!
DON'T WORRY, WE'RE JUST GOING TO TALK.
HE IS FAMILY, AFTER ALL.

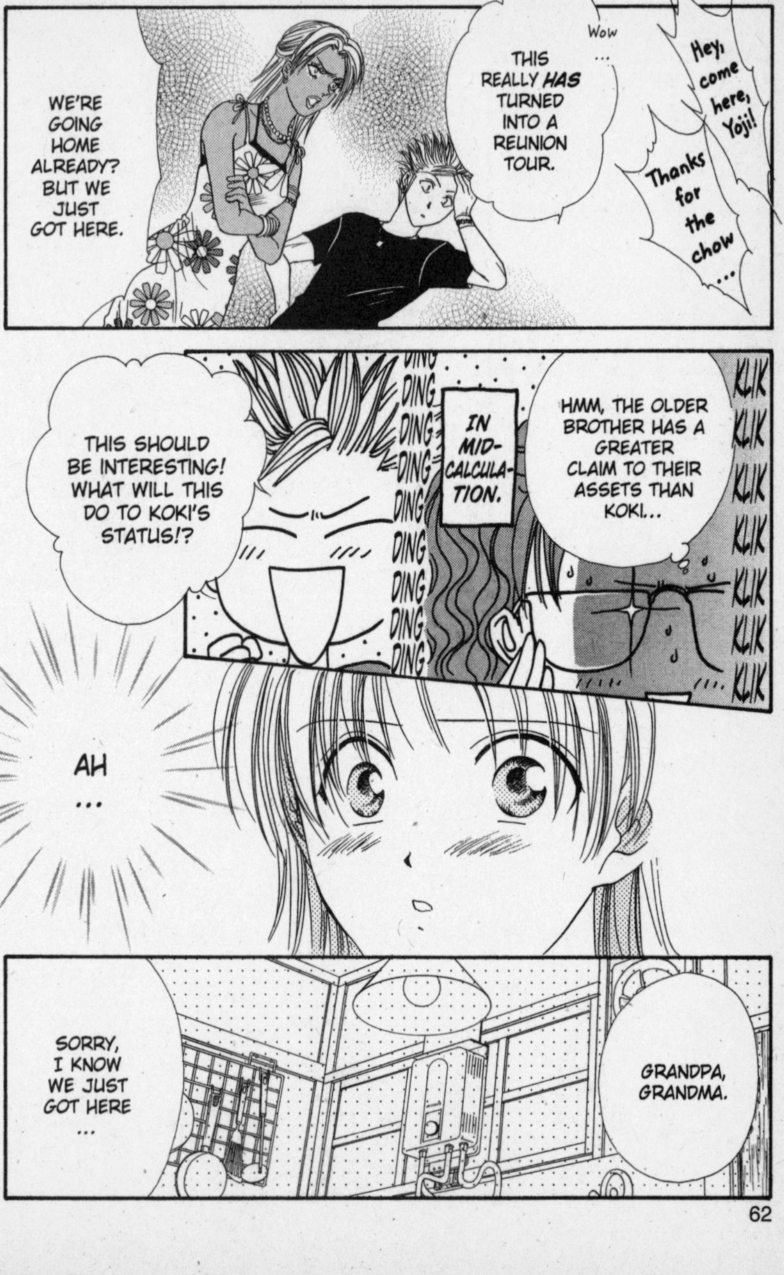
Hey, come here, Yoji!
Thanks for the chow ...
Wow ...
THIS REALLY *HAS* TURNED INTO A REUNION TOUR.
WE'RE GOING HOME ALREADY? BUT WE JUST GOT HERE.
KLIK KLIK KLIK KLIK KLIK KLIK KLIK KLIK KLIK
HMM, THE OLDER BROTHER HAS A GREATER CLAIM TO THEIR ASSETS THAN KOKI...
IN MID-CALCULATION.
DING DING DING DING DING DING DING DING DING DING DING
THIS SHOULD BE INTERESTING! WHAT WILL THIS DO TO KOKI'S STATUS!?
AH ...
GRANDPA, GRANDMA.
SORRY, I KNOW WE JUST GOT HERE ...

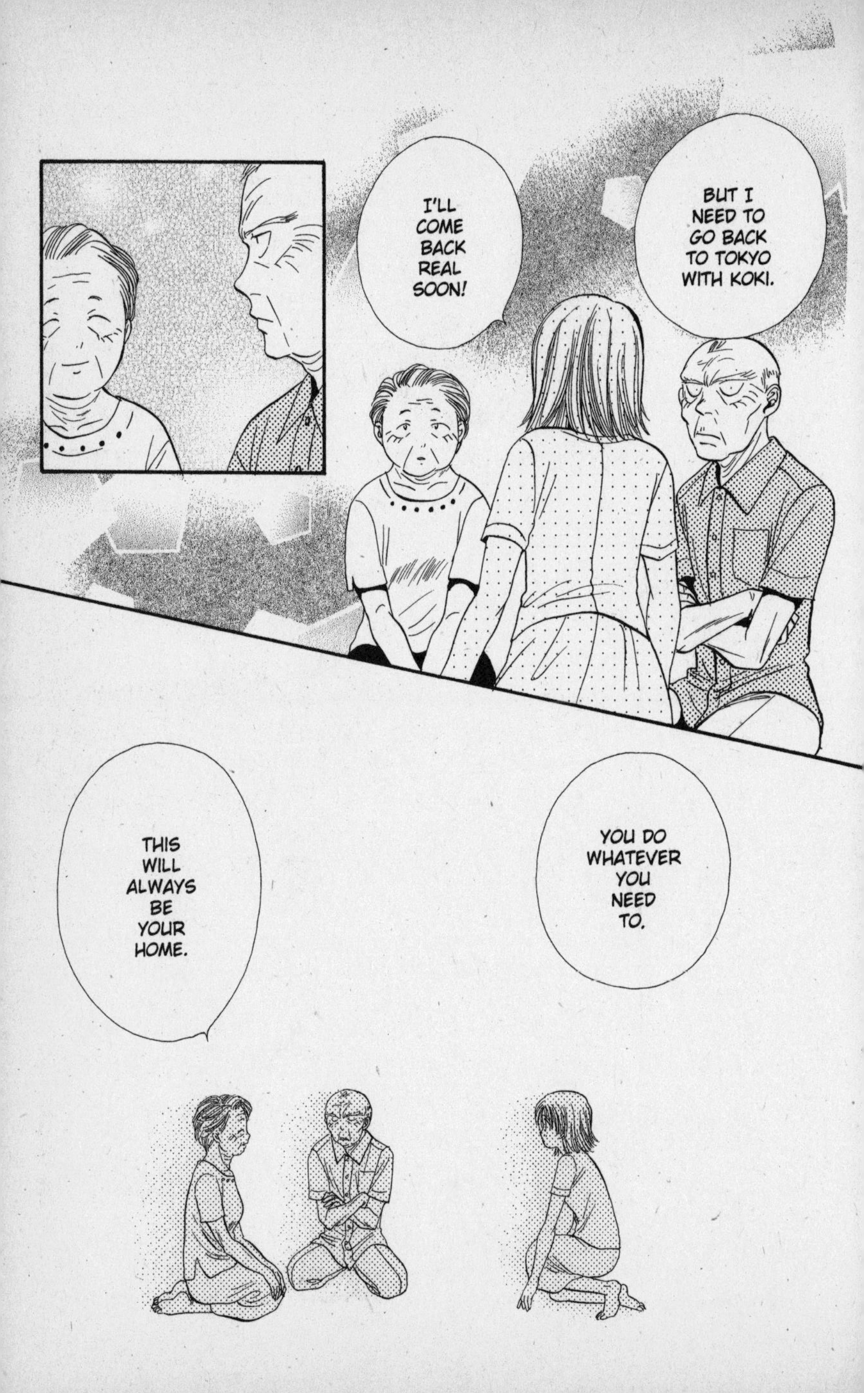
BUT I NEED TO GO BACK TO TOKYO WITH KOKI.
I'LL COME BACK REAL SOON!
YOU DO WHATEVER YOU NEED TO.
THIS WILL ALWAYS BE YOUR HOME.

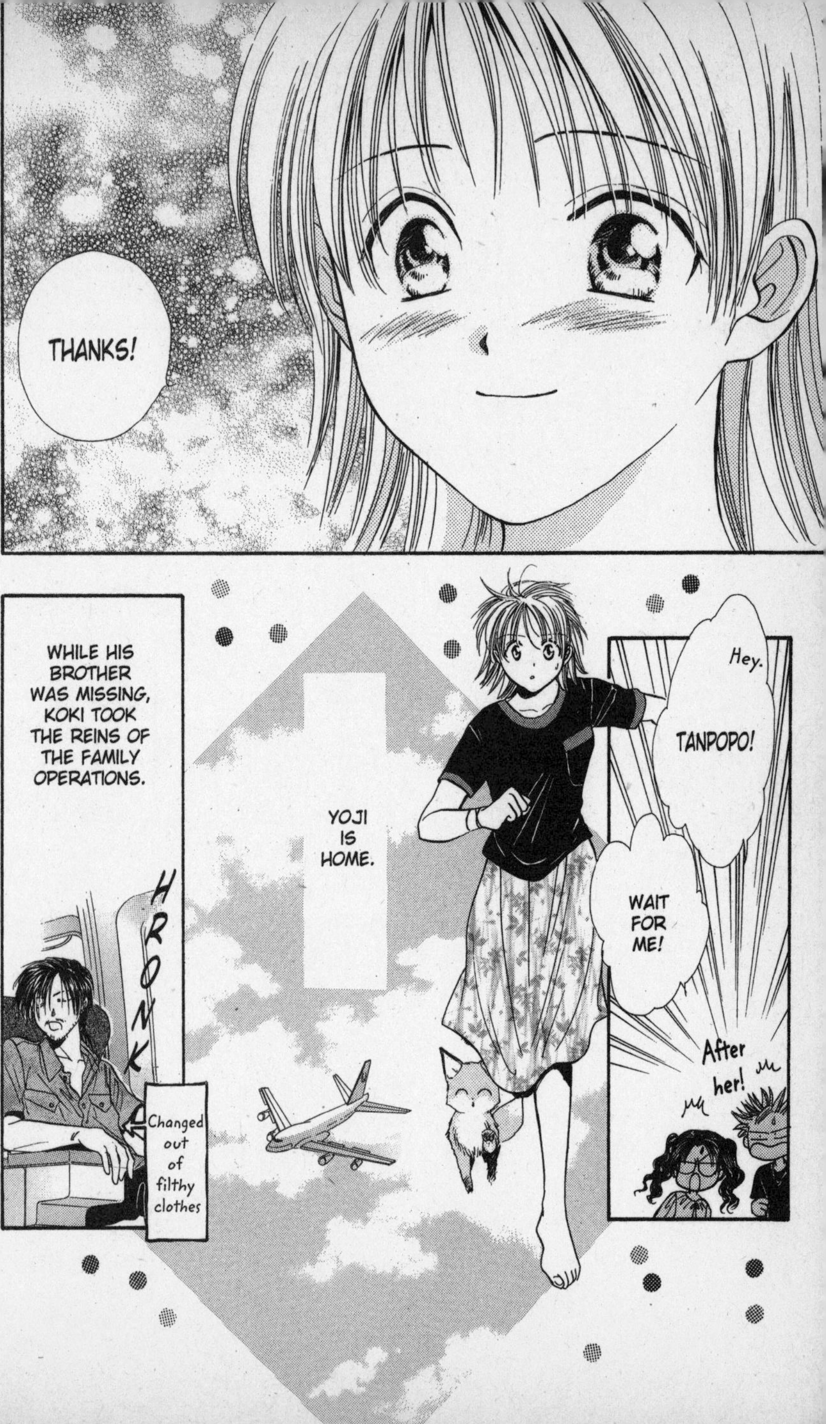
THANKS!
Hey.
TANPOPO!
WAIT FOR ME!
After her!
YOJI IS HOME.
WHILE HIS BROTHER WAS MISSING, KOKI TOOK THE REINS OF THE FAMILY OPERATIONS.
HRONK
Changed out of filthy clothes

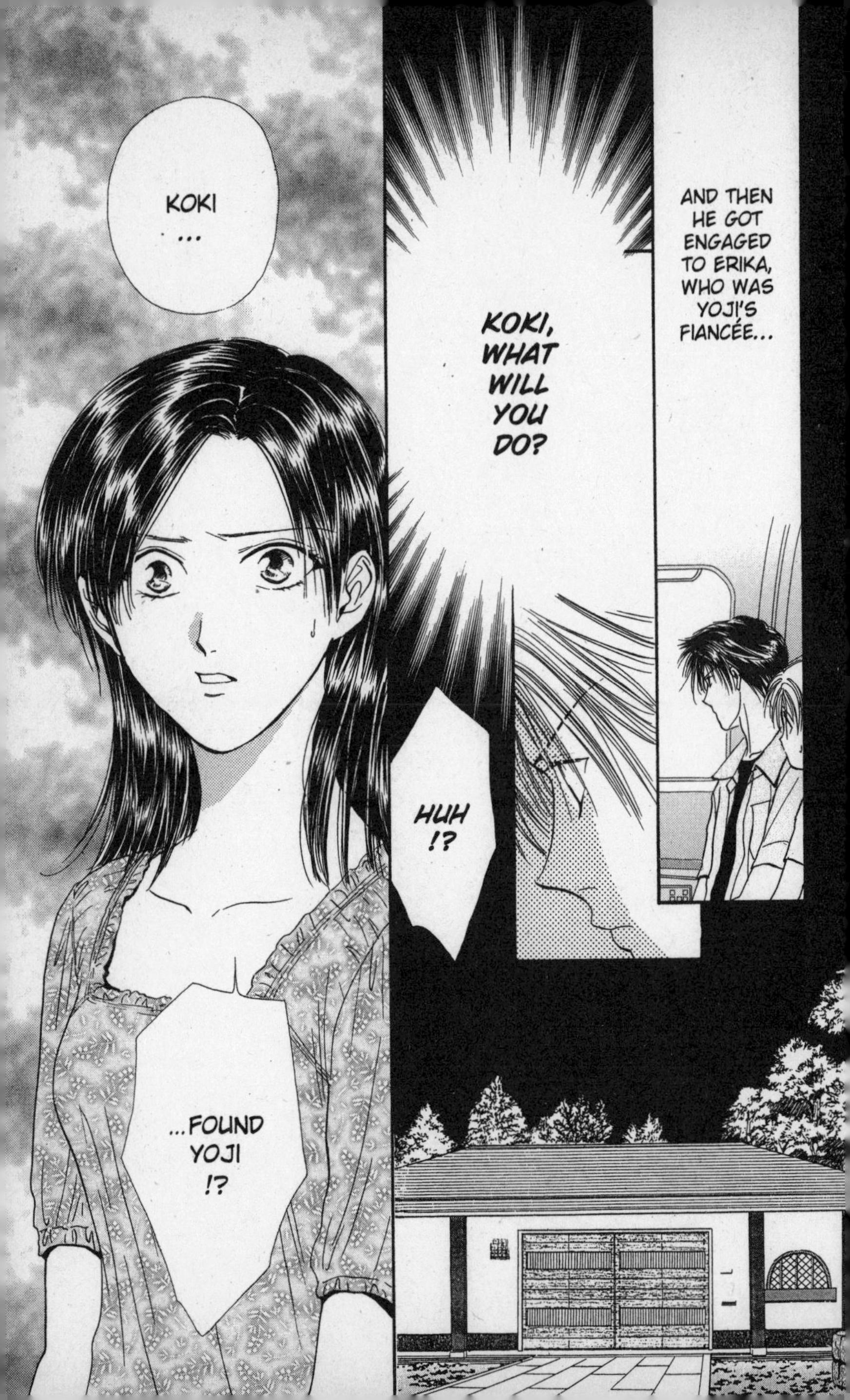
AND THEN HE GOT ENGAGED TO ERIKA, WHO WAS YOJI'S FIANCÉE...
KOKI, WHAT WILL YOU DO?
HUH !?
KOKI ...
...FOUND YOJI !?

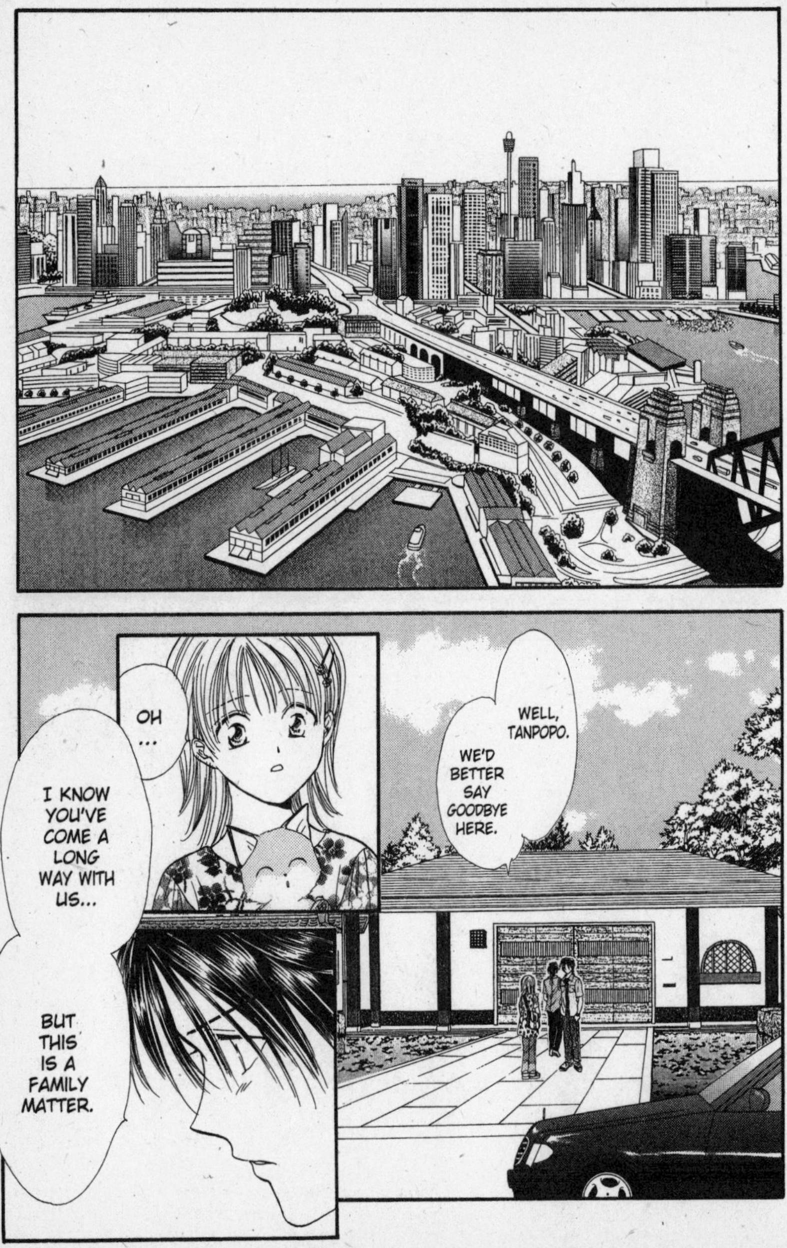
WELL, TANPOPO.
WE'D BETTER SAY GOODBYE HERE.
OH ...
I KNOW YOU'VE COME A LONG WAY WITH US...
BUT THIS IS A FAMILY MATTER.

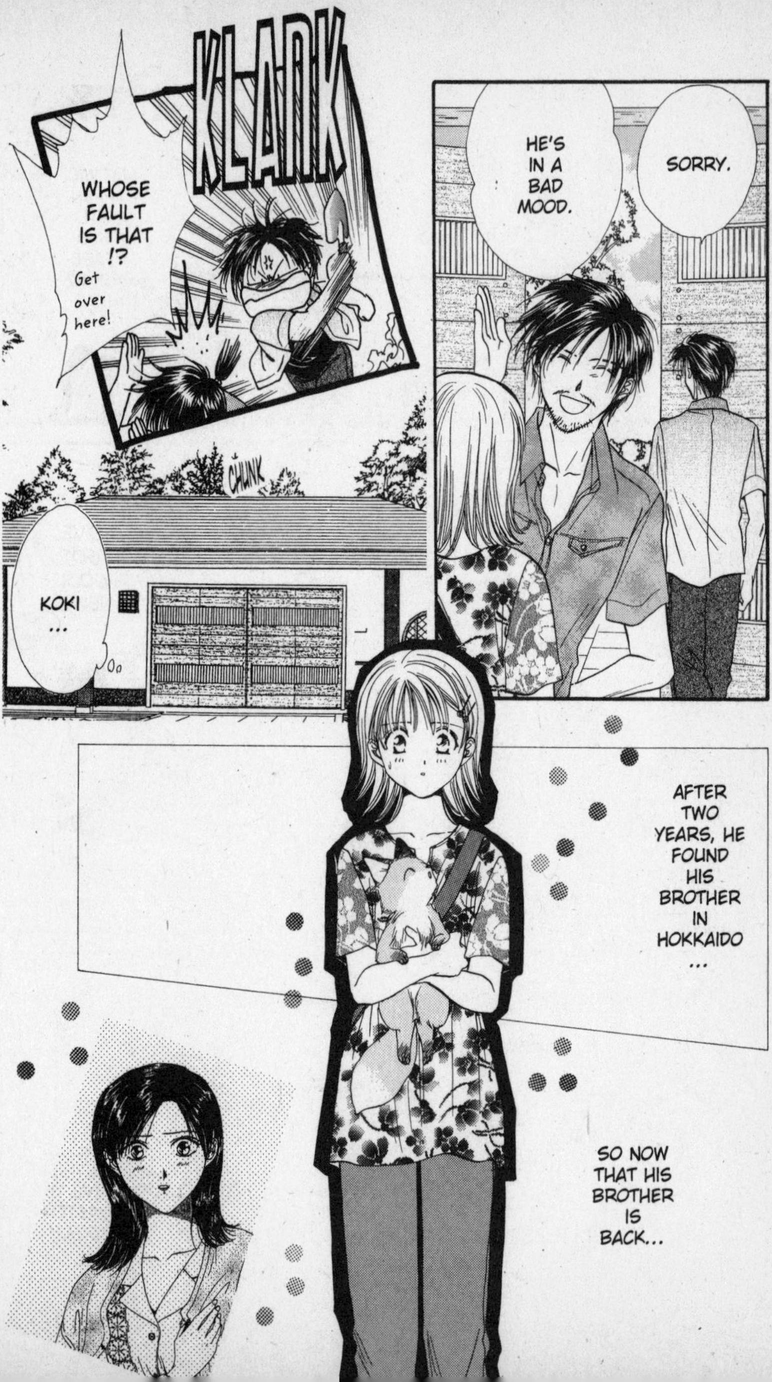
SORRY.
HE'S IN A BAD MOOD.
KLANK
WHOSE FAULT IS THAT !?
Get over here!
CHUNK
KOKI ...
AFTER TWO YEARS, HE FOUND HIS BROTHER IN HOKKAIDO ...
SO NOW THAT HIS BROTHER IS BACK...

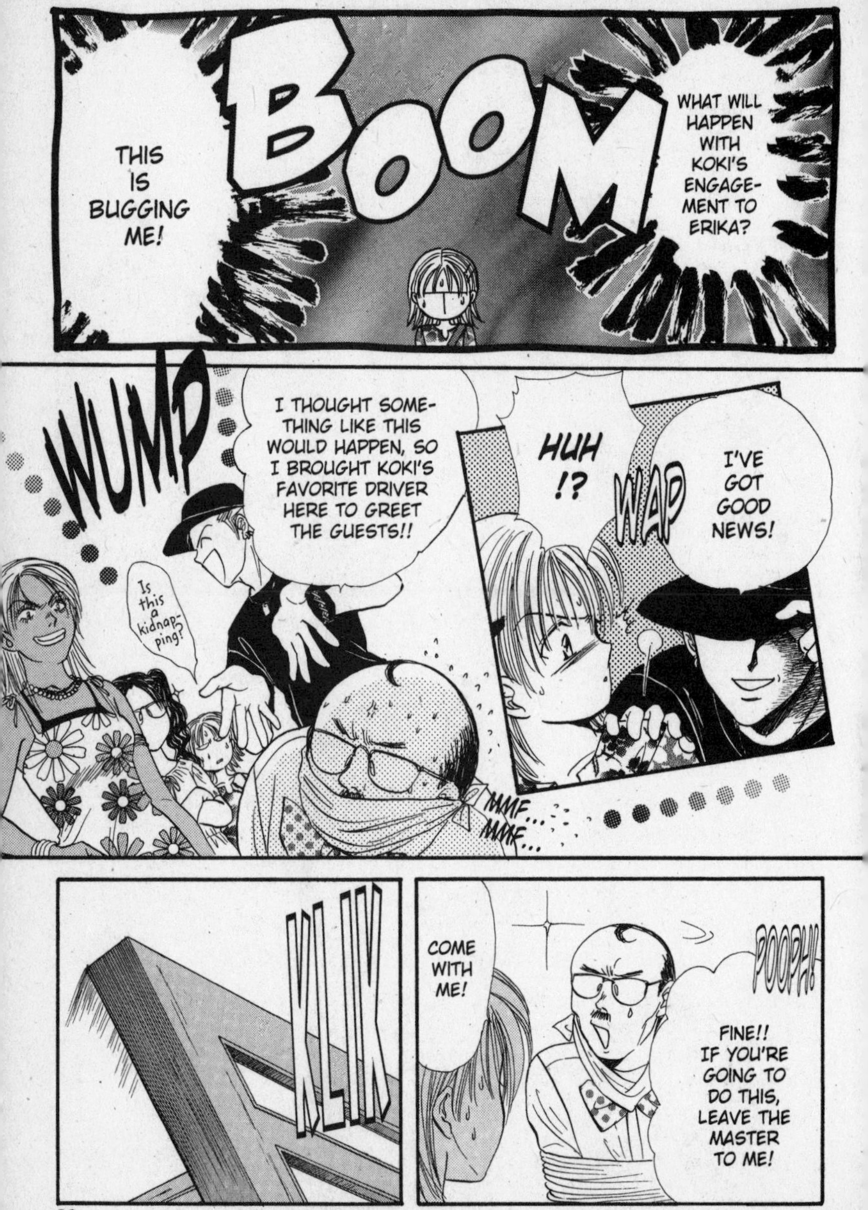
WHAT WILL HAPPEN WITH KOKI'S ENGAGE-MENT TO ERIKA?
BOOM
THIS IS BUGGING ME!
HUH !?
I'VE GOT GOOD NEWS!
WAP
I THOUGHT SOME-THING LIKE THIS WOULD HAPPEN, SO I BROUGHT KOKI'S FAVORITE DRIVER HERE TO GREET THE GUESTS!!
WUMP
Is this a kidnap-ping?
MMF... MMF...
POOPH!
FINE!! IF YOU'RE GOING TO DO THIS, LEAVE THE MASTER TO ME!
COME WITH ME!
KLIK

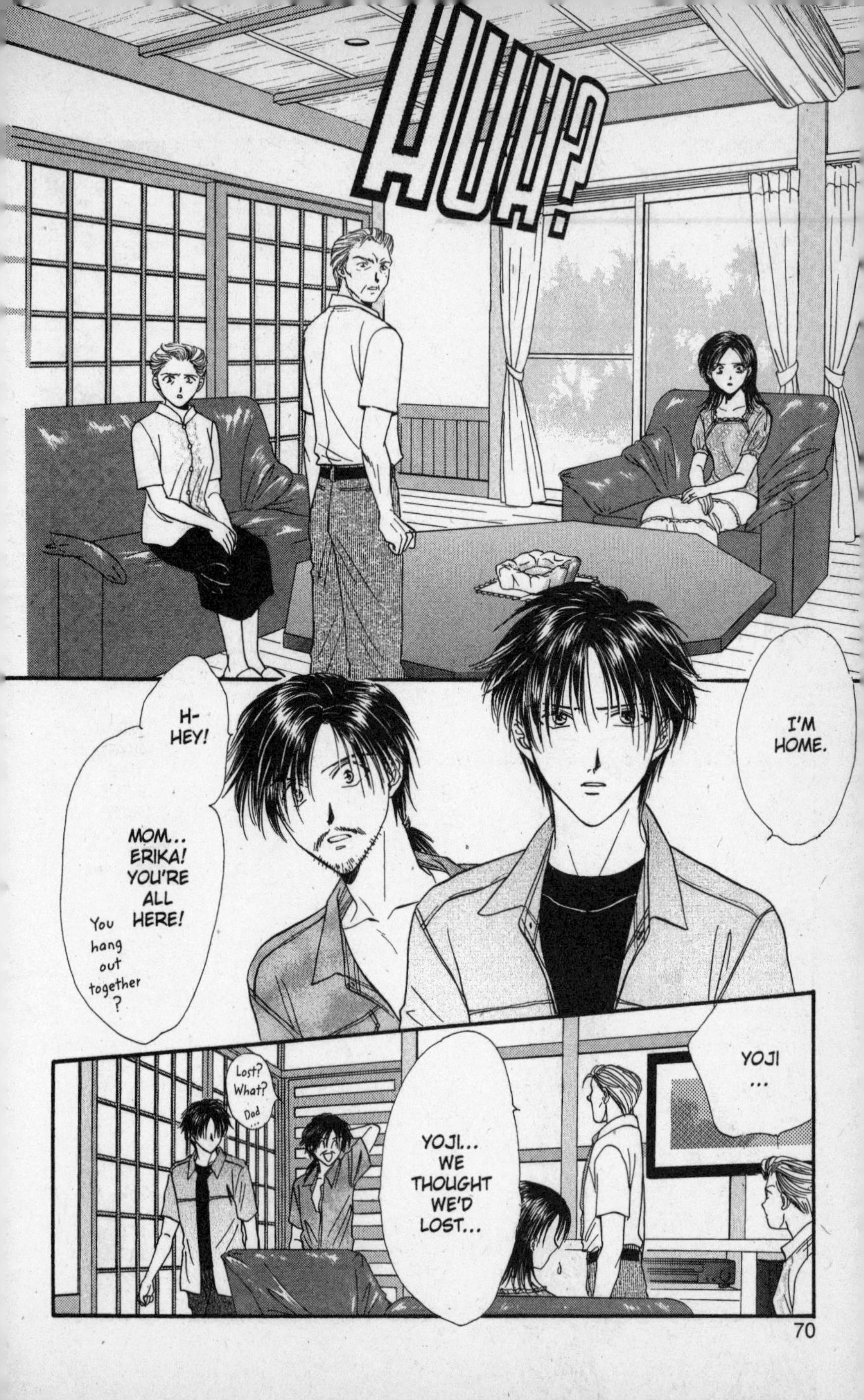
HUH?
I'M HOME.
H- HEY!
MOM... ERIKA! YOU'RE ALL HERE!
You hang out together?
YOJI ...
YOJI... WE THOUGHT WE'D LOST...
Lost? What? Dad ...

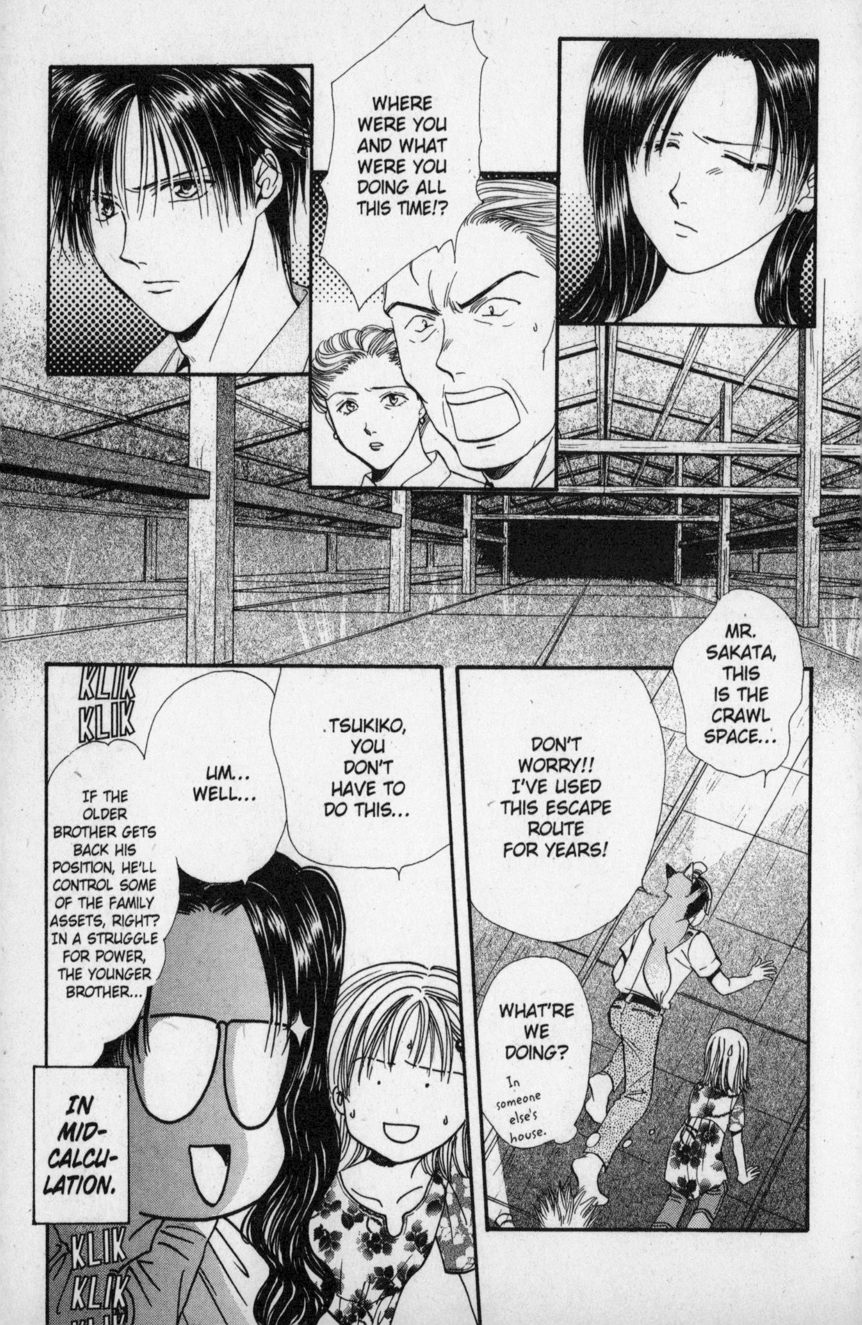
WHERE WERE YOU AND WHAT WERE YOU DOING ALL THIS TIME!?
MR. SAKATA, THIS IS THE CRAWL SPACE...
DON'T WORRY!! I'VE USED THIS ESCAPE ROUTE FOR YEARS!
WHAT'RE WE DOING?
In someone else's house.
TSUKIKO, YOU DON'T HAVE TO DO THIS...
UM... WELL...
KLIK KLIK
IF THE OLDER BROTHER GETS BACK HIS POSITION, HE'LL CONTROL SOME OF THE FAMILY ASSETS, RIGHT? IN A STRUGGLE FOR POWER, THE YOUNGER BROTHER...
IN MID-CALCULATION.
KLIK KLIK

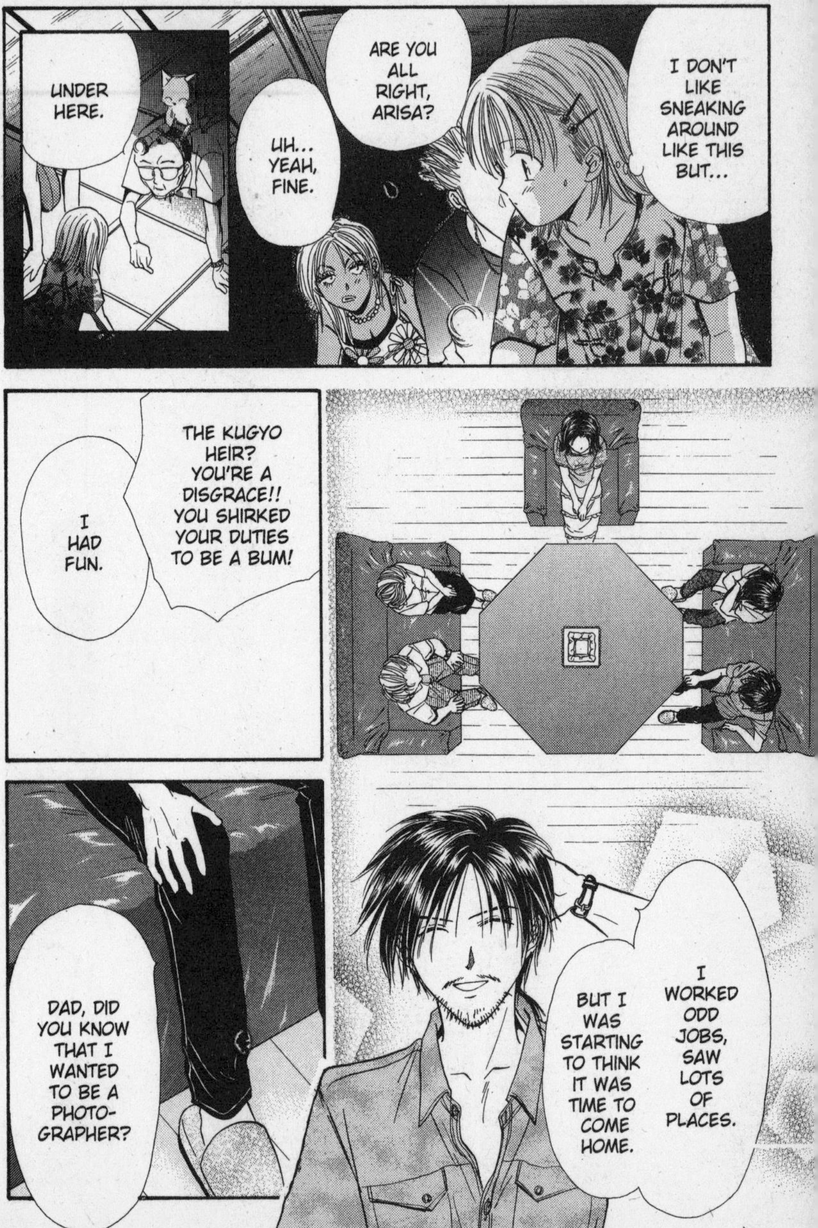
I DON'T LIKE SNEAKING AROUND LIKE THIS BUT...
ARE YOU ALL RIGHT, ARISA?
UH... YEAH, FINE.
UNDER HERE.
I WORKED ODD JOBS, SAW LOTS OF PLACES.
BUT I WAS STARTING TO THINK IT WAS TIME TO COME HOME.
THE KUGYO HEIR? YOU'RE A DISGRACE!! YOU SHIRKED YOUR DUTIES TO BE A BUM!
I HAD FUN.
DAD, DID YOU KNOW THAT I WANTED TO BE A PHOTOGRAPHER?

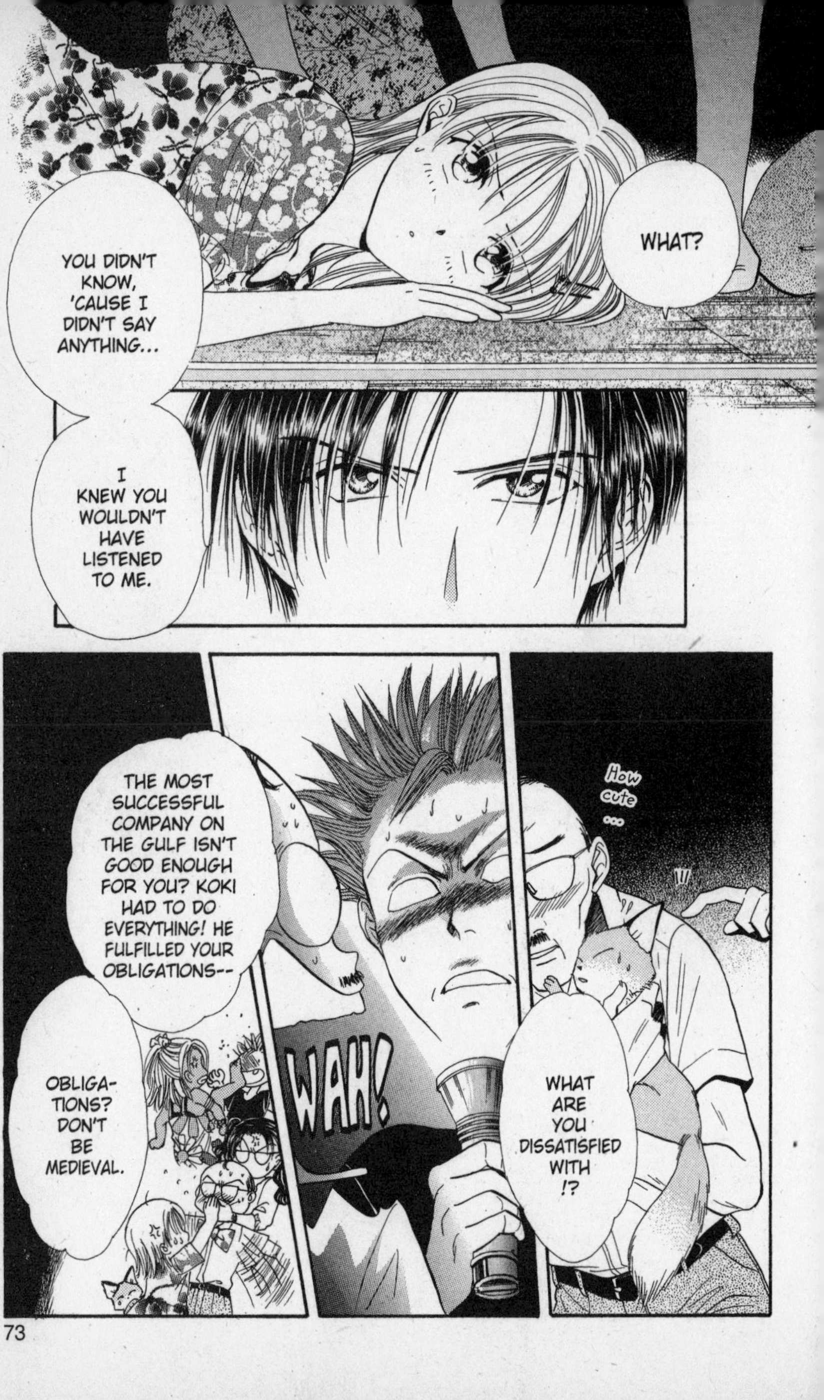
WHAT?
YOU DIDN'T KNOW, 'CAUSE I DIDN'T SAY ANYTHING...
I KNEW YOU WOULDN'T HAVE LISTENED TO ME.
How cute...
WHAT ARE YOU DISSATISFIED WITH !?
WAH!
THE MOST SUCCESSFUL COMPANY ON THE GULF ISN'T GOOD ENOUGH FOR YOU? KOKI HAD TO DO EVERYTHING! HE FULFILLED YOUR OBLIGATIONS--
OBLIGA-TIONS? DON'T BE MEDIEVAL.

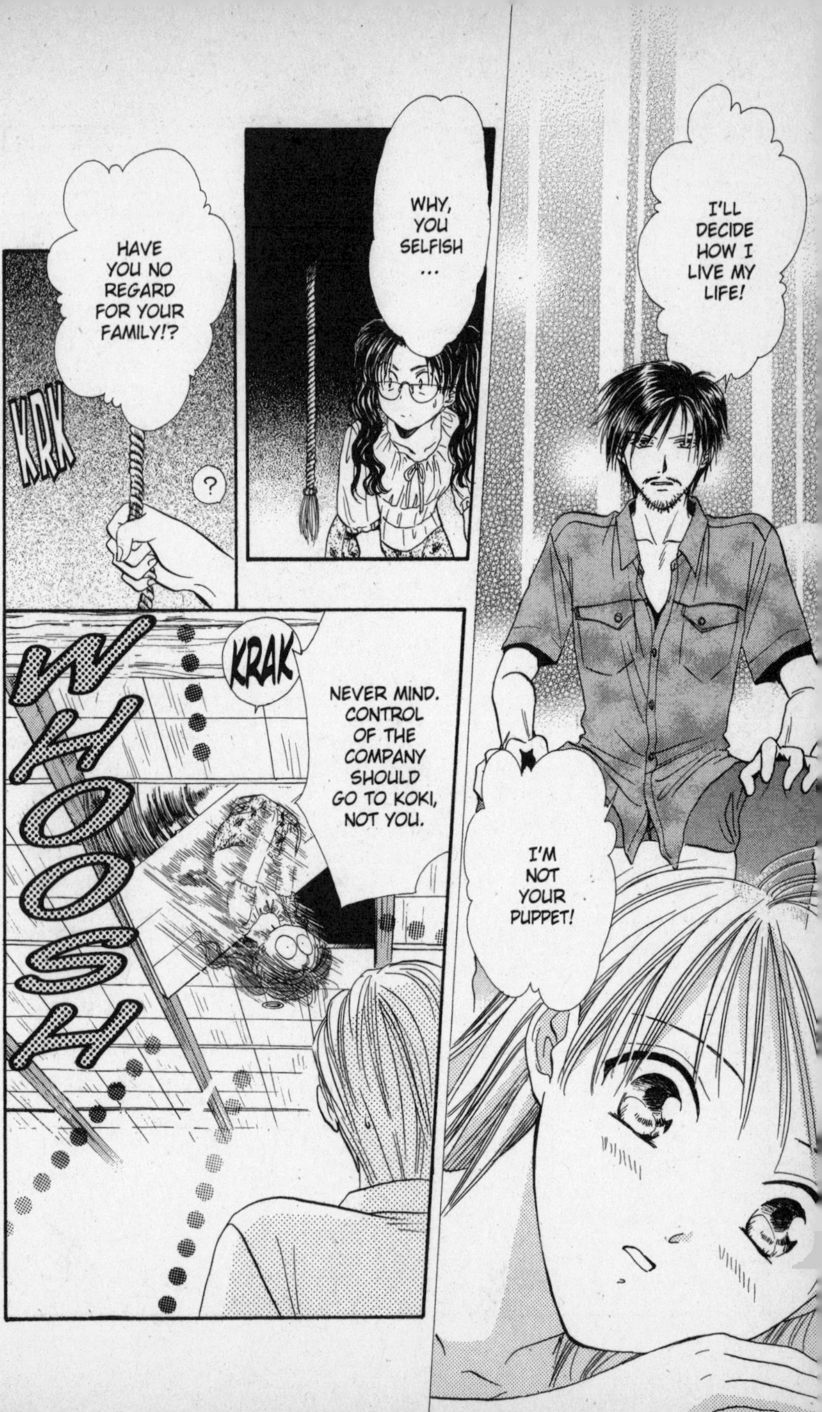
I'LL DECIDE HOW I LIVE MY LIFE!
I'M NOT YOUR PUPPET!
WHY, YOU SELFISH ...
HAVE YOU NO REGARD FOR YOUR FAMILY!?
KRK
?
KRAK
NEVER MIND. CONTROL OF THE COMPANY SHOULD GO TO KOKI, NOT YOU.
WHOOSH

KLIK
WHAT'S WRONG, DEAR?
...
Success !!
WHAT IS HE TALKING ABOUT !?
WHAT'S WITH THE GADGET!?
THROB THROB
IS THAT WHY YOU'RE SO MAD, KOKI?
I must be seeing things.

There were a lot of TV specials at the end of the year, weren't there? Nostalgic retrospectives on the twentieth century, etc...

One was a special about Osamu Tezuka. Did any of you see it? They showed an original animation during the show. I thought they said some good things. After all, a work affects the viewers' hopes and dreams. That's what I thought. I'd include "thought-provoking" as part of the creative process.

I mentioned before (in Volume 2) that I'd never read a school story before drawing **Imadoki**, but I did read one that the person in charge of this project had read long ago, called **Lemons and Cherries** by Yoko Nishitani. It served as a template since it was a popular school story in its day...although I wasn't even been born when it came out. It was written in 1966, and was interesting from a number of different perspectives and interpretations. I really felt the "youth!" part. I wonder what Yumiko's hairstyle is like now. Lately I've been in the mood to read old manga.

I'm surprisingly unfamiliar with them because I grew up watching anime on TV. That's why when they show those "Nostalgic Anime" shows on TV, I know most of them. Years ago there weren't as many forms of entertainment as there are today, so you read manga or watched anime even if you weren't a "nerd." Especially in Osaka--they showed reruns all the time. I think those older anime were more interesting. Anyway, I don't know the works of famous young girl comic writers like Taika...

Two years ago, my assistant lent me her copies of Shōjo Comic writer Moto Hagio's works and I read them for the first time. **Pono Ichizoku** and **Toma no Shinzo.** Most women older than me have probably read these. Amazing! I'm a child of the '70's. To be continued.

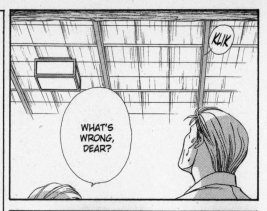

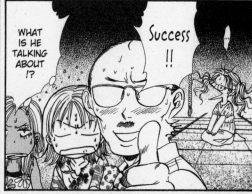

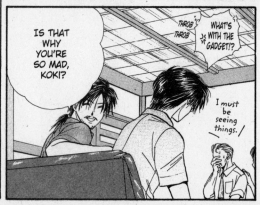

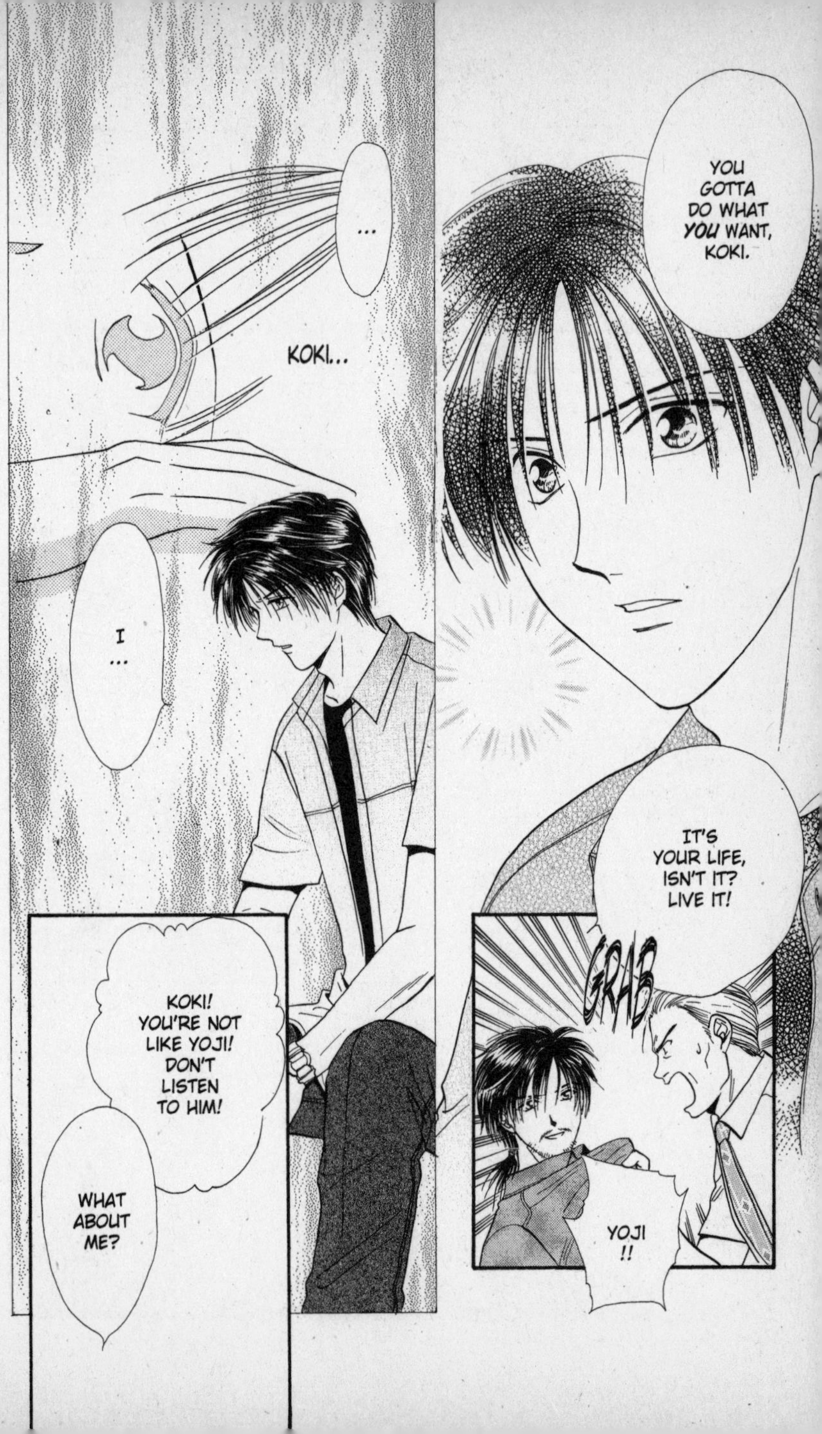
YOU GOTTA DO WHAT *YOU* WANT, KOKI.
IT'S YOUR LIFE, ISN'T IT? LIVE IT!
GRAB
YOJI !!
...
KOKI...
I ...
KOKI! YOU'RE NOT LIKE YOJI! DON'T LISTEN TO HIM!
WHAT ABOUT ME?

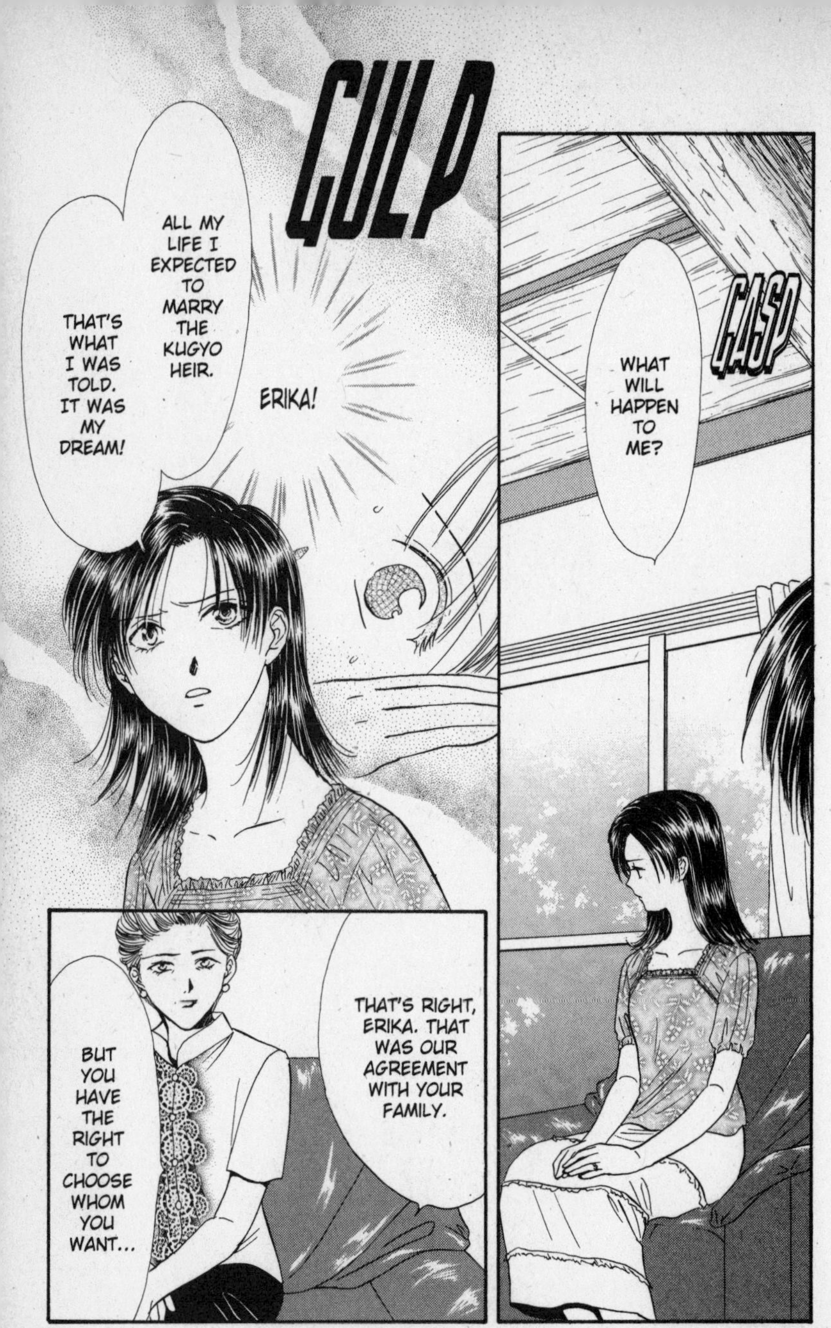
GASP
WHAT WILL HAPPEN TO ME?
GULP
ERIKA!
ALL MY LIFE I EXPECTED TO MARRY THE KUGYO HEIR.
THAT'S WHAT I WAS TOLD. IT WAS MY DREAM!
THAT'S RIGHT, ERIKA. THAT WAS OUR AGREEMENT WITH YOUR FAMILY.
BUT YOU HAVE THE RIGHT TO CHOOSE WHOM YOU WANT...

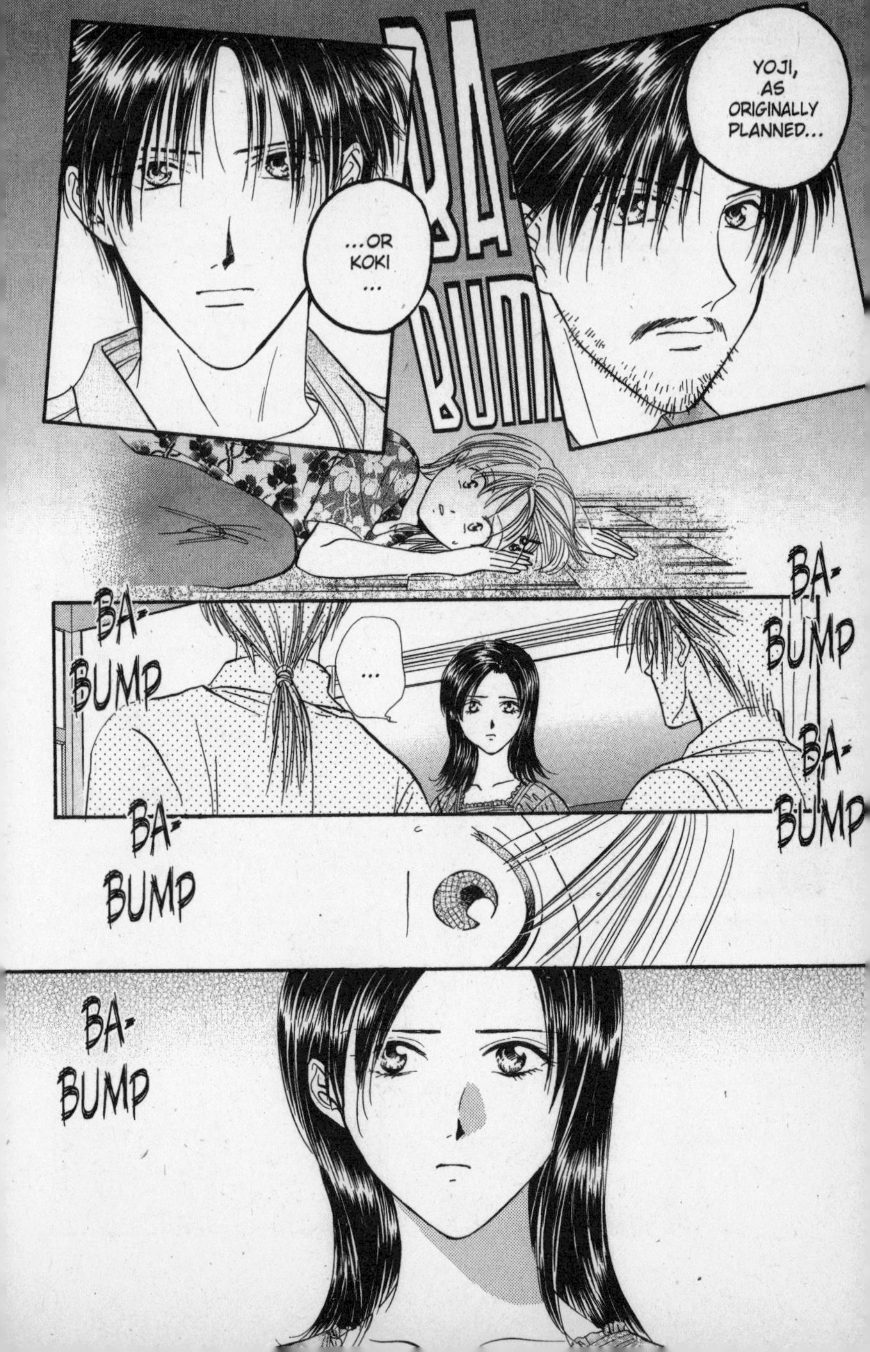
YOJI, AS ORIGINALLY PLANNED...
BA BUM
...OR KOKI ...
BA-BUMP
BA-BUMP
...
BA-BUMP
BA-BUMP
BA-BUMP

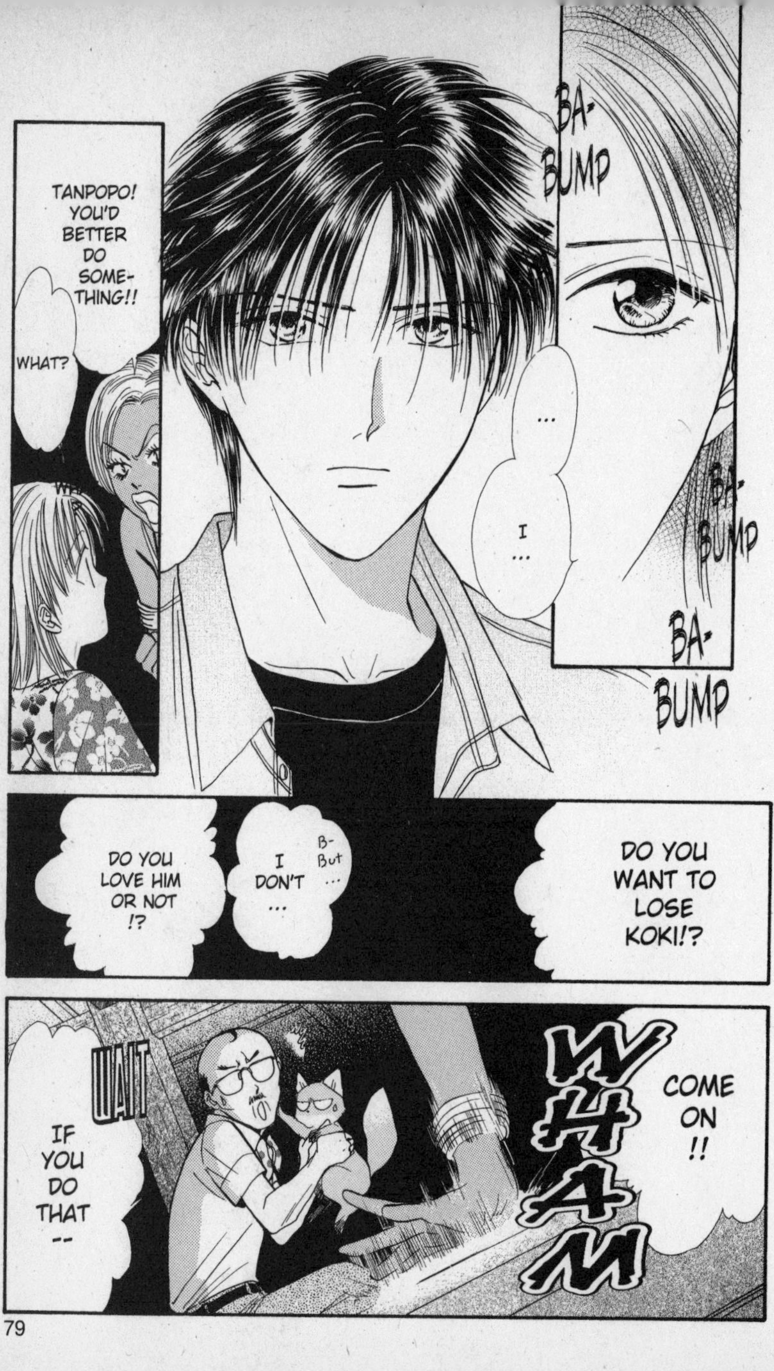
BA-BUMP
BA-BUMP
BA-BUMP
... I ...
TANPOPO! YOU'D BETTER DO SOME-THING!!
WHAT?
DO YOU WANT TO LOSE KOKI!?
B-But ...
I DON'T ...
DO YOU LOVE HIM OR NOT !?
COME ON !!
WHAM
WAIT
IF YOU DO THAT --

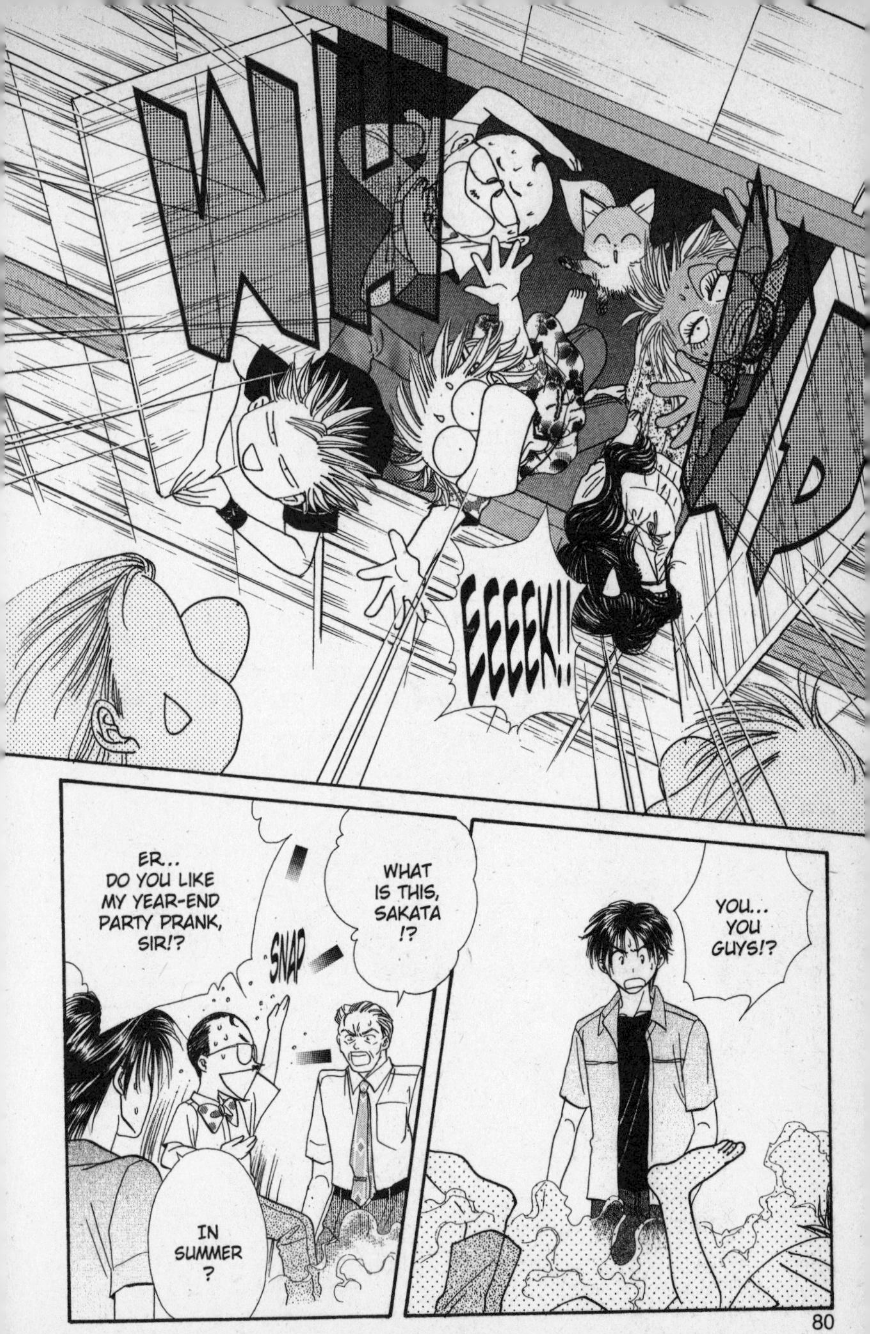
EEEEK!!
YOU... YOU GUYS!?
WHAT IS THIS, SAKATA !?
SNAP
ER.. DO YOU LIKE MY YEAR-END PARTY PRANK, SIR!?
IN SUMMER ?

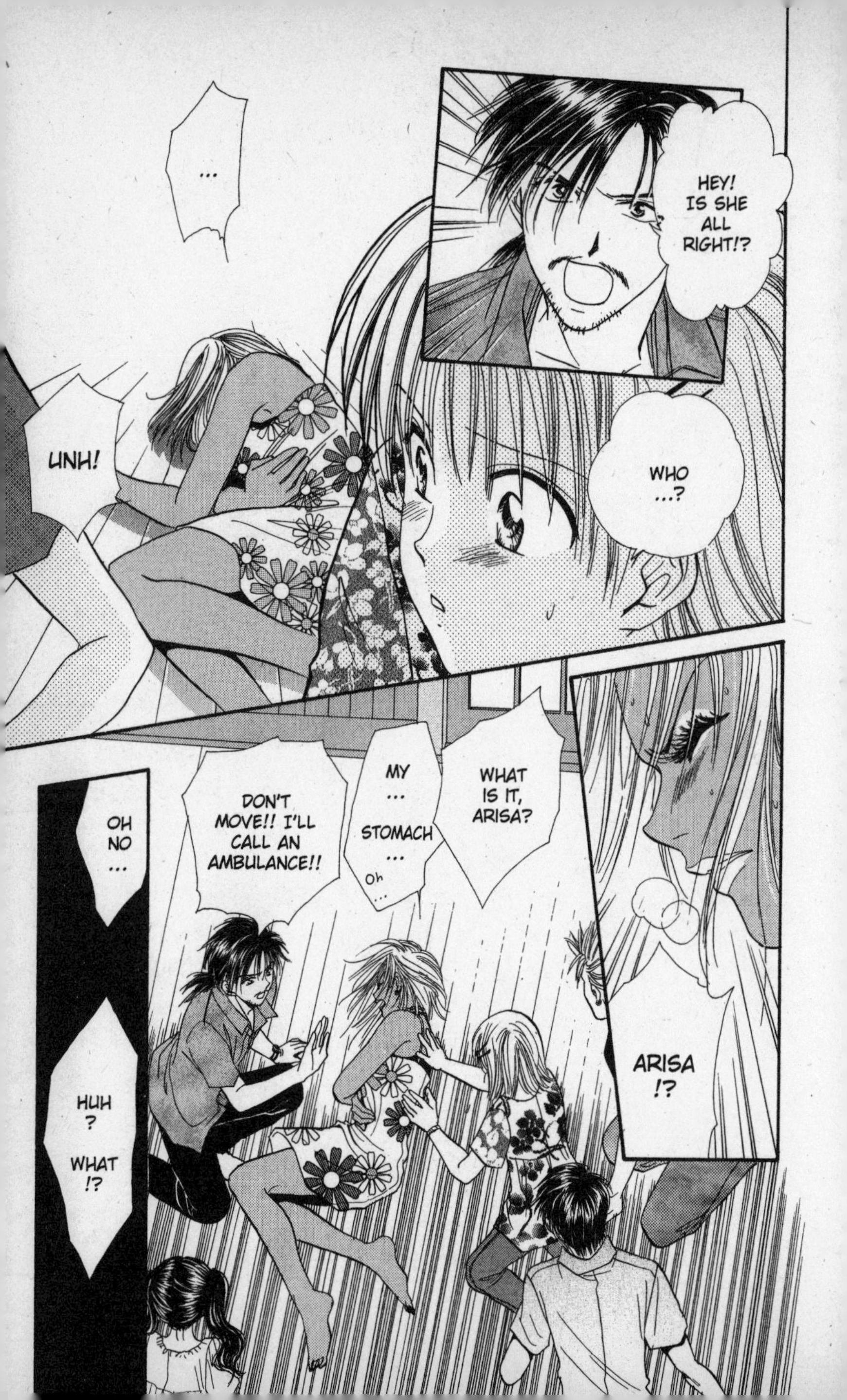
HEY! IS SHE ALL RIGHT!?
...
WHO ...?
UNH!
ARISA !?
WHAT IS IT, ARISA?
MY ... STOMACH ...
Oh ...
DON'T MOVE!! I'LL CALL AN AMBULANCE!!
OH NO ...
HUH ? WHAT !?

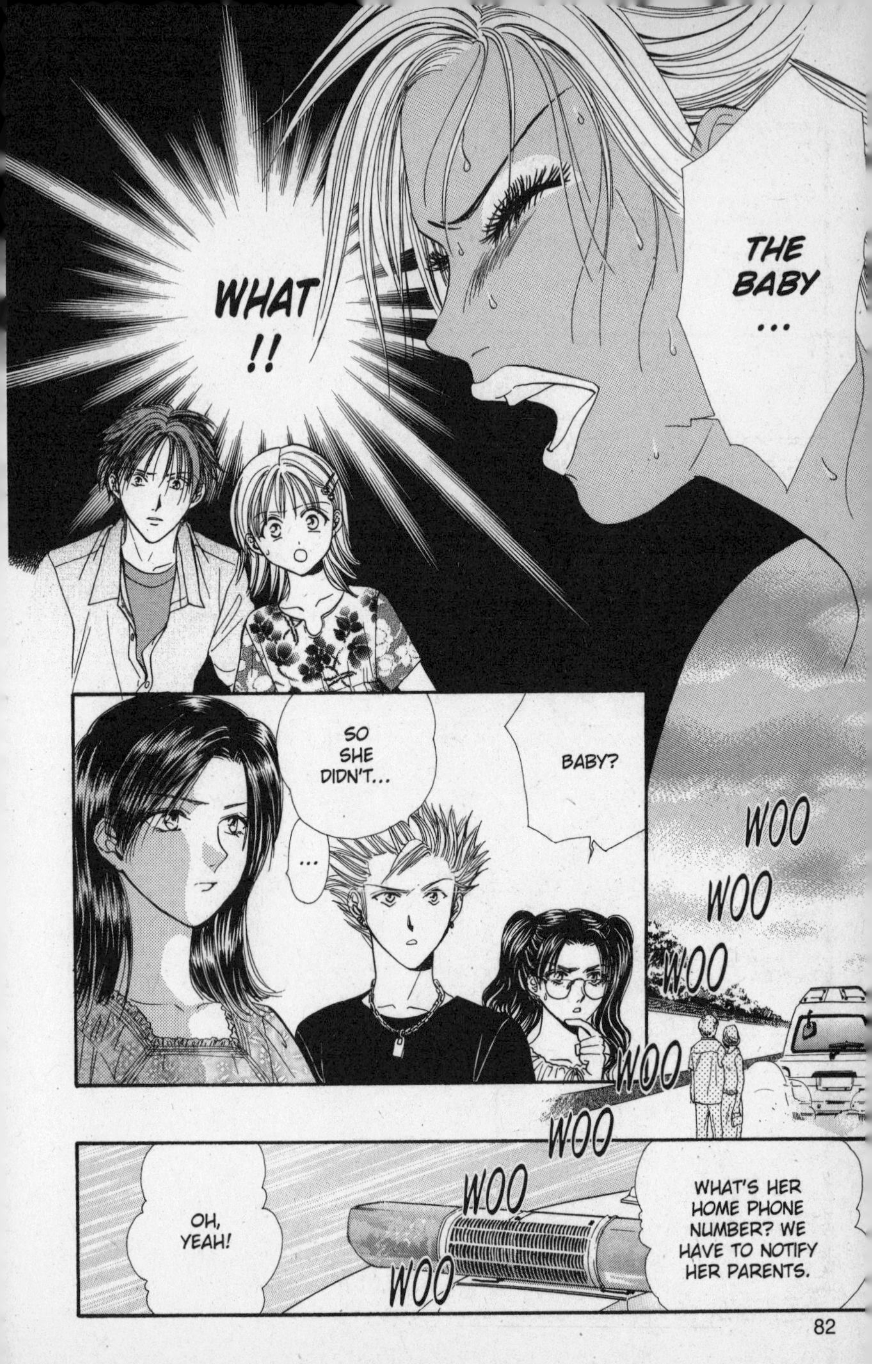
THE BABY ...
WHAT !!
BABY?
SO SHE DIDN'T...
...
WOO
WOO
WOO
WOO
WOO
WOO
WOO
WHAT'S HER HOME PHONE NUMBER? WE HAVE TO NOTIFY HER PARENTS.
OH, YEAH!

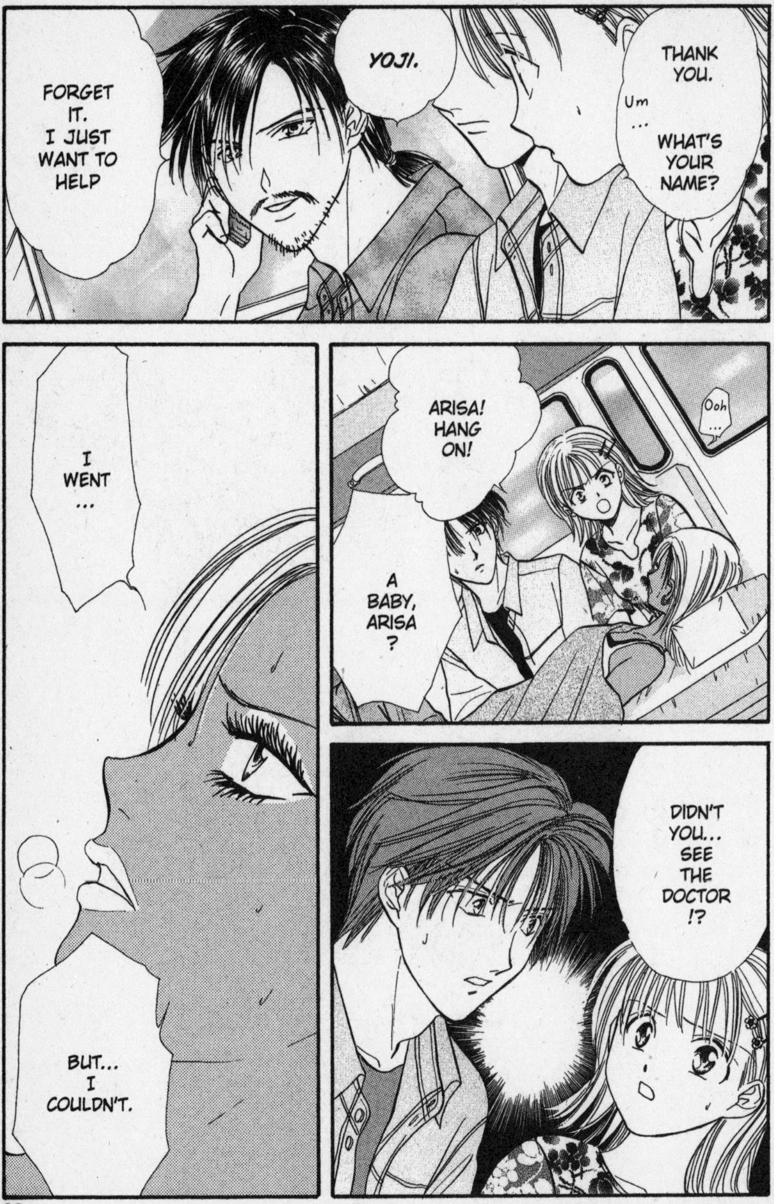
THANK YOU.
Um ...
WHAT'S YOUR NAME?
YOJI.
FORGET IT. I JUST WANT TO HELP
Ooh ...
ARISA! HANG ON!
A BABY, ARISA?
DIDN'T YOU... SEE THE DOCTOR!?
I WENT ...
BUT... I COULDN'T.

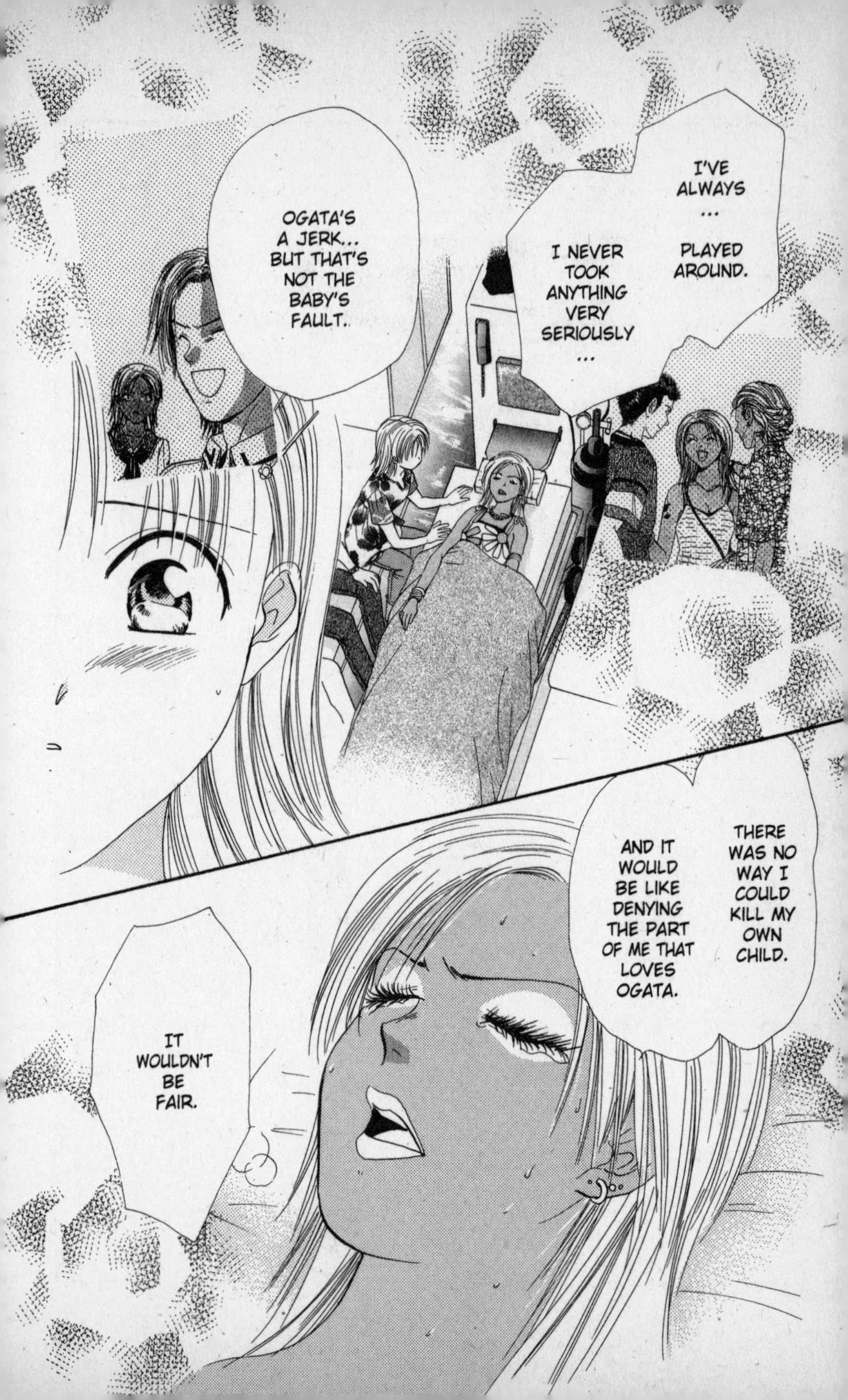
I'VE ALWAYS... PLAYED AROUND.
I NEVER TOOK ANYTHING VERY SERIOUSLY...
OGATA'S A JERK... BUT THAT'S NOT THE BABY'S FAULT.
THERE WAS NO WAY I COULD KILL MY OWN CHILD.
AND IT WOULD BE LIKE DENYING THE PART OF ME THAT LOVES OGATA.
IT WOULDN'T BE FAIR.

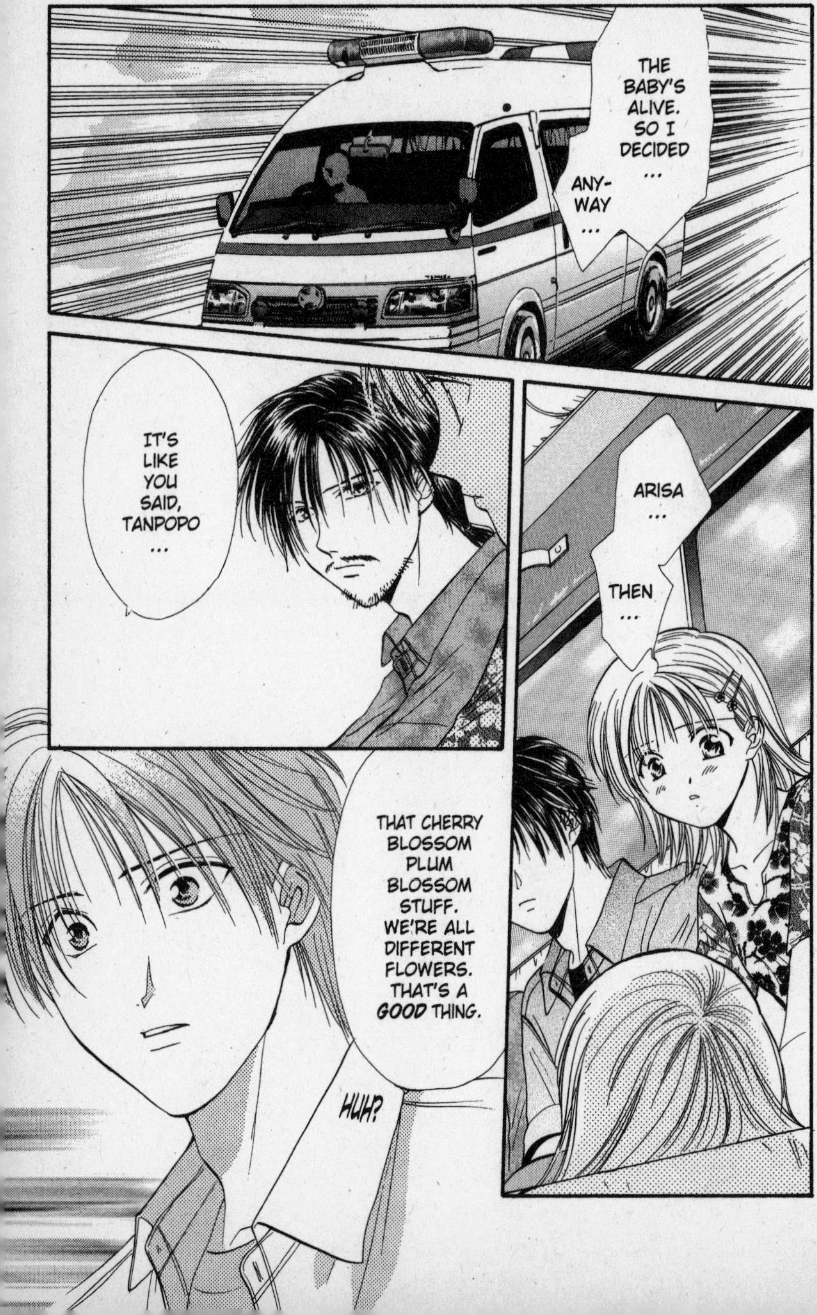
THE BABY'S ALIVE. SO I DECIDED...
ANY-WAY...
ARISA...
THEN...
IT'S LIKE YOU SAID, TANPOPO...
THAT CHERRY BLOSSOM PLUM BLOSSOM STUFF. WE'RE ALL DIFFERENT FLOWERS. THAT'S A *GOOD* THING.
HUH?

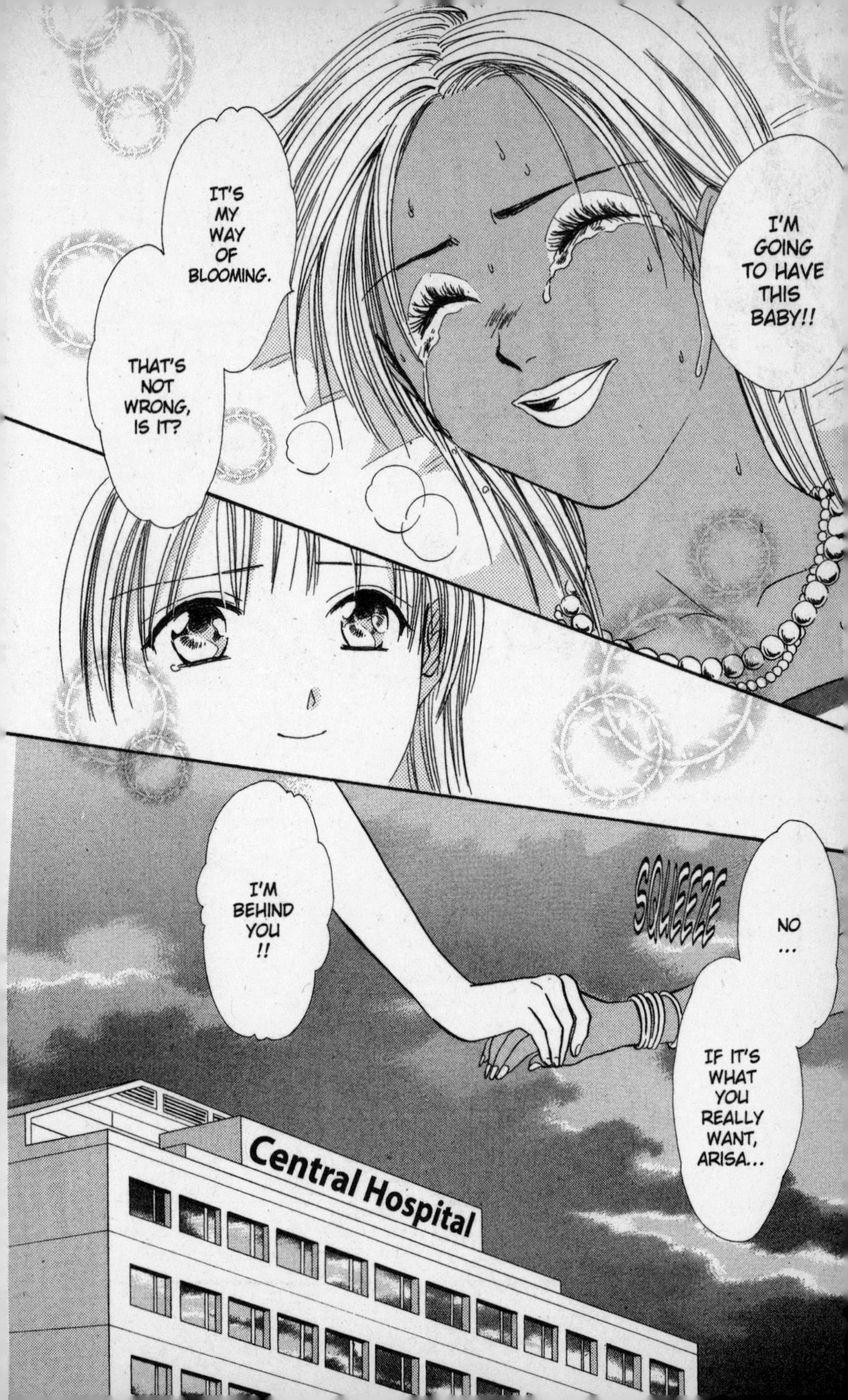
I'M GOING TO HAVE THIS BABY!!
IT'S MY WAY OF BLOOMING.
THAT'S NOT WRONG, IS IT?
NO...
IF IT'S WHAT YOU REALLY WANT, ARISA...
SQUEEZE
I'M BEHIND YOU!!
Central Hospital

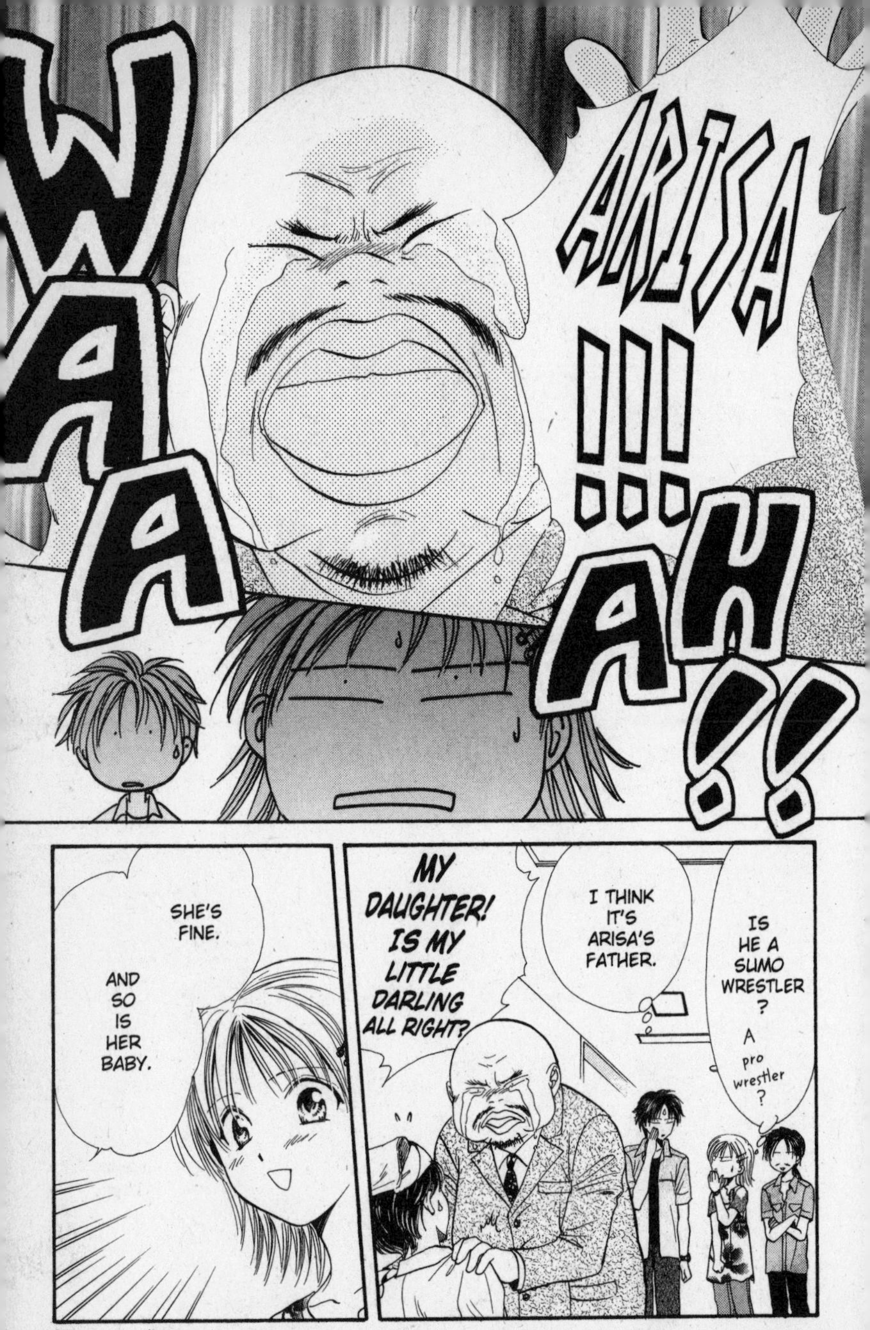
ARISA!!!
WAAAH!!
IS HE A SUMO WRESTLER?
A pro wrestler?
I THINK IT'S ARISA'S FATHER.
MY DAUGHTER! IS MY LITTLE DARLING ALL RIGHT?
SHE'S FINE.
AND SO IS HER BABY.

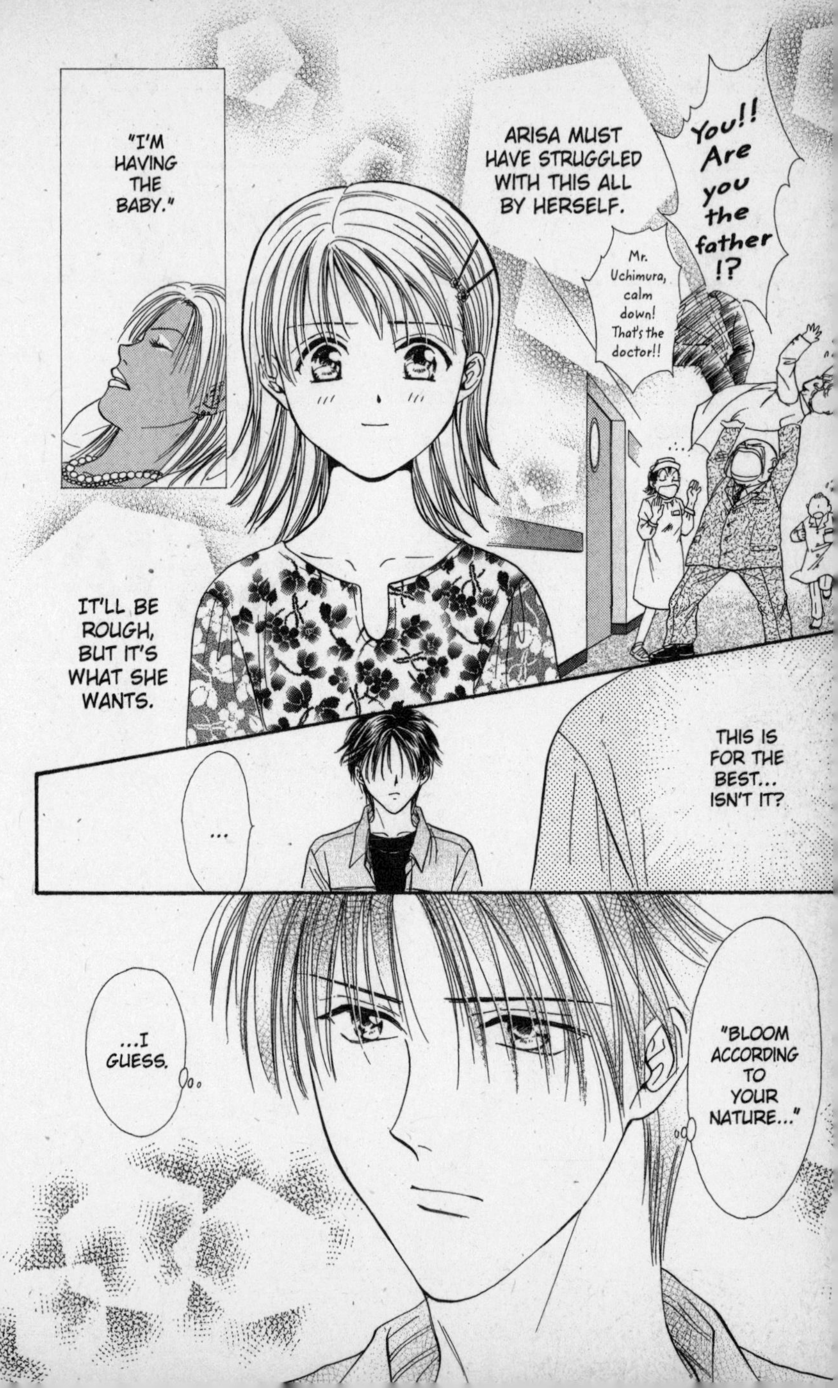
You!! Are you the father !?
Mr. Uchimura, calm down! That's the doctor!!
ARISA MUST HAVE STRUGGLED WITH THIS ALL BY HERSELF.
"I'M HAVING THE BABY."
IT'LL BE ROUGH, BUT IT'S WHAT SHE WANTS.
THIS IS FOR THE BEST... ISN'T IT?
...
"BLOOM ACCORDING TO YOUR NATURE..."
...I GUESS.

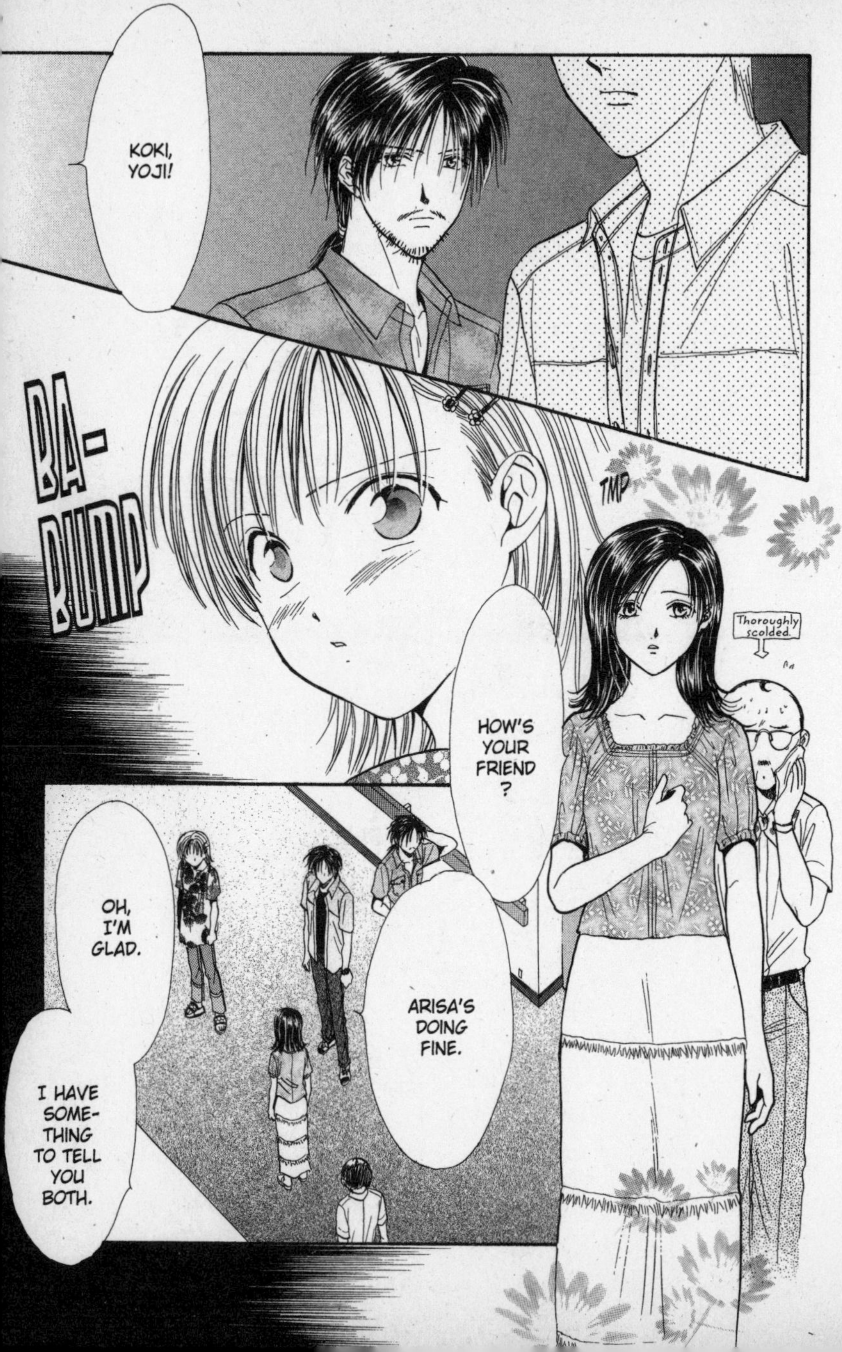
KOKI, YOJI!
TMP
Thoroughly scolded.
HOW'S YOUR FRIEND?
BA-BUMP
ARISA'S DOING FINE.
OH, I'M GLAD.
I HAVE SOMETHING TO TELL YOU BOTH.

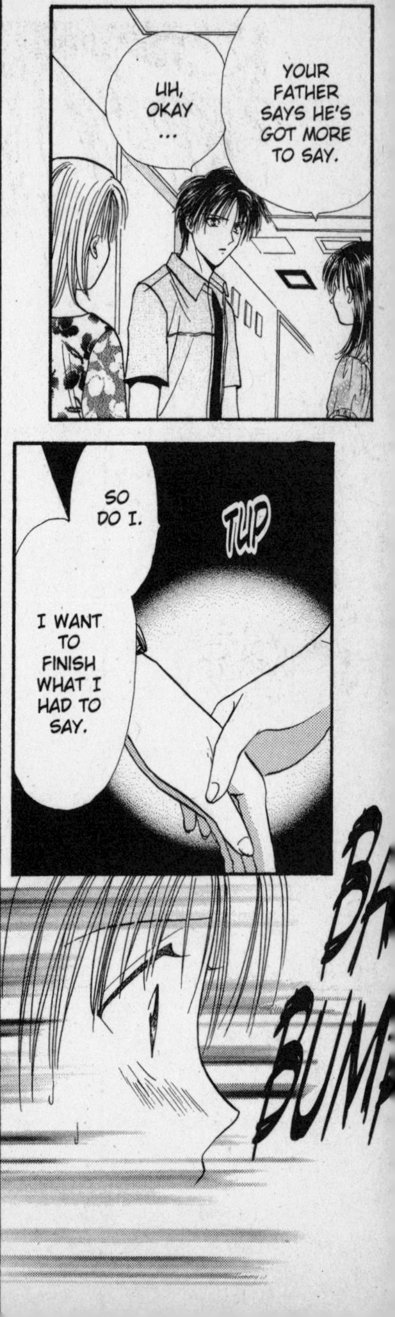
YOUR FATHER SAYS HE'S GOT MORE TO SAY.
UH, OKAY ...
SO DO I.
TUP
I WANT TO FINISH WHAT I HAD TO SAY.

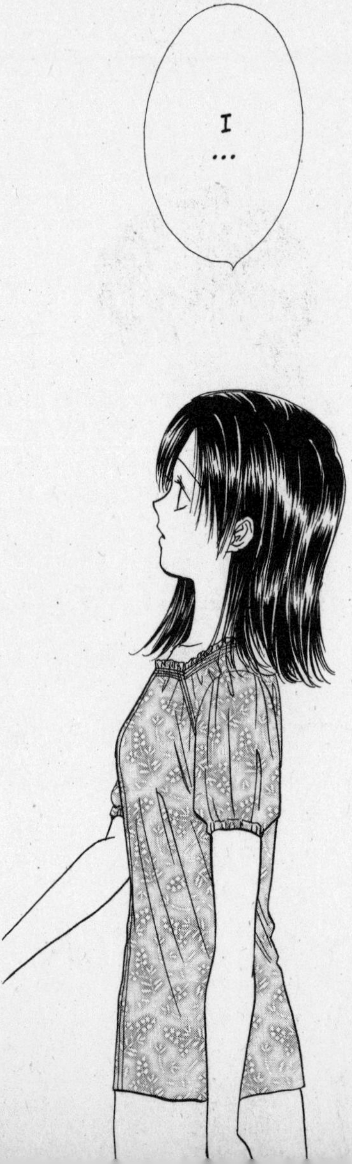
I ...

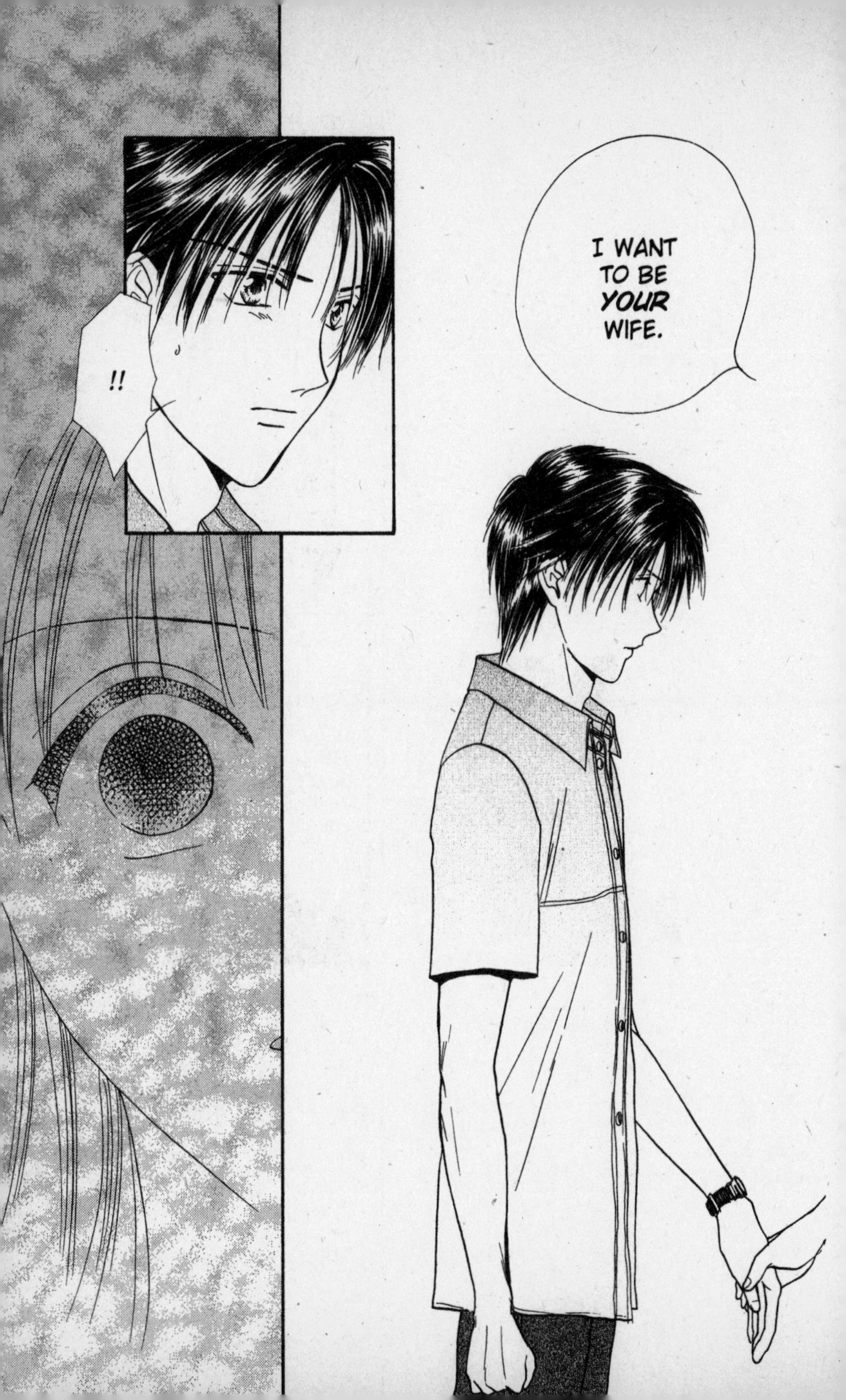
I WANT TO BE *YOUR* WIFE.
!!

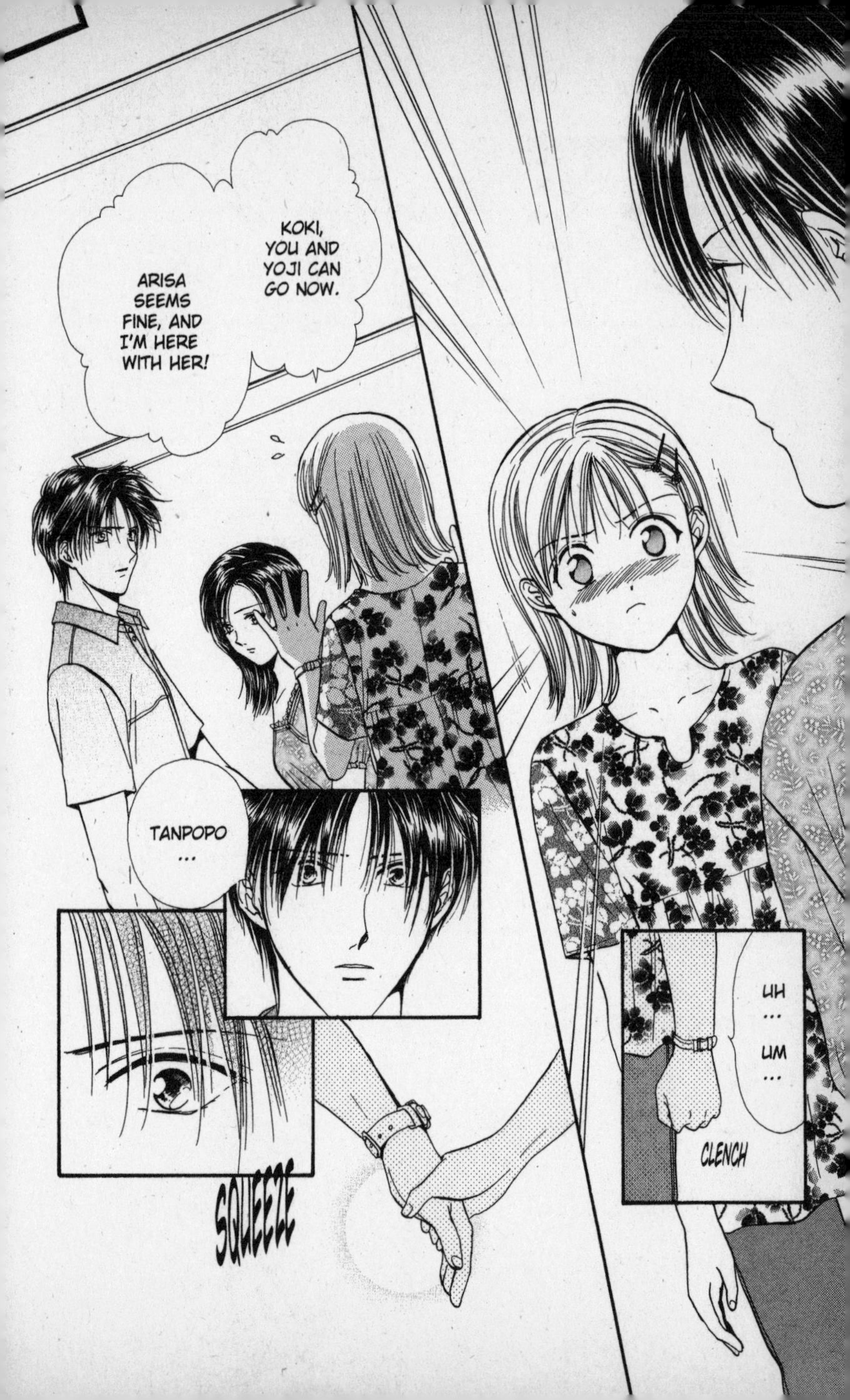
UH ... UM ...
CLENCH
KOKI, YOU AND YOJI CAN GO NOW.
ARISA SEEMS FINE, AND I'M HERE WITH HER!
TANPOPO ...
SQUEEZE

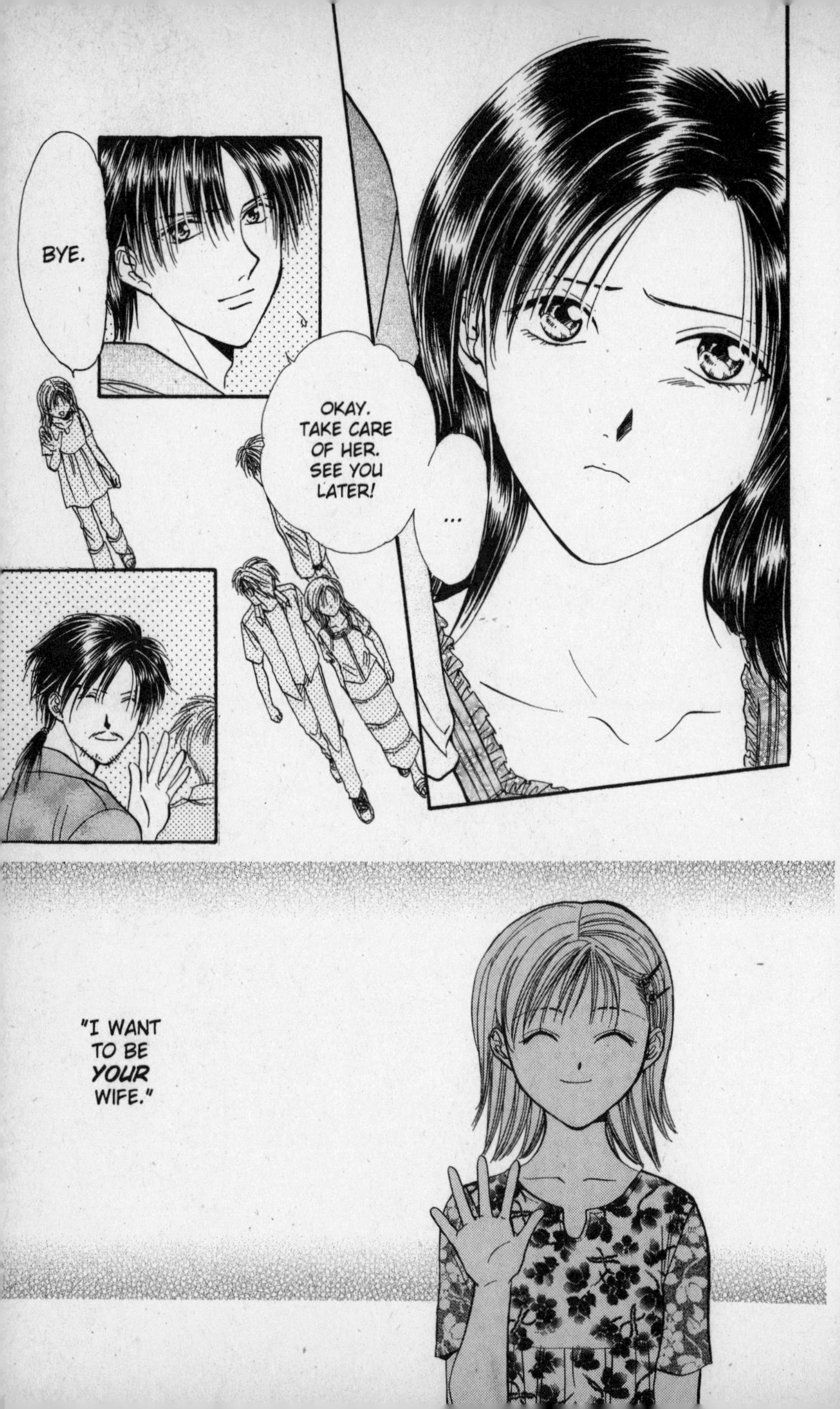
OKAY. TAKE CARE OF HER. SEE YOU LATER!
...
BYE.
"I WANT TO BE *YOUR* WIFE."

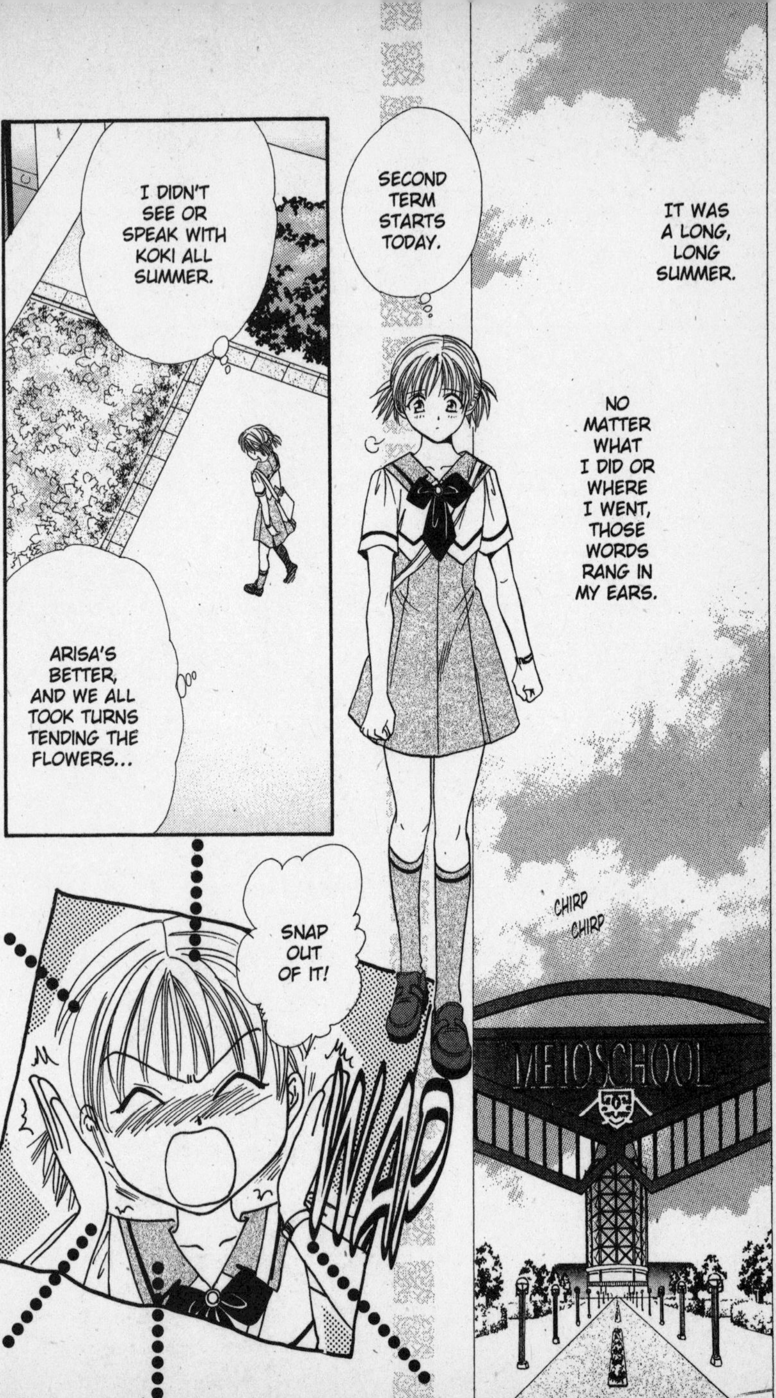

IT WAS A LONG, LONG SUMMER.
NO MATTER WHAT I DID OR WHERE I WENT, THOSE WORDS RANG IN MY EARS.
CHIRP
CHIRP
MEIOSCHOOL
SECOND TERM STARTS TODAY.
I DIDN'T SEE OR SPEAK WITH KOKI ALL SUMMER.
ARISA'S BETTER, AND WE ALL TOOK TURNS TENDING THE FLOWERS...
SNAP OUT OF IT!
WAP

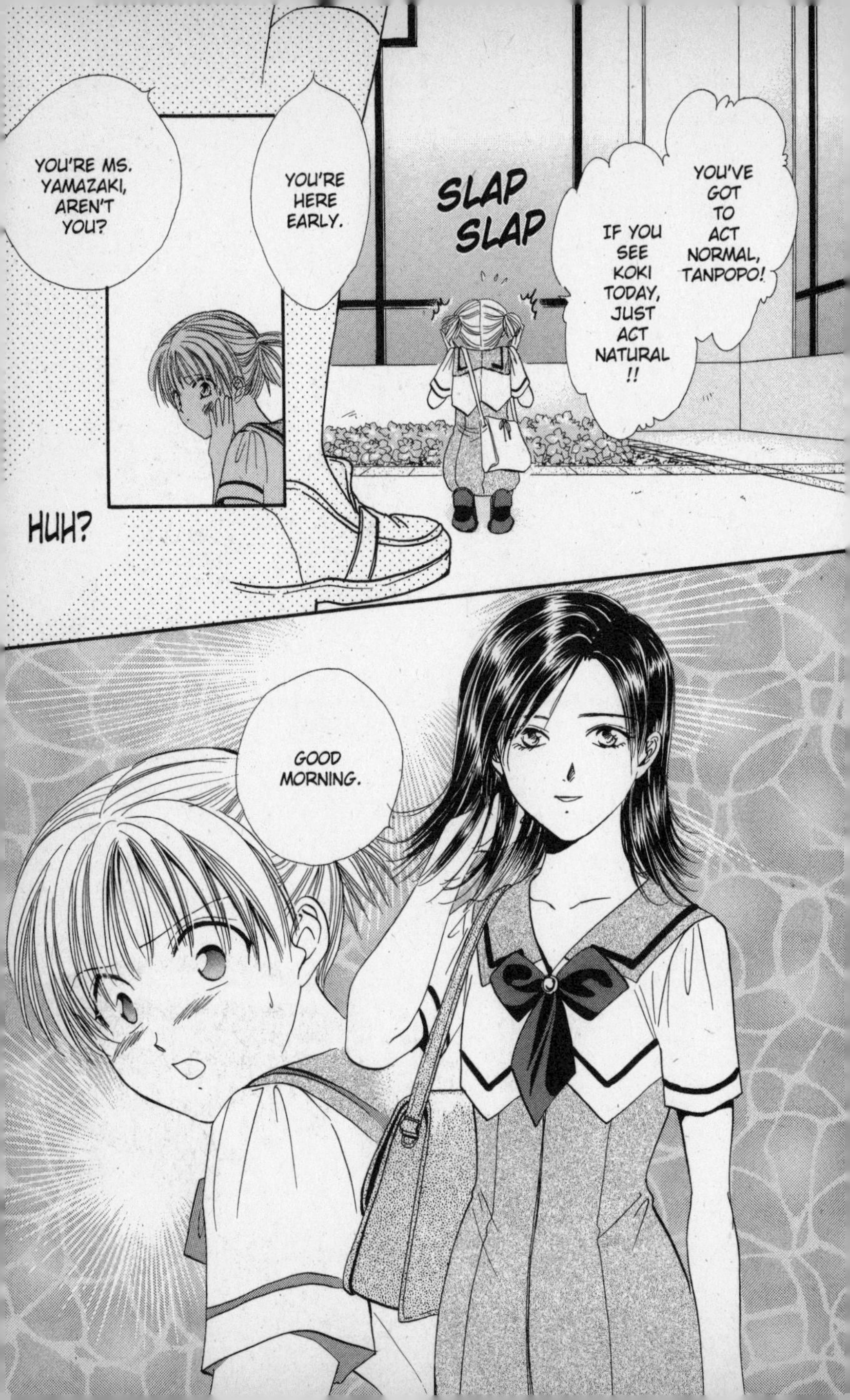
YOU'VE GOT TO ACT NORMAL, TANPOPO!
IF YOU SEE KOKI TODAY, JUST ACT NATURAL !!
SLAP SLAP
YOU'RE HERE EARLY.
YOU'RE MS. YAMAZAKI, AREN'T YOU?
HUH?
GOOD MORNING.

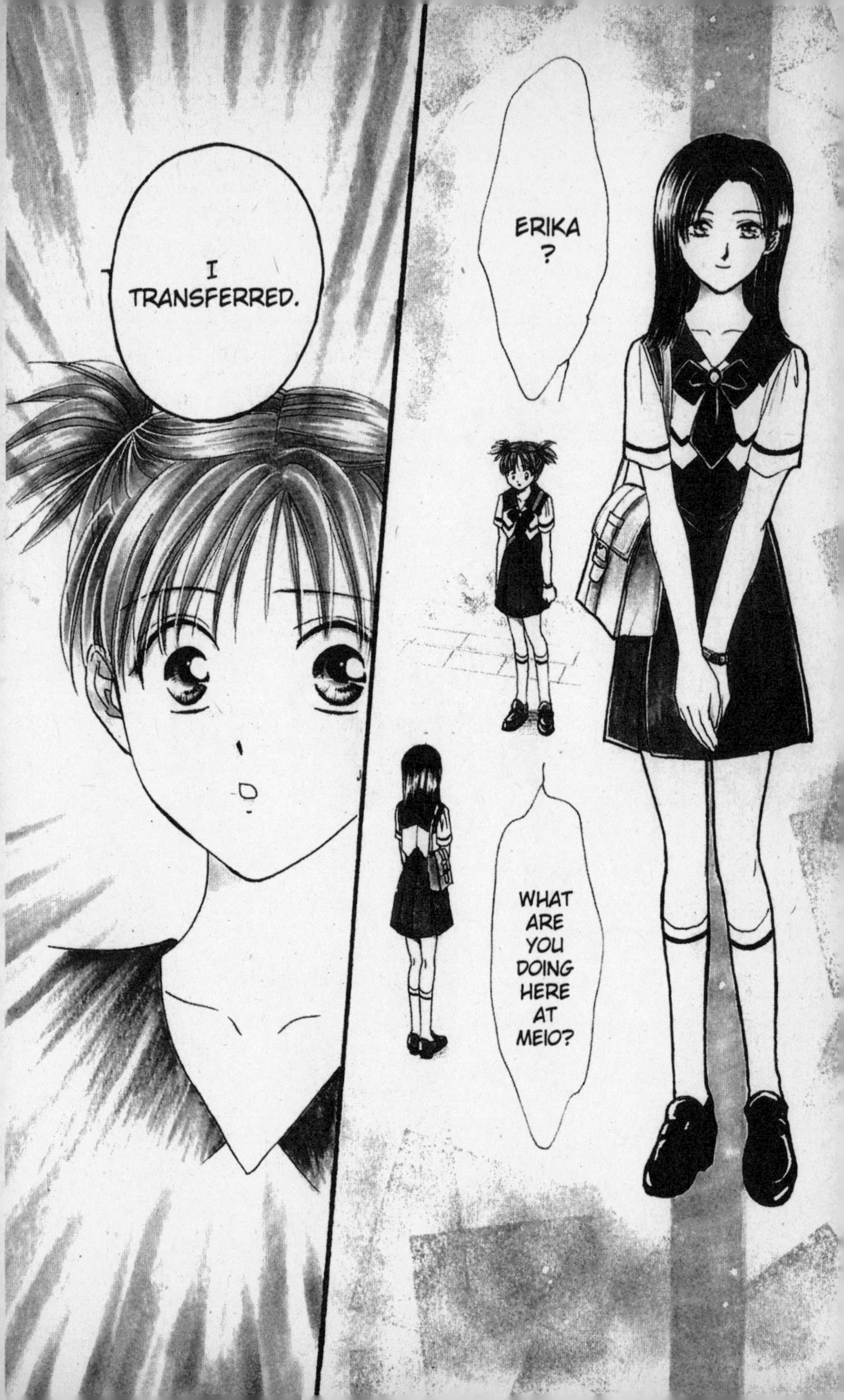
ERIKA?
WHAT ARE YOU DOING HERE AT MEIO?
I TRANSFERRED.

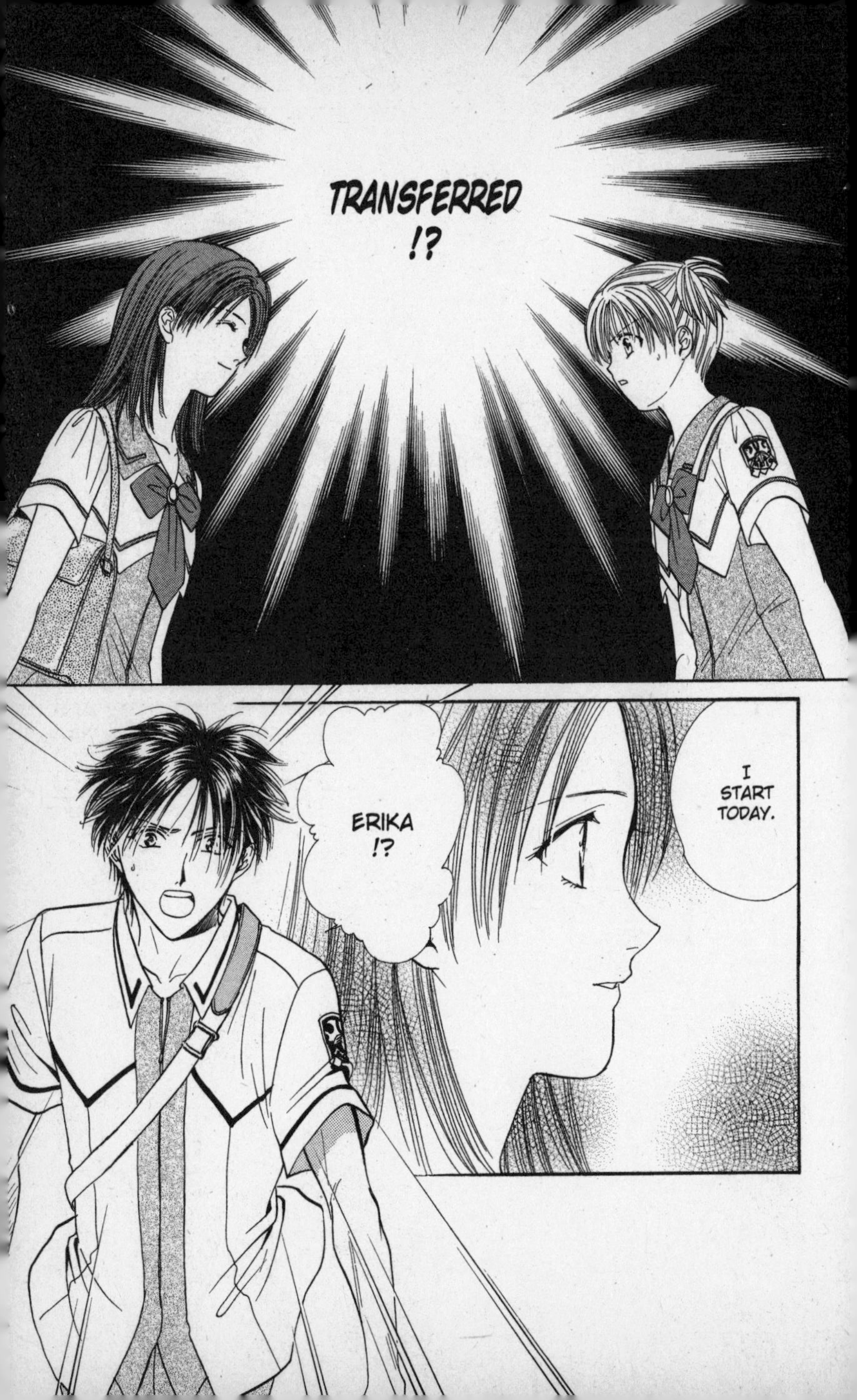
TRANSFERRED !?
I START TODAY.
ERIKA !?

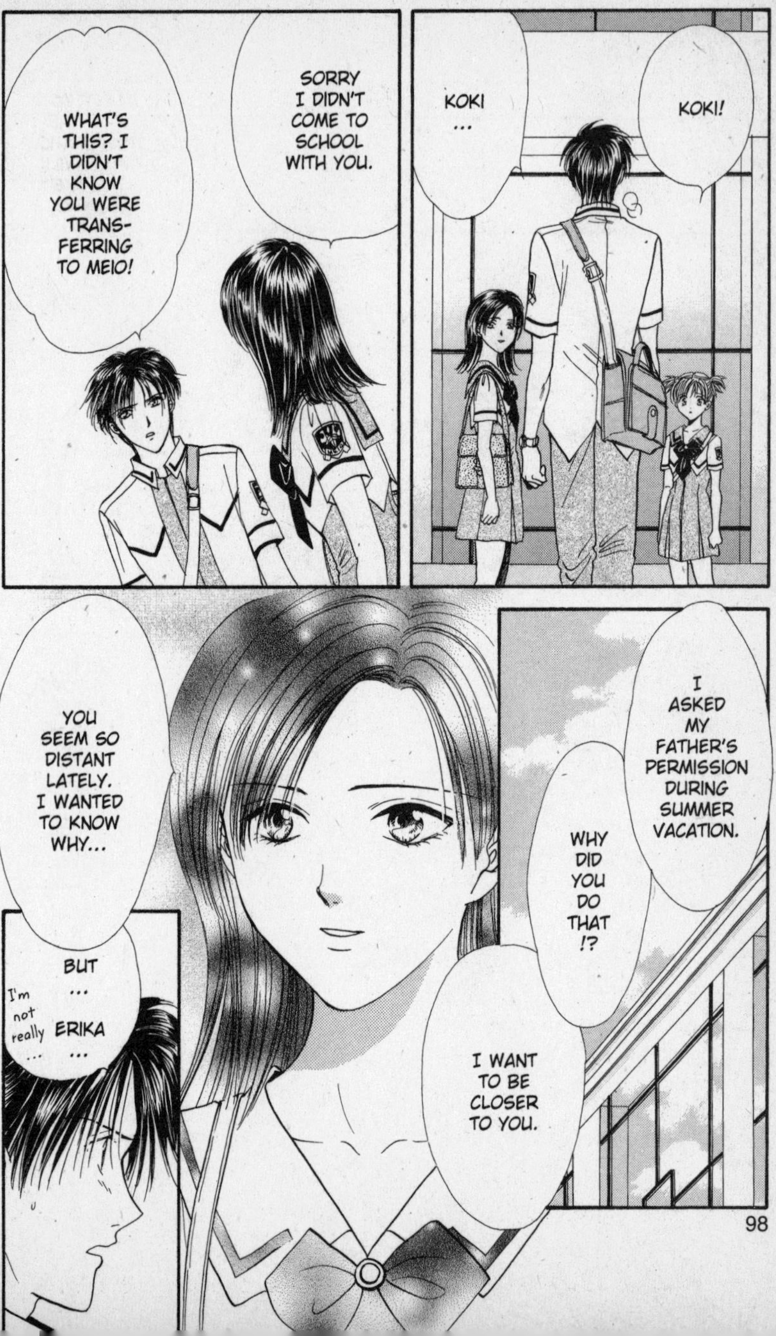
KOKI!
KOKI ...
SORRY I DIDN'T COME TO SCHOOL WITH YOU.
WHAT'S THIS? I DIDN'T KNOW YOU WERE TRANS-FERRING TO MEIO!
I ASKED MY FATHER'S PERMISSION DURING SUMMER VACATION.
WHY DID YOU DO THAT !?
I WANT TO BE CLOSER TO YOU.
YOU SEEM SO DISTANT LATELY. I WANTED TO KNOW WHY...
BUT ... ERIKA ...
I'm not really ...

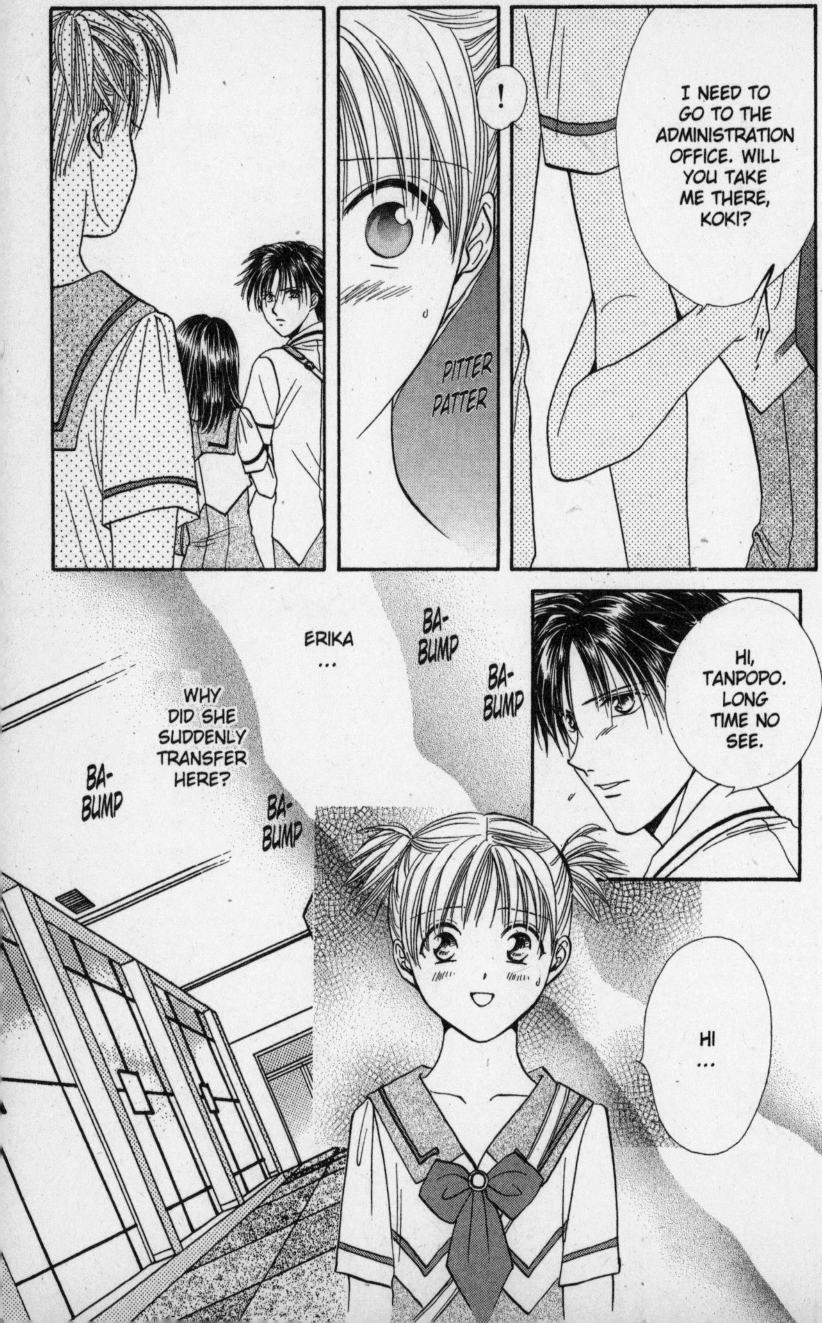
I NEED TO GO TO THE ADMINISTRATION OFFICE. WILL YOU TAKE ME THERE, KOKI?
!
PITTER PATTER
HI, TANPOPO. LONG TIME NO SEE.
BA-BUMP
BA-BUMP
ERIKA ...
WHY DID SHE SUDDENLY TRANSFER HERE?
BA-BUMP
BA-BUMP
HI ...

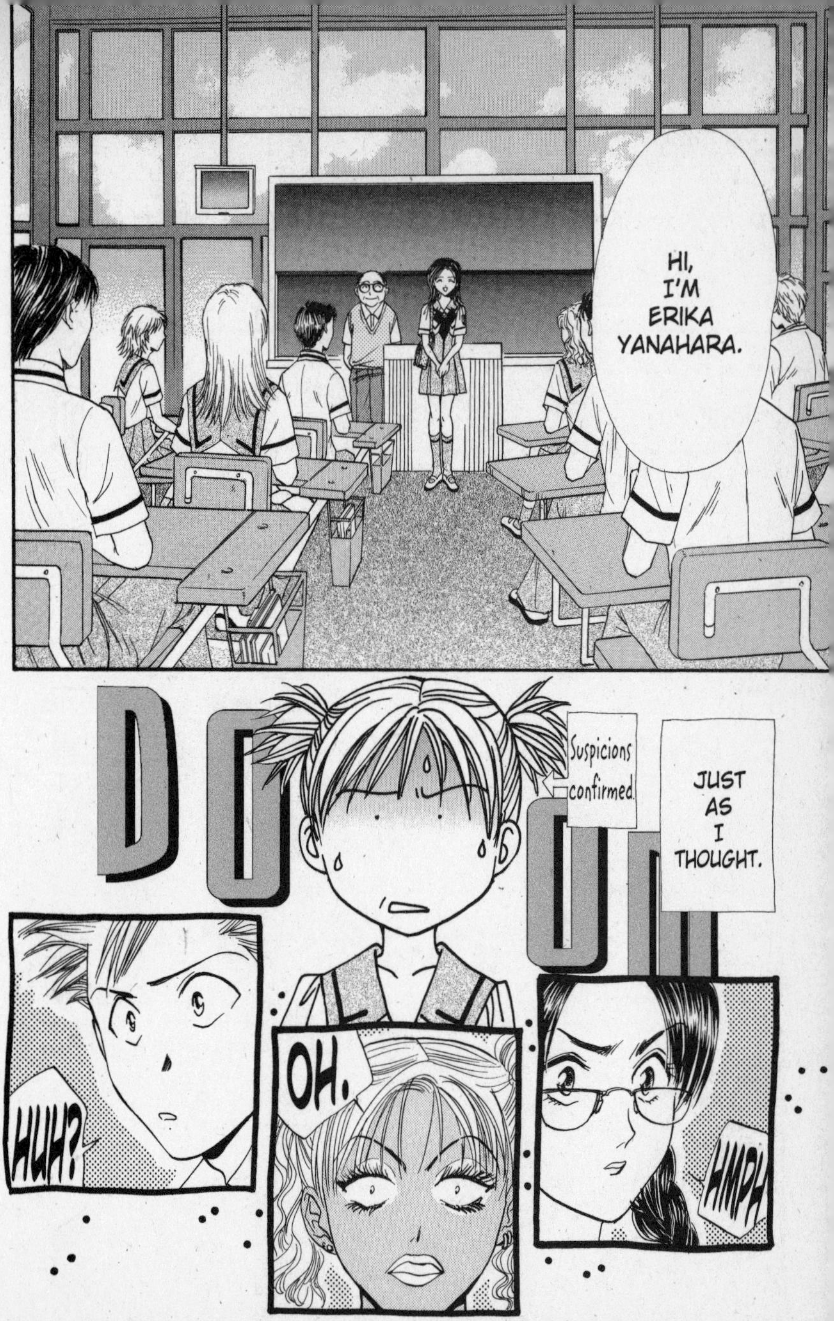
HI, I'M ERIKA YANAHARA.
JUST AS I THOUGHT.
Suspicions confirmed.
DOOM
HMPH
OH.
HUH?

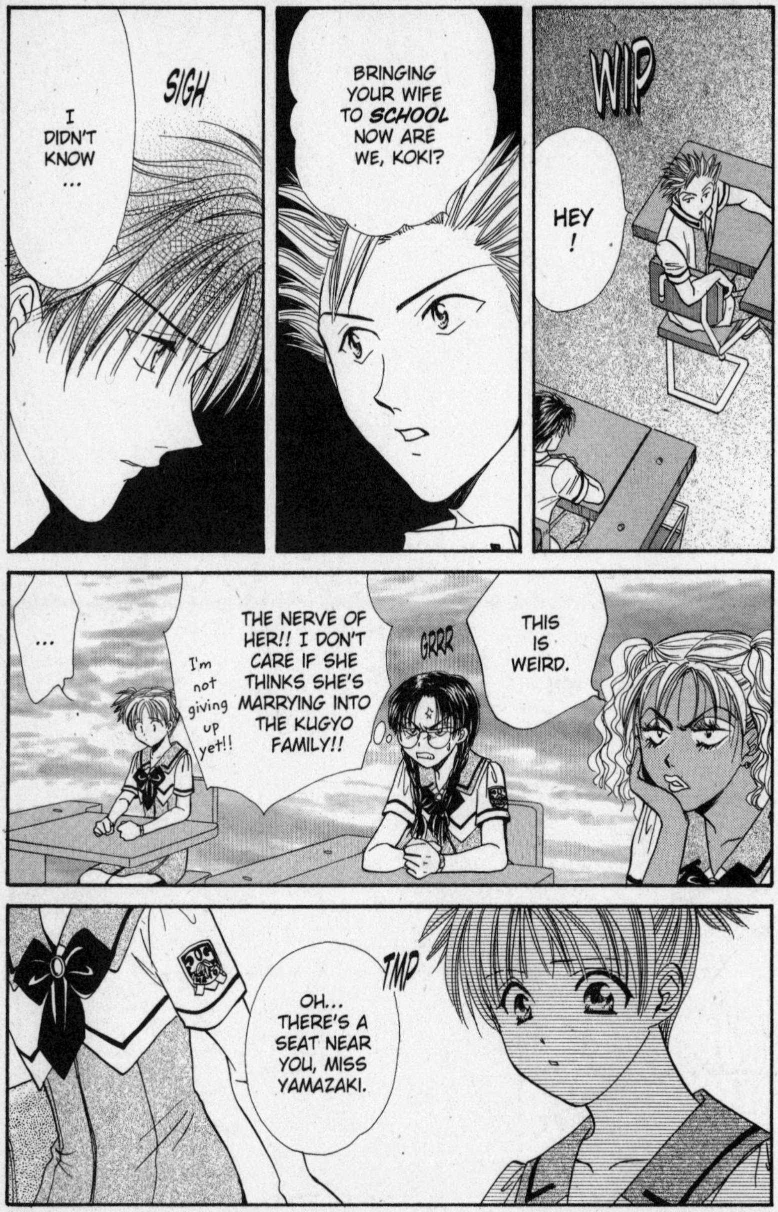
WIP
HEY!
BRINGING YOUR WIFE TO SCHOOL NOW ARE WE, KOKI?
SIGH
I DIDN'T KNOW ...
THIS IS WEIRD.
GRRR
THE NERVE OF HER!! I DON'T CARE IF SHE THINKS SHE'S MARRYING INTO THE KUGYO FAMILY!!
I'm not giving up yet!!
...
TMP
OH... THERE'S A SEAT NEAR YOU, MISS YAMAZAKI.

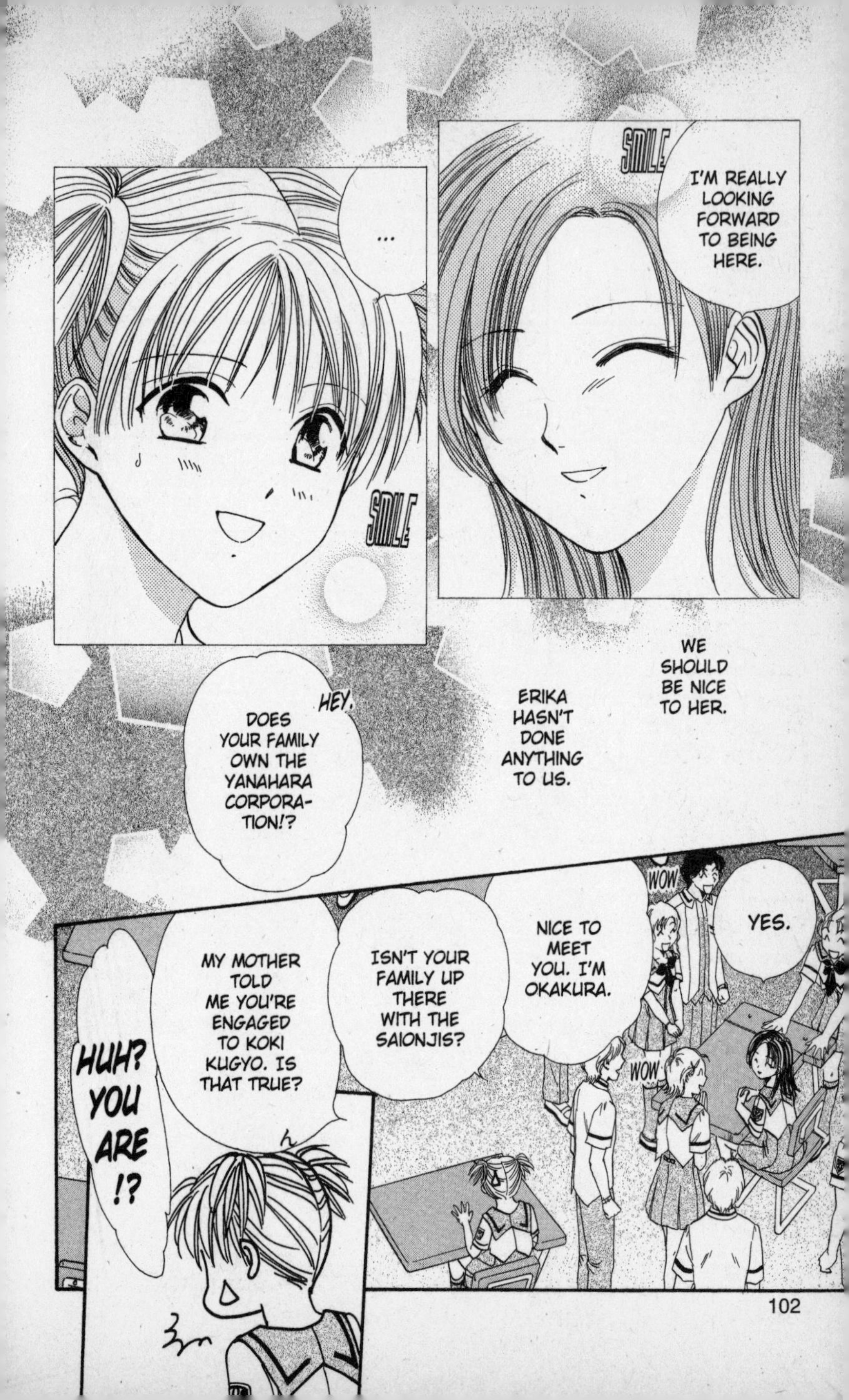
SMILE
I'M REALLY LOOKING FORWARD TO BEING HERE.
...
SMILE
WE SHOULD BE NICE TO HER.
ERIKA HASN'T DONE ANYTHING TO US.
HEY.
DOES YOUR FAMILY OWN THE YANAHARA CORPORATION!?
WOW
YES.
NICE TO MEET YOU. I'M OKAKURA.
WOW
ISN'T YOUR FAMILY UP THERE WITH THE SAIONJIS?
MY MOTHER TOLD ME YOU'RE ENGAGED TO KOKI KUGYO. IS THAT TRUE?
HUH? YOU ARE!?

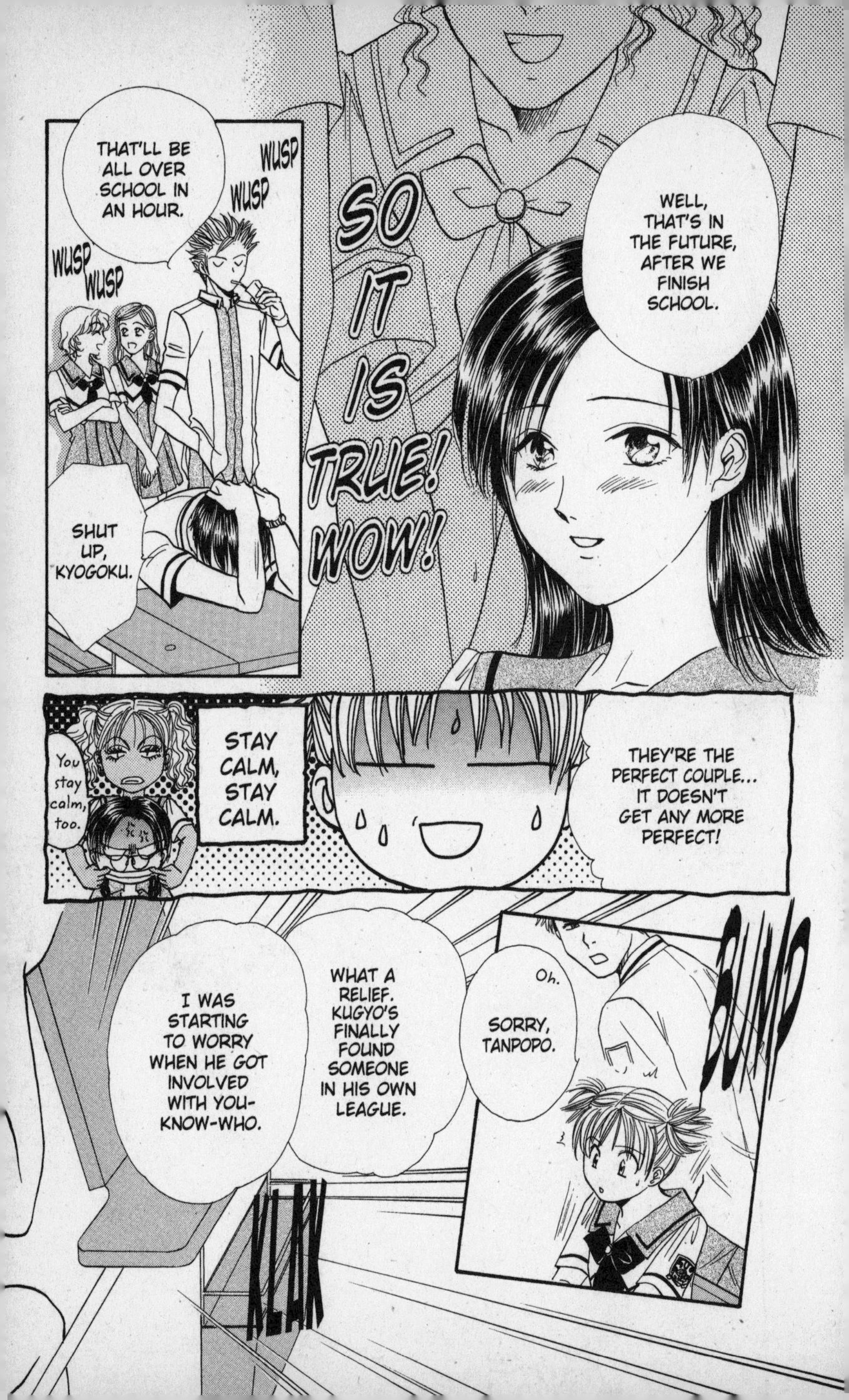
WELL, THAT'S IN THE FUTURE, AFTER WE FINISH SCHOOL.
SO IT IS TRUE! WOW!
WUSP WUSP
WUSP WUSP
THAT'LL BE ALL OVER SCHOOL IN AN HOUR.
SHUT UP, KYOGOKU.
THEY'RE THE PERFECT COUPLE... IT DOESN'T GET ANY MORE PERFECT!
STAY CALM, STAY CALM.
You stay calm, too.
BUMP
Oh.
SORRY, TANPOPO.
WHAT A RELIEF. KUGYO'S FINALLY FOUND SOMEONE IN HIS OWN LEAGUE.
I WAS STARTING TO WORRY WHEN HE GOT INVOLVED WITH YOU-KNOW-WHO.
KLAK

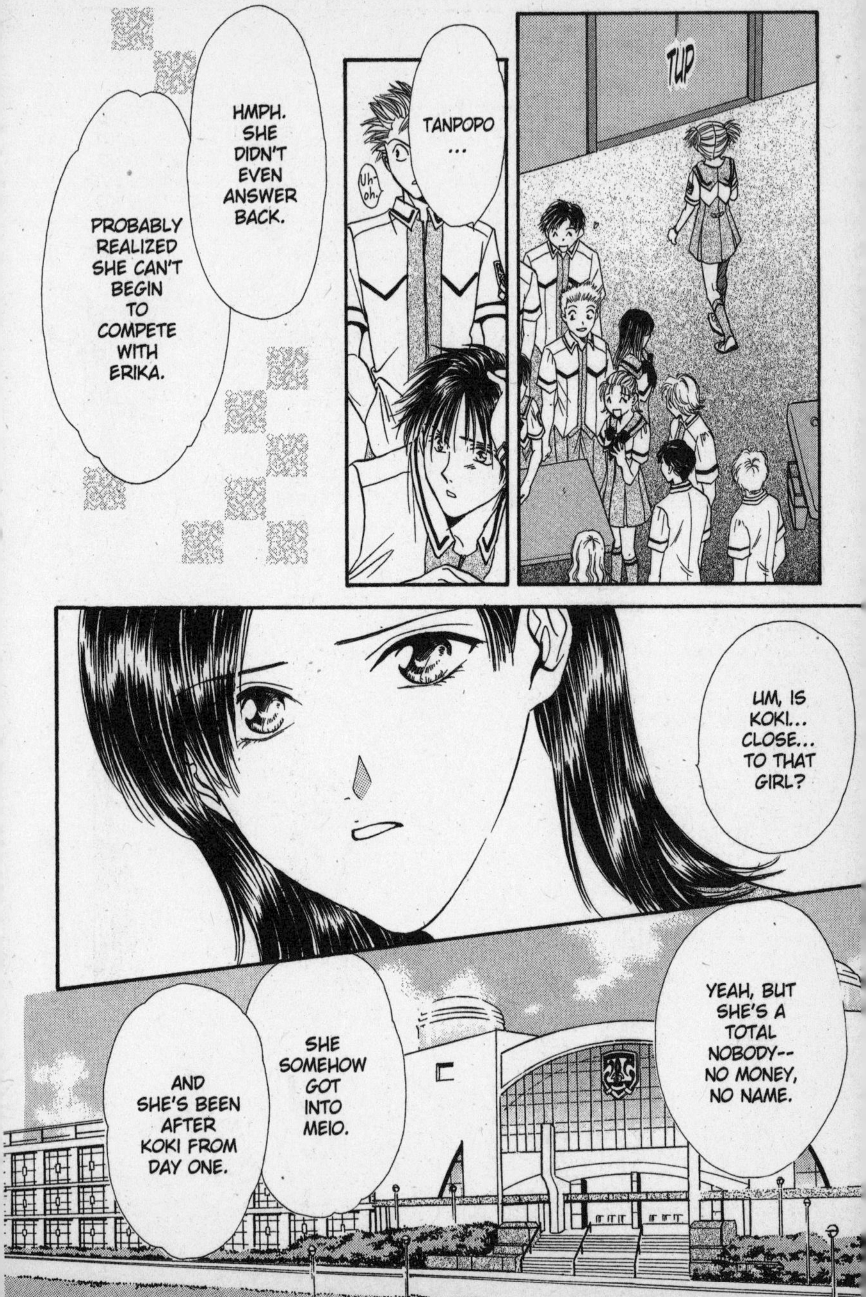
TUP
TANPOPO ...
Uh-oh.
HMPH. SHE DIDN'T EVEN ANSWER BACK.
PROBABLY REALIZED SHE CAN'T BEGIN TO COMPETE WITH ERIKA.
UM, IS KOKI... CLOSE... TO THAT GIRL?
YEAH, BUT SHE'S A TOTAL NOBODY-- NO MONEY, NO NAME.
SHE SOMEHOW GOT INTO MEIO.
AND SHE'S BEEN AFTER KOKI FROM DAY ONE.

They say there's a "Gundam" Generation and an "Ashita no Joe" Generation. When I was little, the big hit show was "Candy Candy". Does that make me the "Candy Candy" Generation? And after that, is it the "899" Generation? Ha! "Z Gundam (including ZZ)".... Oh, how about "Macross"?
I don't know. Heh! Teenagers these days would be part of the "Sailor Moon" and "Evangelion" Generation, right? I'm getting confused!
But to create something so influential that a whole generation would be called the "-----" Generation is really amazing.
Anyway, I'd like to see some old manga (anime). I'm reading some today, too. Hee hee! Bit by bit. Hmm...This is the age of the "Game" Generation, I think.
Speaking of games, I once said that the character Skol in FF8 was "Gakuto" (I don't know the spelling), and someone corrected me, saying "That's Teru!" (see **Ayashi no Ceres** comic book). But it was "Gakuto" apparently.
Someone at Square (the company that produced FF) told me so (that's what my assistant says). But that doesn't matter. So why write about it? It just came to my mind.
Games are fun, but I prefer meeting real live people. E-mail is convenient, but you can't beat meeting someone face to face. I was so far behind on my New Year's cards that I sent some e-cards. But I prefer paper. At least the e-mails got the job done. "I'll see you when I see you," right?
But when your body stops responding because of overwork, it can be rough. Lately, after finishing a production, I try not to go out the next day. Otherwise I get anemic.

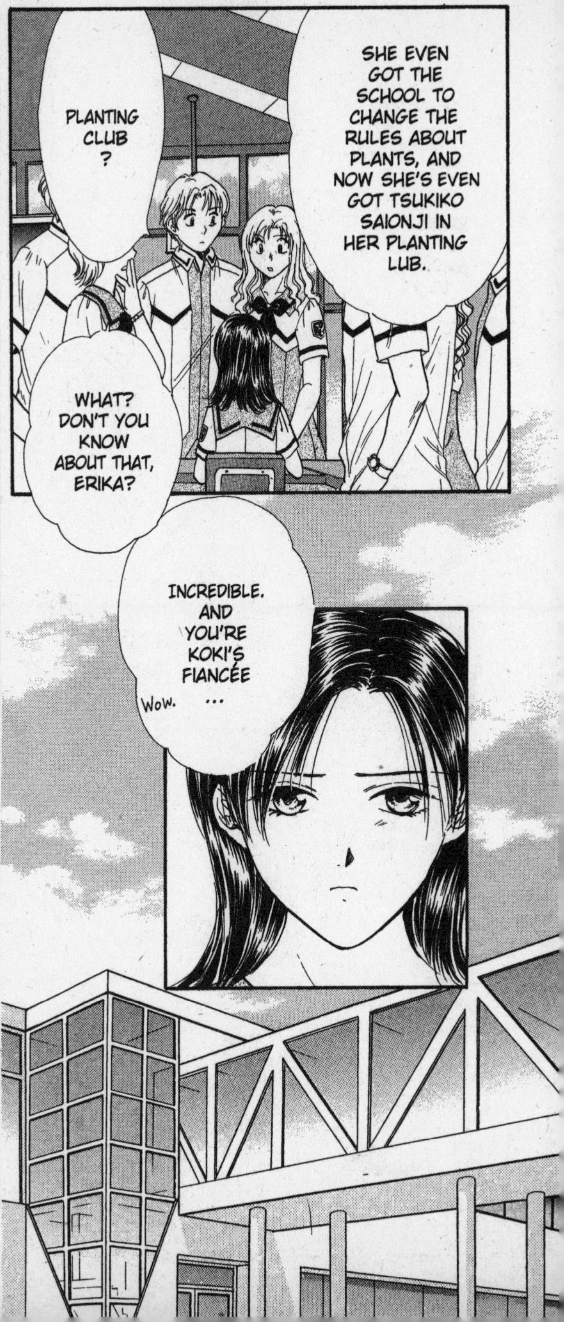
SHE EVEN GOT THE SCHOOL TO CHANGE THE RULES ABOUT PLANTS, AND NOW SHE'S EVEN GOT TSUKIKO SAIONJI IN HER PLANTING LUB.
PLANTING CLUB ?
WHAT? DON'T YOU KNOW ABOUT THAT, ERIKA?
INCREDIBLE. AND YOU'RE KOKI'S FIANCÉE ...
Wow.

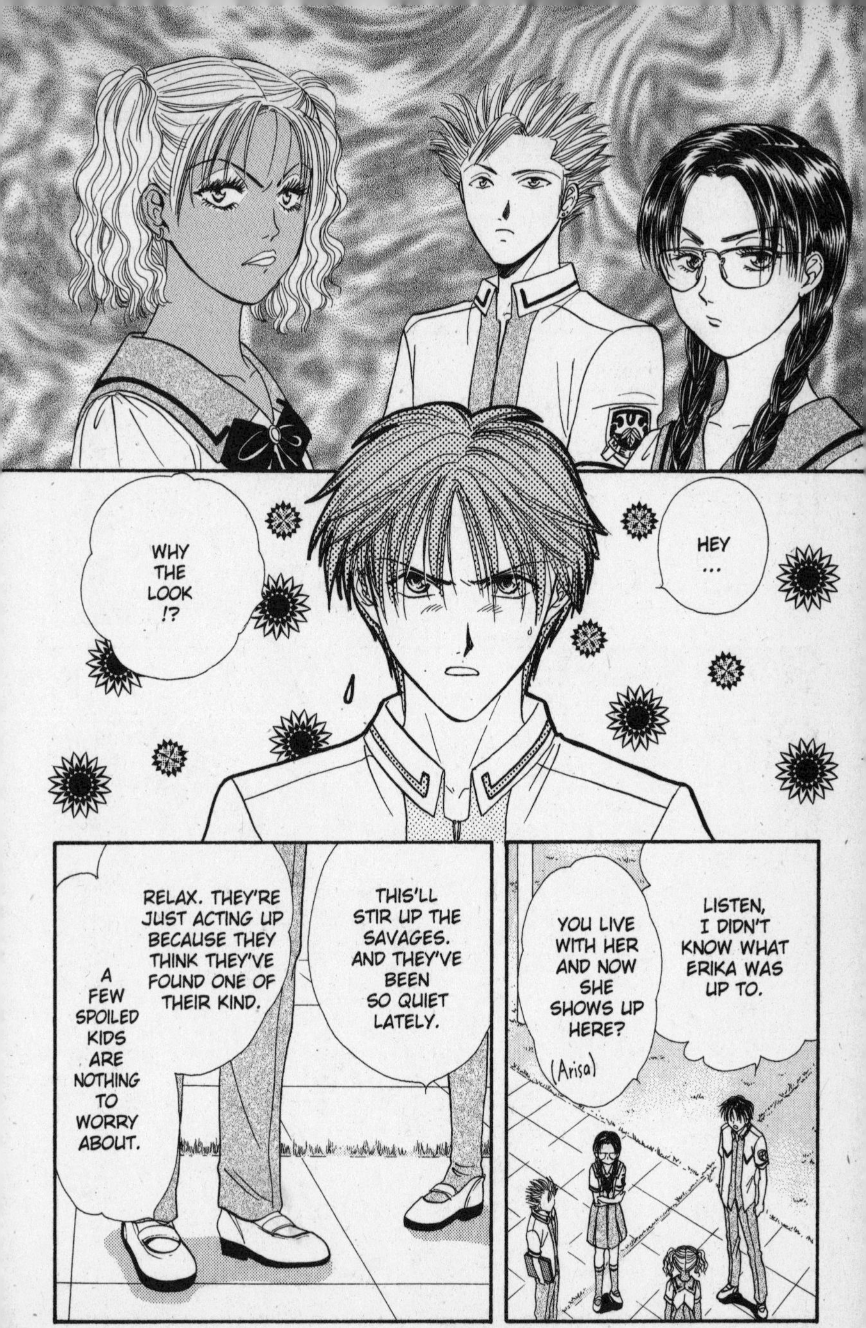
HEY ...
WHY THE LOOK !?
LISTEN, I DIDN'T KNOW WHAT ERIKA WAS UP TO.
YOU LIVE WITH HER AND NOW SHE SHOWS UP HERE?
(Arisa)
THIS'LL STIR UP THE SAVAGES. AND THEY'VE BEEN SO QUIET LATELY.
RELAX. THEY'RE JUST ACTING UP BECAUSE THEY THINK THEY'VE FOUND ONE OF THEIR KIND.
A FEW SPOILED KIDS ARE NOTHING TO WORRY ABOUT.

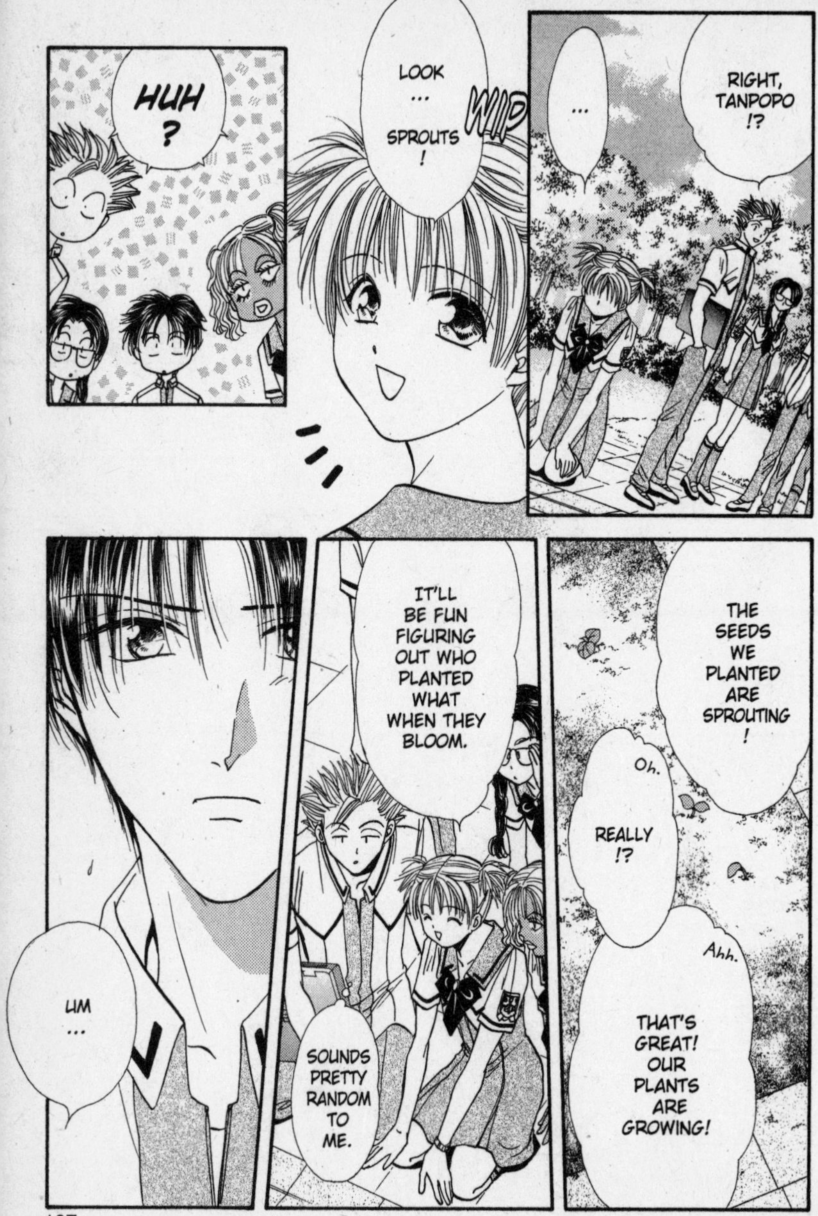
RIGHT, TANPOPO !?
...
LOOK ... SPROUTS !
WIP
HUH ?
THE SEEDS WE PLANTED ARE SPROUTING !
Oh.
REALLY !?
Ahh.
THAT'S GREAT! OUR PLANTS ARE GROWING!
IT'LL BE FUN FIGURING OUT WHO PLANTED WHAT WHEN THEY BLOOM.
SOUNDS PRETTY RANDOM TO ME.
UM ...

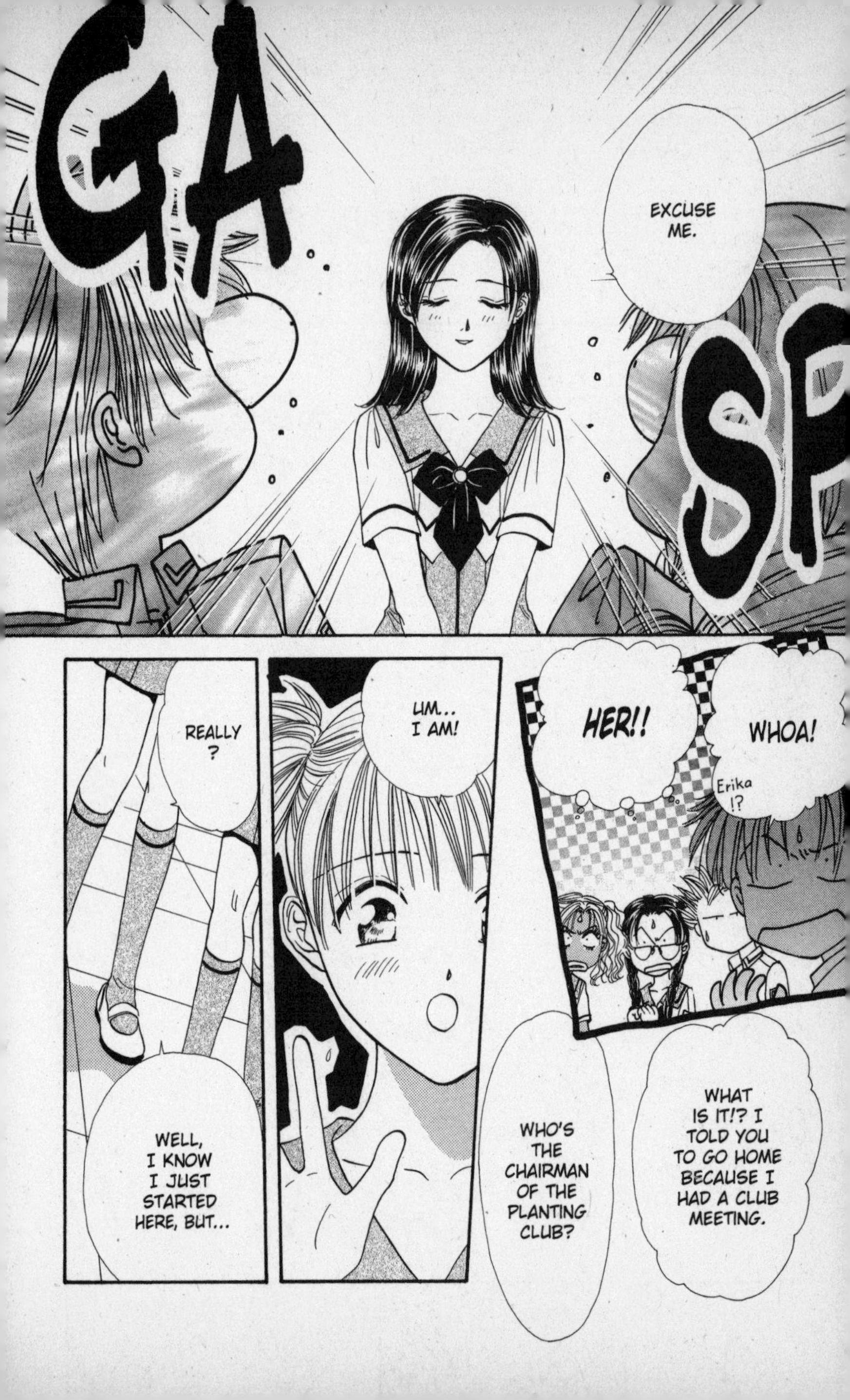
EXCUSE ME.
GA
SP
WHOA!
Erika !?
HER!!
WHAT IS IT!? I TOLD YOU TO GO HOME BECAUSE I HAD A CLUB MEETING.
WHO'S THE CHAIRMAN OF THE PLANTING CLUB?
UM... I AM!
REALLY ?
WELL, I KNOW I JUST STARTED HERE, BUT...

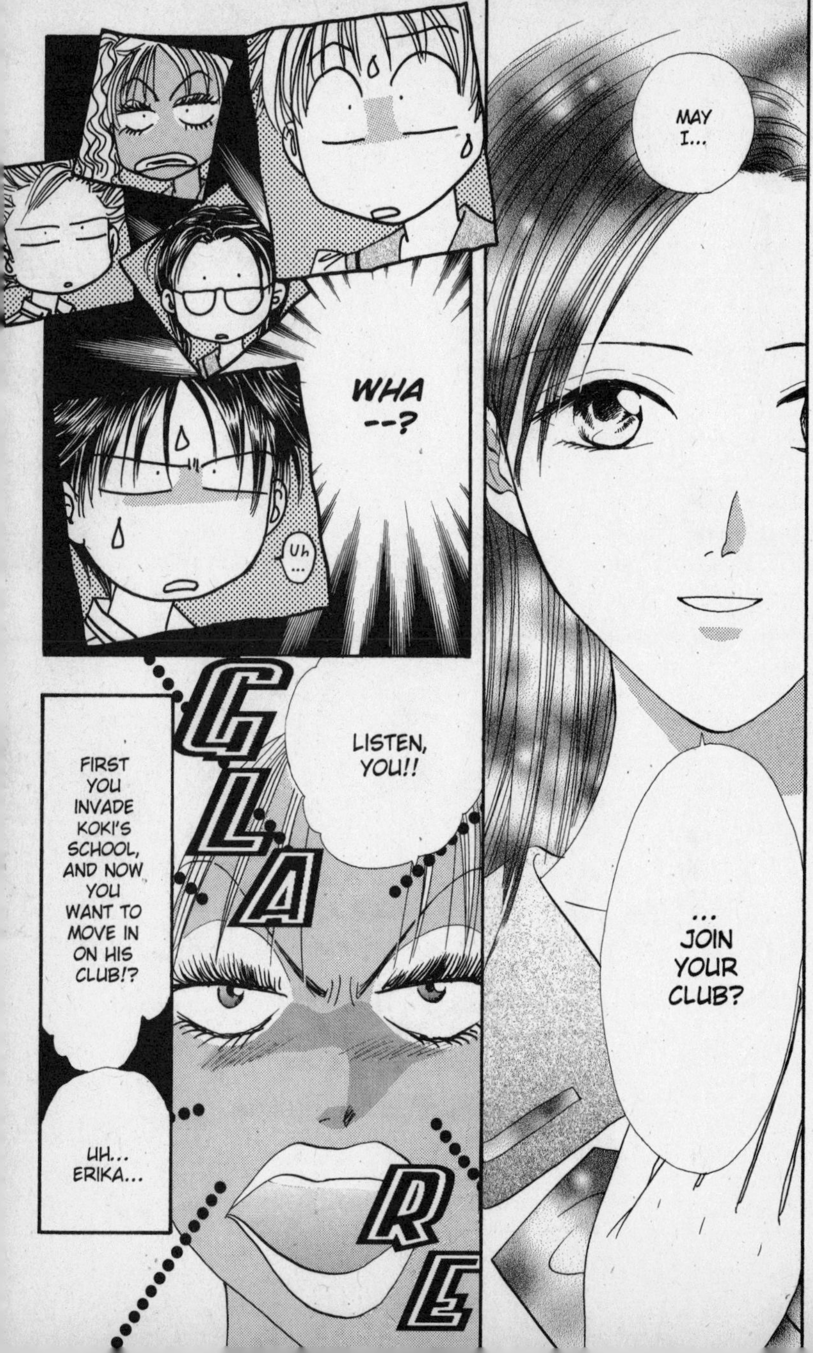
MAY I...
... JOIN YOUR CLUB?
WHA --?
Uh ...
LISTEN, YOU!!
FIRST YOU INVADE KOKI'S SCHOOL, AND NOW YOU WANT TO MOVE IN ON HIS CLUB!?
CLARE
UH... ERIKA...

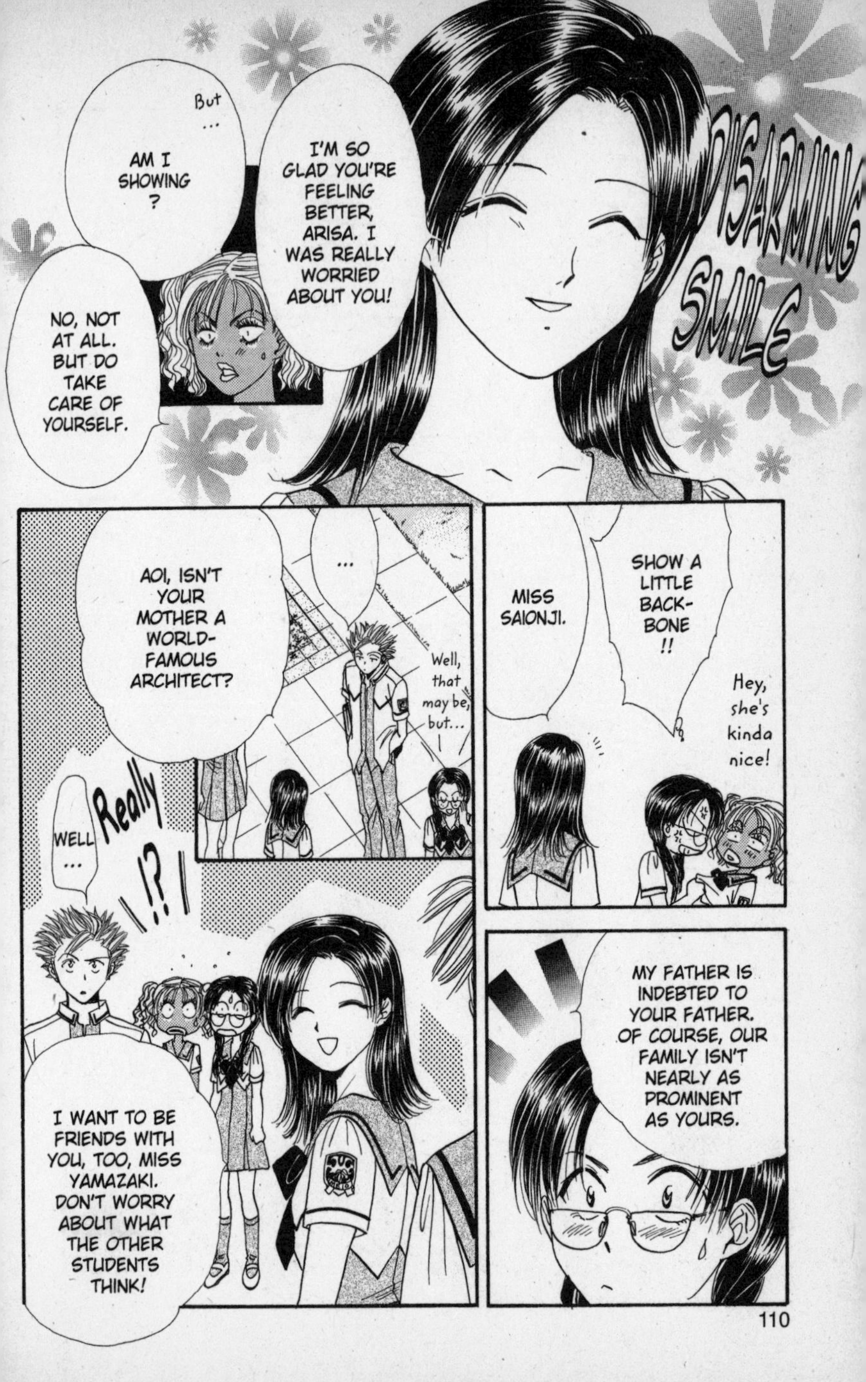
DISARMING SMILE
I'M SO GLAD YOU'RE FEELING BETTER, ARISA. I WAS REALLY WORRIED ABOUT YOU!
But ... AM I SHOWING?
NO, NOT AT ALL. BUT DO TAKE CARE OF YOURSELF.
SHOW A LITTLE BACK-BONE!!
MISS SAIONJI.
Hey, she's kinda nice!
...
AOI, ISN'T YOUR MOTHER A WORLD-FAMOUS ARCHITECT?
Well, that may be, but...
MY FATHER IS INDEBTED TO YOUR FATHER. OF COURSE, OUR FAMILY ISN'T NEARLY AS PROMINENT AS YOURS.
Really !?
WELL ...
I WANT TO BE FRIENDS WITH YOU, TOO, MISS YAMAZAKI. DON'T WORRY ABOUT WHAT THE OTHER STUDENTS THINK!

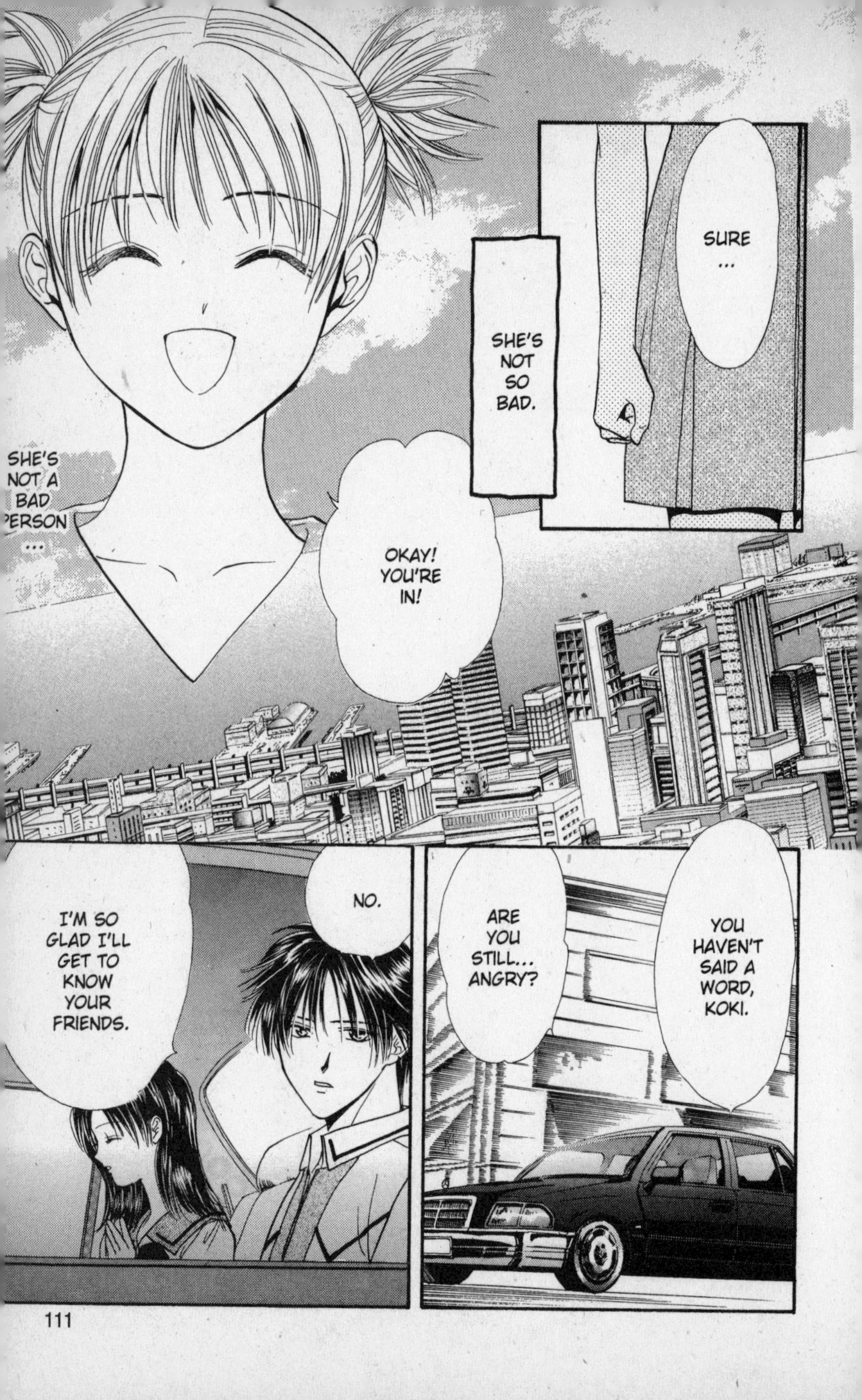
SURE ...
SHE'S NOT SO BAD.
OKAY! YOU'RE IN!
SHE'S NOT A BAD PERSON ...
YOU HAVEN'T SAID A WORD, KOKI.
ARE YOU STILL... ANGRY?
NO.
I'M SO GLAD I'LL GET TO KNOW YOUR FRIENDS.

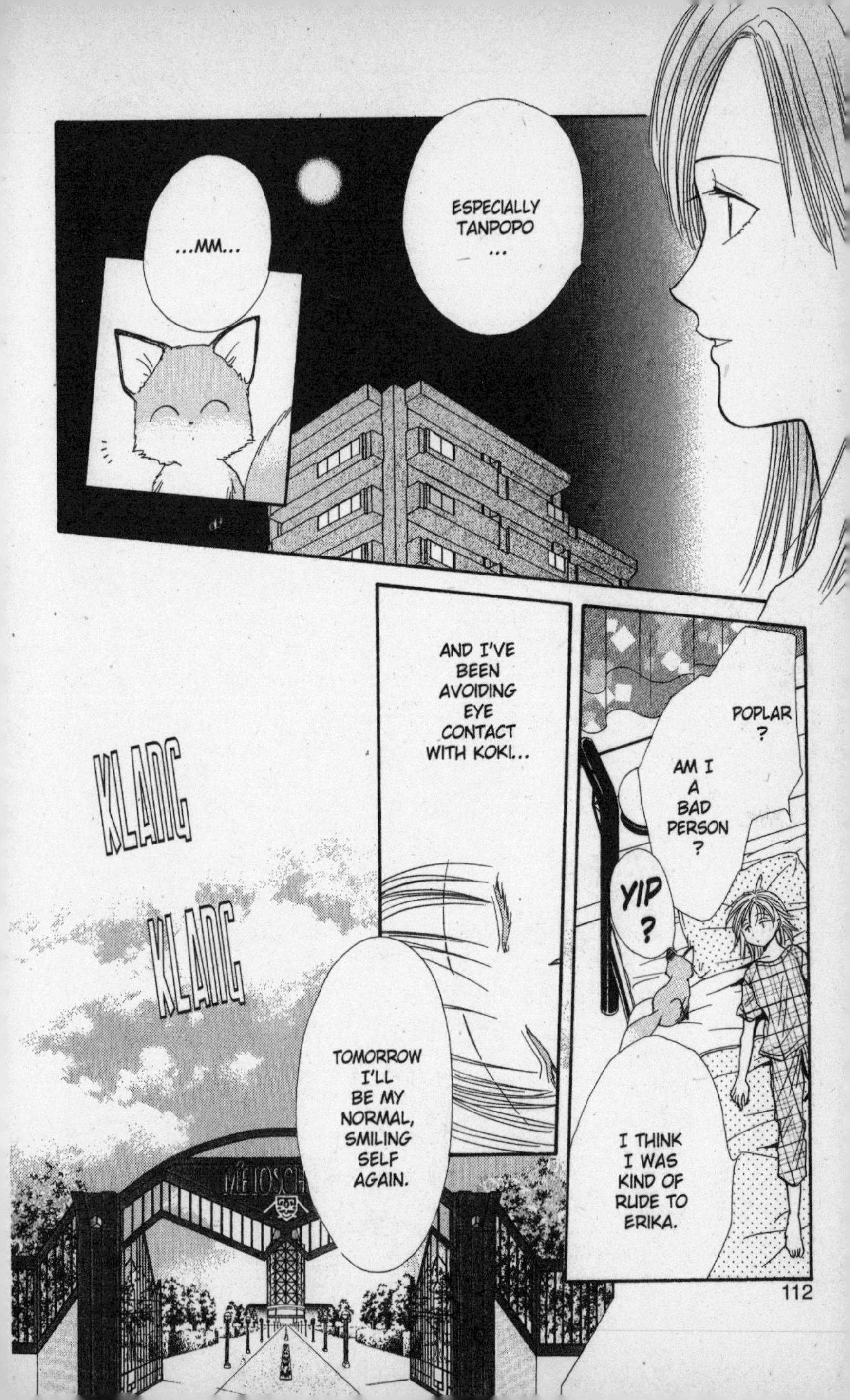
ESPECIALLY TANPOPO ...
...MM...
POPLAR ?
AM I A BAD PERSON ?
YIP ?
I THINK I WAS KIND OF RUDE TO ERIKA.
AND I'VE BEEN AVOIDING EYE CONTACT WITH KOKI...
TOMORROW I'LL BE MY NORMAL, SMILING SELF AGAIN.
KLANG
KLANG

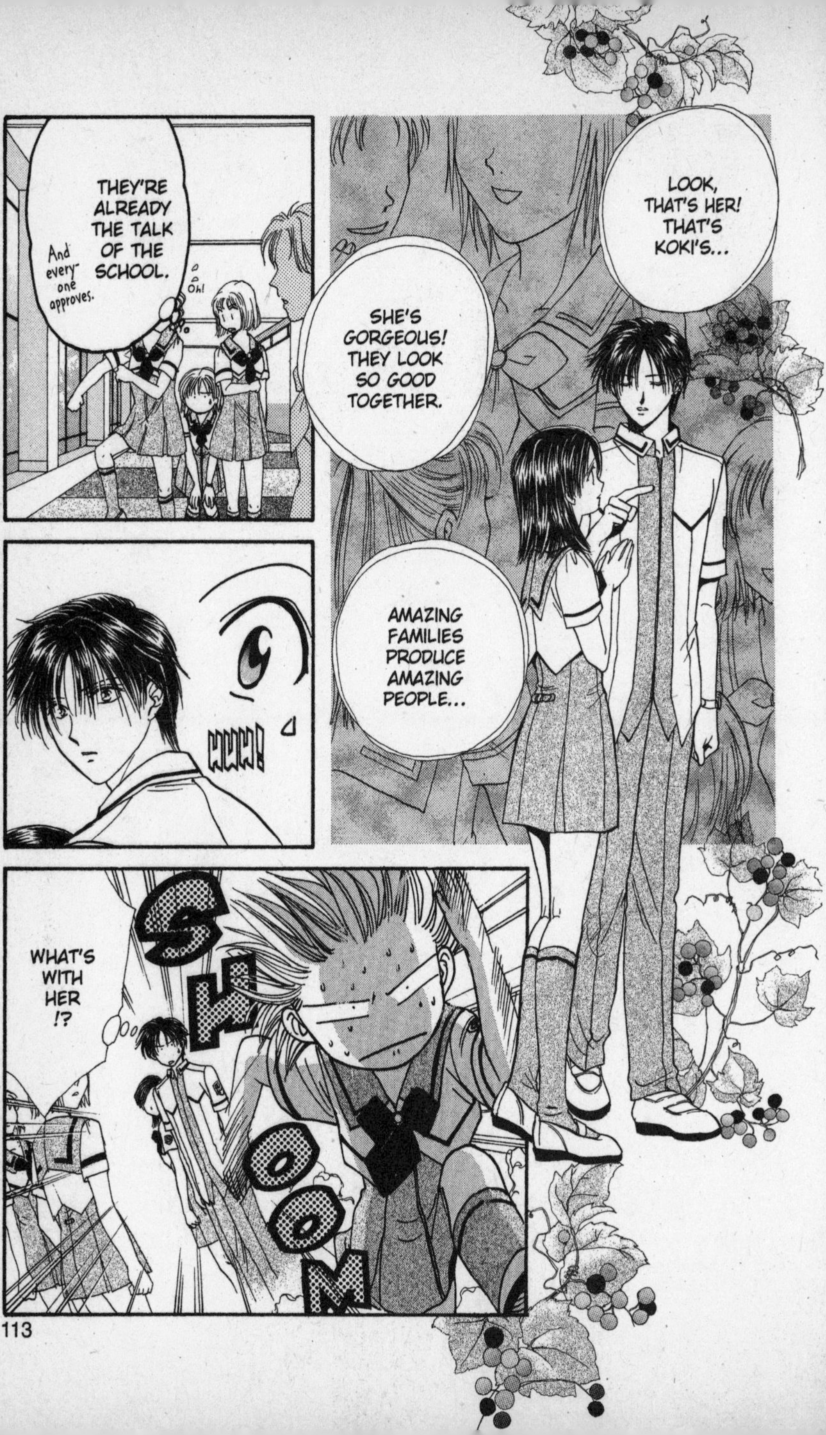
LOOK, THAT'S HER! THAT'S KOKI'S...
SHE'S GORGEOUS! THEY LOOK SO GOOD TOGETHER.
AMAZING FAMILIES PRODUCE AMAZING PEOPLE...
THEY'RE ALREADY THE TALK OF THE SCHOOL.
And every-one approves.
Oh!
HUH!
SHOOOM
WHAT'S WITH HER !?

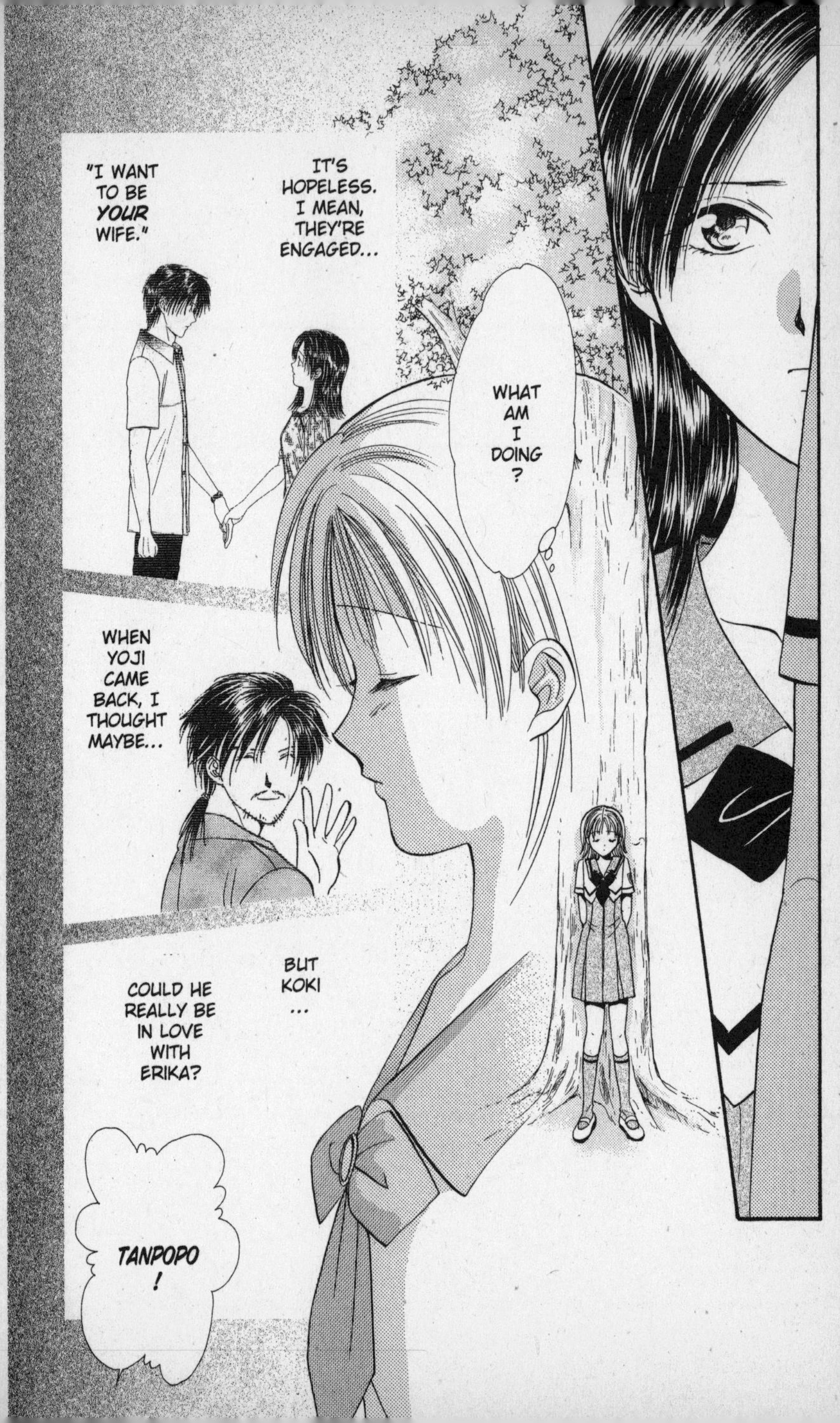
WHAT AM I DOING?
IT'S HOPELESS. I MEAN, THEY'RE ENGAGED...
"I WANT TO BE *YOUR* WIFE."
WHEN YOJI CAME BACK, I THOUGHT MAYBE...
BUT KOKI...
COULD HE REALLY BE IN LOVE WITH ERIKA?
TANPOPO!

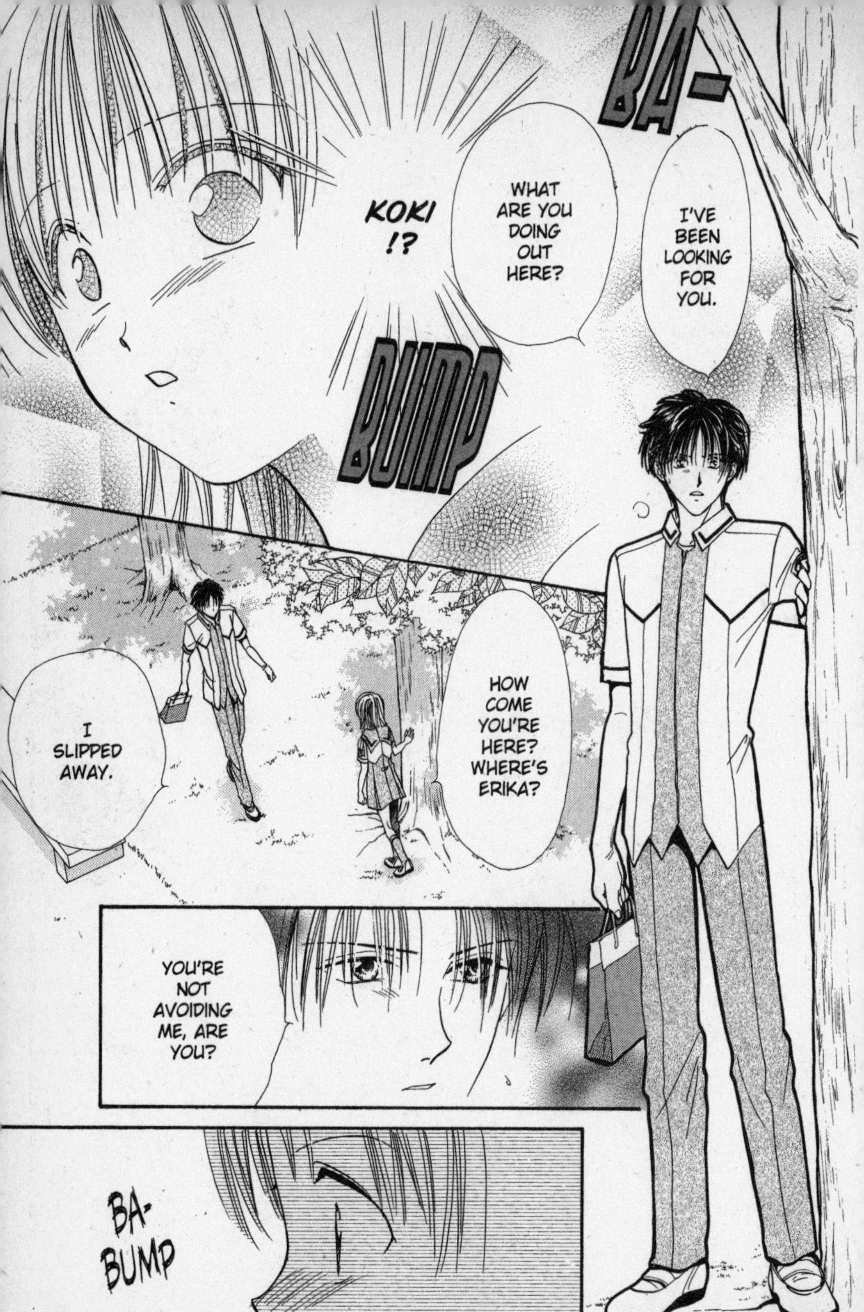
BA-
I'VE BEEN LOOKING FOR YOU.
WHAT ARE YOU DOING OUT HERE?
KOKI!?
BUMP
HOW COME YOU'RE HERE? WHERE'S ERIKA?
I SLIPPED AWAY.
YOU'RE NOT AVOIDING ME, ARE YOU?
BA-BUMP

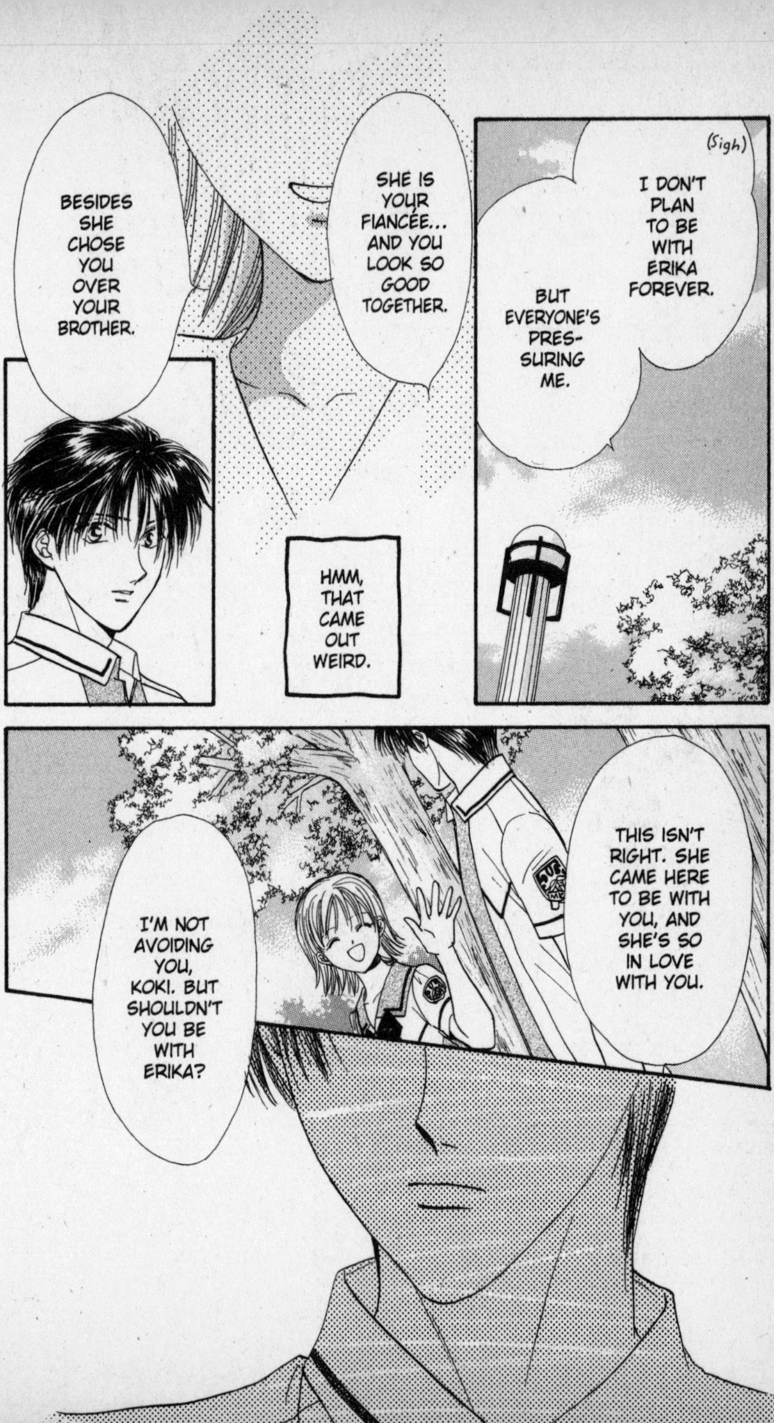
(Sigh)
I DON'T PLAN TO BE WITH ERIKA FOREVER.
BUT EVERYONE'S PRES-SURING ME.
SHE IS YOUR FIANCÉE... AND YOU LOOK SO GOOD TOGETHER.
BESIDES SHE CHOSE YOU OVER YOUR BROTHER.
HMM, THAT CAME OUT WEIRD.
THIS ISN'T RIGHT. SHE CAME HERE TO BE WITH YOU, AND SHE'S SO IN LOVE WITH YOU.
I'M NOT AVOIDING YOU, KOKI. BUT SHOULDN'T YOU BE WITH ERIKA?

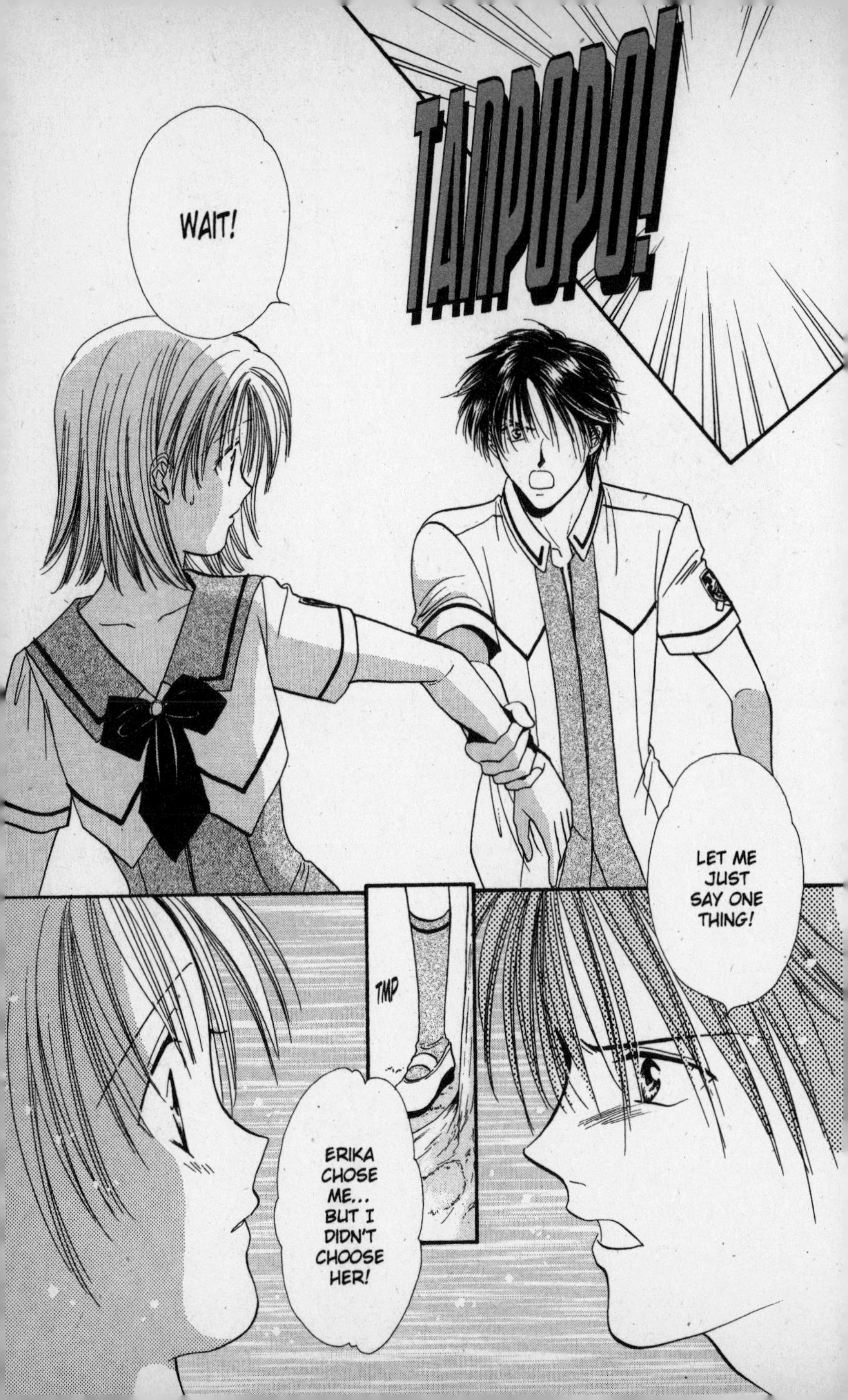
TANPOPO!
WAIT!
LET ME JUST SAY ONE THING!
TMP
ERIKA CHOSE ME... BUT I DIDN'T CHOOSE HER!

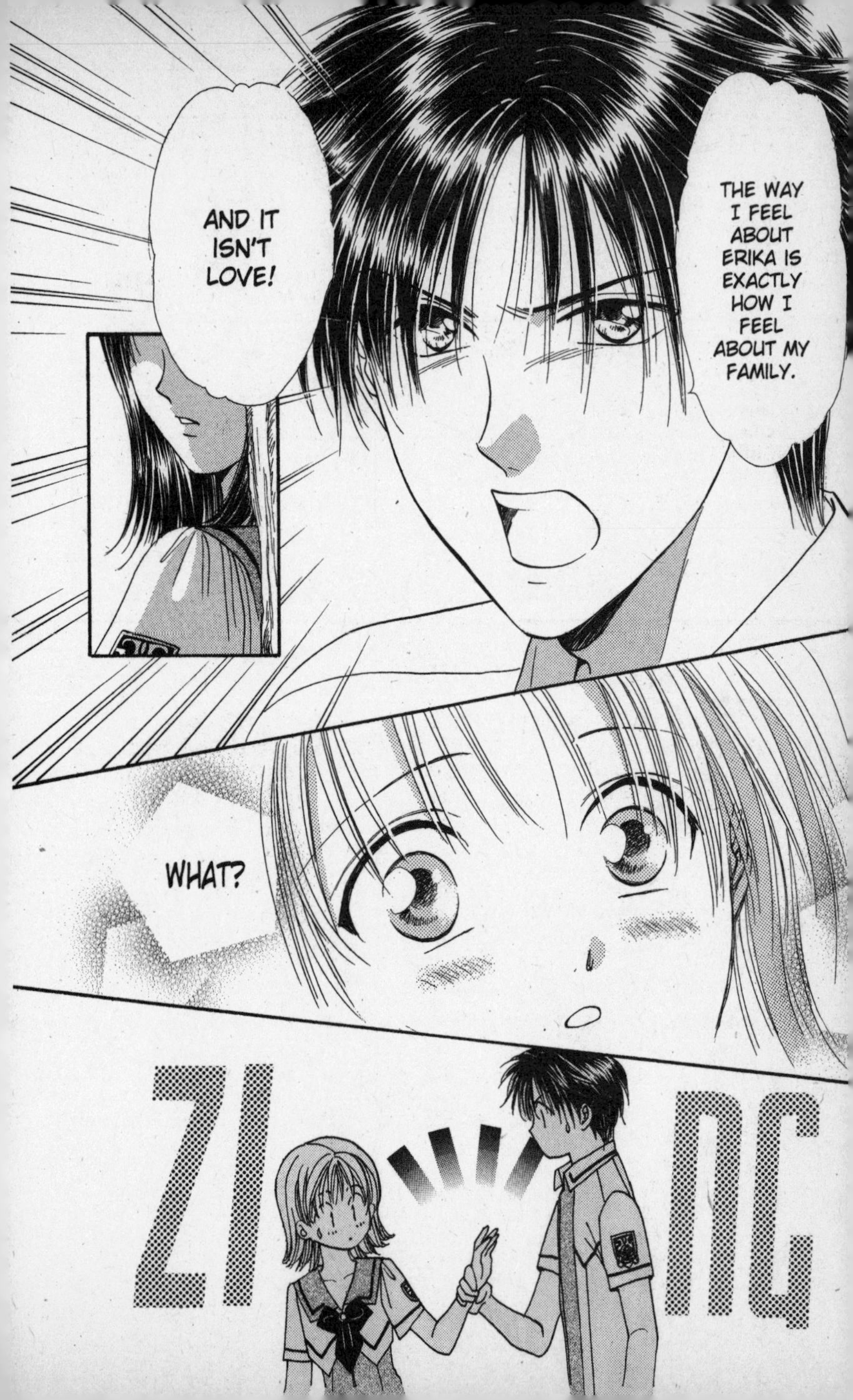
THE WAY I FEEL ABOUT ERIKA IS EXACTLY HOW I FEEL ABOUT MY FAMILY.
AND IT ISN'T LOVE!
WHAT?
ZING

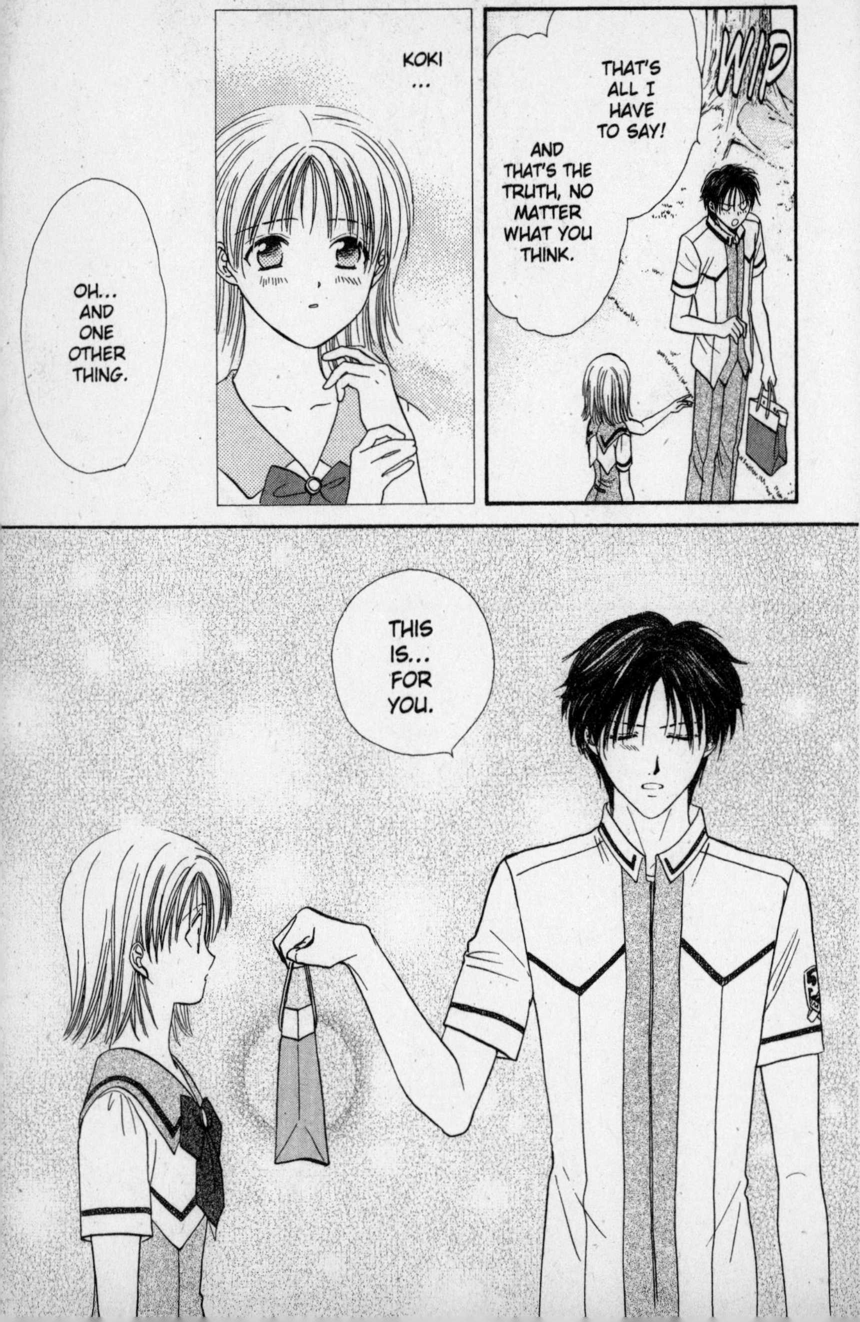
WIP
THAT'S ALL I HAVE TO SAY!
AND THAT'S THE TRUTH, NO MATTER WHAT YOU THINK.
KOKI ...
OH... AND ONE OTHER THING.
THIS IS... FOR YOU.

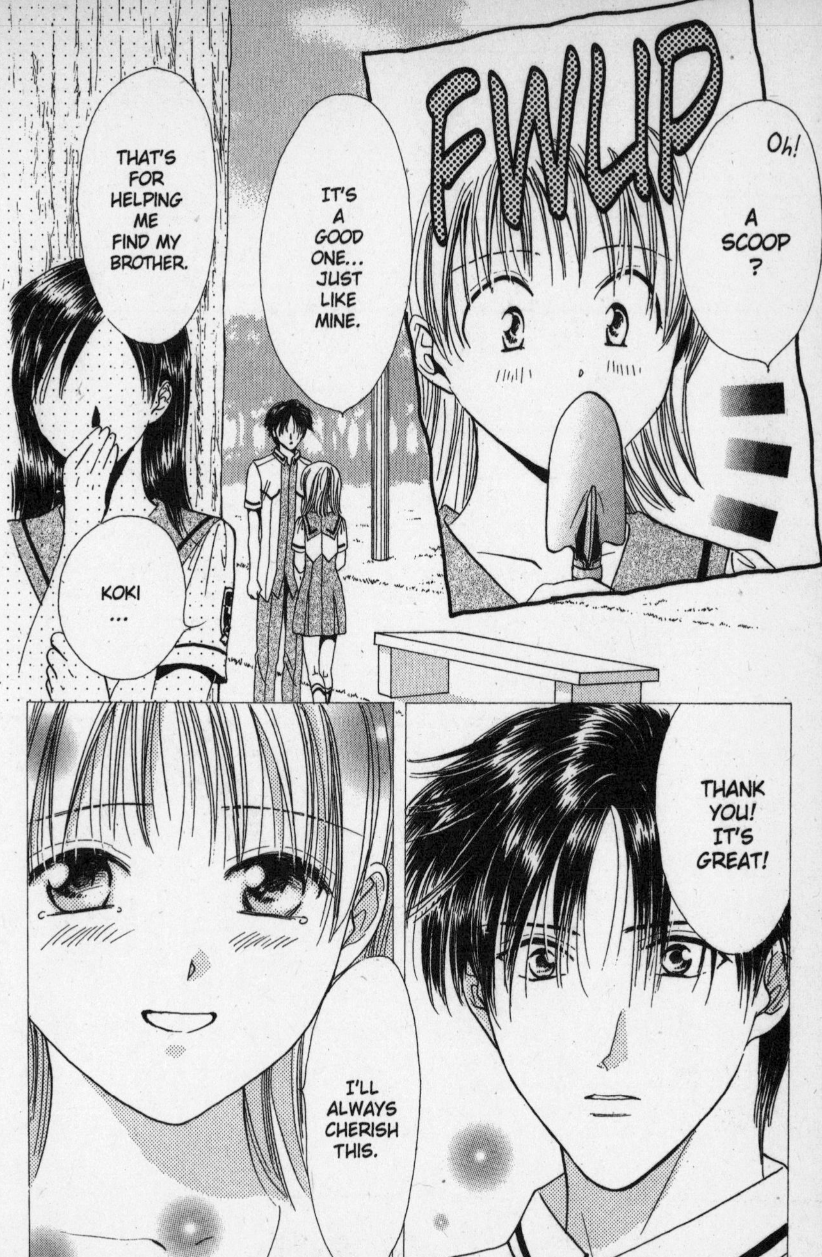
FWUP
Oh! A SCOOP?
IT'S A GOOD ONE... JUST LIKE MINE.
THAT'S FOR HELPING ME FIND MY BROTHER.
KOKI...
THANK YOU! IT'S GREAT!
I'LL ALWAYS CHERISH THIS.

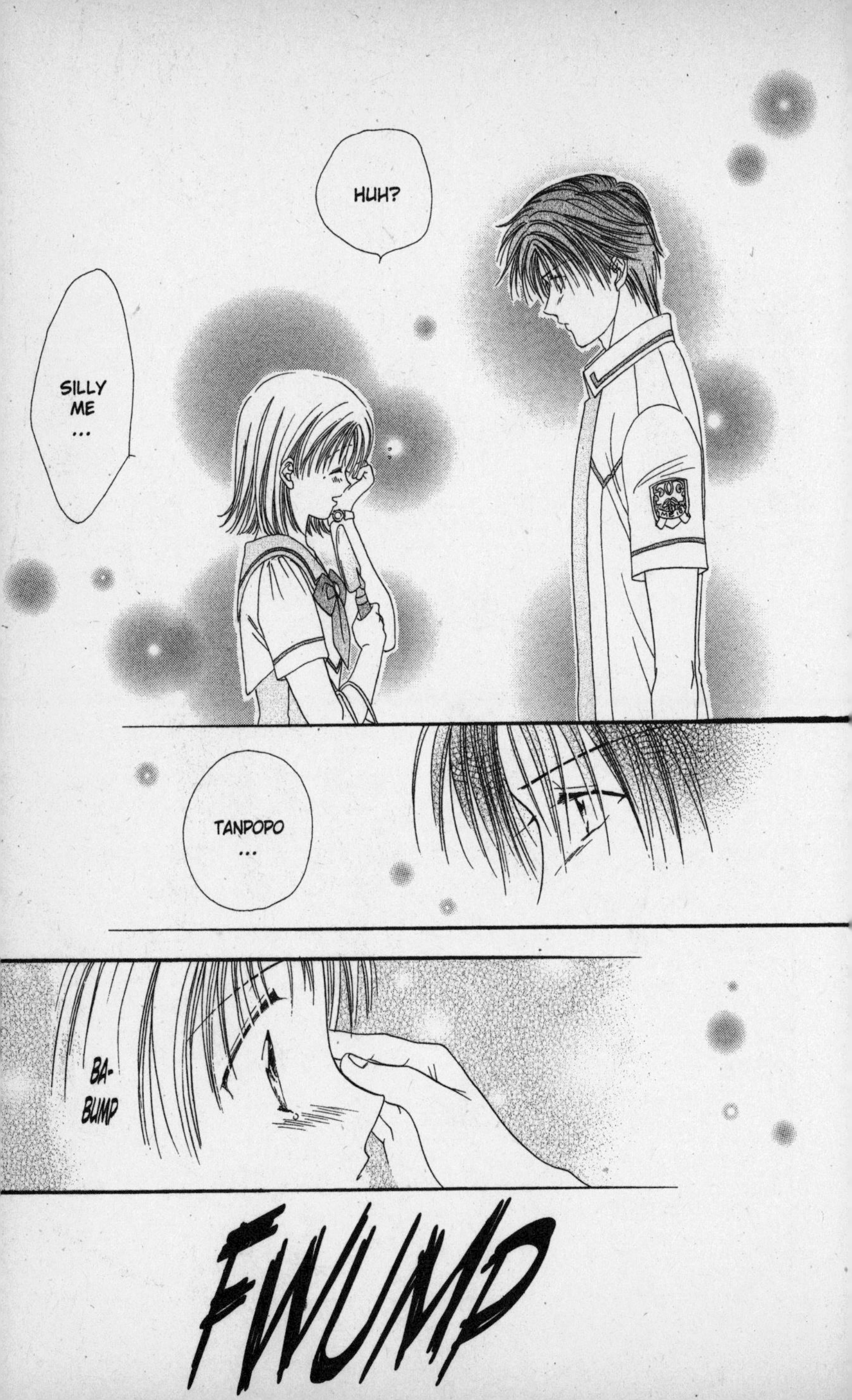
HUH?
SILLY ME ...
TANPOPO ...
BA-BUMP
FWUMP

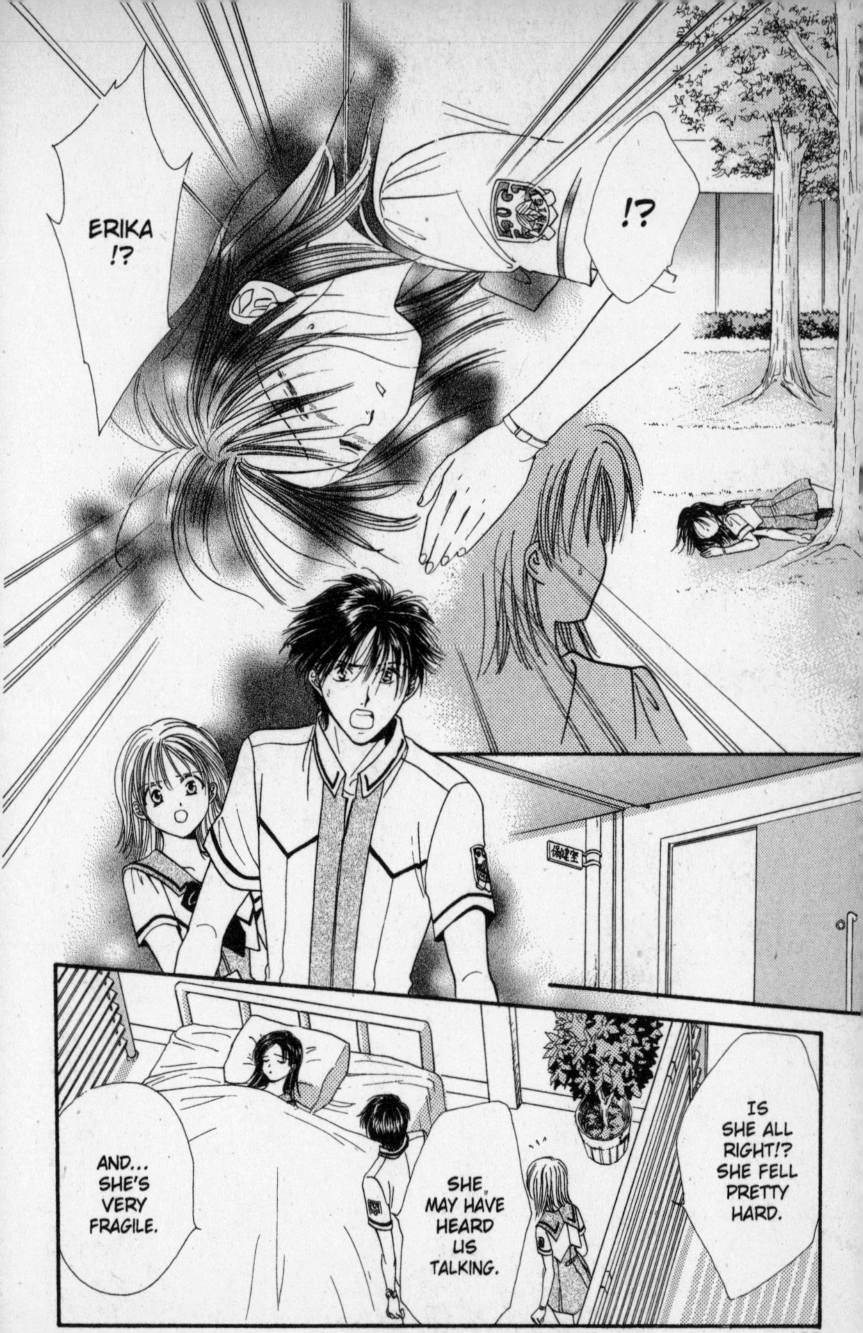
!?
ERIKA !?
IS SHE ALL RIGHT!? SHE FELL PRETTY HARD.
SHE MAY HAVE HEARD US TALKING.
AND... SHE'S VERY FRAGILE.

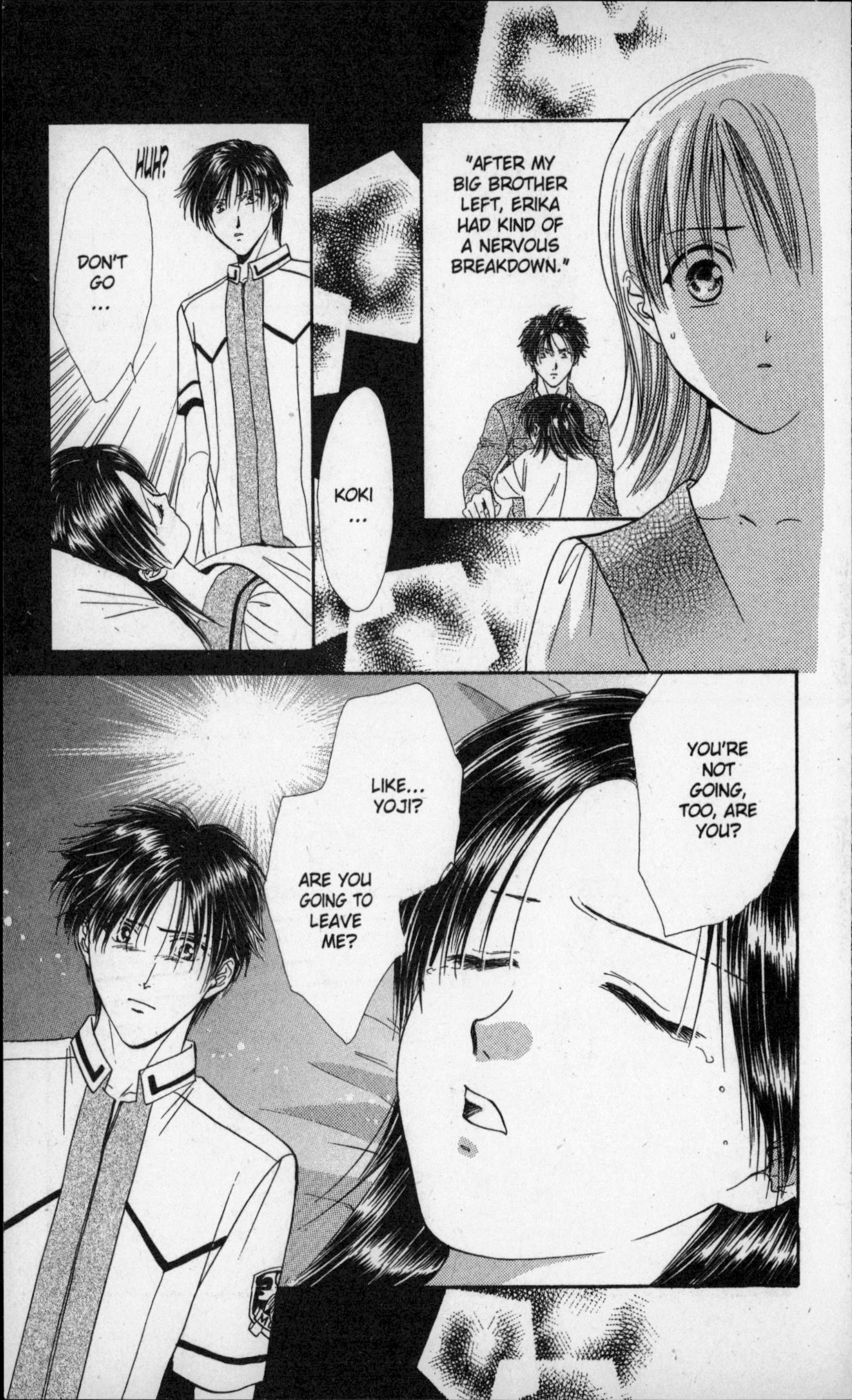
"AFTER MY BIG BROTHER LEFT, ERIKA HAD KIND OF A NERVOUS BREAKDOWN."
KOKI ...
HUH?
DON'T GO ...
YOU'RE NOT GOING, TOO, ARE YOU?
LIKE... YOJI?
ARE YOU GOING TO LEAVE ME?

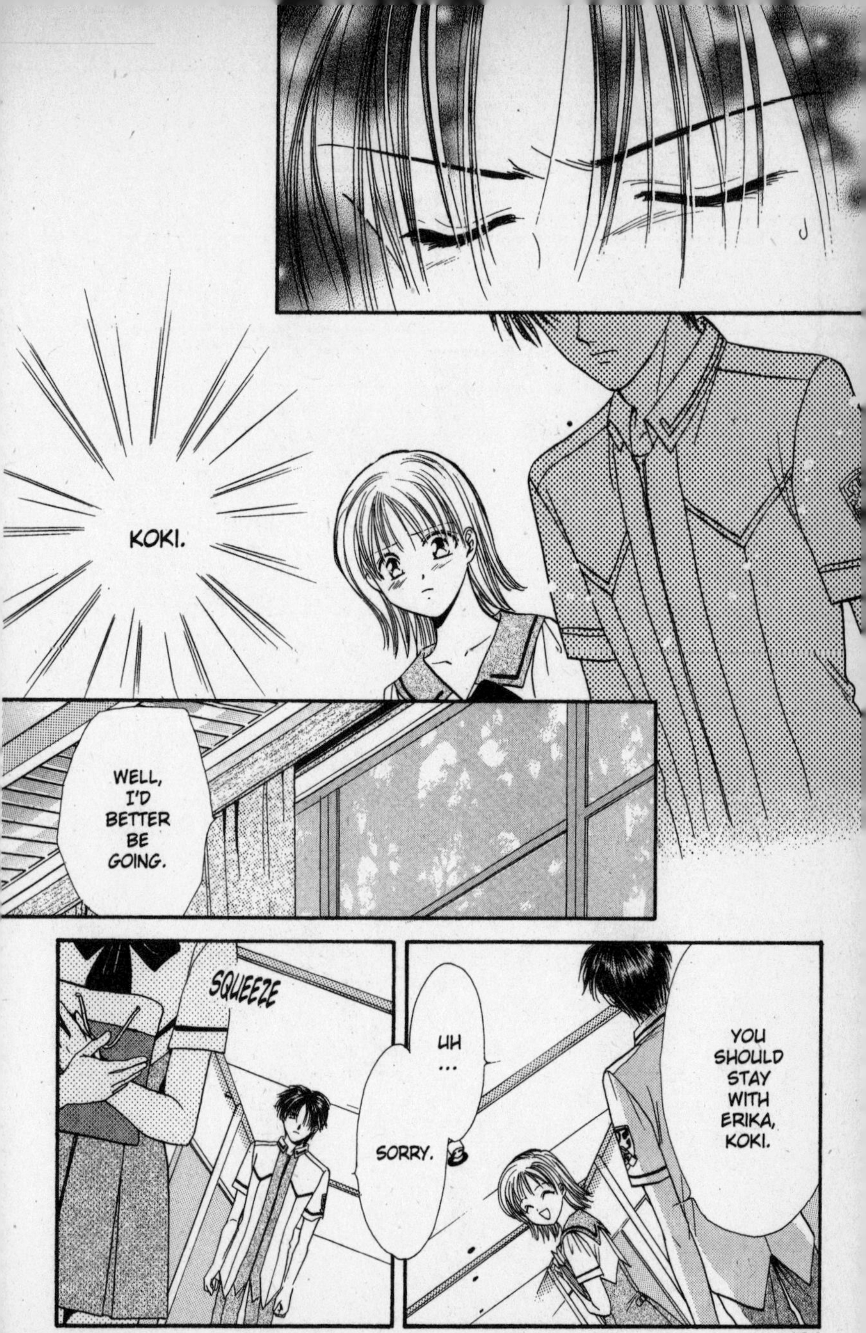
KOKI.
WELL, I'D BETTER BE GOING.
YOU SHOULD STAY WITH ERIKA, KOKI.
UH ...
SORRY.
SQUEEZE

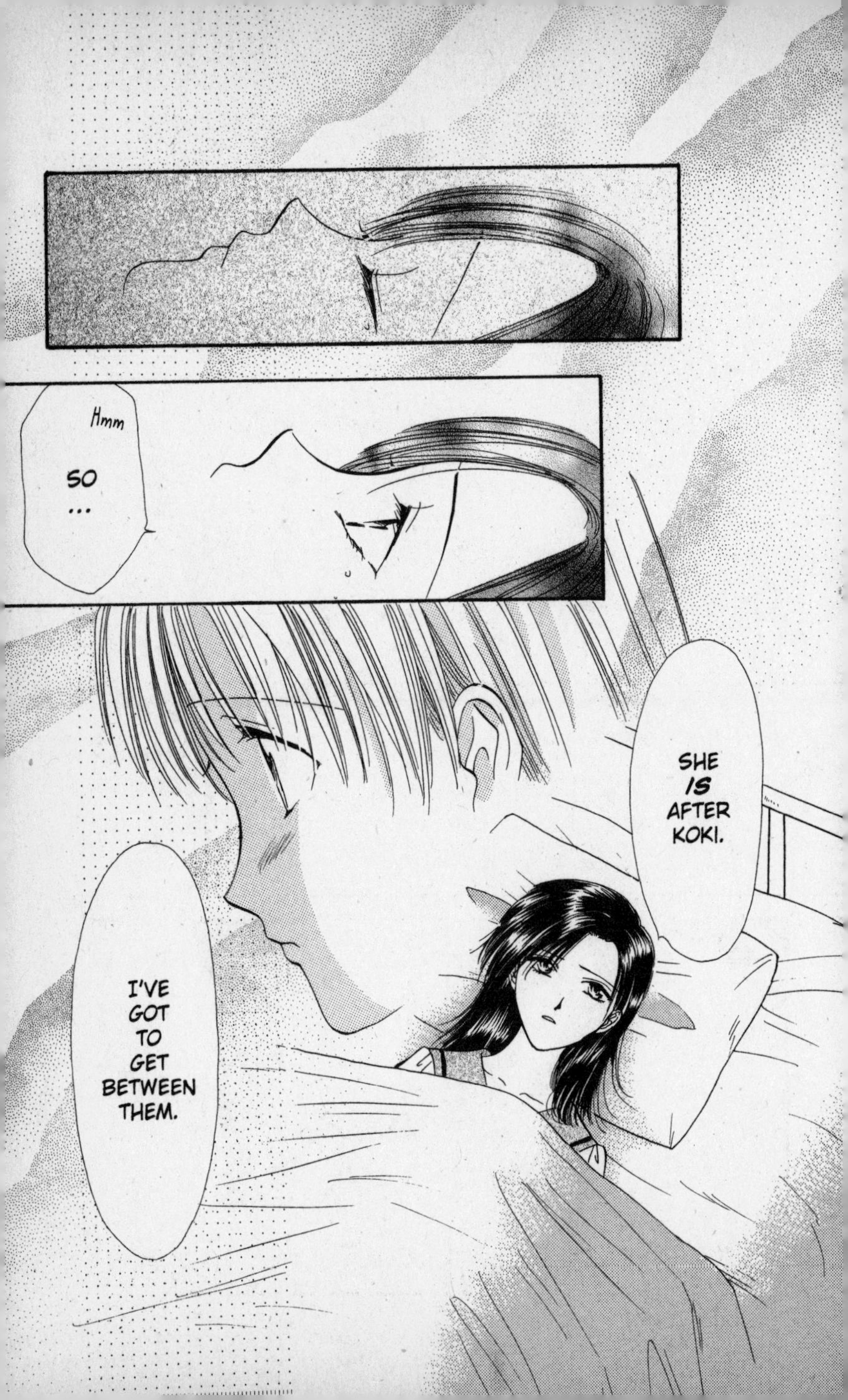
Hmm
SO ...
SHE *IS* AFTER KOKI.
I'VE GOT TO GET BETWEEN THEM.

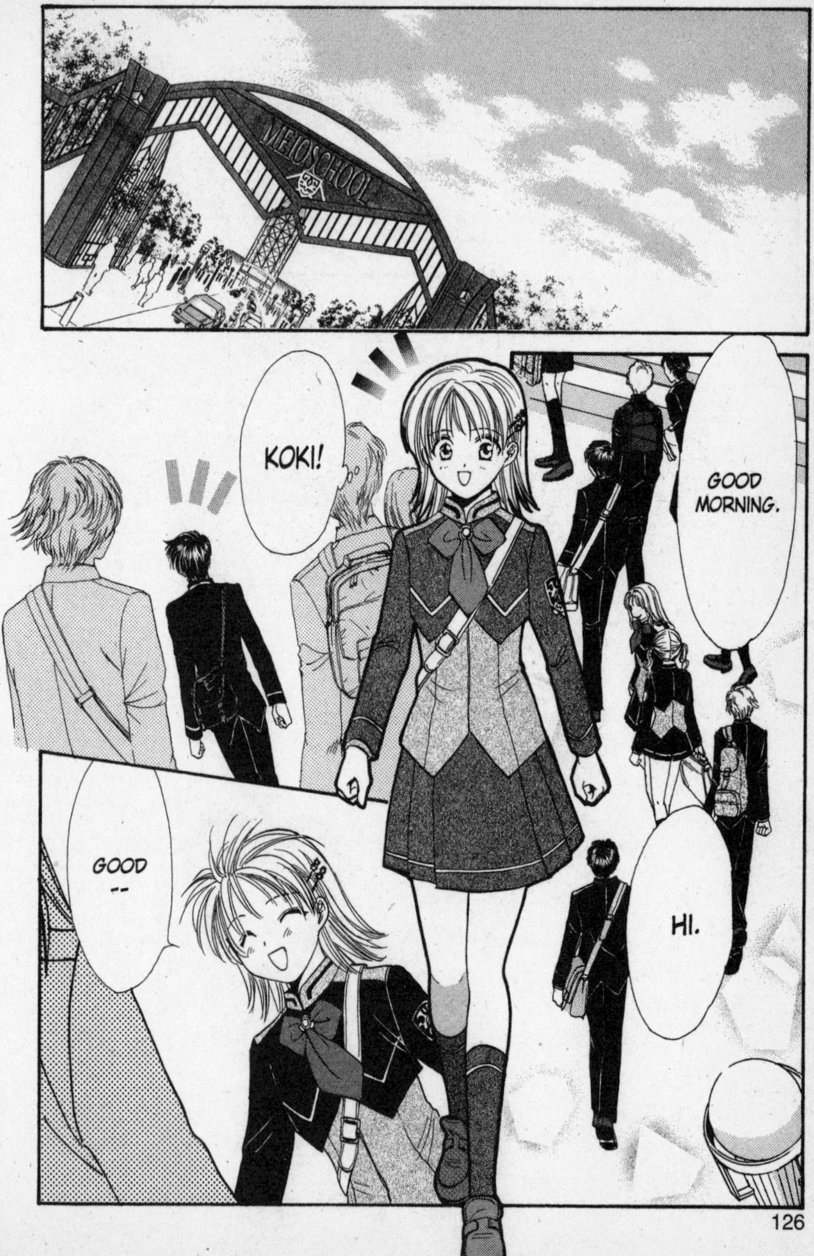
MEIOSCHOOL
GOOD MORNING.
KOKI!
HI.
GOOD --

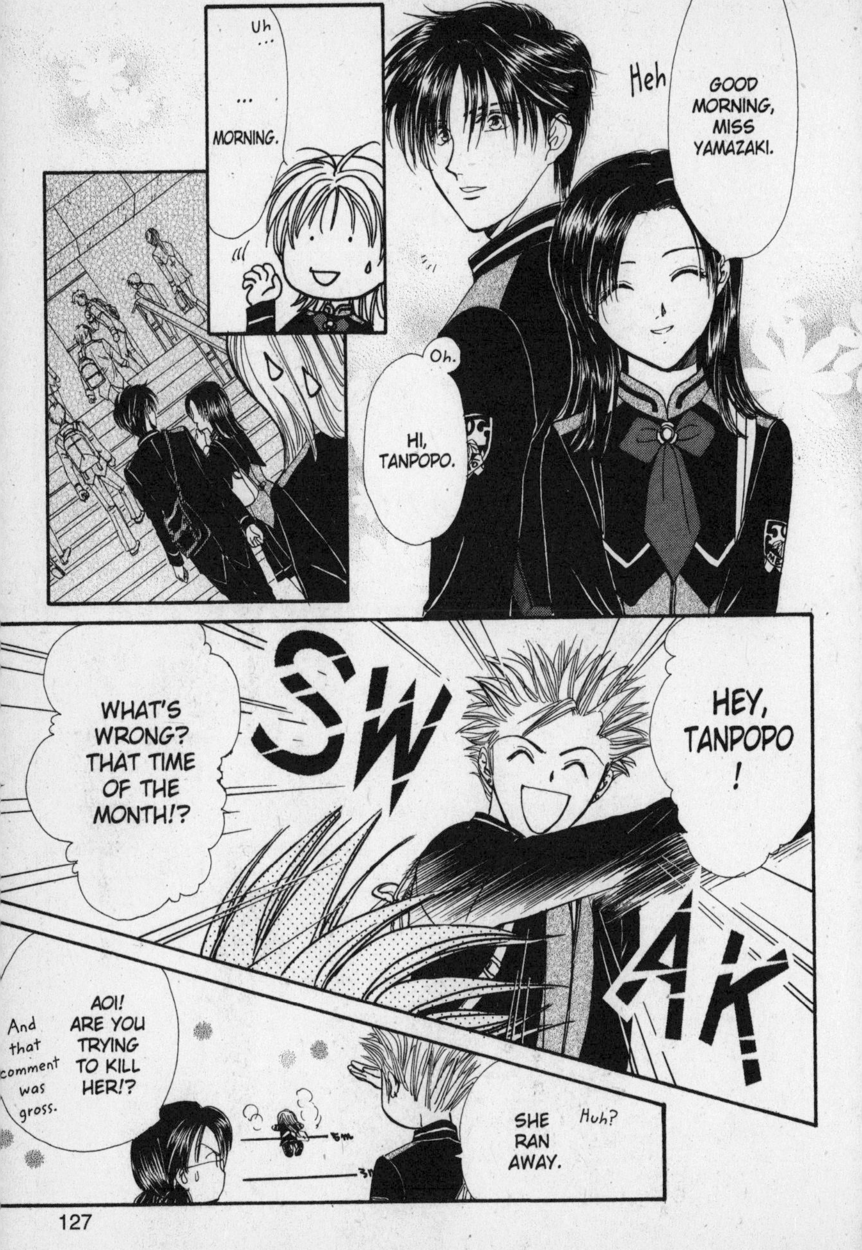
Heh
GOOD MORNING, MISS YAMAZAKI.
Oh.
HI, TANPOPO.
Uh ...
... MORNING.
HEY, TANPOPO!
SWAK
WHAT'S WRONG? THAT TIME OF THE MONTH!?
Huh?
SHE RAN AWAY.
AOI! ARE YOU TRYING TO KILL HER!?
And that comment was gross.

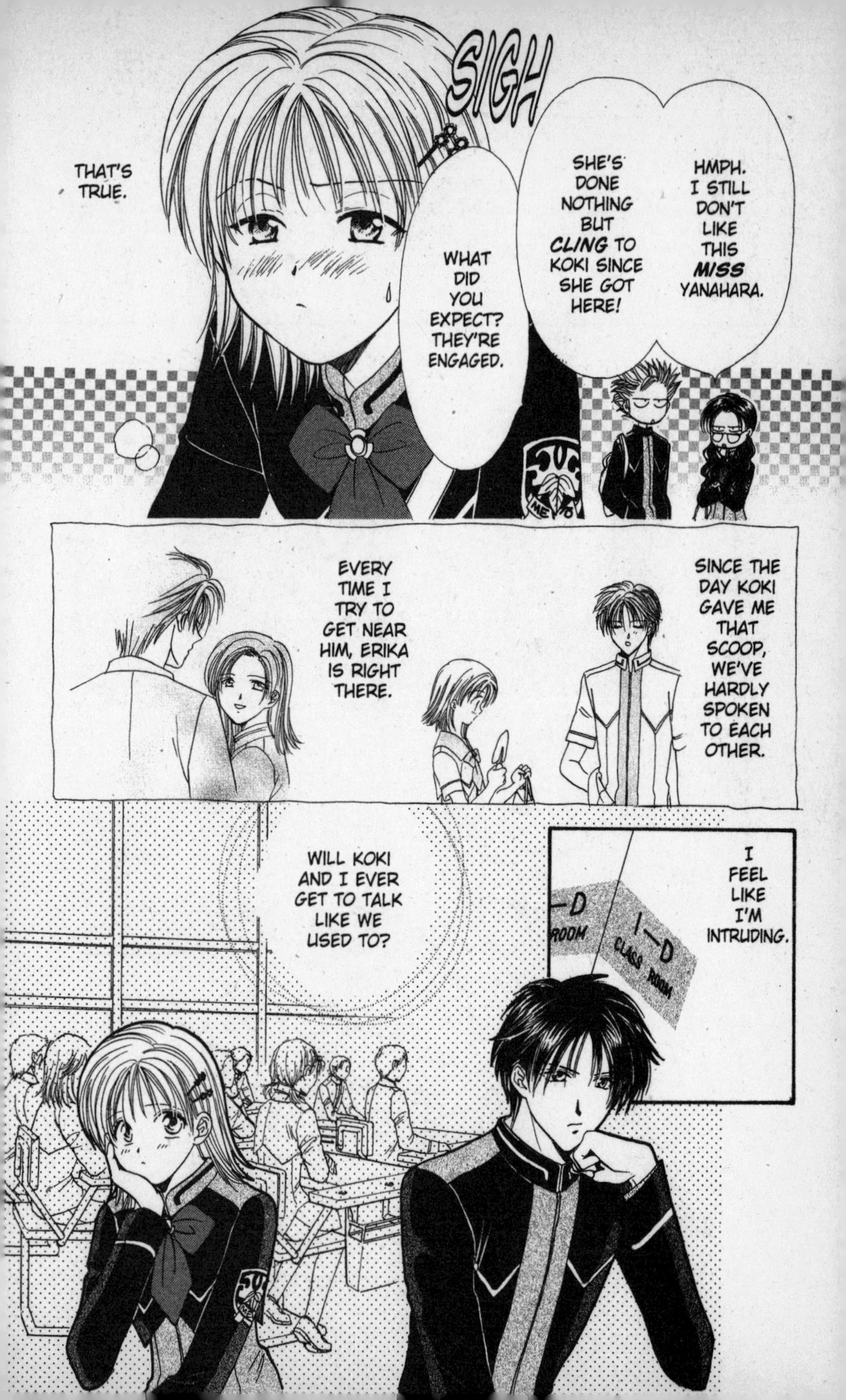
SIGH
HMPH. I STILL DON'T LIKE THIS *MISS* YANAHARA.
SHE'S DONE NOTHING BUT *CLING* TO KOKI SINCE SHE GOT HERE!
WHAT DID YOU EXPECT? THEY'RE ENGAGED.
THAT'S TRUE.
SINCE THE DAY KOKI GAVE ME THAT SCOOP, WE'VE HARDLY SPOKEN TO EACH OTHER.
EVERY TIME I TRY TO GET NEAR HIM, ERIKA IS RIGHT THERE.
I FEEL LIKE I'M INTRUDING.
1-D CLASS ROOM
-D ROOM
WILL KOKI AND I EVER GET TO TALK LIKE WE USED TO?

Speaking of e-mail, there's the Internet. Homepages (HP). There are a lot of problems these days, aren't there? My friend's HP, Life of the Laughing Elderly is safe so far. I contribute on occasion.

I wouldn't call it a storm of controversy, but the keyword when looking at other websites is "net manners."

I don't know a lot about this, but it makes me think we have to be more careful.

There are a lot of problems. Looking at the BBS (bulletin boards where people exchange opinions) on some HPs, people just ignore warnings by the administrators. You guys! Does this concern Ayashi no Ceres...? Oh! My lettering is starting to slant upward!

On a friend's site, there's a corner dedicated to me called Watase's BBS. I'm so grateful.

When I contribute to it, sometimes it bothers me that I'm the subject of the discussion. Hee! I can't always be promoting my comics. Sometimes I just want to tell people something totally unrelated to work. Should Watase be allowed to contribute to Watase's Corner? Ha! Sometimes, I wonder if there was some sort of mistake. It's just a place for discussions about my work. Maybe creating a Watase-Free Talk Corner is the answer? Or a corner for discussing life issues? Ha! I don't have much advice to give, though. I can't reply to all my paper mail. But I worry about some people. To others it might not be a big deal, but to the person writing in it is. All it takes is a comforting comment. Since the start of this year, I've been thinking about this seriously. Actually, I've been thinking about this for some time.

Anyway, it's all about balancing work and health.

Getting back to net manners, there are an awful lot of bad kids in elementary and middle schools! A lot only talk amongst themselves. If you ignore the rest of the world, problems will arise!

NOW ABOUT THE UPCOMING SCHOOL FESTIVAL...
SCHOOL FESTIVAL !?
UM, WE DON'T HAVE TO DO ANYTHING, DO WE? WON'T THERE BE VENDORS AND STUFF?
TSUKIKO, THERE'S A SCHOOL FESTIVAL?
LOOKS THAT WAY. BUT I'M NOT SMELLING ANY SCHOOL SPIRIT.
WUSP WUSP
EVEN SO, WE'D LIKE YOU STUDENTS TO PLAN AN EVENT.
Geez. What a pain.
!

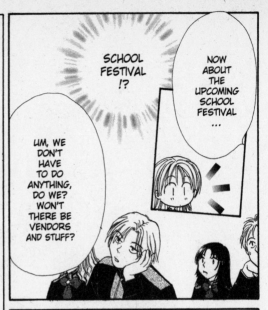

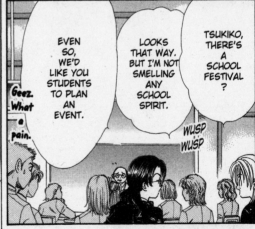

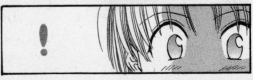

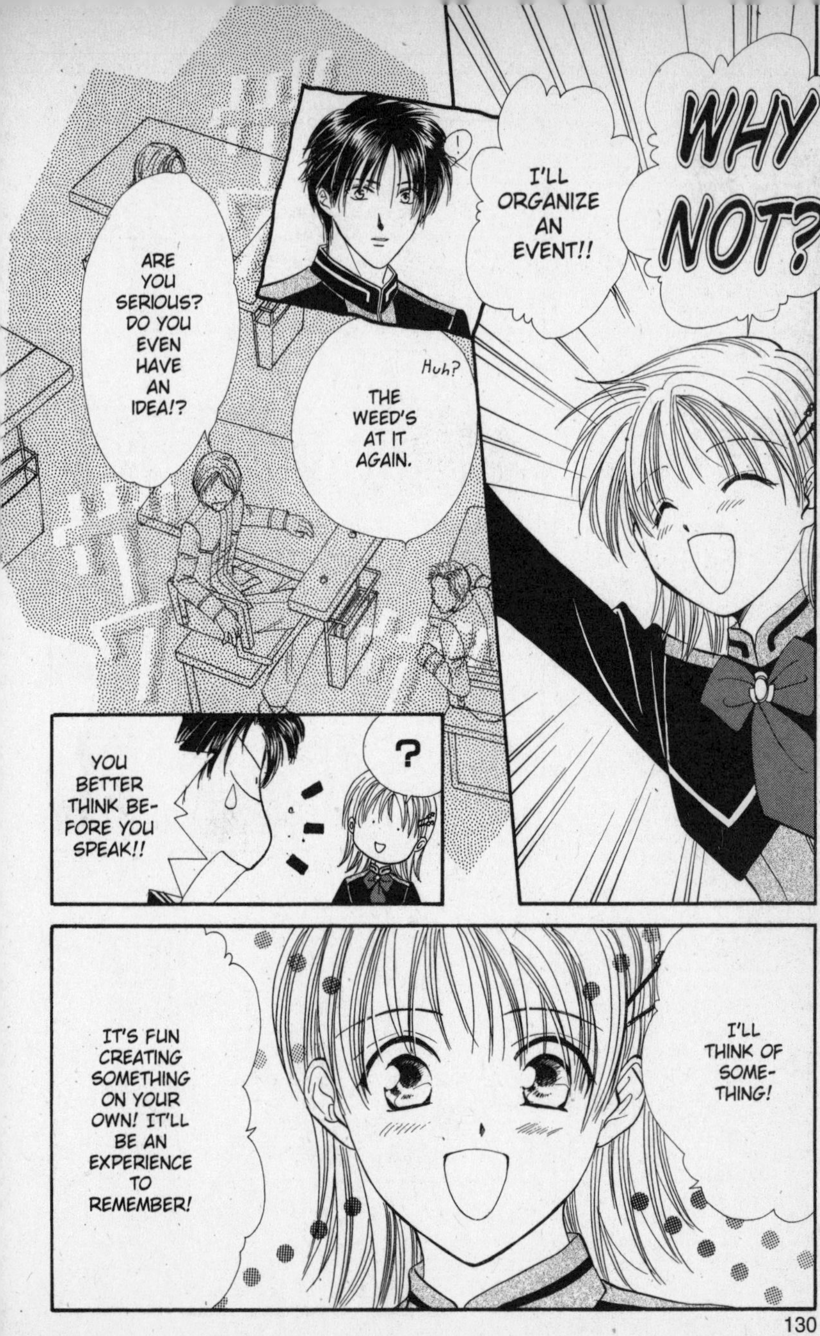
WHY NOT?
I'LL ORGANIZE AN EVENT!!
!
Huh?
THE WEED'S AT IT AGAIN.
ARE YOU SERIOUS? DO YOU EVEN HAVE AN IDEA!?
?
YOU BETTER THINK BE-FORE YOU SPEAK!!
I'LL THINK OF SOME-THING!
IT'S FUN CREATING SOMETHING ON YOUR OWN! IT'LL BE AN EXPERIENCE TO REMEMBER!

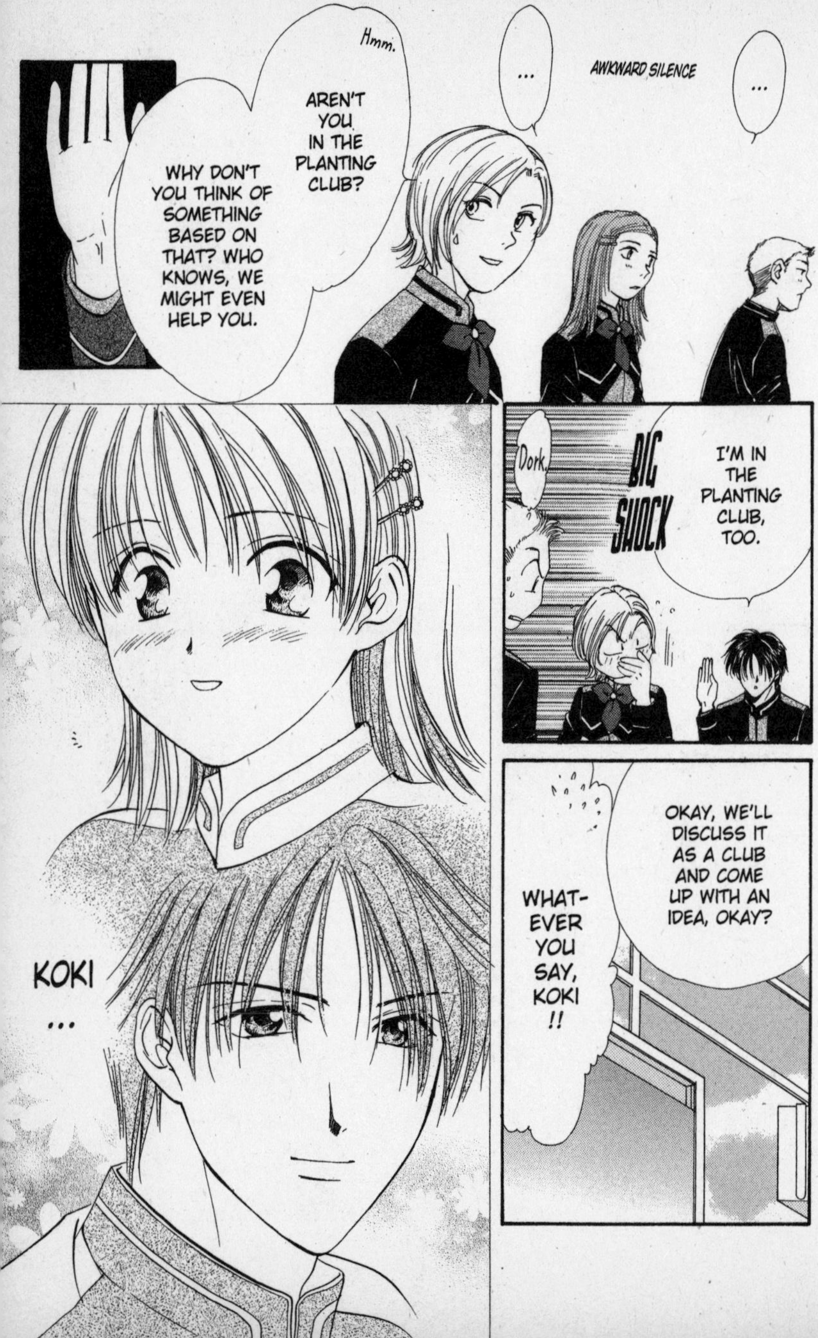
...
AWKWARD SILENCE
...
Hmm.
AREN'T YOU IN THE PLANTING CLUB?
WHY DON'T YOU THINK OF SOMETHING BASED ON THAT? WHO KNOWS, WE MIGHT EVEN HELP YOU.
I'M IN THE PLANTING CLUB, TOO.
BIG SHOCK
Dork.
OKAY, WE'LL DISCUSS IT AS A CLUB AND COME UP WITH AN IDEA, OKAY?
WHAT-EVER YOU SAY, KOKI !!
KOKI ...

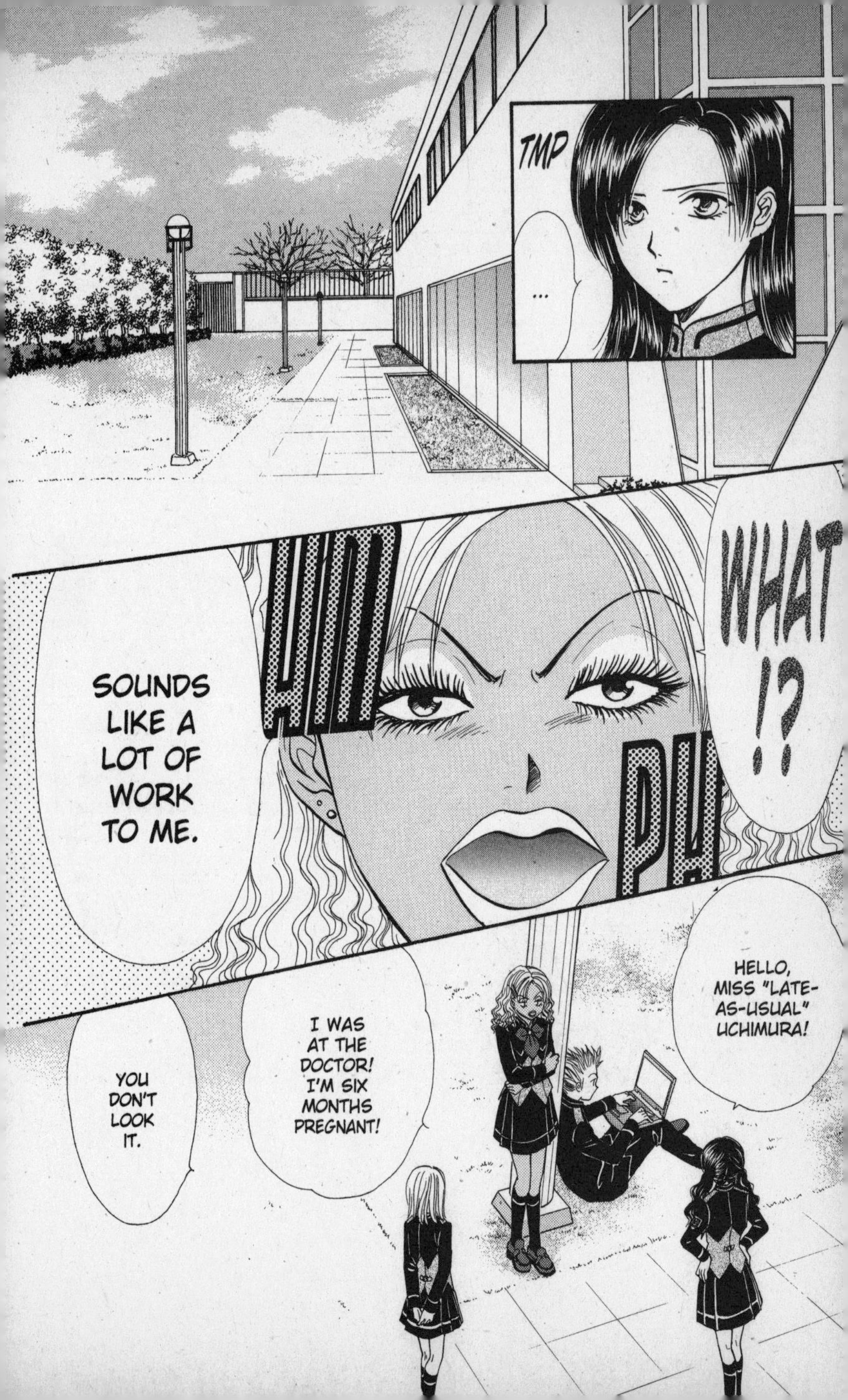
TMP
...
WHAT !?
SOUNDS LIKE A LOT OF WORK TO ME.
HELLO, MISS "LATE-AS-USUAL" UCHIMURA!
I WAS AT THE DOCTOR! I'M SIX MONTHS PREGNANT!
YOU DON'T LOOK IT.

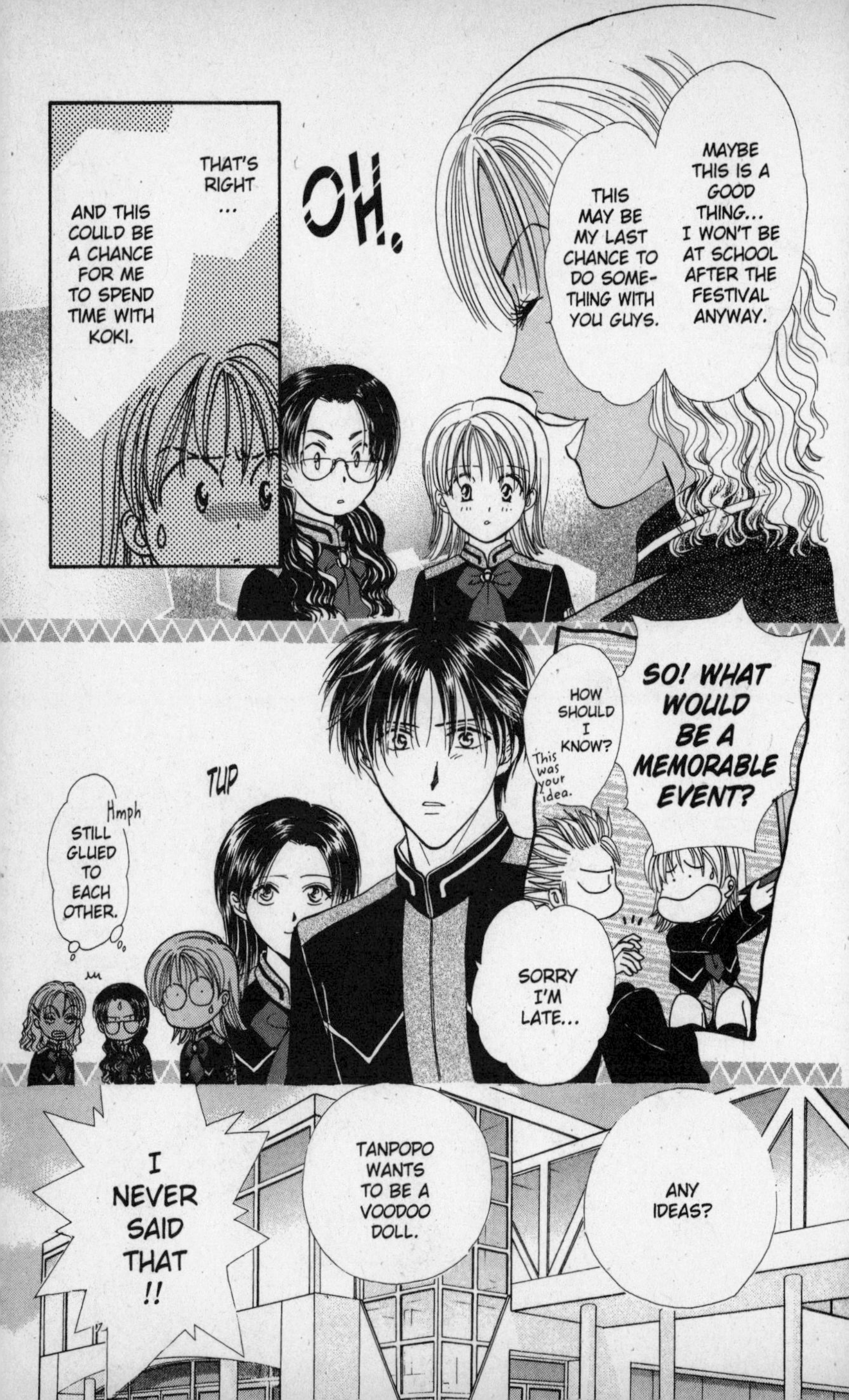
MAYBE THIS IS A GOOD THING... I WON'T BE AT SCHOOL AFTER THE FESTIVAL ANYWAY.
THIS MAY BE MY LAST CHANCE TO DO SOME-THING WITH YOU GUYS.
OH.
THAT'S RIGHT ...
AND THIS COULD BE A CHANCE FOR ME TO SPEND TIME WITH KOKI.
SO! WHAT WOULD BE A MEMORABLE EVENT?
HOW SHOULD I KNOW?
This was your idea.
SORRY I'M LATE...
TUP
Hmph
STILL GLUED TO EACH OTHER.
ANY IDEAS?
TANPOPO WANTS TO BE A VOODOO DOLL.
I NEVER SAID THAT !!

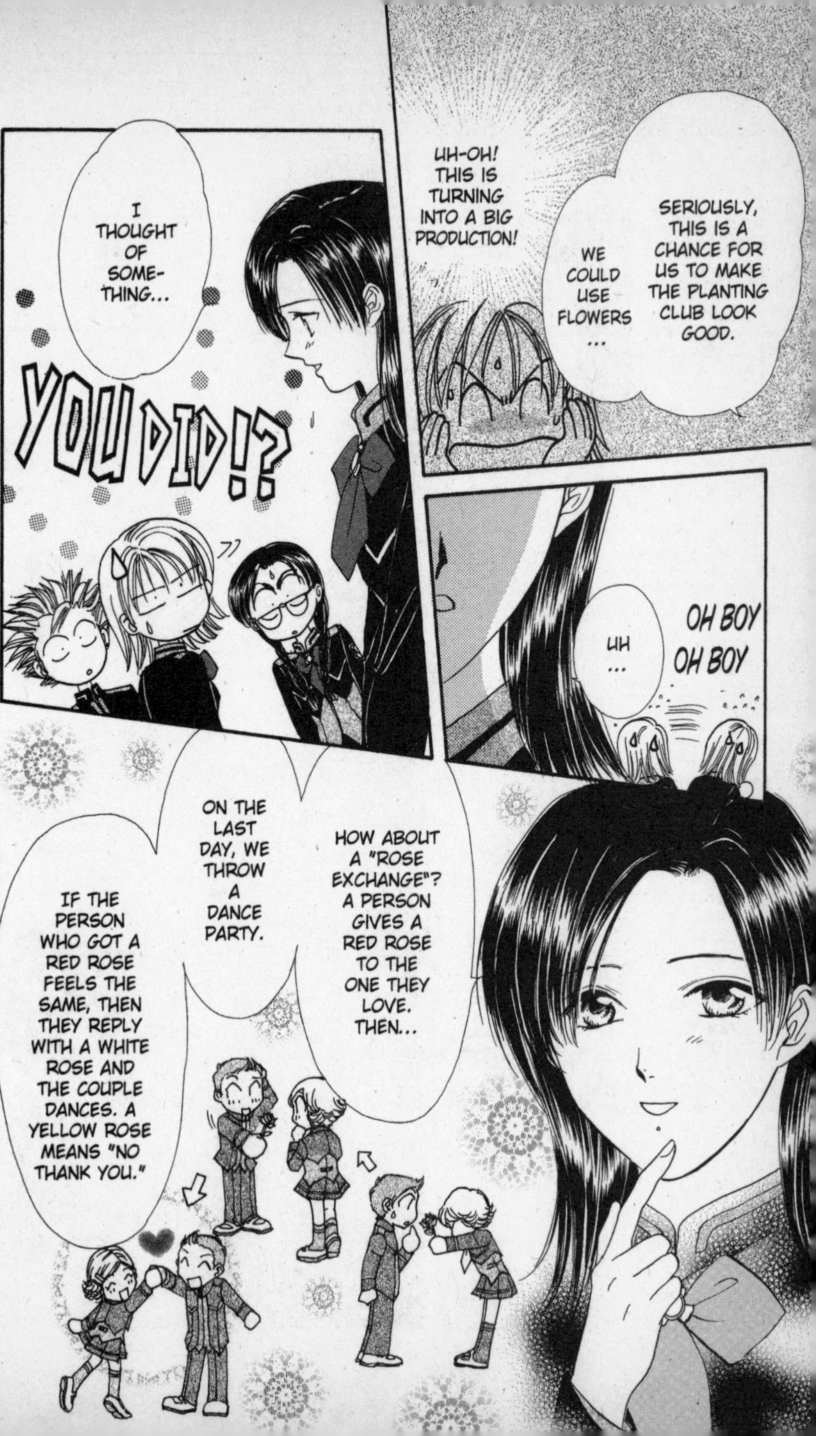
SERIOUSLY, THIS IS A CHANCE FOR US TO MAKE THE PLANTING CLUB LOOK GOOD.
WE COULD USE FLOWERS...
UH-OH! THIS IS TURNING INTO A BIG PRODUCTION!
UH...
OH BOY OH BOY
I THOUGHT OF SOME-THING...
YOU DID!?
ON THE LAST DAY, WE THROW A DANCE PARTY.
HOW ABOUT A "ROSE EXCHANGE"? A PERSON GIVES A RED ROSE TO THE ONE THEY LOVE. THEN...
IF THE PERSON WHO GOT A RED ROSE FEELS THE SAME, THEN THEY REPLY WITH A WHITE ROSE AND THE COUPLE DANCES. A YELLOW ROSE MEANS "NO THANK YOU."

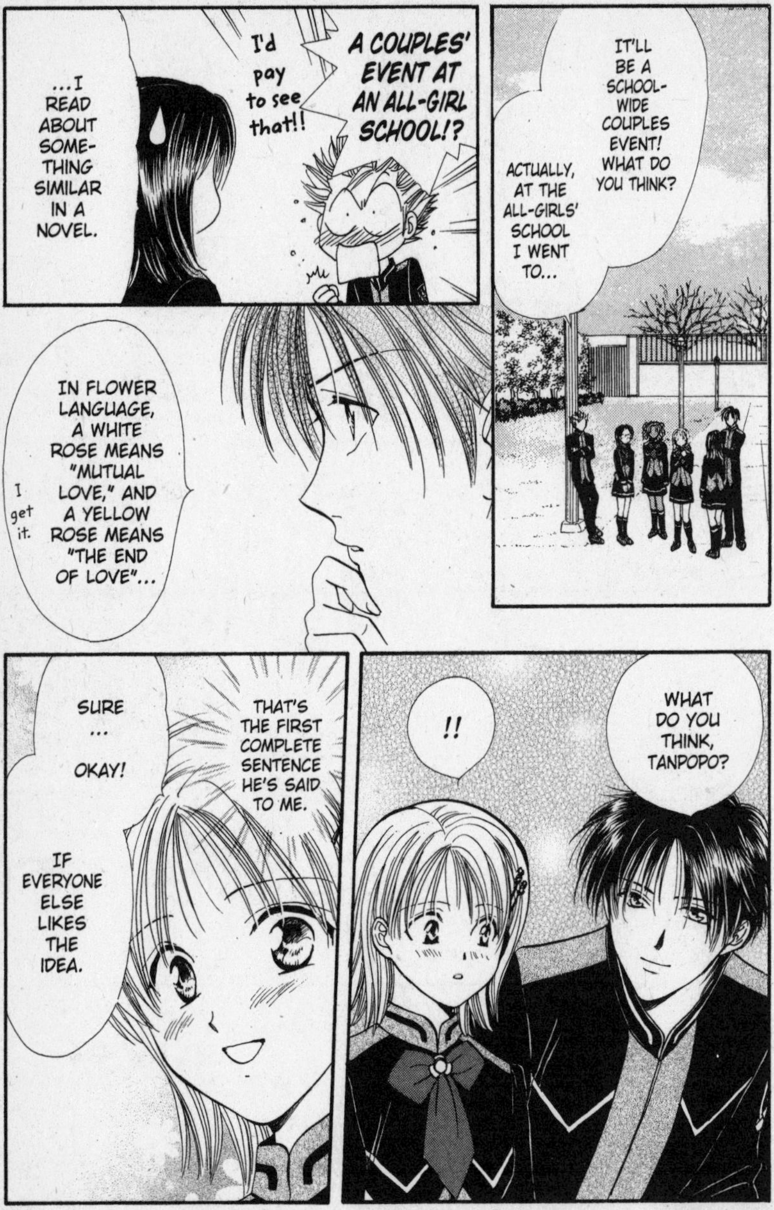
IT'LL BE A SCHOOL-WIDE COUPLES EVENT! WHAT DO YOU THINK?
ACTUALLY, AT THE ALL-GIRLS' SCHOOL I WENT TO...
A COUPLES' EVENT AT AN ALL-GIRL SCHOOL!?
I'd pay to see that!!
...I READ ABOUT SOMETHING SIMILAR IN A NOVEL.
IN FLOWER LANGUAGE, A WHITE ROSE MEANS "MUTUAL LOVE," AND A YELLOW ROSE MEANS "THE END OF LOVE"...
I get it.
WHAT DO YOU THINK, TANPOPO?
!!
THAT'S THE FIRST COMPLETE SENTENCE HE'S SAID TO ME.
SURE ... OKAY!
IF EVERYONE ELSE LIKES THE IDEA.

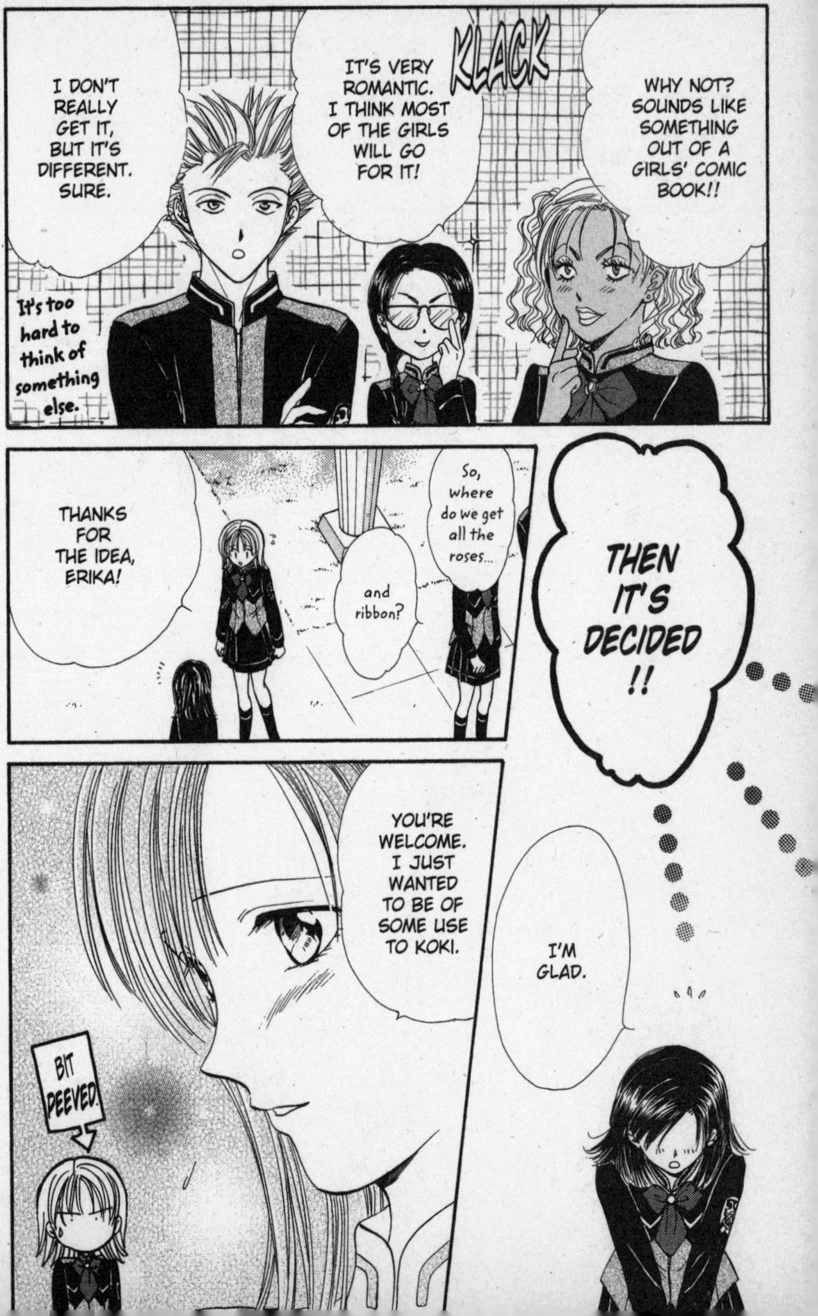
WHY NOT? SOUNDS LIKE SOMETHING OUT OF A GIRLS' COMIC BOOK!!
KLACK
IT'S VERY ROMANTIC. I THINK MOST OF THE GIRLS WILL GO FOR IT!
I DON'T REALLY GET IT, BUT IT'S DIFFERENT. SURE.
It's too hard to think of something else.
THEN IT'S DECIDED!!
So, where do we get all the roses...
and ribbon?
THANKS FOR THE IDEA, ERIKA!
I'M GLAD.
YOU'RE WELCOME. I JUST WANTED TO BE OF SOME USE TO KOKI.
BIT PEEVED.

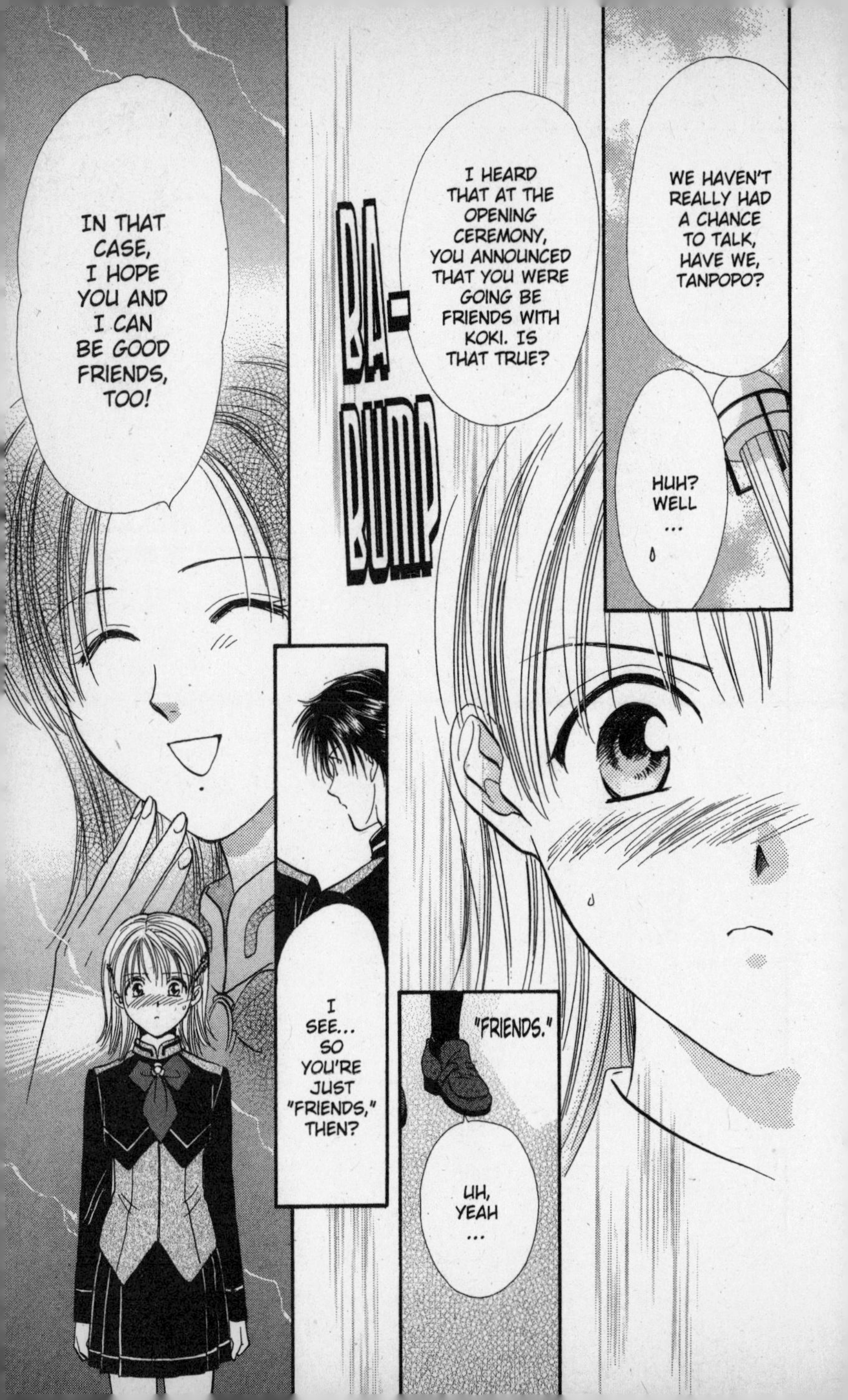
WE HAVEN'T REALLY HAD A CHANCE TO TALK, HAVE WE, TANPOPO?
HUH? WELL ...
I HEARD THAT AT THE OPENING CEREMONY, YOU ANNOUNCED THAT YOU WERE GOING BE FRIENDS WITH KOKI. IS THAT TRUE?
BA-BUMP
"FRIENDS."
UH, YEAH ...
I SEE... SO YOU'RE JUST "FRIENDS," THEN?
IN THAT CASE, I HOPE YOU AND I CAN BE GOOD FRIENDS, TOO!

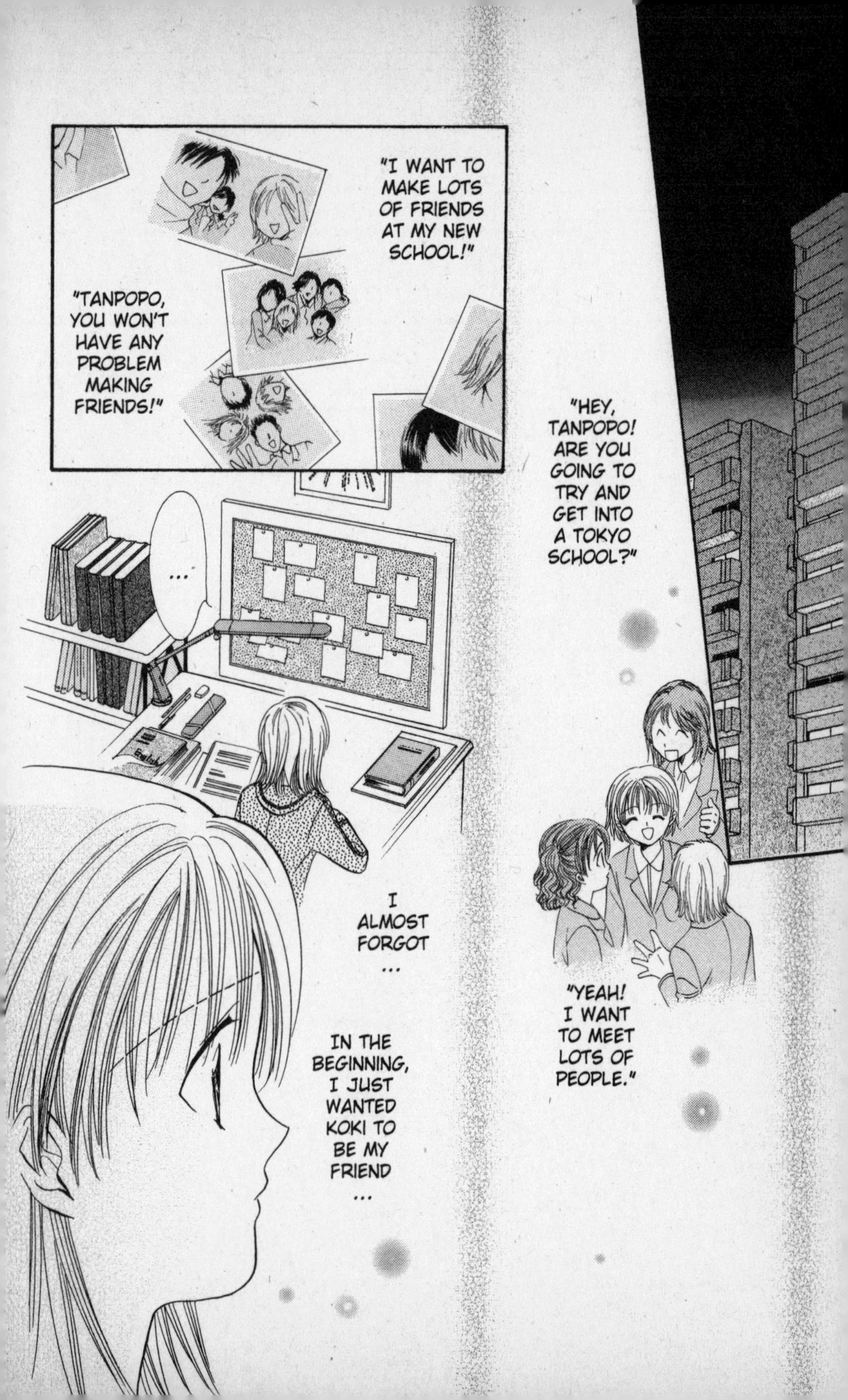
"HEY, TANPOPO! ARE YOU GOING TO TRY AND GET INTO A TOKYO SCHOOL?"
"YEAH! I WANT TO MEET LOTS OF PEOPLE."
"I WANT TO MAKE LOTS OF FRIENDS AT MY NEW SCHOOL!"
"TANPOPO, YOU WON'T HAVE ANY PROBLEM MAKING FRIENDS!"
...
I ALMOST FORGOT ...
IN THE BEGINNING, I JUST WANTED KOKI TO BE MY FRIEND ...

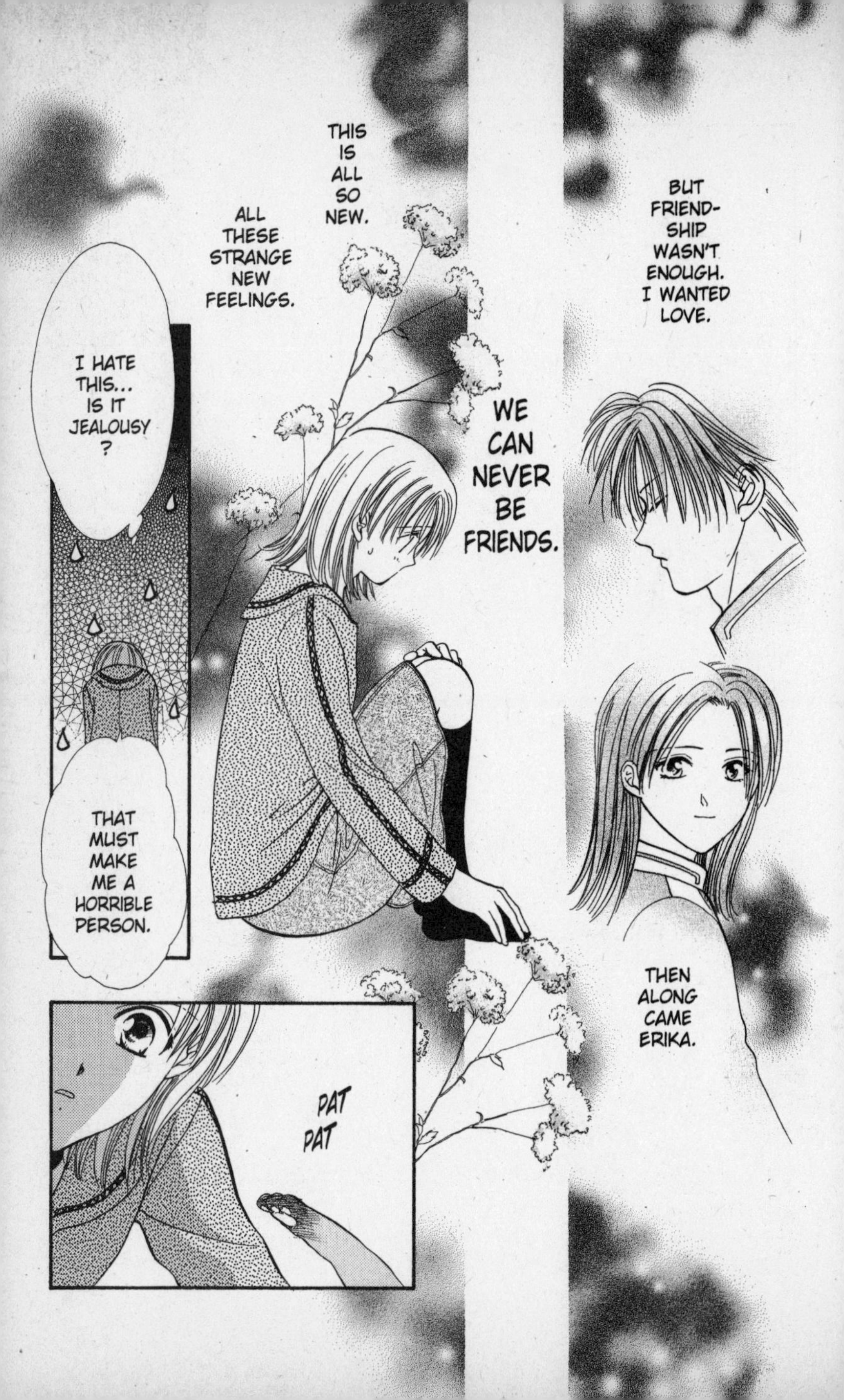
BUT FRIENDSHIP WASN'T ENOUGH. I WANTED LOVE.
THEN ALONG CAME ERIKA.
WE CAN NEVER BE FRIENDS.
THIS IS ALL SO NEW.
ALL THESE STRANGE NEW FEELINGS.
I HATE THIS... IS IT JEALOUSY?
THAT MUST MAKE ME A HORRIBLE PERSON.
PAT PAT

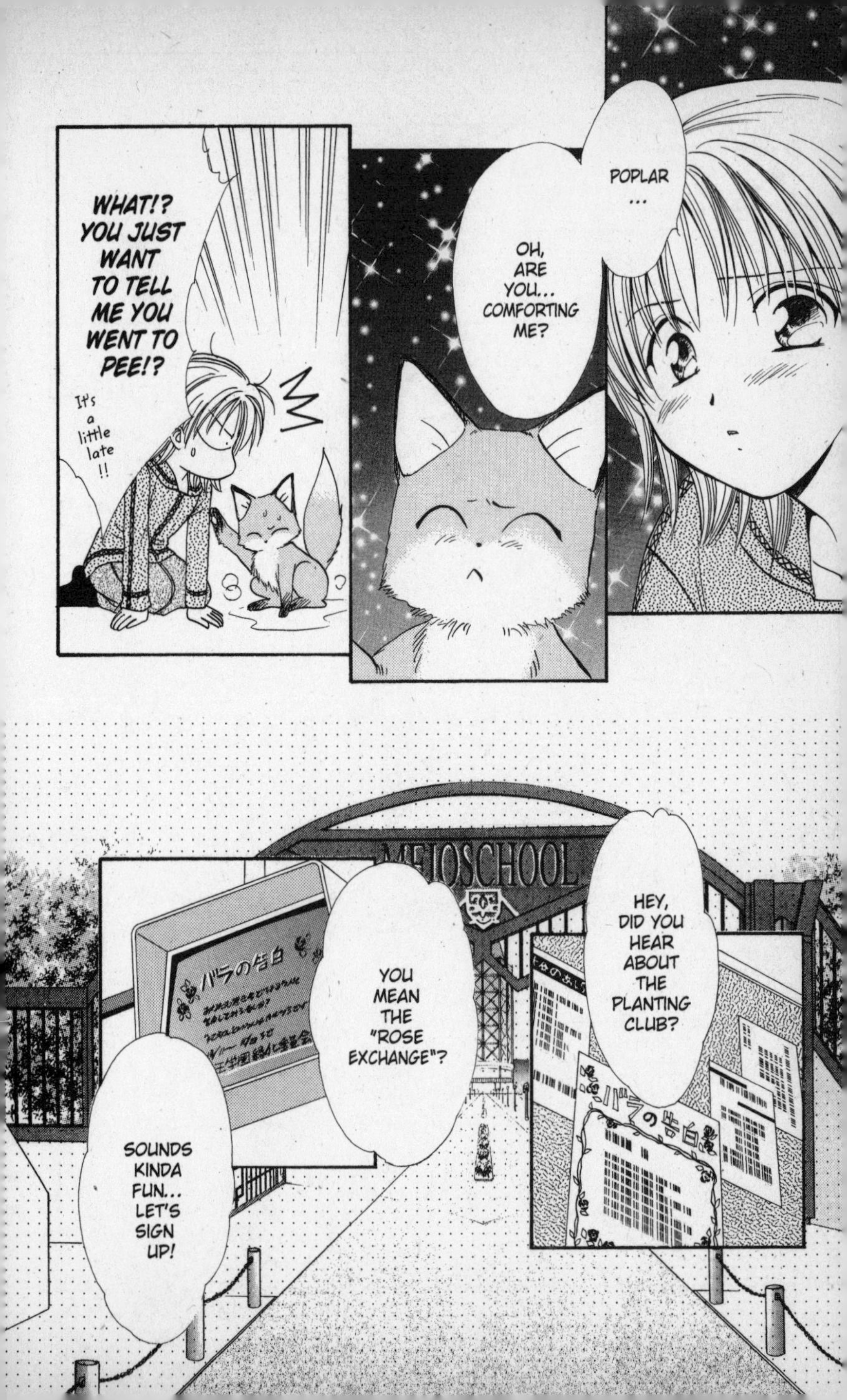
POPLAR ...
OH, ARE YOU... COMFORTING ME?
WHAT!? YOU JUST WANT TO TELL ME YOU WENT TO PEE!?
It's a little late !!
MEIOSCHOOL
HEY, DID YOU HEAR ABOUT THE PLANTING CLUB?
YOU MEAN THE "ROSE EXCHANGE"?
SOUNDS KINDA FUN... LET'S SIGN UP!
バラの告白
バラの告白

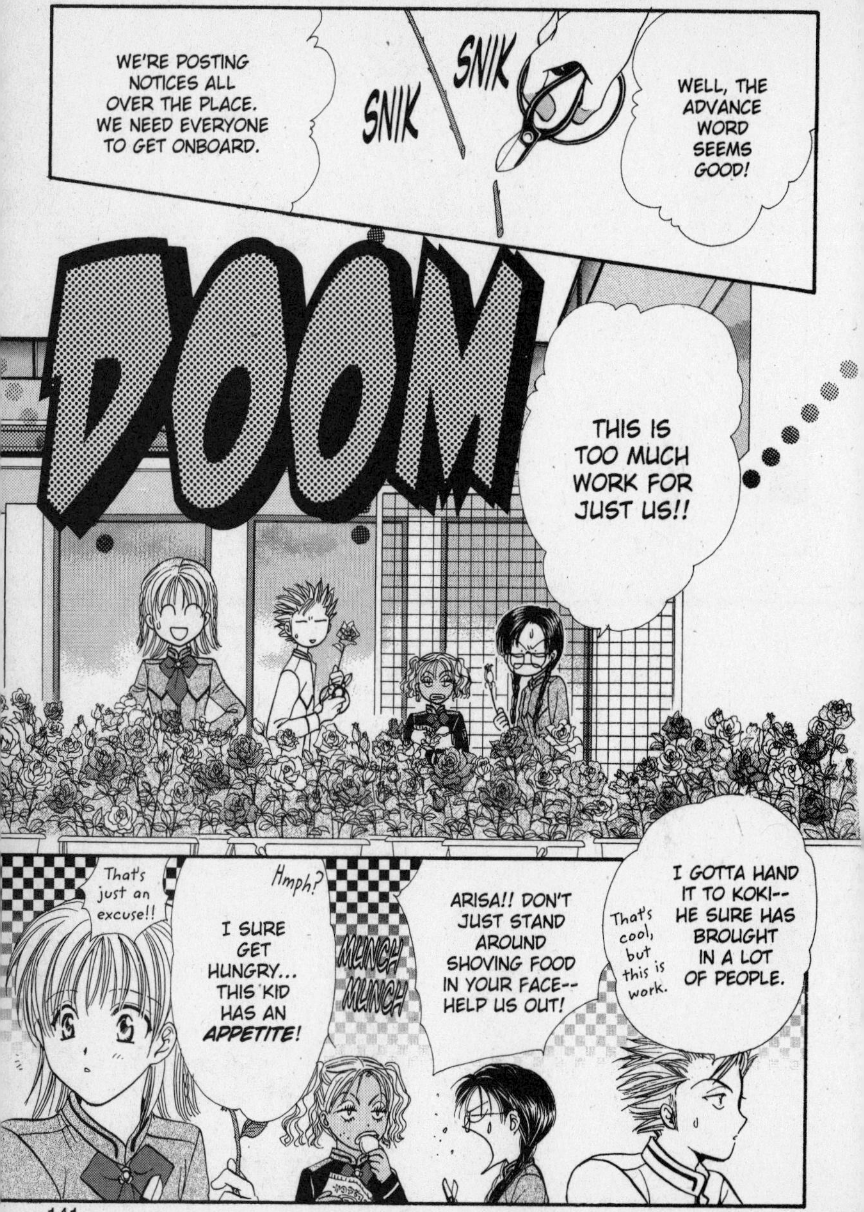
WELL, THE ADVANCE WORD SEEMS GOOD!
SNIK
SNIK
WE'RE POSTING NOTICES ALL OVER THE PLACE. WE NEED EVERYONE TO GET ONBOARD.
DOOM
THIS IS TOO MUCH WORK FOR JUST US!!
I GOTTA HAND IT TO KOKI-- HE SURE HAS BROUGHT IN A LOT OF PEOPLE.
That's cool, but this is work.
ARISA!! DON'T JUST STAND AROUND SHOVING FOOD IN YOUR FACE-- HELP US OUT!
MUNCH MUNCH
Hmph?
I SURE GET HUNGRY... THIS KID HAS AN APPETITE!
That's just an excuse!!

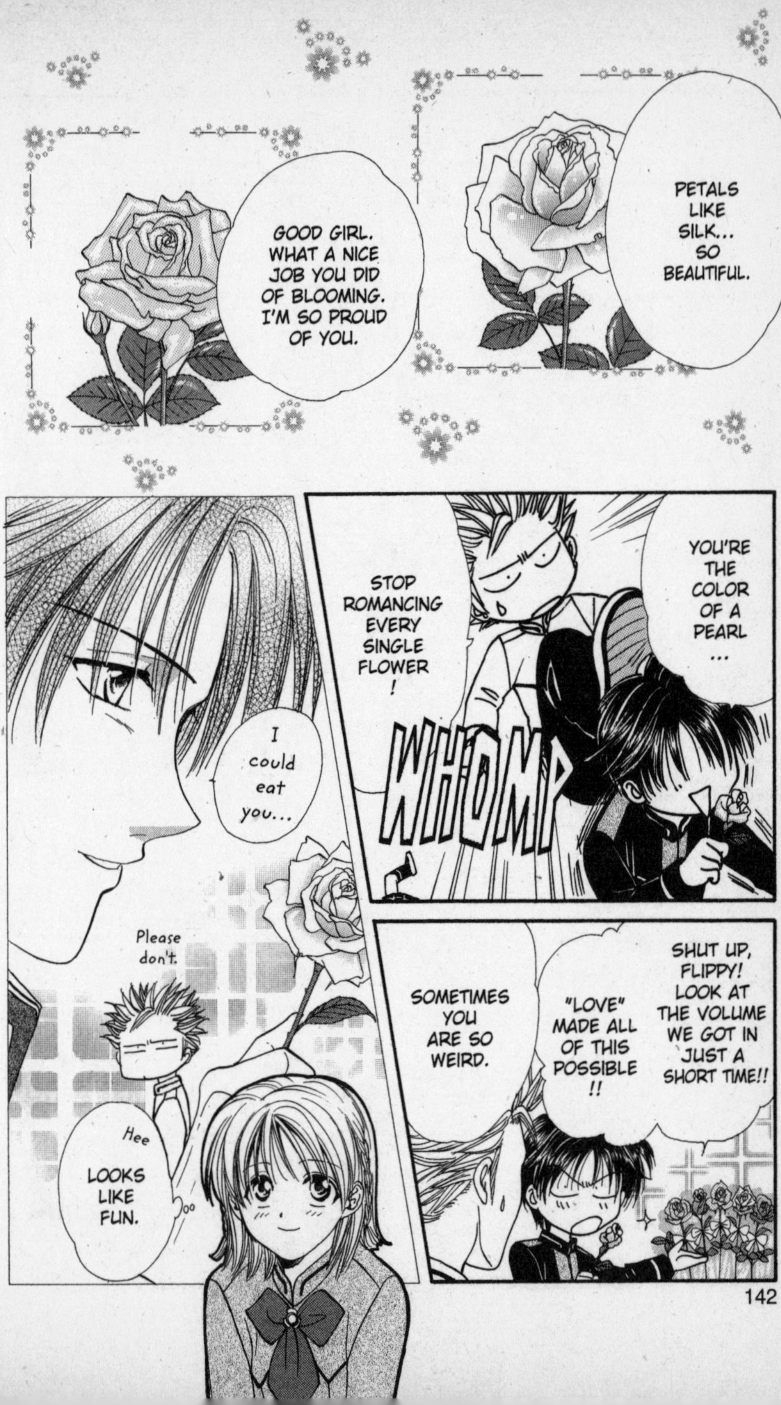
PETALS LIKE SILK... SO BEAUTIFUL.
GOOD GIRL. WHAT A NICE JOB YOU DID OF BLOOMING. I'M SO PROUD OF YOU.
YOU'RE THE COLOR OF A PEARL...
STOP ROMANCING EVERY SINGLE FLOWER!
WHOMP
SHUT UP, FLIPPY! LOOK AT THE VOLUME WE GOT IN JUST A SHORT TIME!!
"LOVE" MADE ALL OF THIS POSSIBLE!!
SOMETIMES YOU ARE SO WEIRD.
I could eat you...
Please don't.
Hee
LOOKS LIKE FUN.

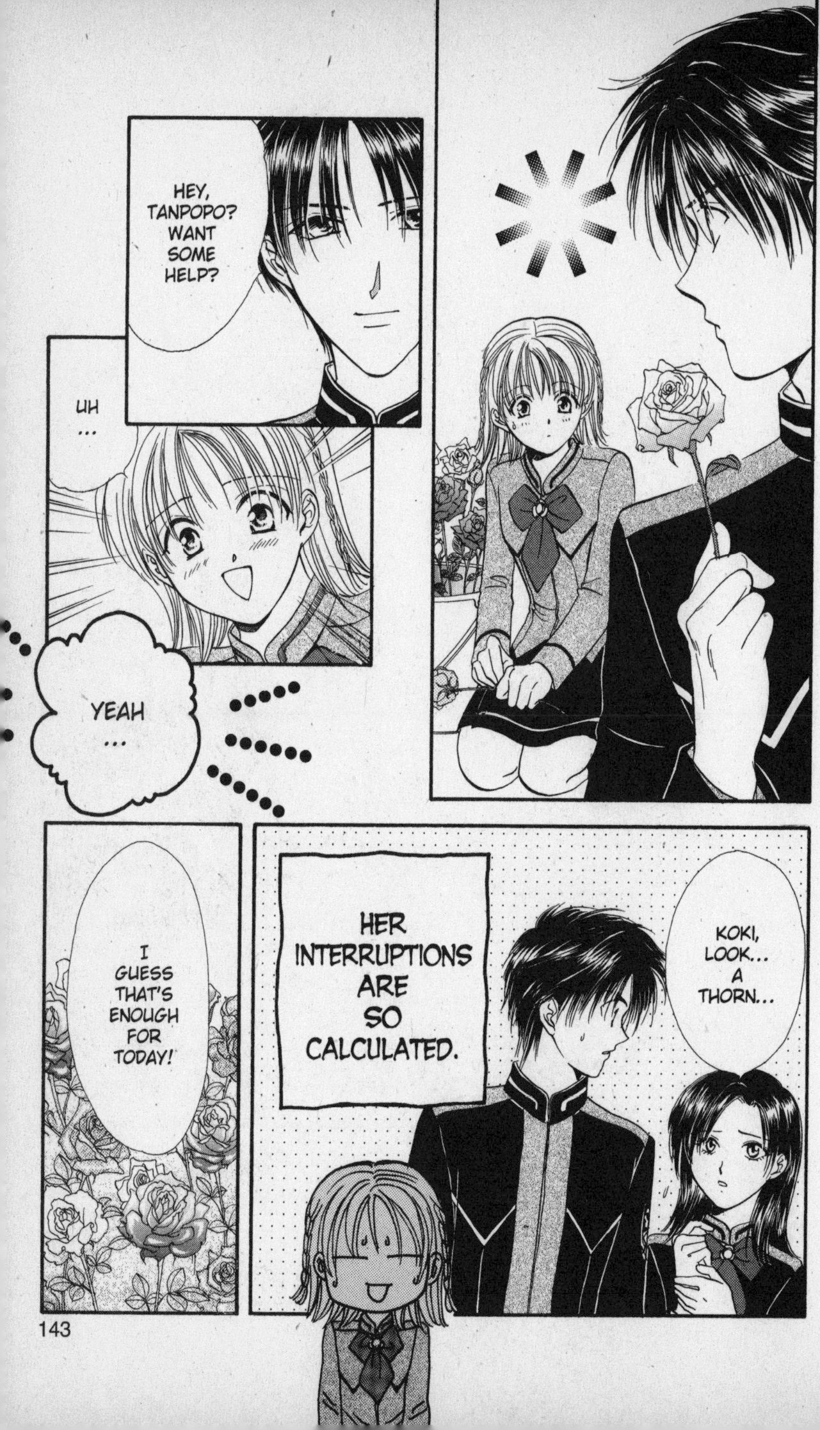
HEY, TANPOPO? WANT SOME HELP?
UH ...
YEAH ...
KOKI, LOOK... A THORN...
HER INTERRUPTIONS ARE SO CALCULATED.
I GUESS THAT'S ENOUGH FOR TODAY!

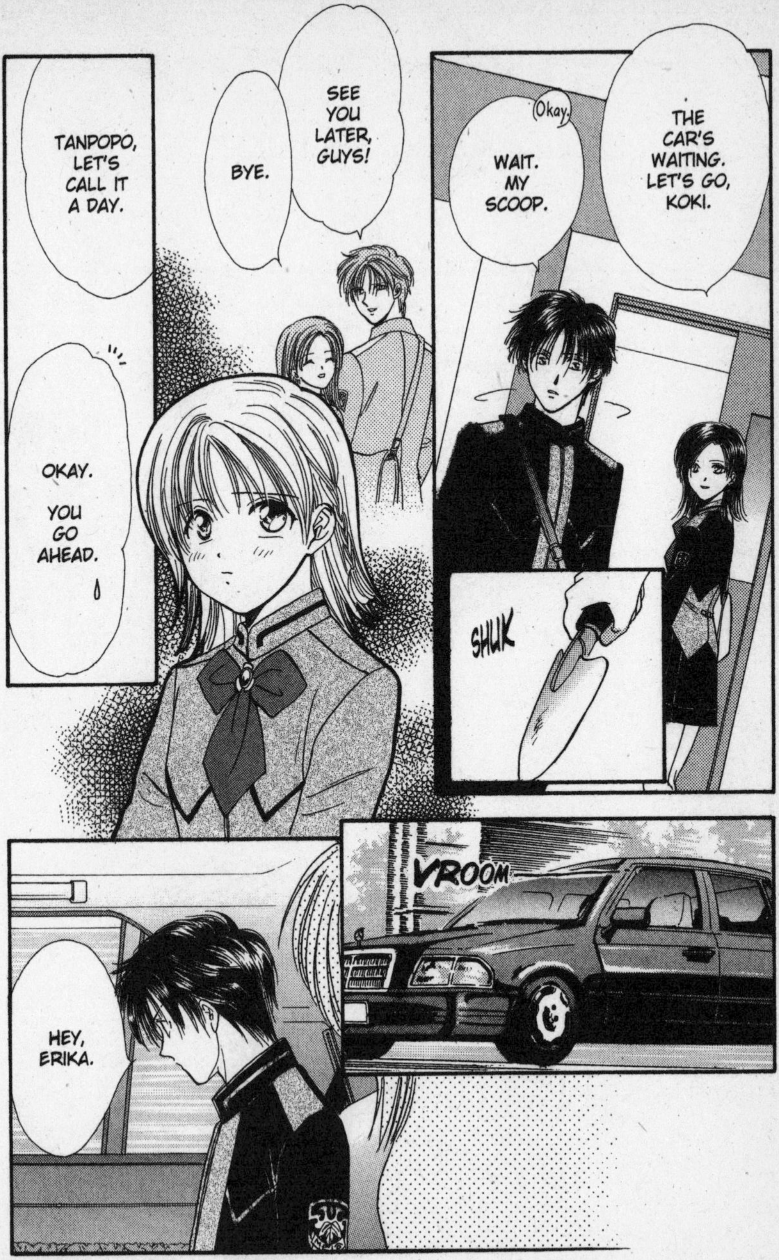
THE CAR'S WAITING. LET'S GO, KOKI.
Okay.
WAIT. MY SCOOP.
SHUK
SEE YOU LATER, GUYS!
BYE.
TANPOPO, LET'S CALL IT A DAY.
OKAY. YOU GO AHEAD.
VROOM
HEY, ERIKA.

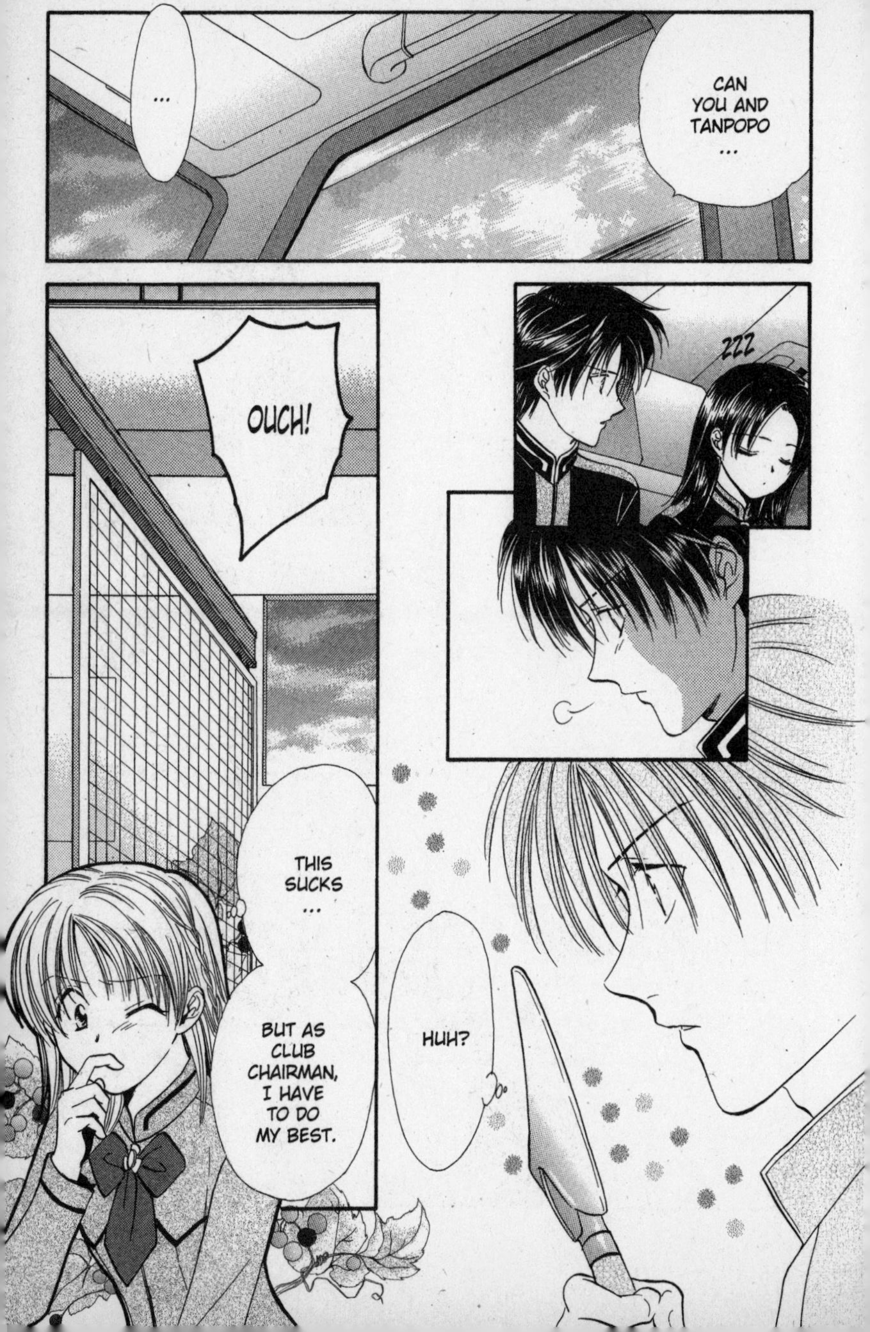
CAN YOU AND TANPOPO ...
...
ZZZ
HUH?
OUCH!
THIS SUCKS ...
BUT AS CLUB CHAIRMAN, I HAVE TO DO MY BEST.

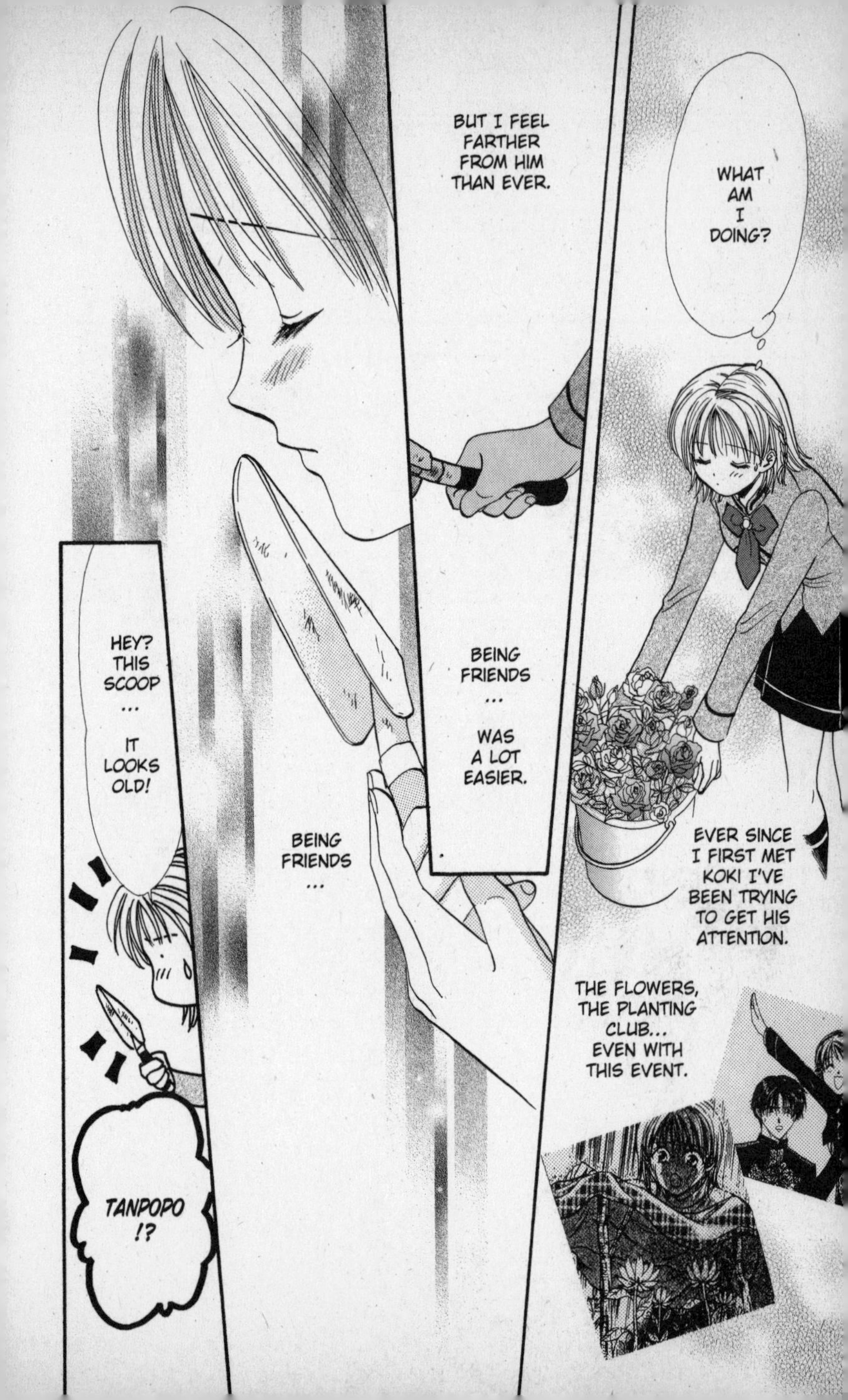
WHAT AM I DOING?
EVER SINCE I FIRST MET KOKI I'VE BEEN TRYING TO GET HIS ATTENTION.
THE FLOWERS, THE PLANTING CLUB... EVEN WITH THIS EVENT.
BUT I FEEL FARTHER FROM HIM THAN EVER.
BEING FRIENDS ... WAS A LOT EASIER.
BEING FRIENDS ...
HEY? THIS SCOOP ... IT LOOKS OLD!
TANPOPO !?

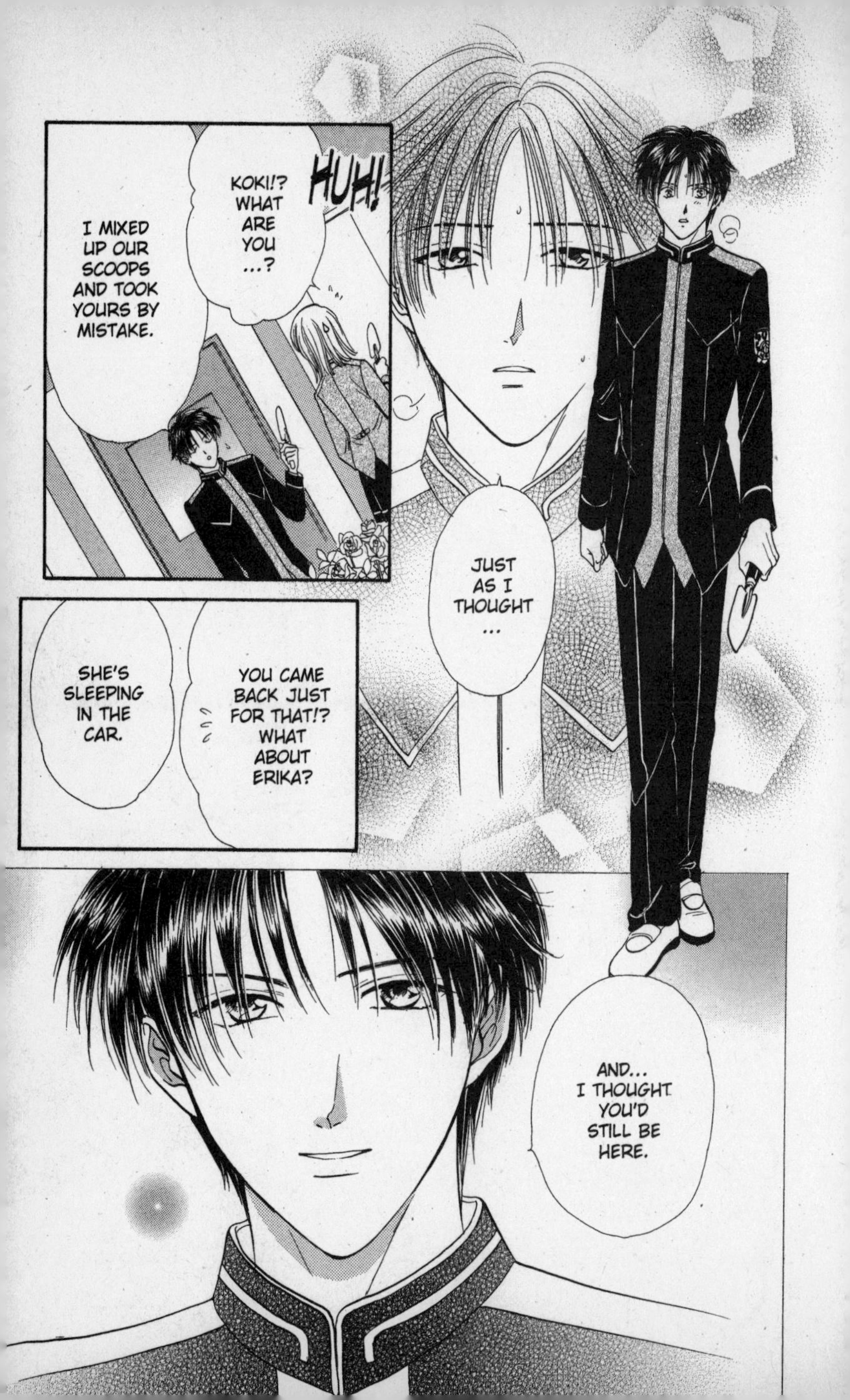
JUST AS I THOUGHT...
HUH!
KOKI!? WHAT ARE YOU ...?
I MIXED UP OUR SCOOPS AND TOOK YOURS BY MISTAKE.
YOU CAME BACK JUST FOR THAT!? WHAT ABOUT ERIKA?
SHE'S SLEEPING IN THE CAR.
AND... I THOUGHT YOU'D STILL BE HERE.

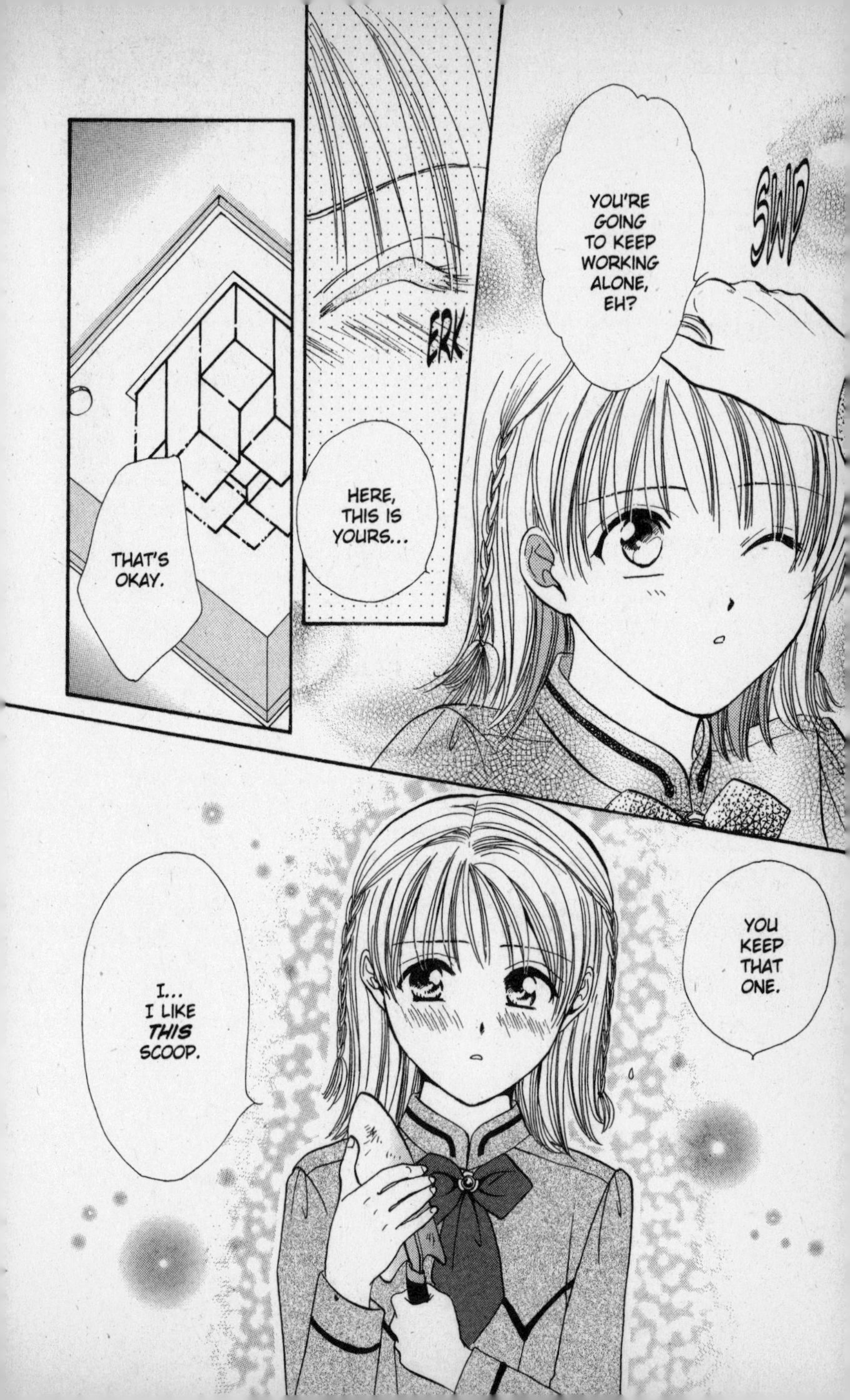
SWP
YOU'RE GOING TO KEEP WORKING ALONE, EH?
ERK
HERE, THIS IS YOURS...
THAT'S OKAY.
YOU KEEP THAT ONE.
I... I LIKE *THIS* SCOOP.

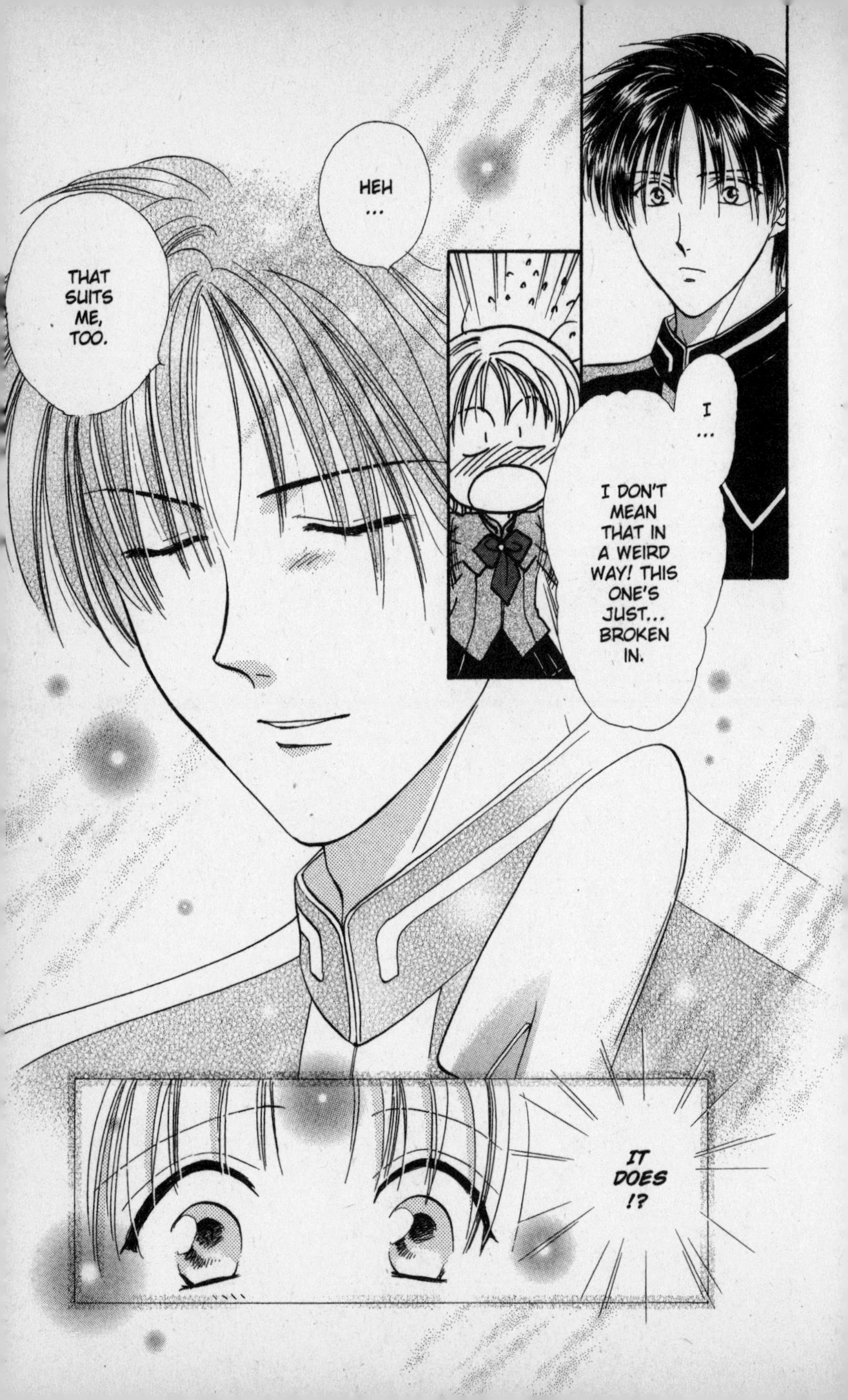
I ...
I DON'T MEAN THAT IN A WEIRD WAY! THIS ONE'S JUST... BROKEN IN.
HEH ...
THAT SUITS ME, TOO.
IT DOES !?

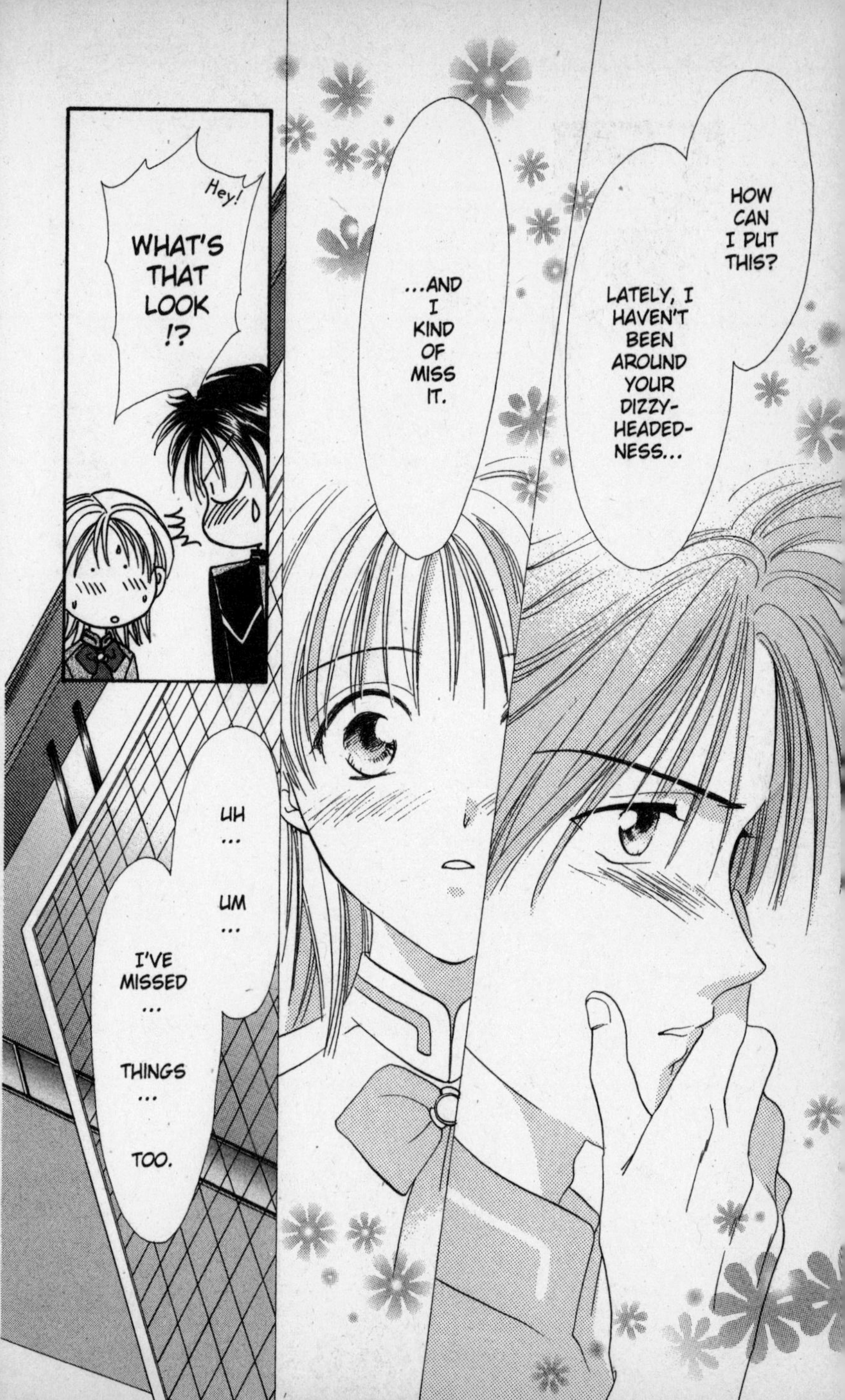
HOW CAN I PUT THIS?
LATELY, I HAVEN'T BEEN AROUND YOUR DIZZY-HEADEDNESS...
...AND I KIND OF MISS IT.
Hey!
WHAT'S THAT LOOK !?
UH ...
UM ...
I'VE MISSED ...
THINGS ...
TOO.

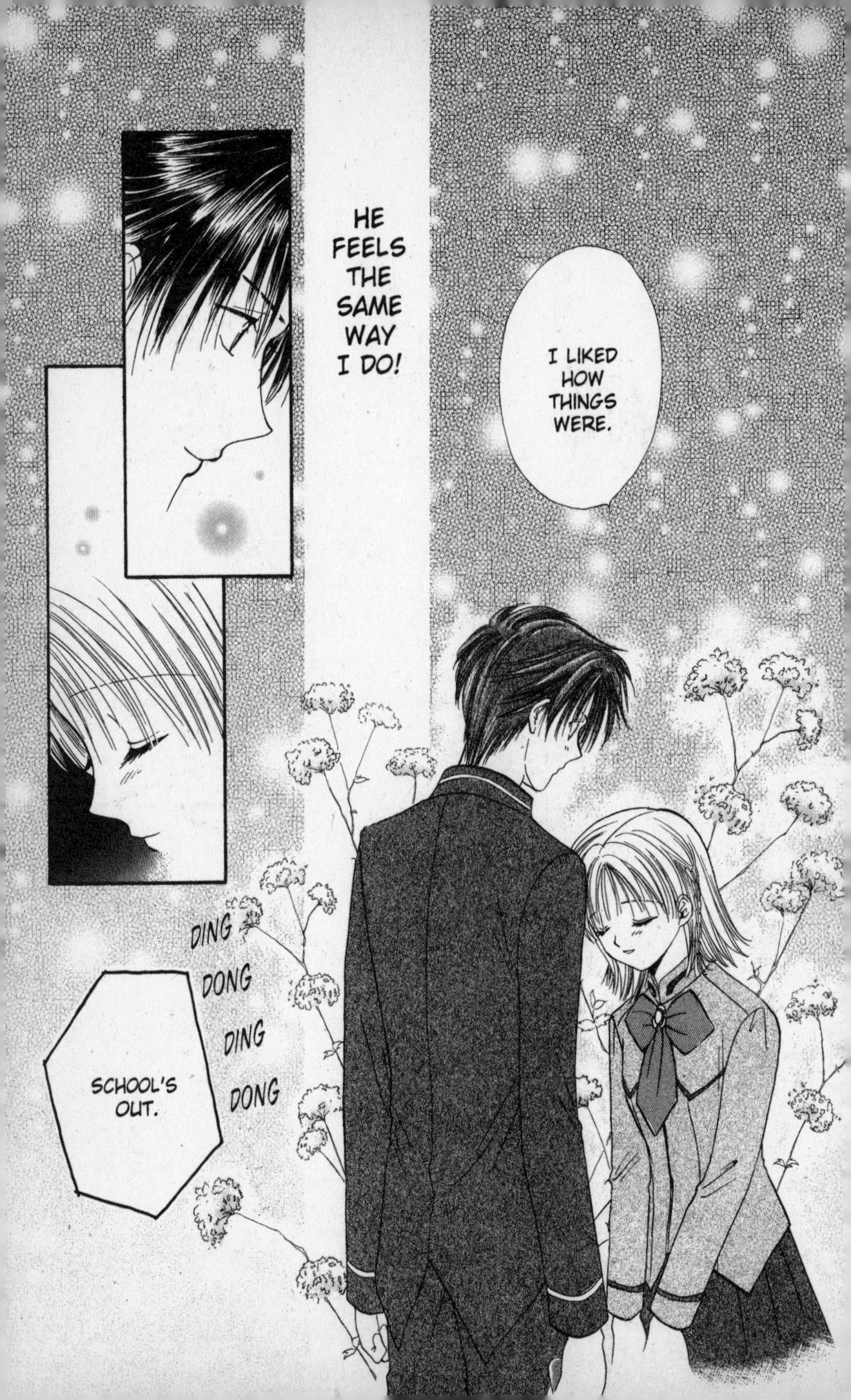
I LIKED HOW THINGS WERE.
HE FEELS THE SAME WAY I DO!
DING DONG DING DONG
SCHOOL'S OUT.

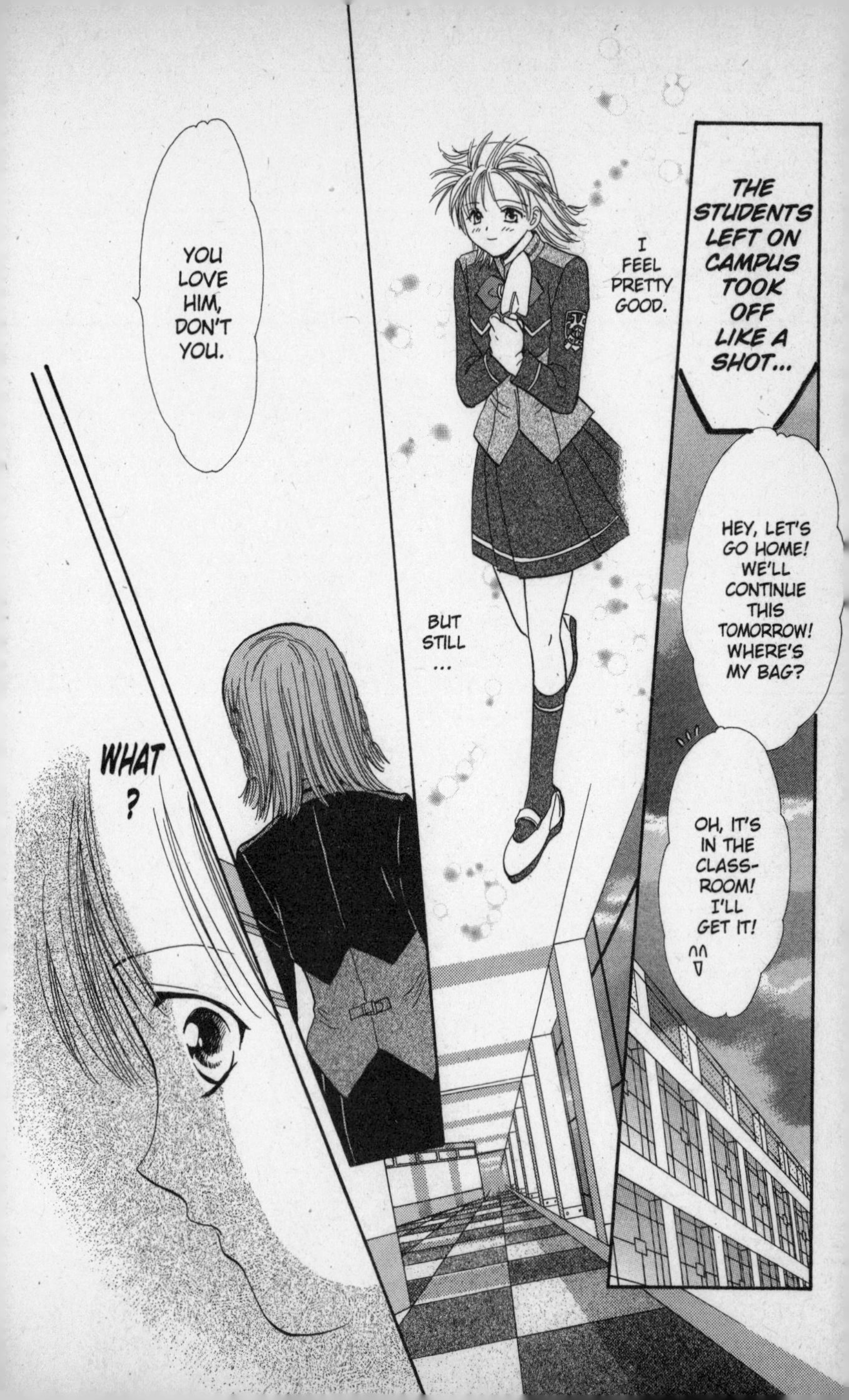
THE STUDENTS LEFT ON CAMPUS TOOK OFF LIKE A SHOT...
HEY, LET'S GO HOME! WE'LL CONTINUE THIS TOMORROW! WHERE'S MY BAG?
OH, IT'S IN THE CLASS-ROOM! I'LL GET IT!
I FEEL PRETTY GOOD.
BUT STILL ...
YOU LOVE HIM, DON'T YOU.
WHAT ?

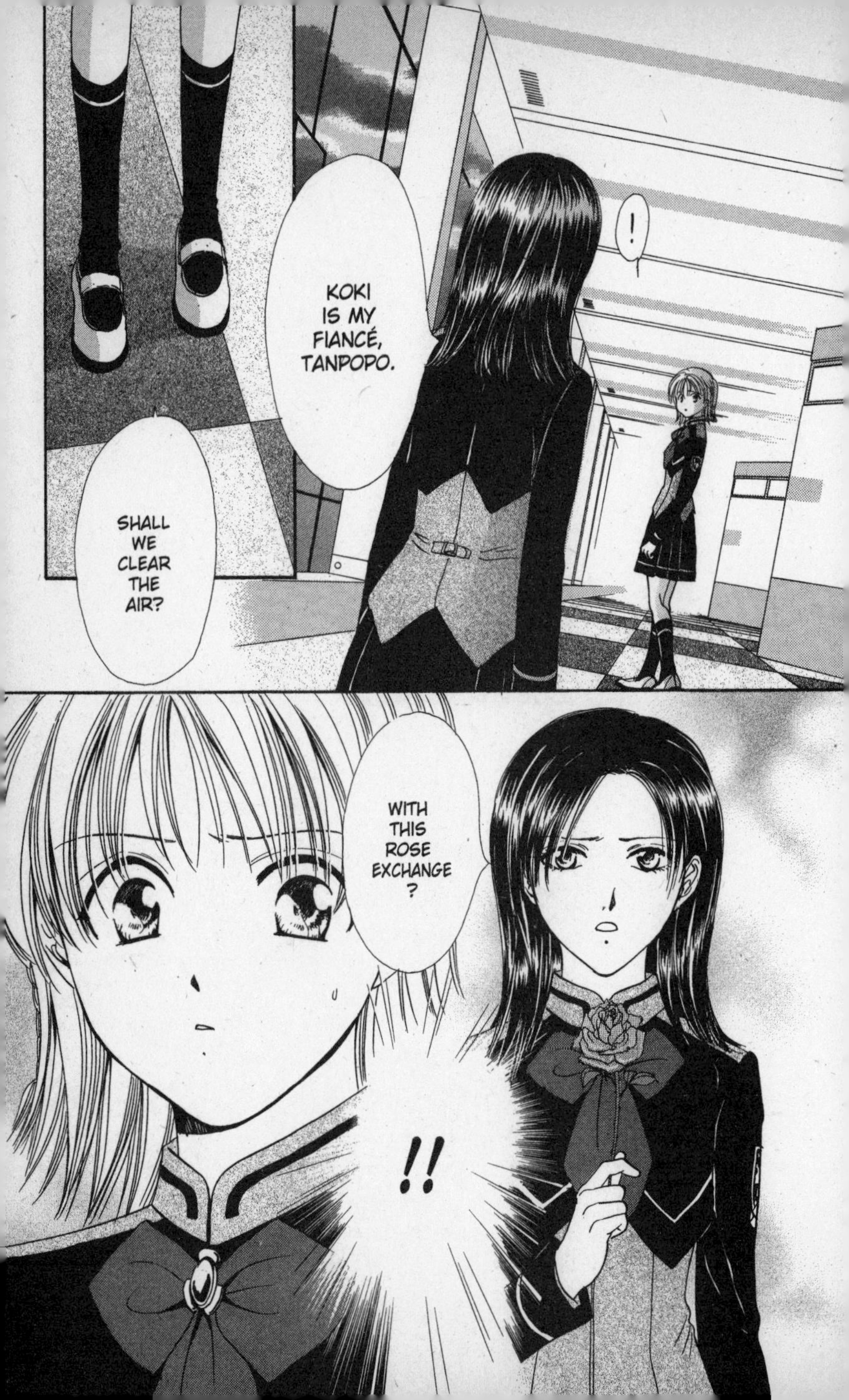
!
KOKI IS MY FIANCÉ, TANPOPO.
SHALL WE CLEAR THE AIR?
WITH THIS ROSE EXCHANGE?
!!

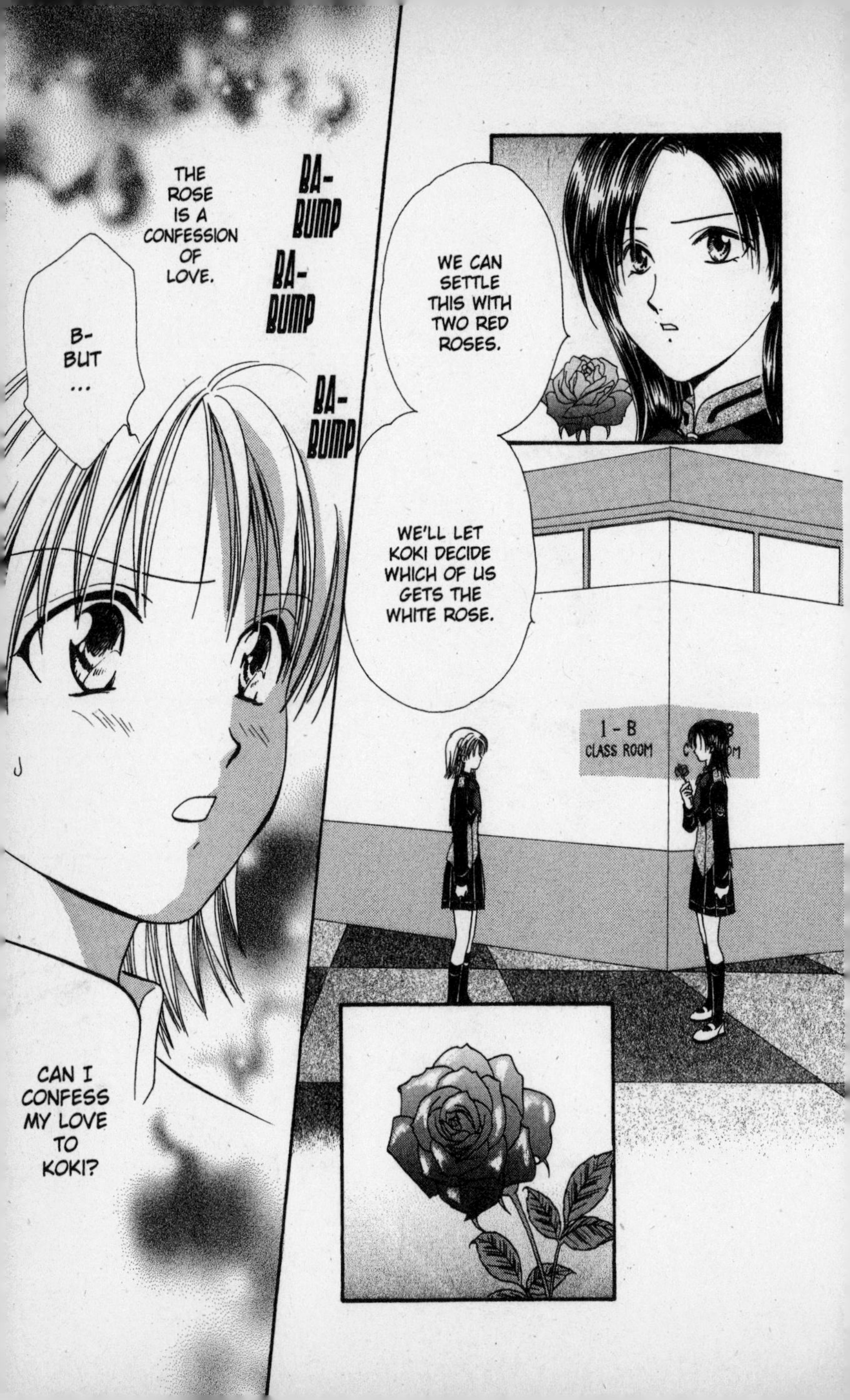
WE CAN SETTLE THIS WITH TWO RED ROSES.
WE'LL LET KOKI DECIDE WHICH OF US GETS THE WHITE ROSE.
1 - B CLASS ROOM
BA-BUMP
BA-BUMP
THE ROSE IS A CONFESSION OF LOVE.
BA-BUMP
B-BUT ...
CAN I CONFESS MY LOVE TO KOKI?

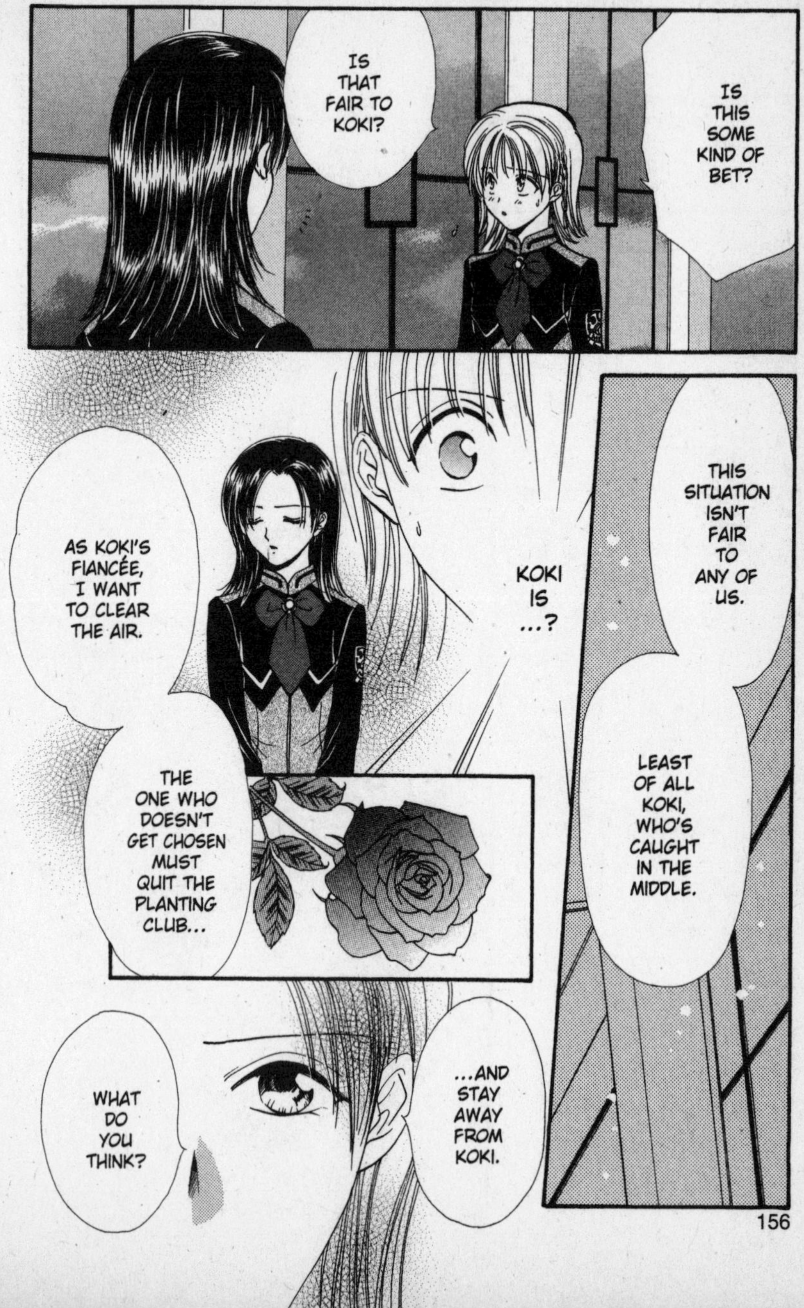
IS THIS SOME KIND OF BET?
IS THAT FAIR TO KOKI?
THIS SITUATION ISN'T FAIR TO ANY OF US.
LEAST OF ALL KOKI, WHO'S CAUGHT IN THE MIDDLE.
KOKI IS ...?
AS KOKI'S FIANCÉE, I WANT TO CLEAR THE AIR.
THE ONE WHO DOESN'T GET CHOSEN MUST QUIT THE PLANTING CLUB...
...AND STAY AWAY FROM KOKI.
WHAT DO YOU THINK?

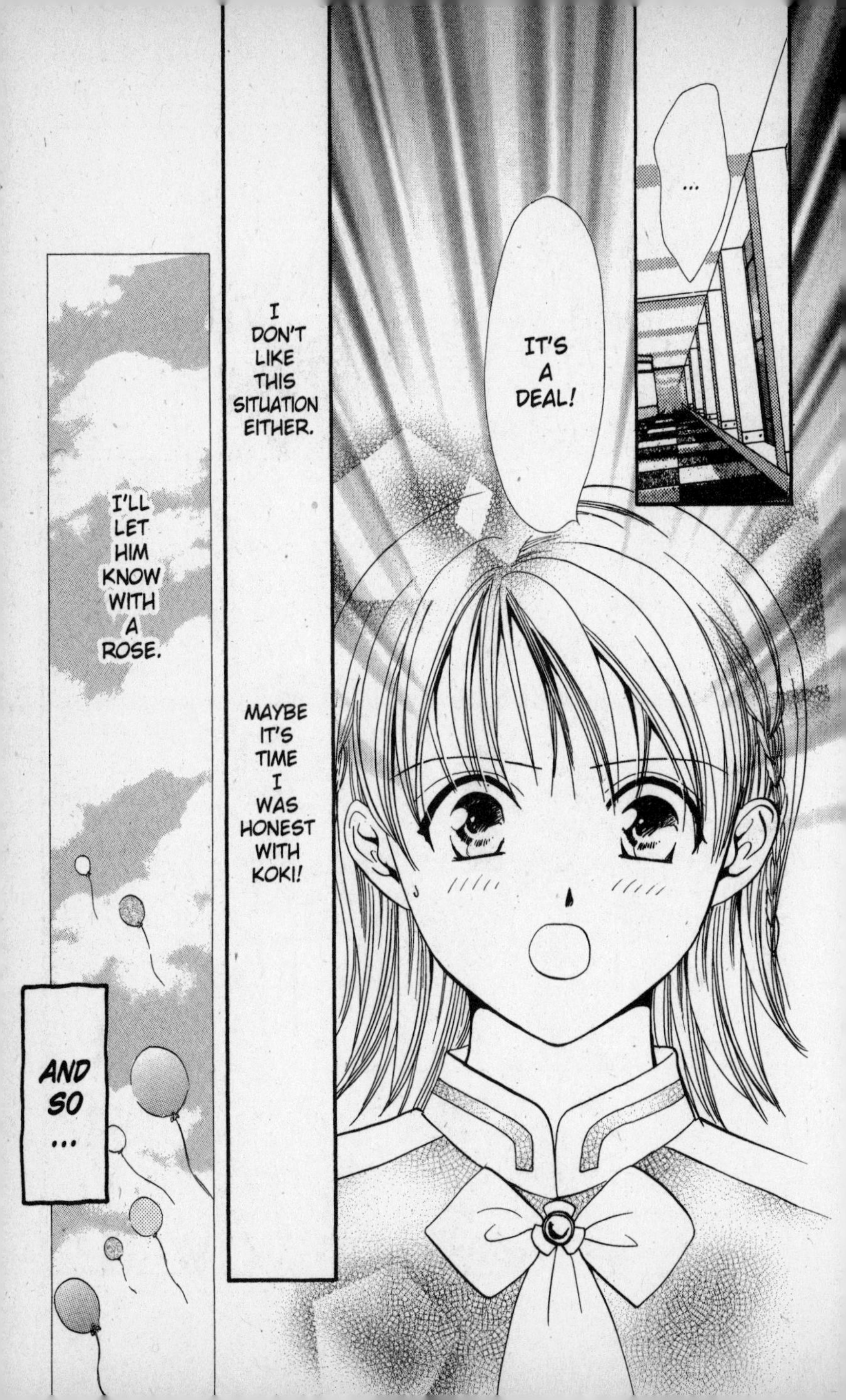
...
IT'S A DEAL!
I DON'T LIKE THIS SITUATION EITHER.
MAYBE IT'S TIME I WAS HONEST WITH KOKI!
I'LL LET HIM KNOW WITH A ROSE.
AND SO ...

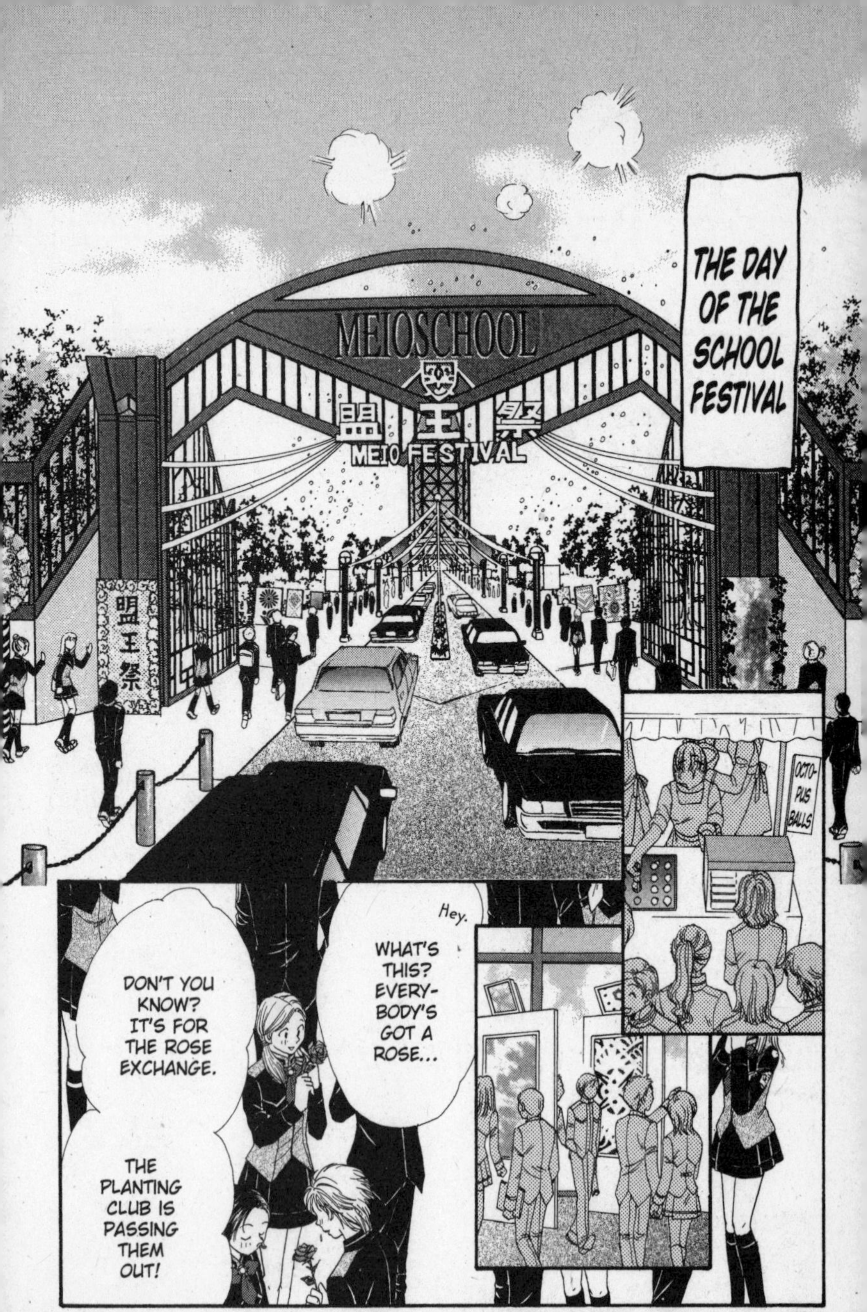
THE DAY OF THE SCHOOL FESTIVAL
MEIOSCHOOL
盟王祭
MEIO FESTIVAL
盟王祭
OCTO-PUS BALLS
Hey.
WHAT'S THIS? EVERY-BODY'S GOT A ROSE...
DON'T YOU KNOW? IT'S FOR THE ROSE EXCHANGE.
THE PLANTING CLUB IS PASSING THEM OUT!

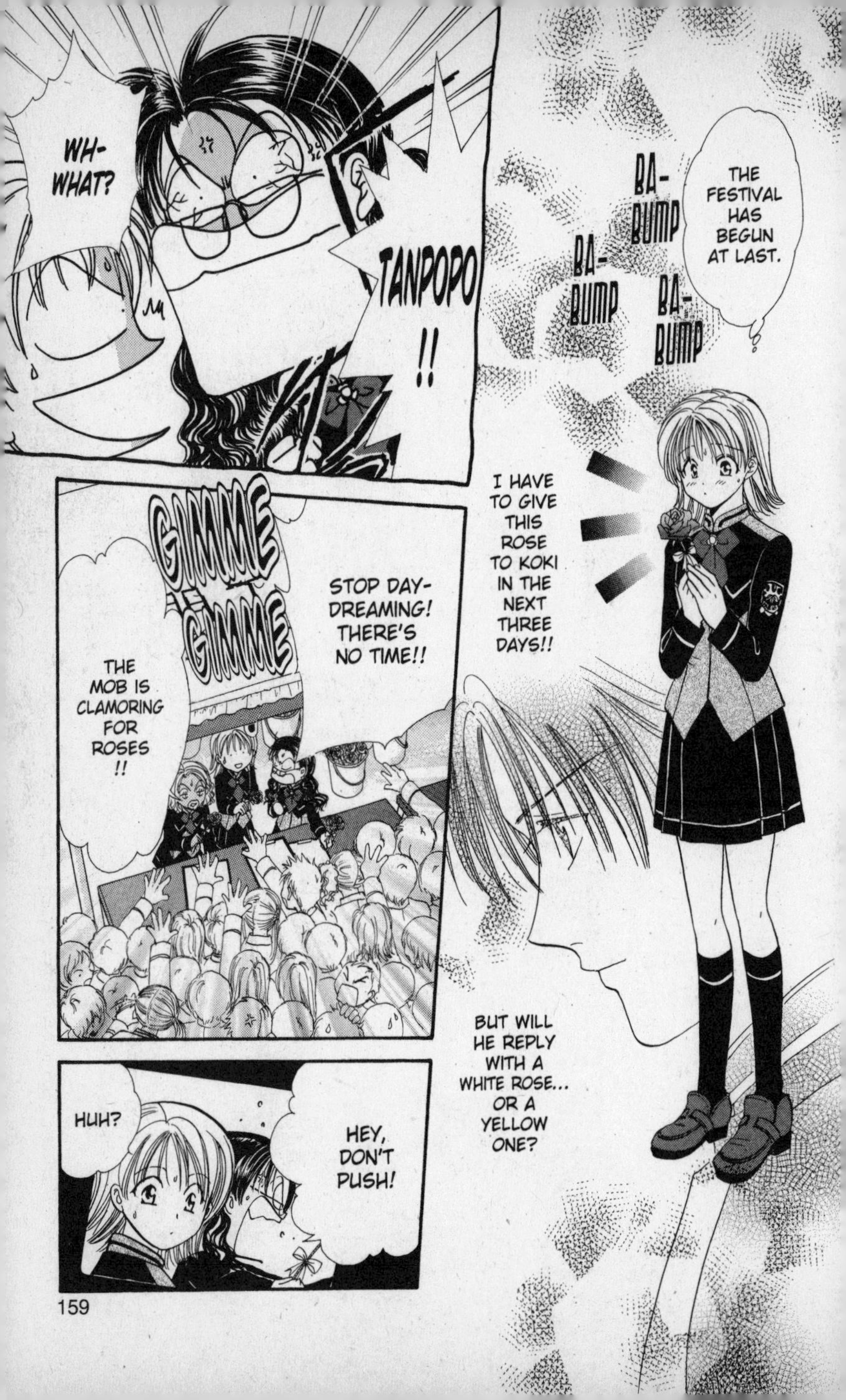
THE FESTIVAL HAS BEGUN AT LAST.
BA-BUMP
BA-BUMP
BA-BUMP
I HAVE TO GIVE THIS ROSE TO KOKI IN THE NEXT THREE DAYS!!
BUT WILL HE REPLY WITH A WHITE ROSE... OR A YELLOW ONE?
TANPOPO!!
WH-WHAT?
STOP DAY-DREAMING! THERE'S NO TIME!!
GIMME GIMME
THE MOB IS CLAMORING FOR ROSES!!
HEY, DON'T PUSH!
HUH?

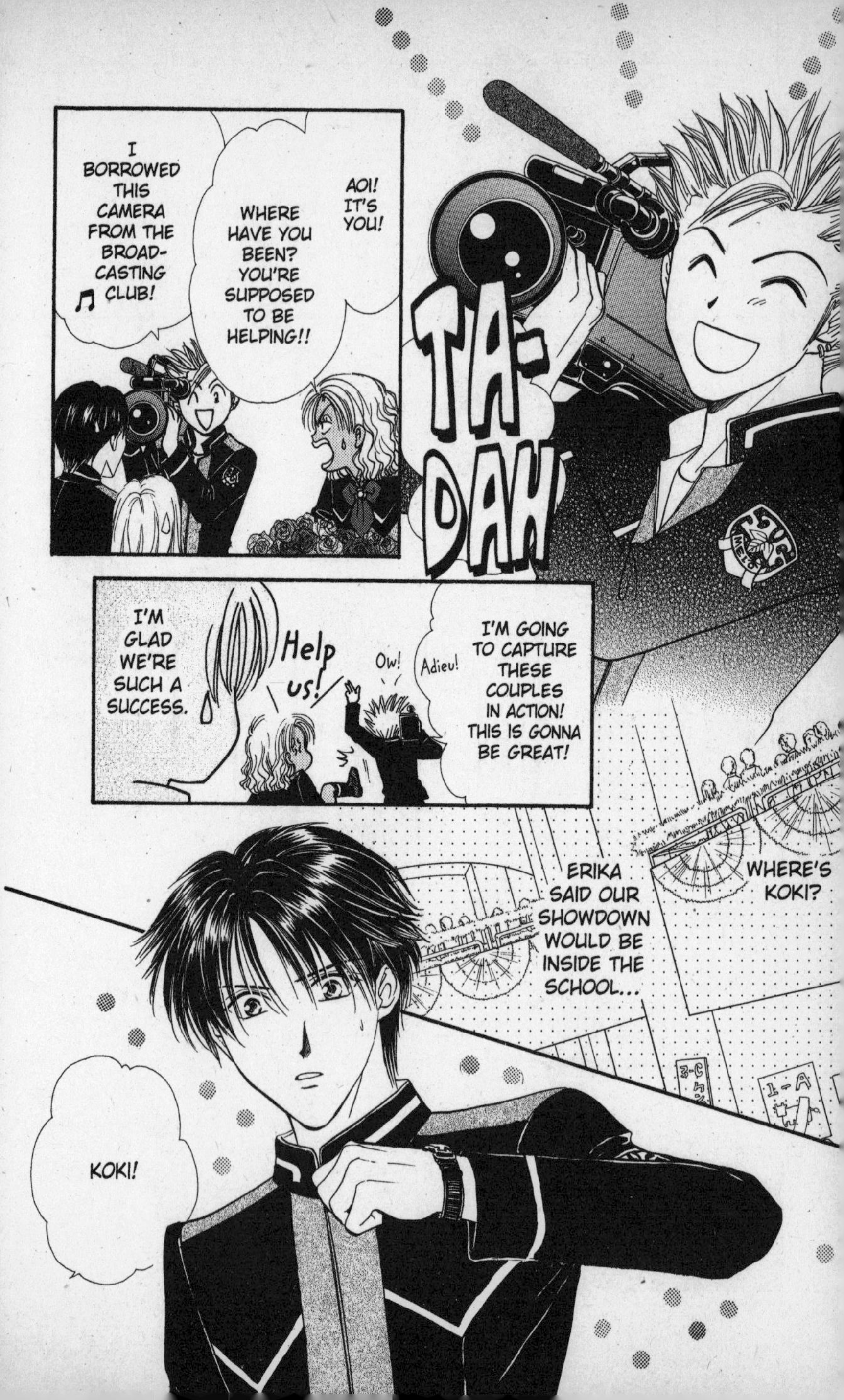
TA-DAH
AOI! IT'S YOU!
WHERE HAVE YOU BEEN? YOU'RE SUPPOSED TO BE HELPING!!
I BORROWED THIS CAMERA FROM THE BROAD-CASTING CLUB! ♫
I'M GOING TO CAPTURE THESE COUPLES IN ACTION! THIS IS GONNA BE GREAT!
Adieu!
Ow!
Help us!
I'M GLAD WE'RE SUCH A SUCCESS.
WHERE'S KOKI?
ERIKA SAID OUR SHOWDOWN WOULD BE INSIDE THE SCHOOL...
KOKI!

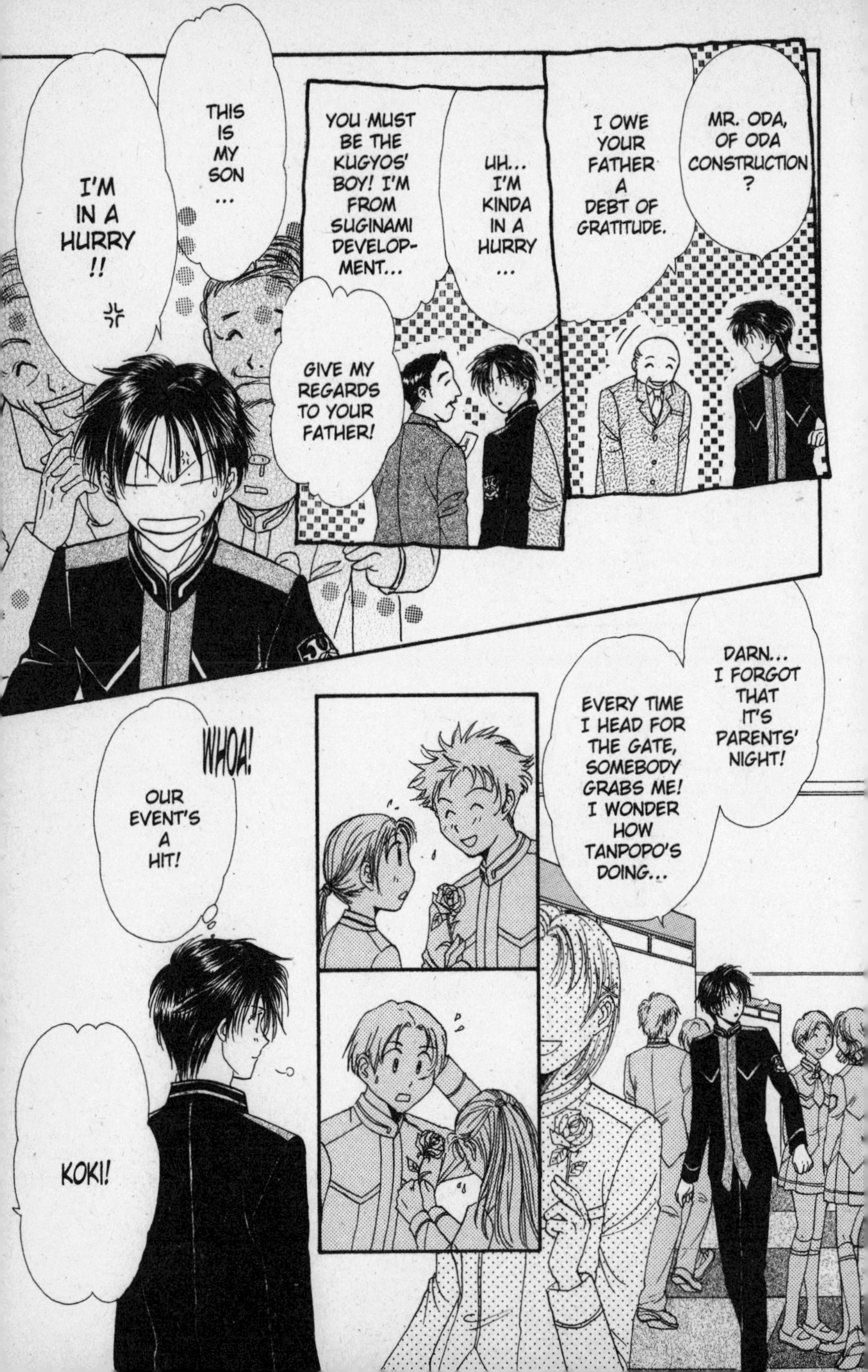
MR. ODA, OF ODA CONSTRUCTION?
I OWE YOUR FATHER A DEBT OF GRATITUDE.
UH... I'M KINDA IN A HURRY...
YOU MUST BE THE KUGYOS' BOY! I'M FROM SUGINAMI DEVELOPMENT...
GIVE MY REGARDS TO YOUR FATHER!
THIS IS MY SON...
I'M IN A HURRY!!
DARN... I FORGOT THAT IT'S PARENTS' NIGHT!
EVERY TIME I HEAD FOR THE GATE, SOMEBODY GRABS ME! I WONDER HOW TANPOPO'S DOING...
WHOA!
OUR EVENT'S A HIT!
KOKI!

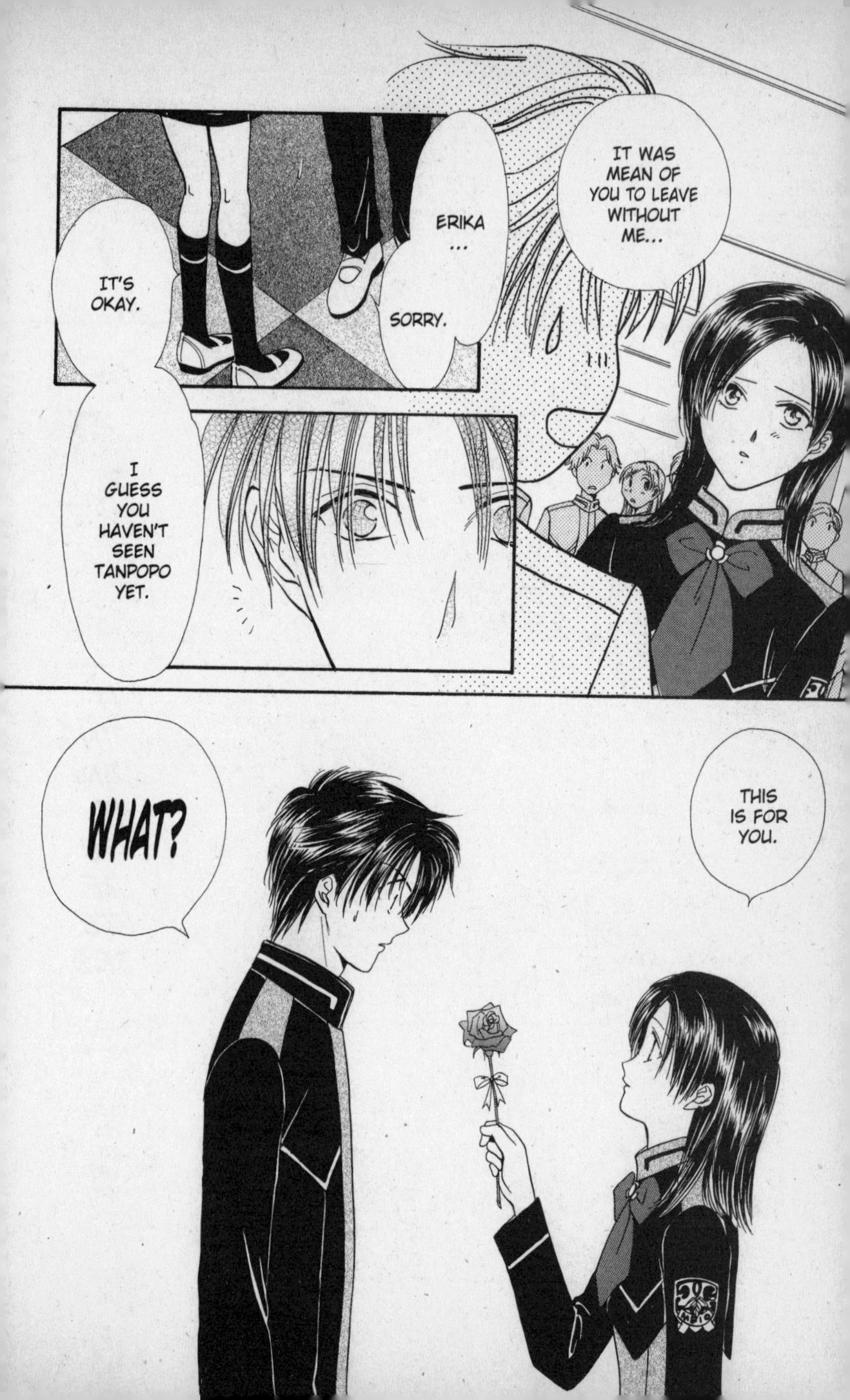
IT WAS MEAN OF YOU TO LEAVE WITHOUT ME...
ERIKA ...
SORRY.
IT'S OKAY.
I GUESS YOU HAVEN'T SEEN TANPOPO YET.
THIS IS FOR YOU.
WHAT?

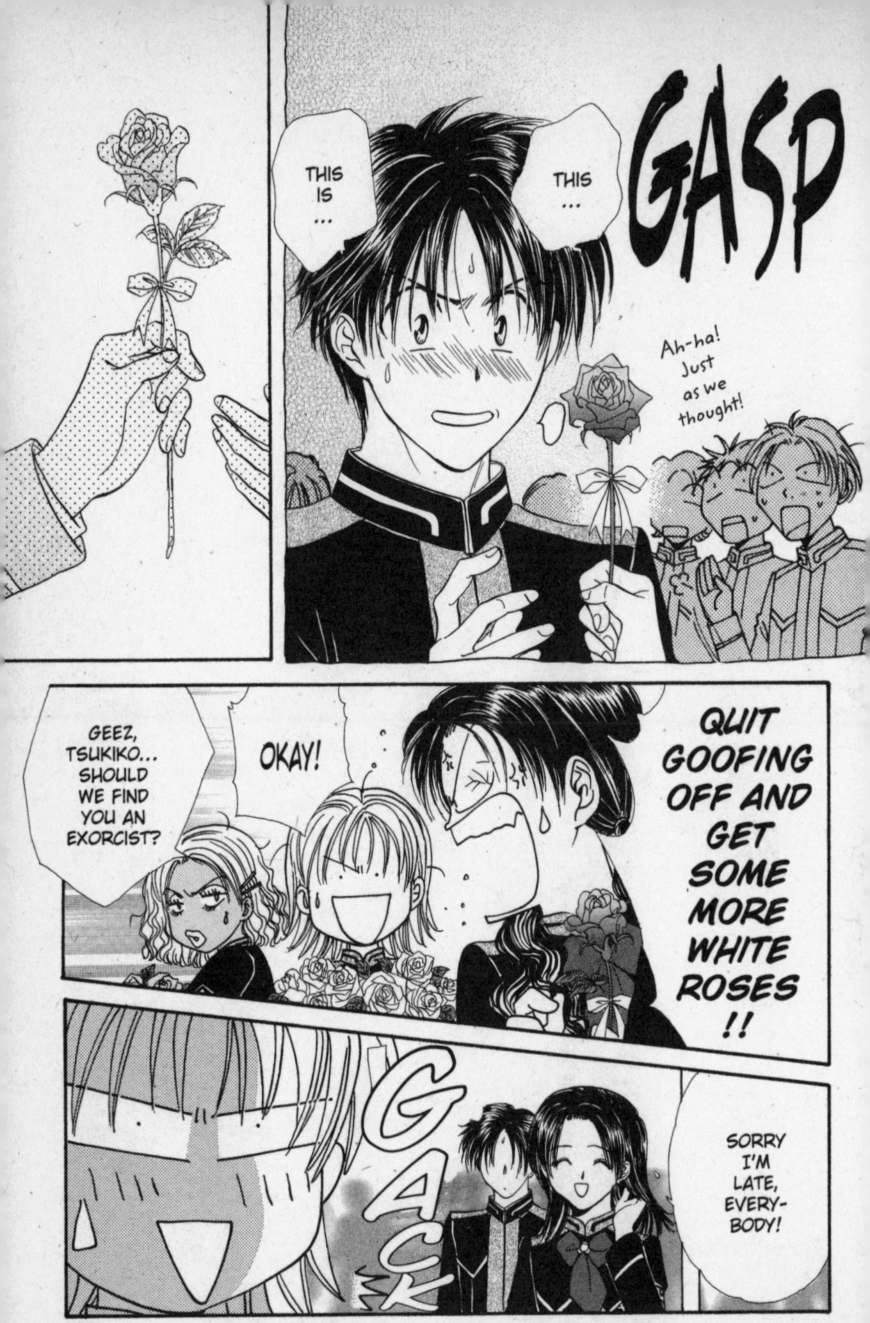
GASP
THIS...
THIS IS...
Ah-ha! Just as we thought!
QUIT GOOFING OFF AND GET SOME MORE WHITE ROSES!!
OKAY!
GEEZ, TSUKIKO... SHOULD WE FIND YOU AN EXORCIST?
SORRY I'M LATE, EVERYBODY!
GACK

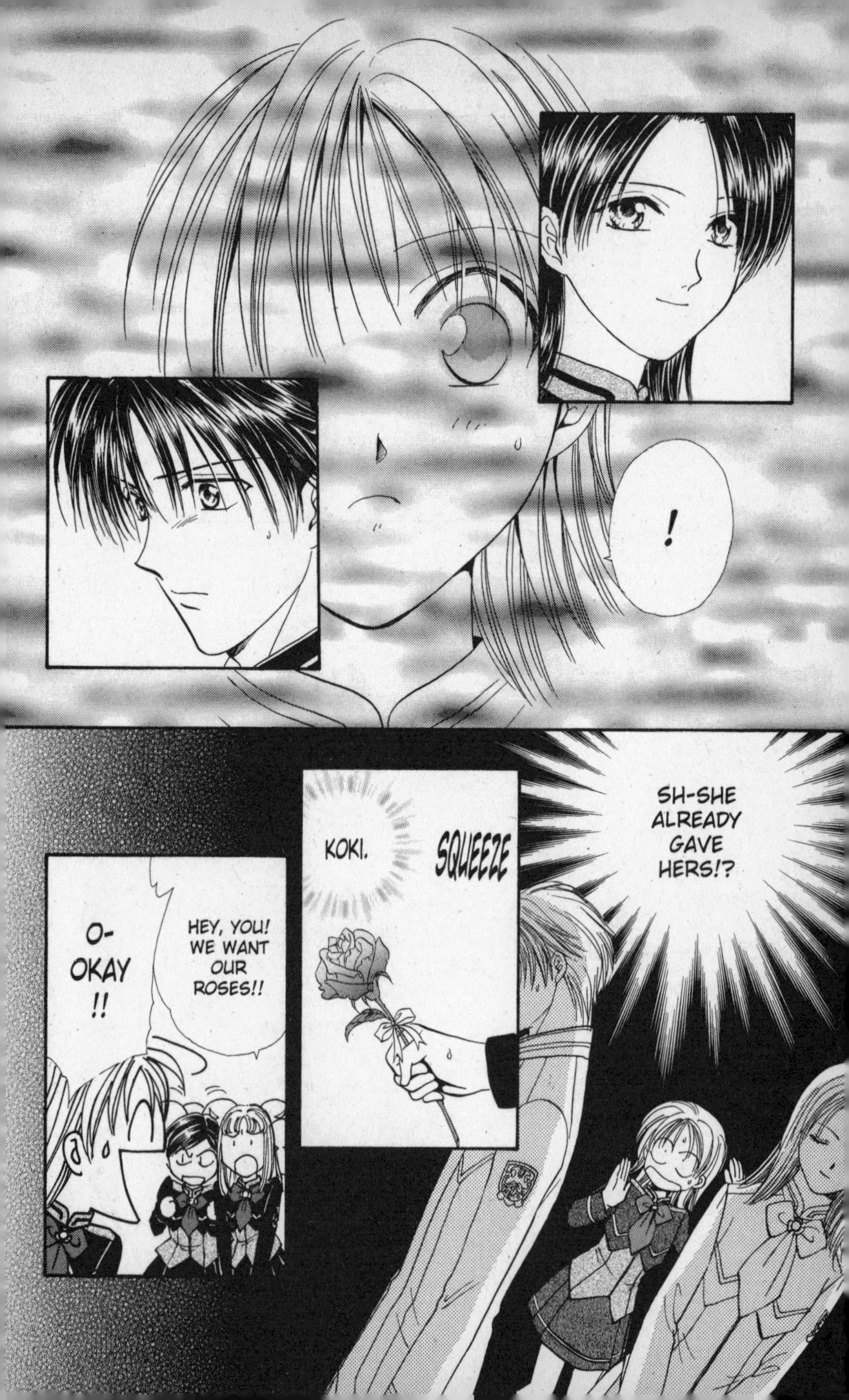
!
SH-SHE ALREADY GAVE HERS!?
KOKI.
SQUEEZE
HEY, YOU! WE WANT OUR ROSES!!
O-OKAY!!

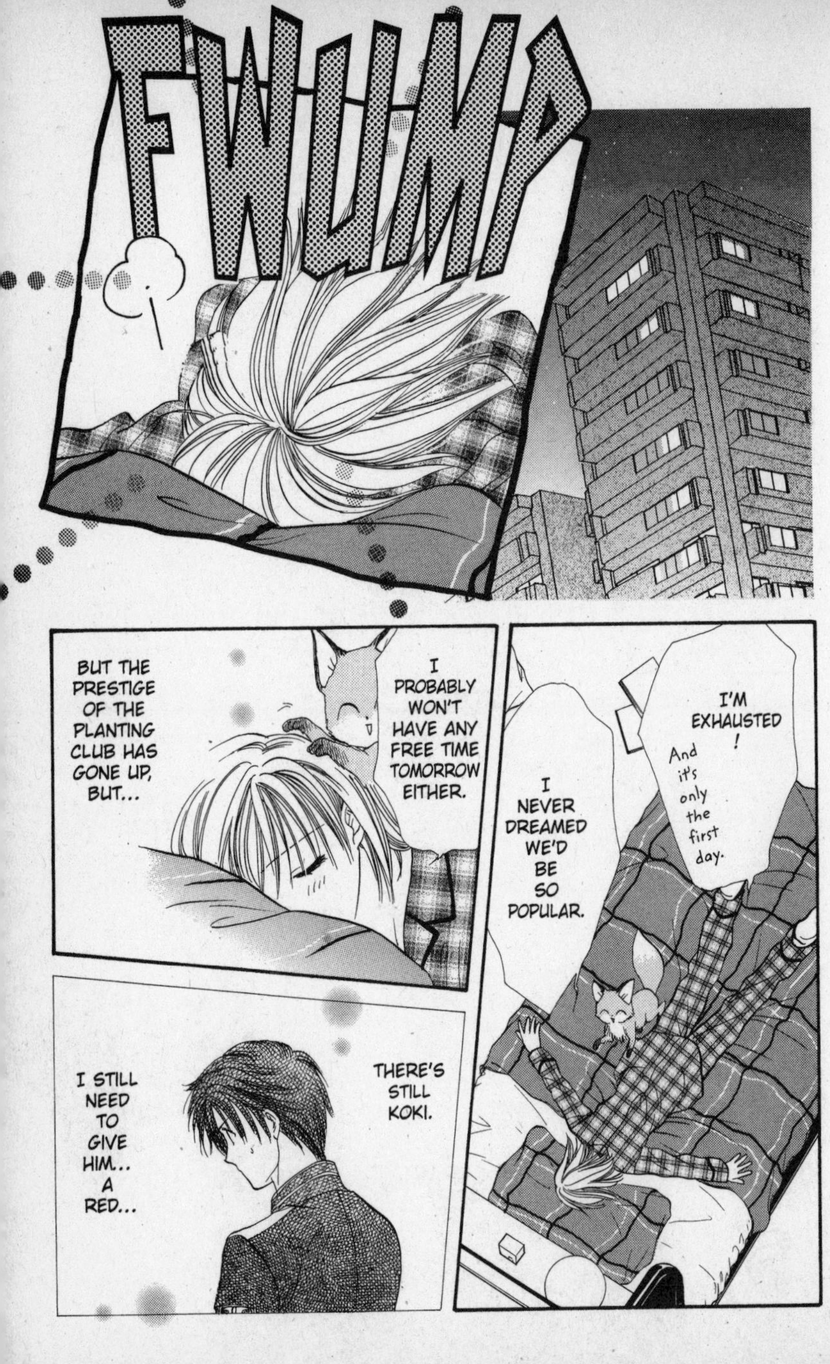
FWUMP
I'M EXHAUSTED!
And it's only the first day.
I NEVER DREAMED WE'D BE SO POPULAR.
I PROBABLY WON'T HAVE ANY FREE TIME TOMORROW EITHER.
BUT THE PRESTIGE OF THE PLANTING CLUB HAS GONE UP, BUT...
THERE'S STILL KOKI.
I STILL NEED TO GIVE HIM... A RED...

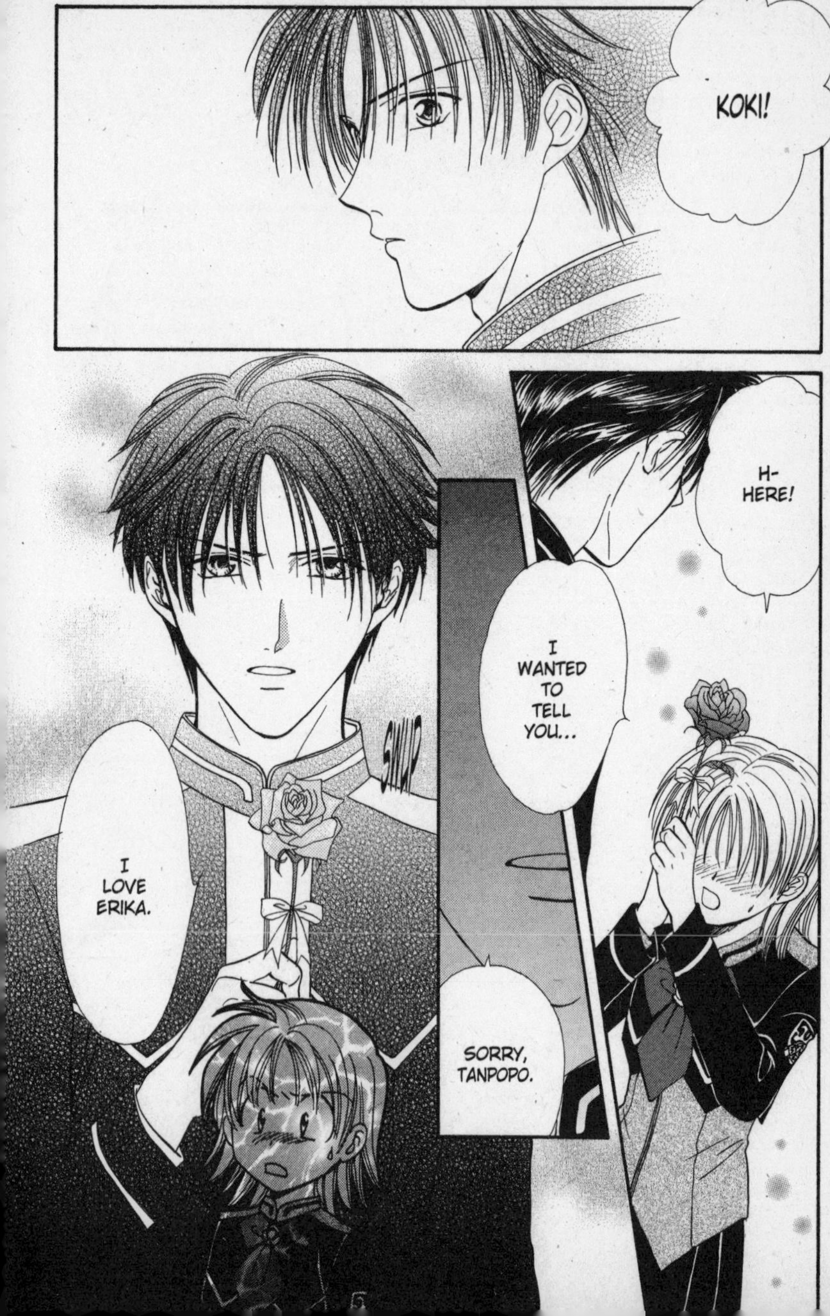
KOKI!
H-HERE!
I WANTED TO TELL YOU...
SORRY, TANPOPO.
SNUP
I LOVE ERIKA.

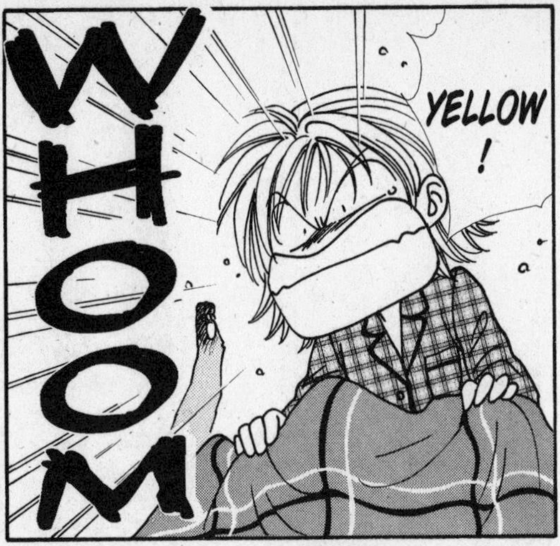
WHOOM
YELLOW!

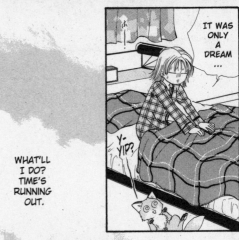

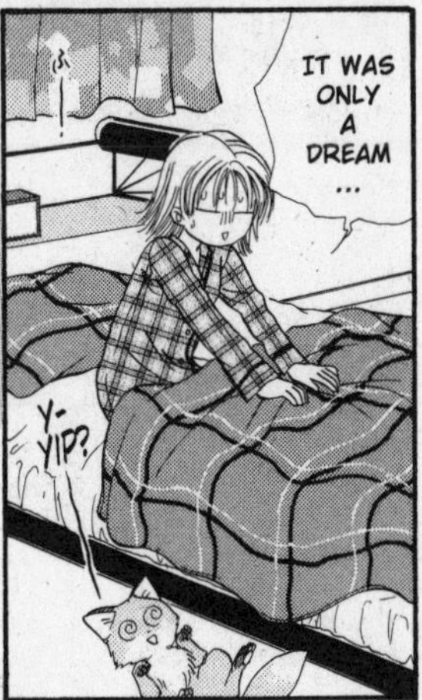
IT WAS ONLY A DREAM ...
Y-YIP?

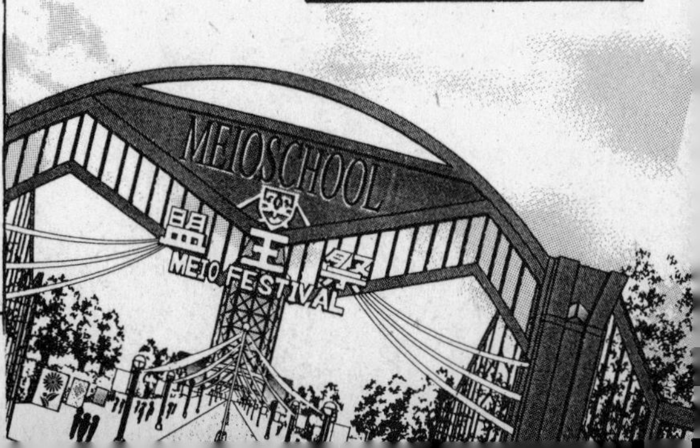
WHAT'LL I DO? TIME'S RUNNING OUT.
MEIO SCHOOL
盟王祭
MEIO FESTIVAL

When it comes to letter writing, there's no such thing as equality. Especially if the writers are starting out, and they're not the same age. Even we cartoonists have to be considerate. Politeness counts. Using the appropriate language can be difficult. But ultimately, it's the thought that counts, and your respect will shine through.

In a verbal exchange you need to understand the other person, right? The world is a tough place, but you could just be making it tougher. If each of us tries to change the world, we might make a difference.

Incidentally, remember when Tanpopo said, "A plum is a plum" and "A cherry blossom is a cherry blossom"? There's a Japanese term for this-- *obaitori.* It's true.

It means that each of us has our own personality. Every one of us was born with a different identity. We are each unique. A plum blossom can't become a cherry blossom or vice versa. You must live according to your own nature. In other words, don't let others tell you how to live. Just be yourself. If something doesn't work out the first time, keep trying and you'll find your own way. *Obaitori* is a Buddhist concept. Isn't it a good word? So all of you believe in yourselves! Tanpopo and her friends are all searching for themselves, too. Take your time and discover what you can and can't do. See you next time!

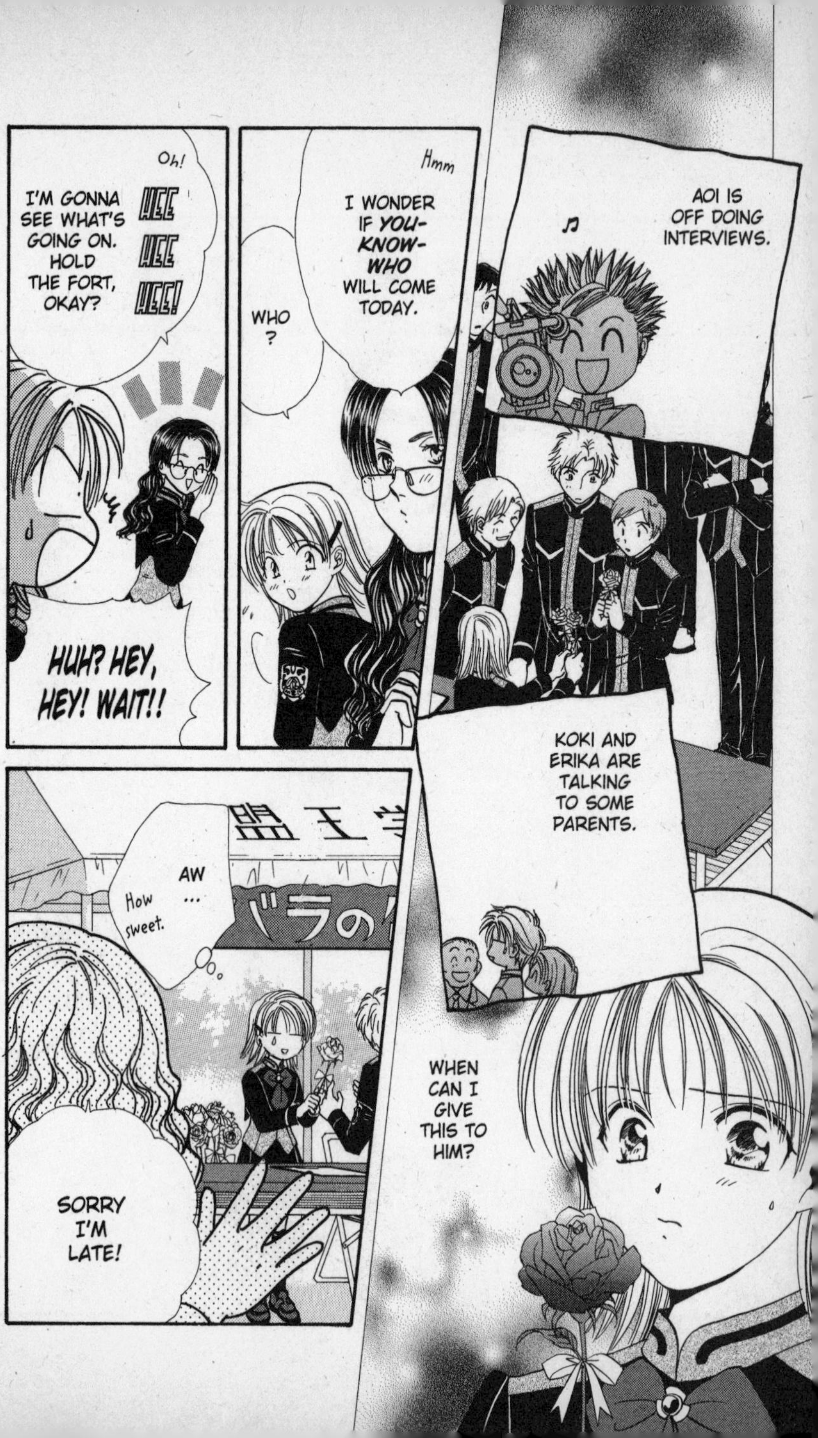
AOI IS OFF DOING INTERVIEWS.
♪
KOKI AND ERIKA ARE TALKING TO SOME PARENTS.
WHEN CAN I GIVE THIS TO HIM?
Hmm
I WONDER IF *YOU-KNOW-WHO* WILL COME TODAY.
WHO?
Oh!
I'M GONNA SEE WHAT'S GOING ON. HOLD THE FORT, OKAY?
HEE HEE HEE!
HUH? HEY, HEY! WAIT!!
AW...
How sweet.
SORRY I'M LATE!

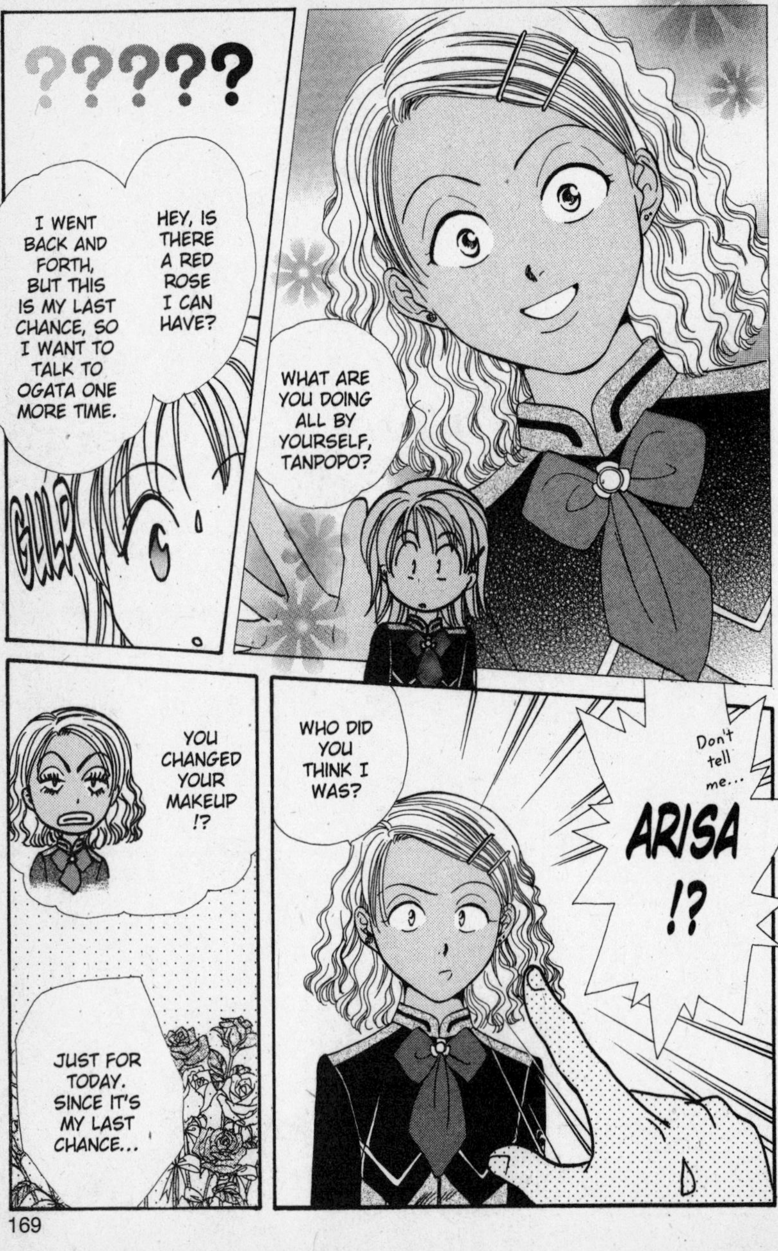
WHAT ARE YOU DOING ALL BY YOURSELF, TANPOPO?
?????
HEY, IS THERE A RED ROSE I CAN HAVE?
I WENT BACK AND FORTH, BUT THIS IS MY LAST CHANCE, SO I WANT TO TALK TO OGATA ONE MORE TIME.
GULP
Don't tell me...
ARISA !?
WHO DID YOU THINK I WAS?
YOU CHANGED YOUR MAKEUP !?
JUST FOR TODAY. SINCE IT'S MY LAST CHANCE...

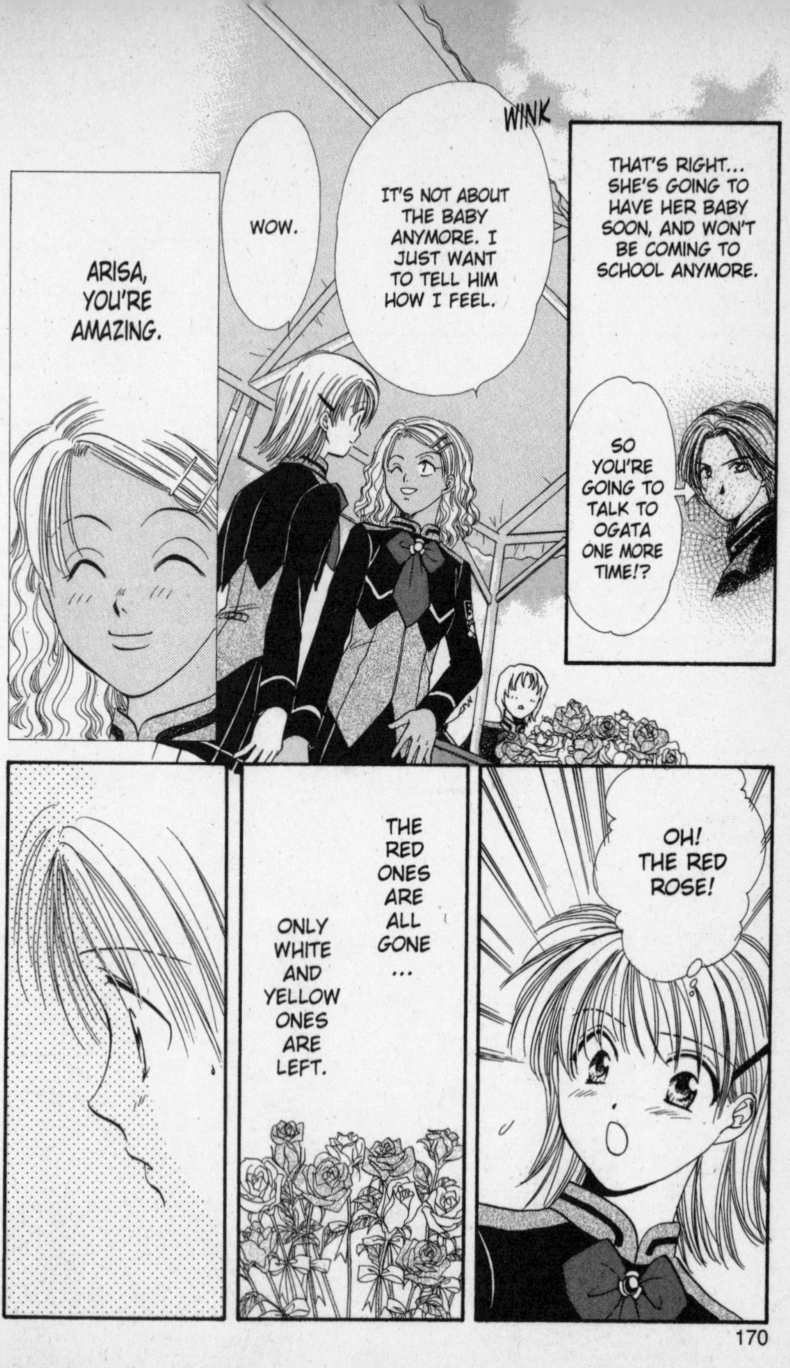
THAT'S RIGHT... SHE'S GOING TO HAVE HER BABY SOON, AND WON'T BE COMING TO SCHOOL ANYMORE.
SO YOU'RE GOING TO TALK TO OGATA ONE MORE TIME!?
WINK
IT'S NOT ABOUT THE BABY ANYMORE. I JUST WANT TO TELL HIM HOW I FEEL.
WOW.
ARISA, YOU'RE AMAZING.
OH! THE RED ROSE!
THE RED ONES ARE ALL GONE...
ONLY WHITE AND YELLOW ONES ARE LEFT.

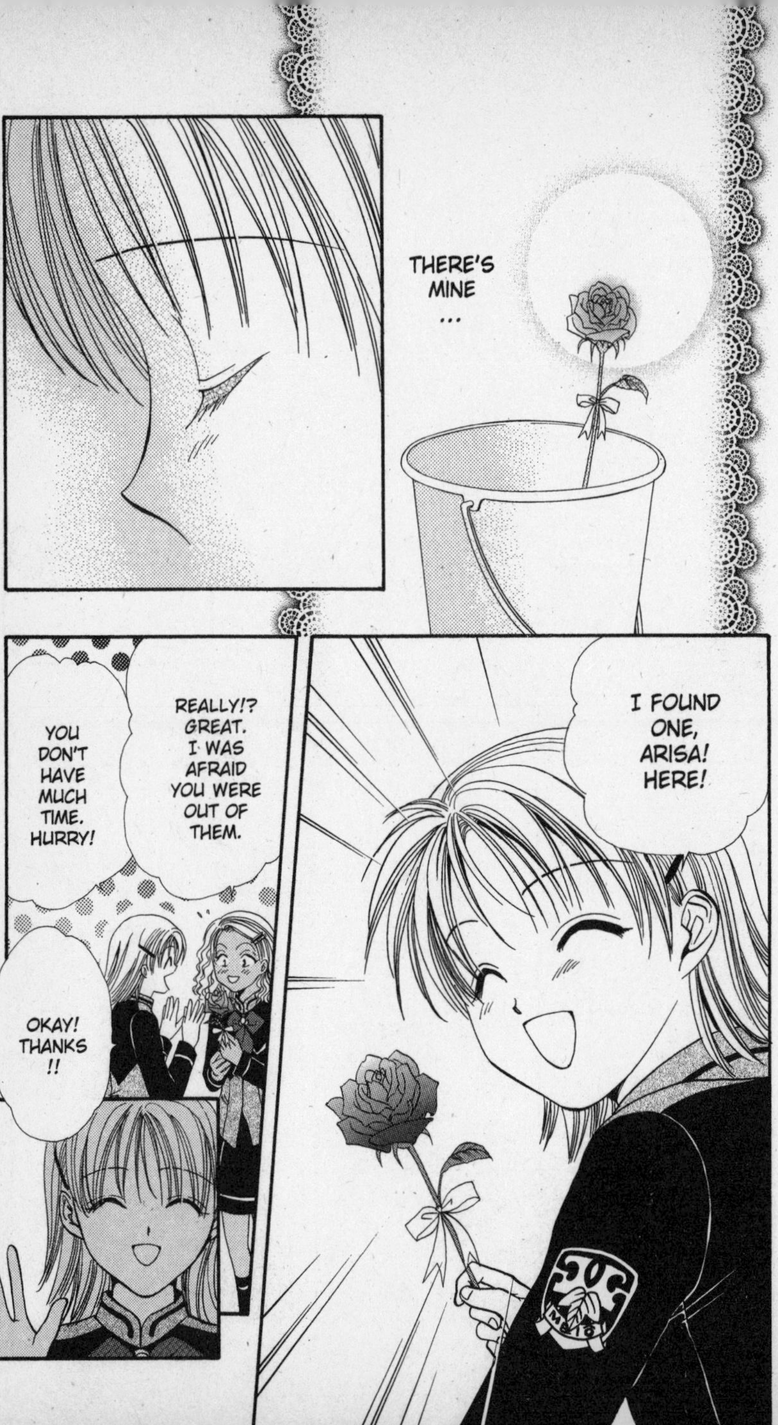
THERE'S MINE ...
I FOUND ONE, ARISA! HERE!
REALLY!? GREAT. I WAS AFRAID YOU WERE OUT OF THEM.
YOU DON'T HAVE MUCH TIME. HURRY!
OKAY! THANKS !!

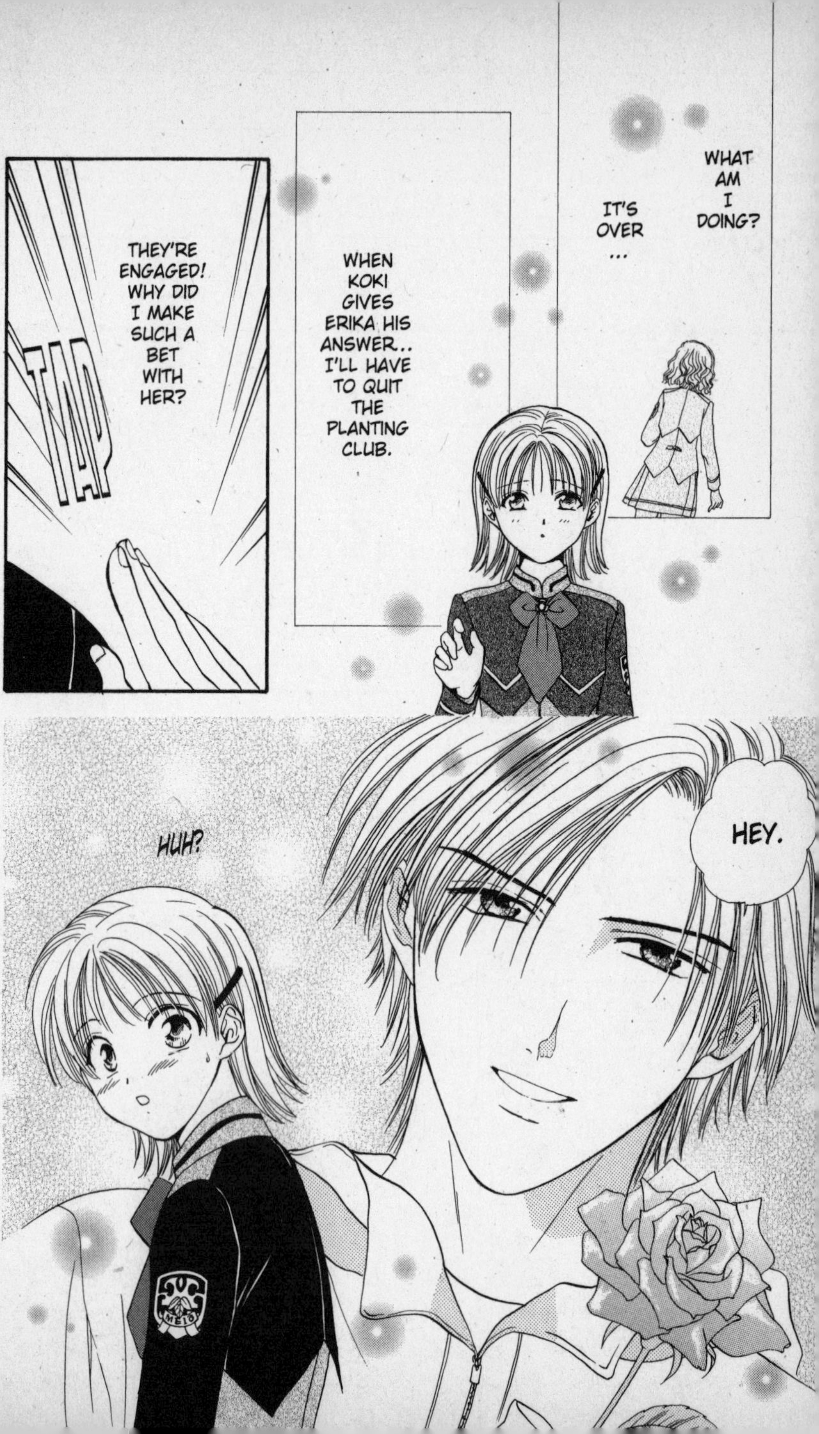
WHAT AM I DOING?
IT'S OVER ...
WHEN KOKI GIVES ERIKA HIS ANSWER.. I'LL HAVE TO QUIT THE PLANTING CLUB.
TAP
THEY'RE ENGAGED! WHY DID I MAKE SUCH A BET WITH HER?
HEY.
HUH?

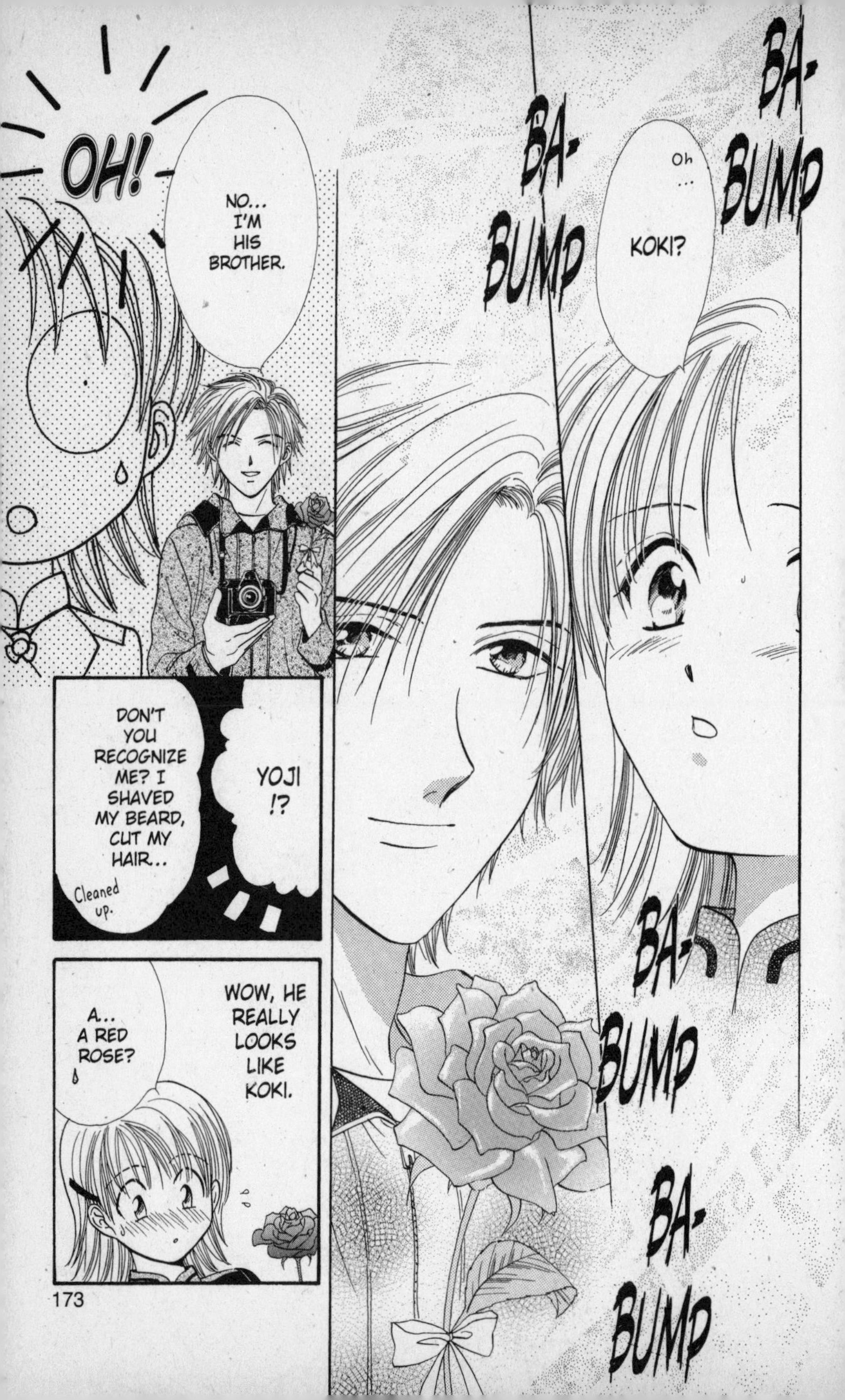

BA-BUMP
Oh... KOKI?
BA-BUMP
BA-BUMP
BA-BUMP
BA-BUMP
OH!
NO... I'M HIS BROTHER.
YOJI !?
DON'T YOU RECOGNIZE ME? I SHAVED MY BEARD, CUT MY HAIR...
Cleaned up.
WOW, HE REALLY LOOKS LIKE KOKI.
A... A RED ROSE?

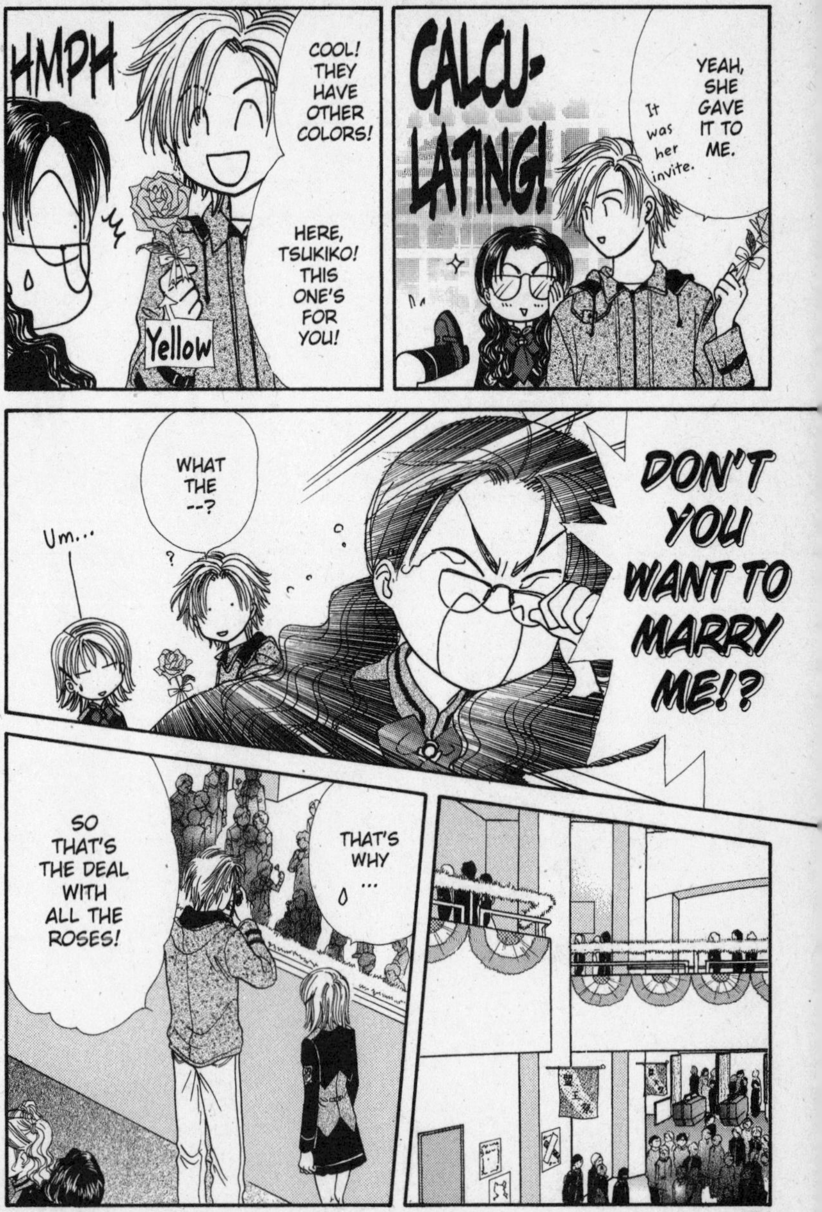
CALCU-LATING!
YEAH, SHE GAVE IT TO ME.
It was her invite.
COOL! THEY HAVE OTHER COLORS!
HMPH
HERE, TSUKIKO! THIS ONE'S FOR YOU!
Yellow
DON'T YOU WANT TO MARRY ME!?
WHAT THE --?
Um...
THAT'S WHY ...
SO THAT'S THE DEAL WITH ALL THE ROSES!

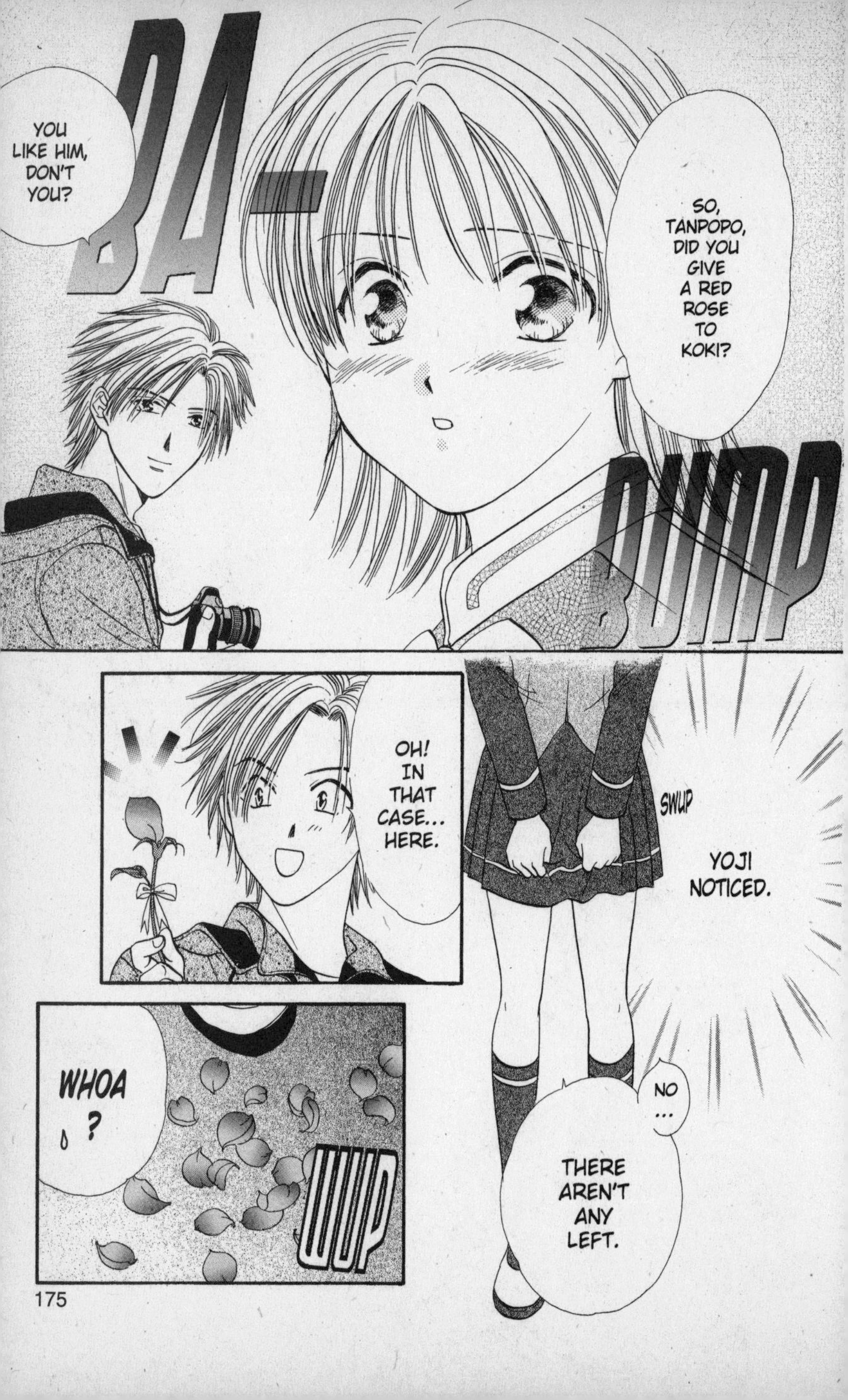
SO, TANPOPO, DID YOU GIVE A RED ROSE TO KOKI?
BA-BUMP
YOU LIKE HIM, DON'T YOU?
SWUP
YOJI NOTICED.
NO...
THERE AREN'T ANY LEFT.
OH! IN THAT CASE... HERE.
WHOA?
WUP

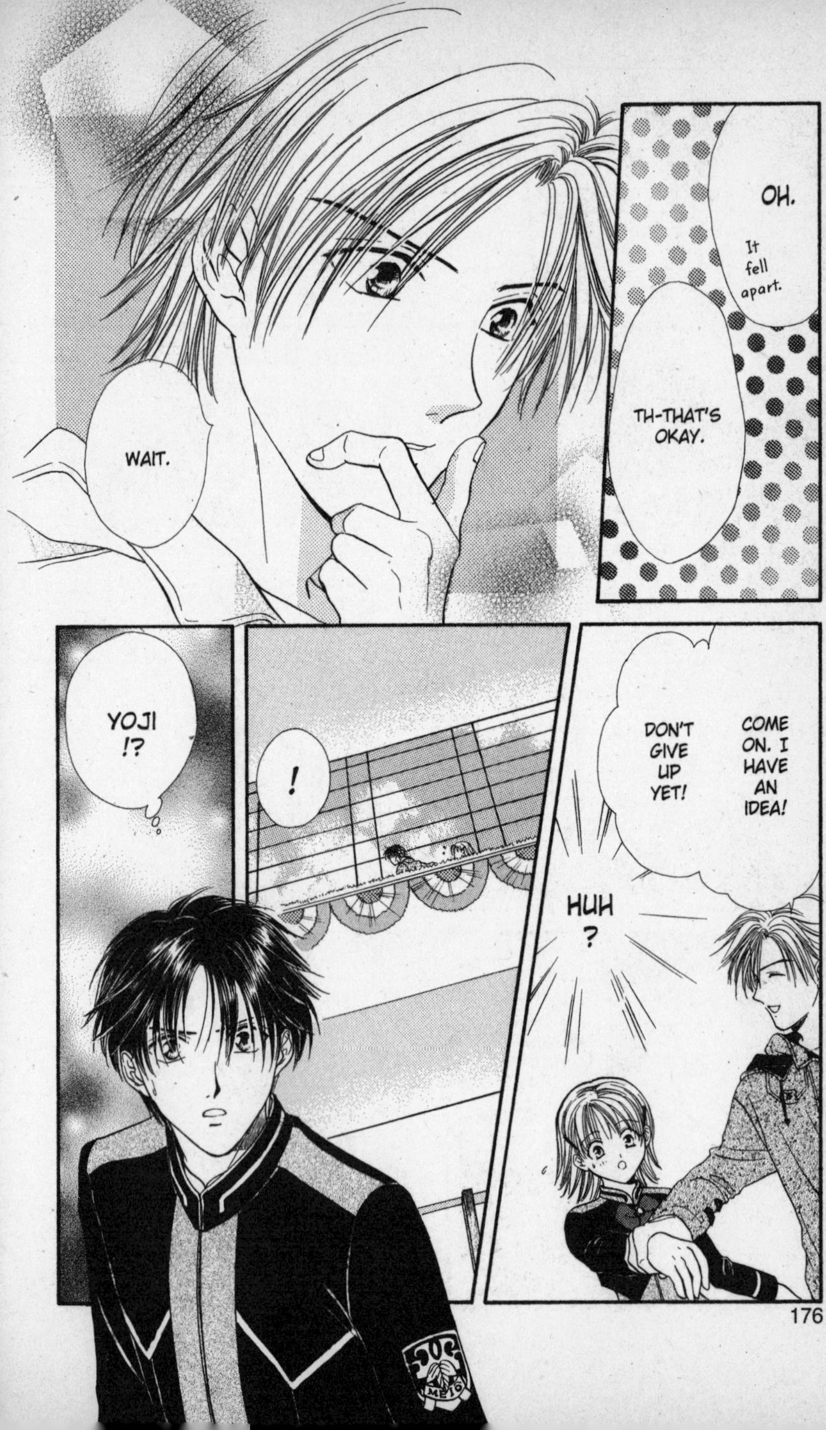
OH.
It fell apart.
TH-THAT'S OKAY.
WAIT.
COME ON. I HAVE AN IDEA!
DON'T GIVE UP YET!
HUH?
!
YOJI!?

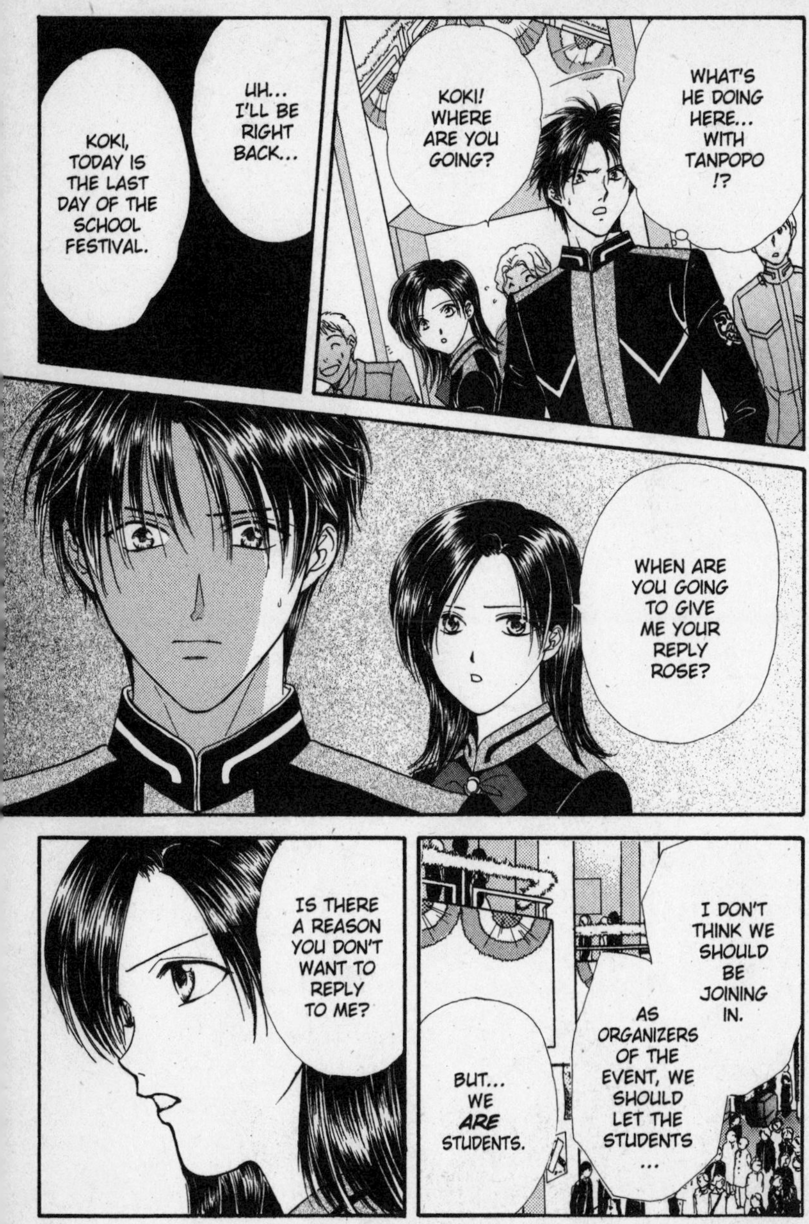
WHAT'S HE DOING HERE... WITH TANPOPO!?
KOKI! WHERE ARE YOU GOING?
UH... I'LL BE RIGHT BACK...
KOKI, TODAY IS THE LAST DAY OF THE SCHOOL FESTIVAL.
WHEN ARE YOU GOING TO GIVE ME YOUR REPLY ROSE?
I DON'T THINK WE SHOULD BE JOINING IN.
AS ORGANIZERS OF THE EVENT, WE SHOULD LET THE STUDENTS...
BUT... WE *ARE* STUDENTS.
IS THERE A REASON YOU DON'T WANT TO REPLY TO ME?

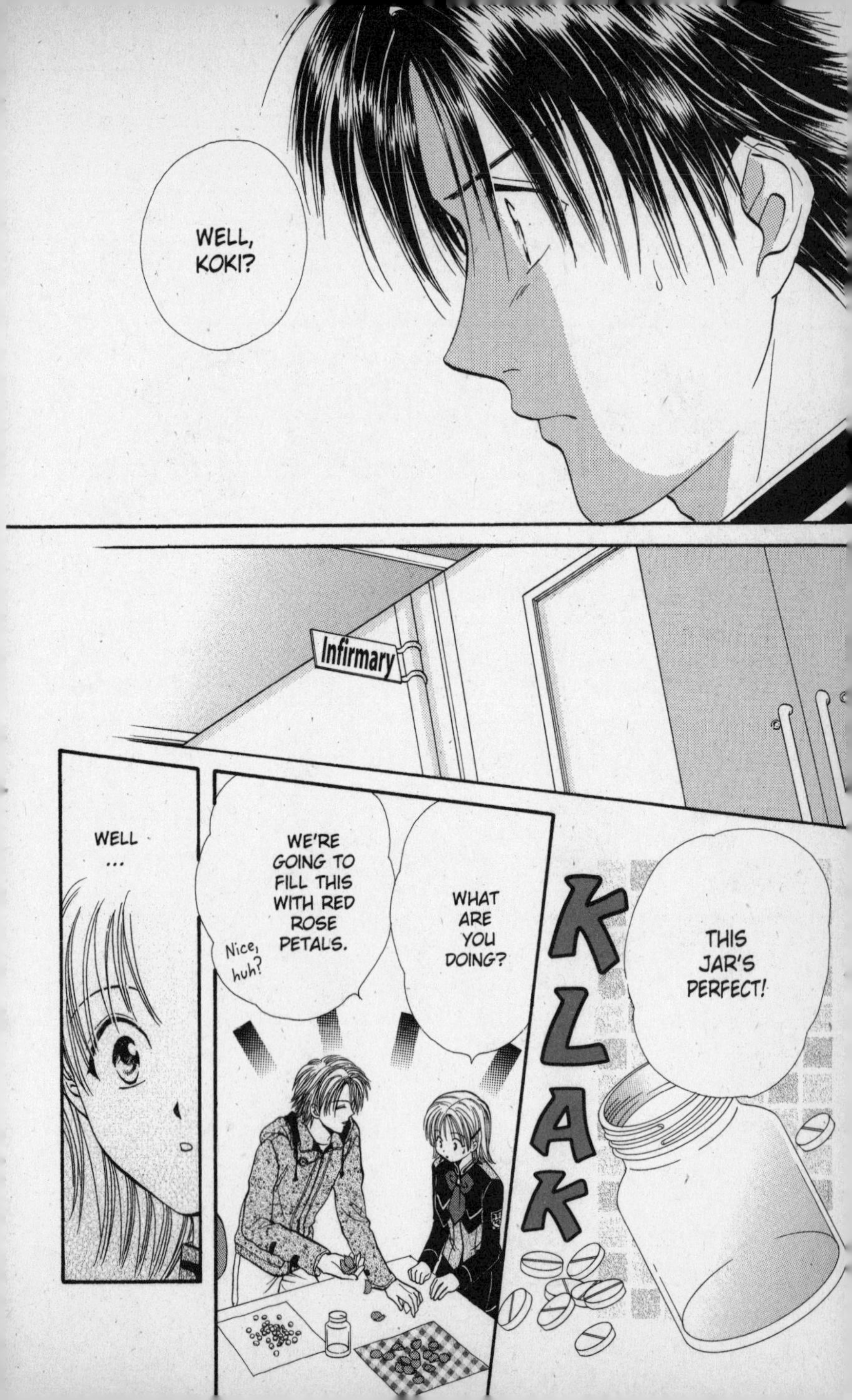
WELL, KOKI?
Infirmary
KLAK
THIS JAR'S PERFECT!
WHAT ARE YOU DOING?
WE'RE GOING TO FILL THIS WITH RED ROSE PETALS.
Nice, huh?
WELL ...

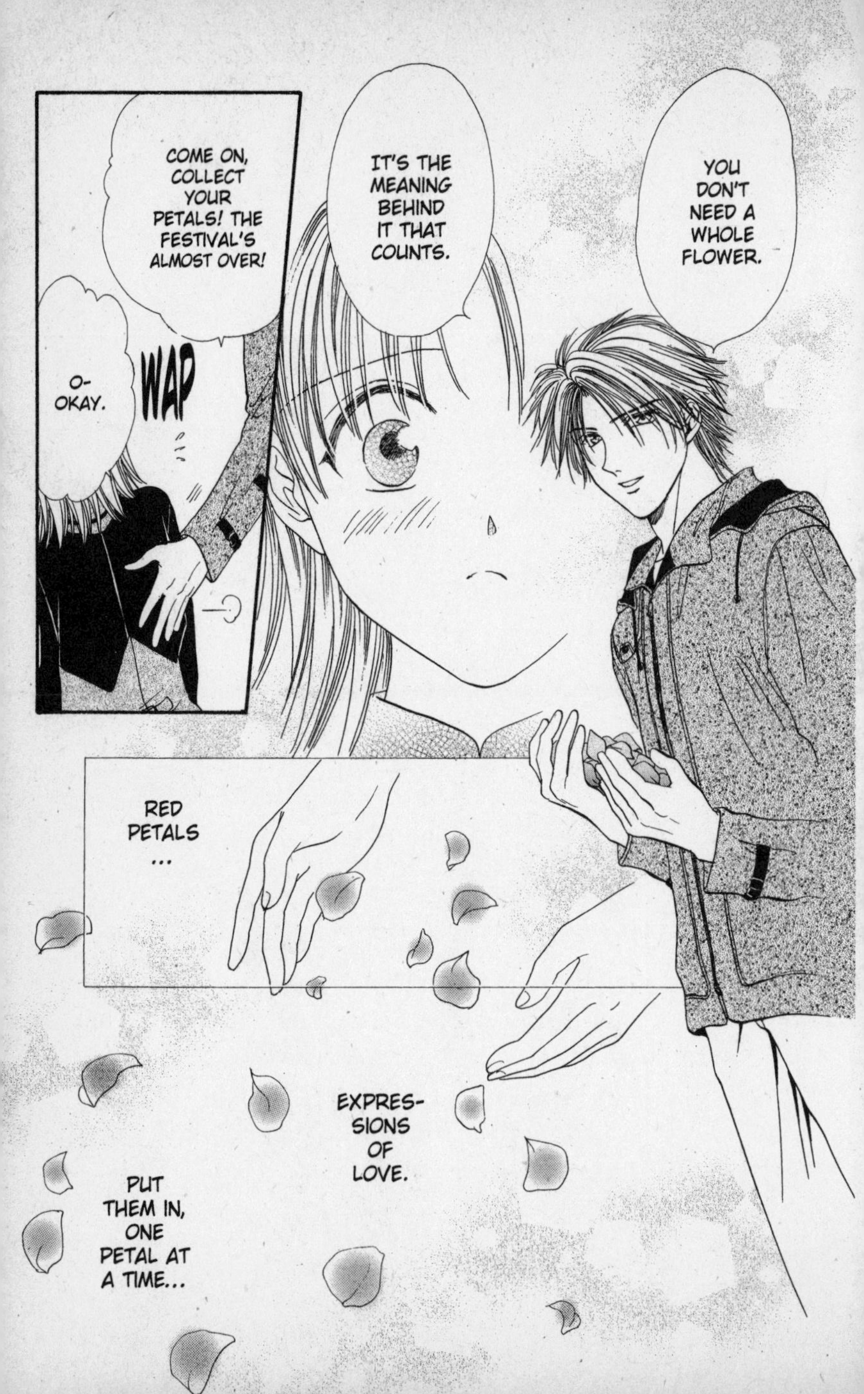
YOU DON'T NEED A WHOLE FLOWER.
IT'S THE MEANING BEHIND IT THAT COUNTS.
COME ON, COLLECT YOUR PETALS! THE FESTIVAL'S ALMOST OVER!
WAP
O-OKAY.
RED PETALS...
EXPRESSIONS OF LOVE.
PUT THEM IN, ONE PETAL AT A TIME...

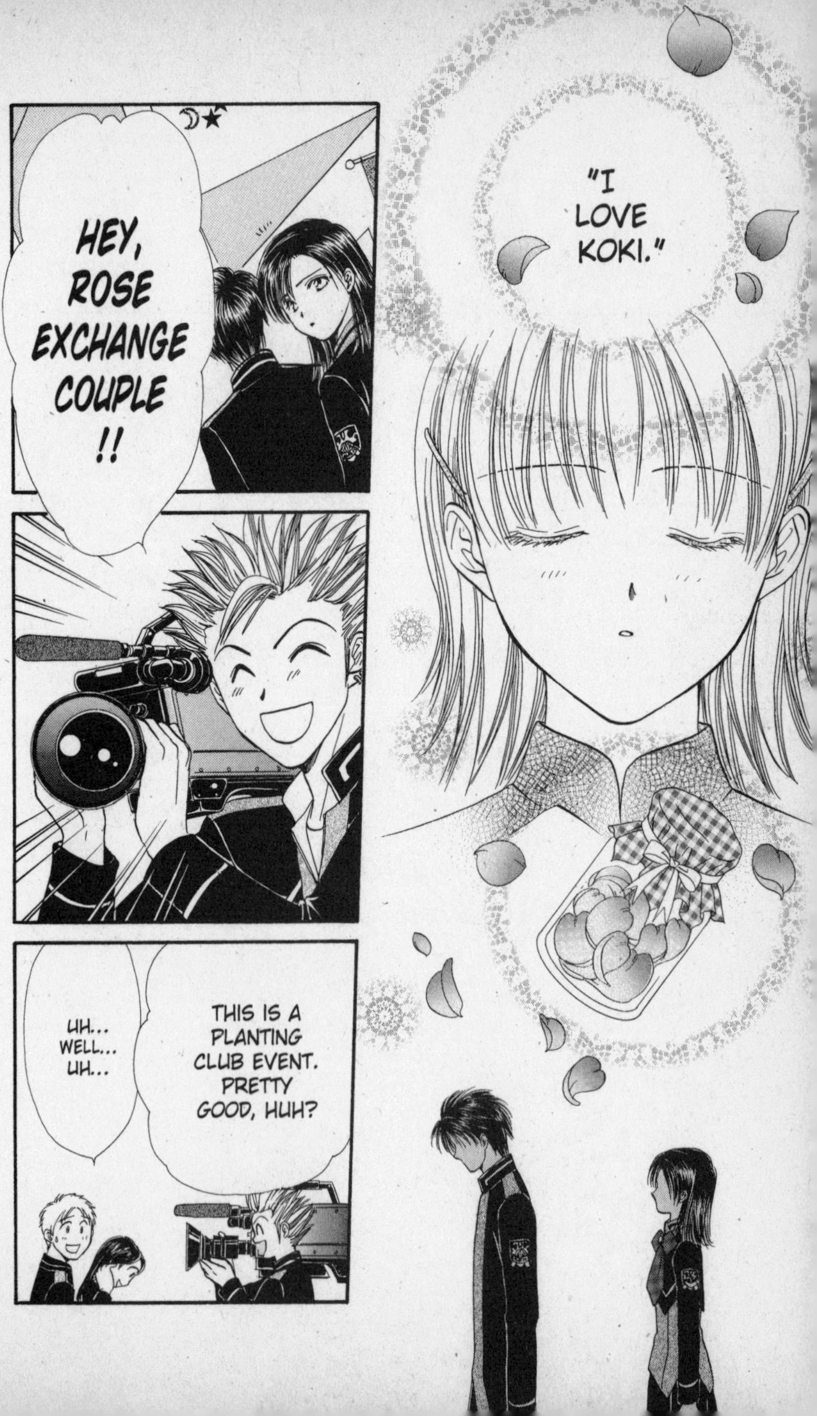
"I LOVE KOKI."
HEY, ROSE EXCHANGE COUPLE !!
THIS IS A PLANTING CLUB EVENT. PRETTY GOOD, HUH?
UH... WELL... UH...

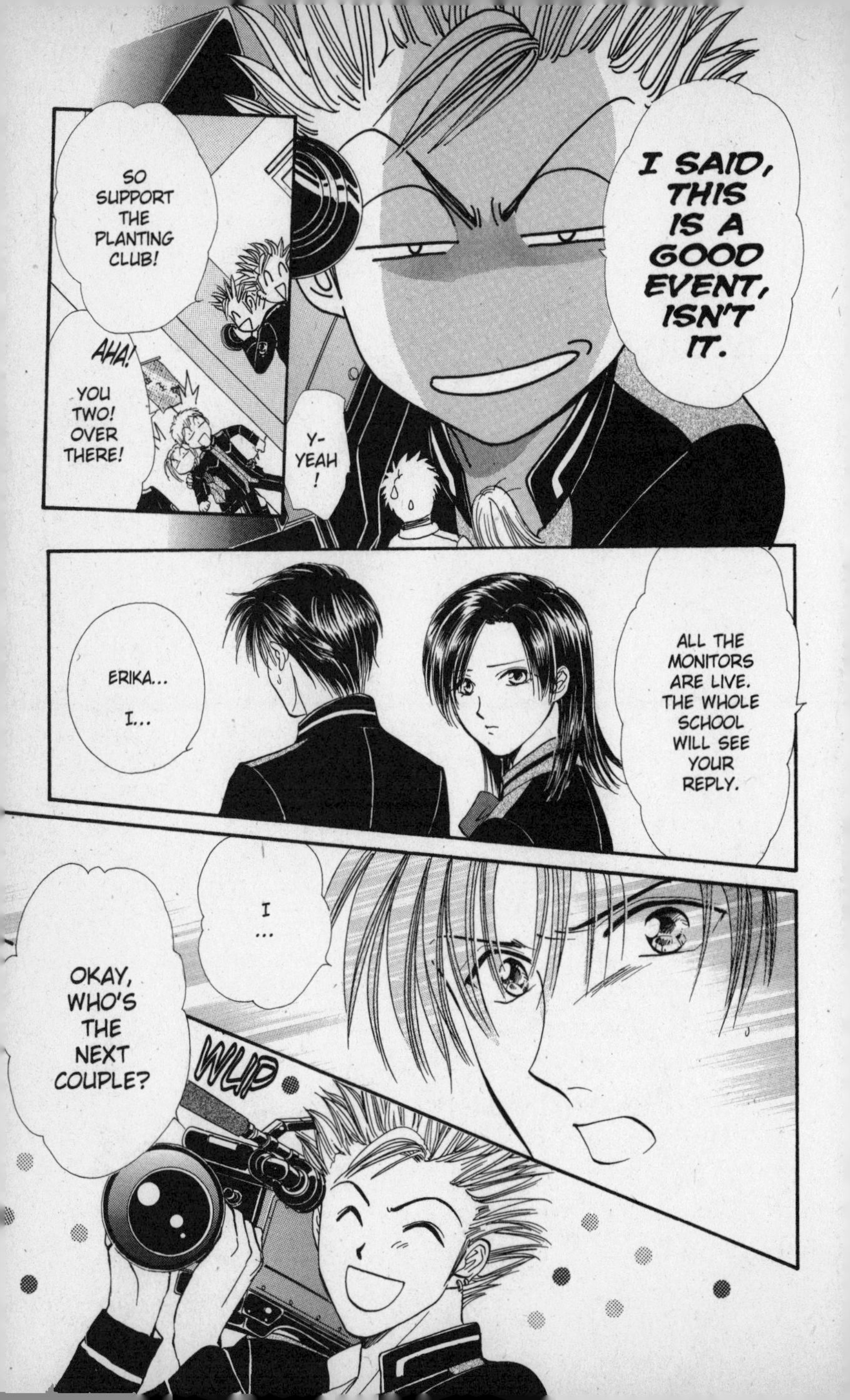
I SAID, THIS IS A GOOD EVENT, ISN'T IT.
Y-YEAH!
SO SUPPORT THE PLANTING CLUB!
AHA!
YOU TWO! OVER THERE!
ALL THE MONITORS ARE LIVE. THE WHOLE SCHOOL WILL SEE YOUR REPLY.
ERIKA... I...
I ...
WUP
OKAY, WHO'S THE NEXT COUPLE?

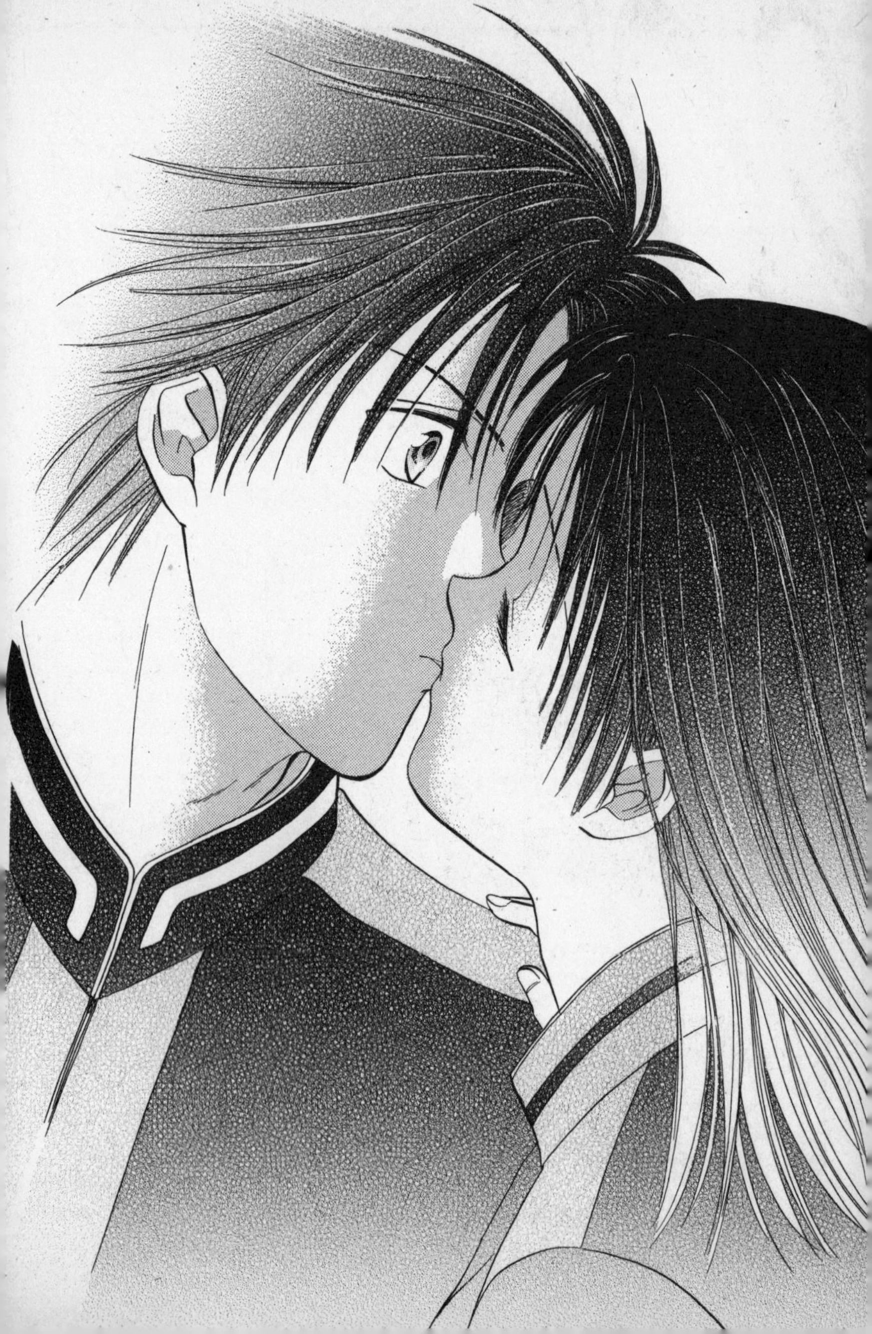

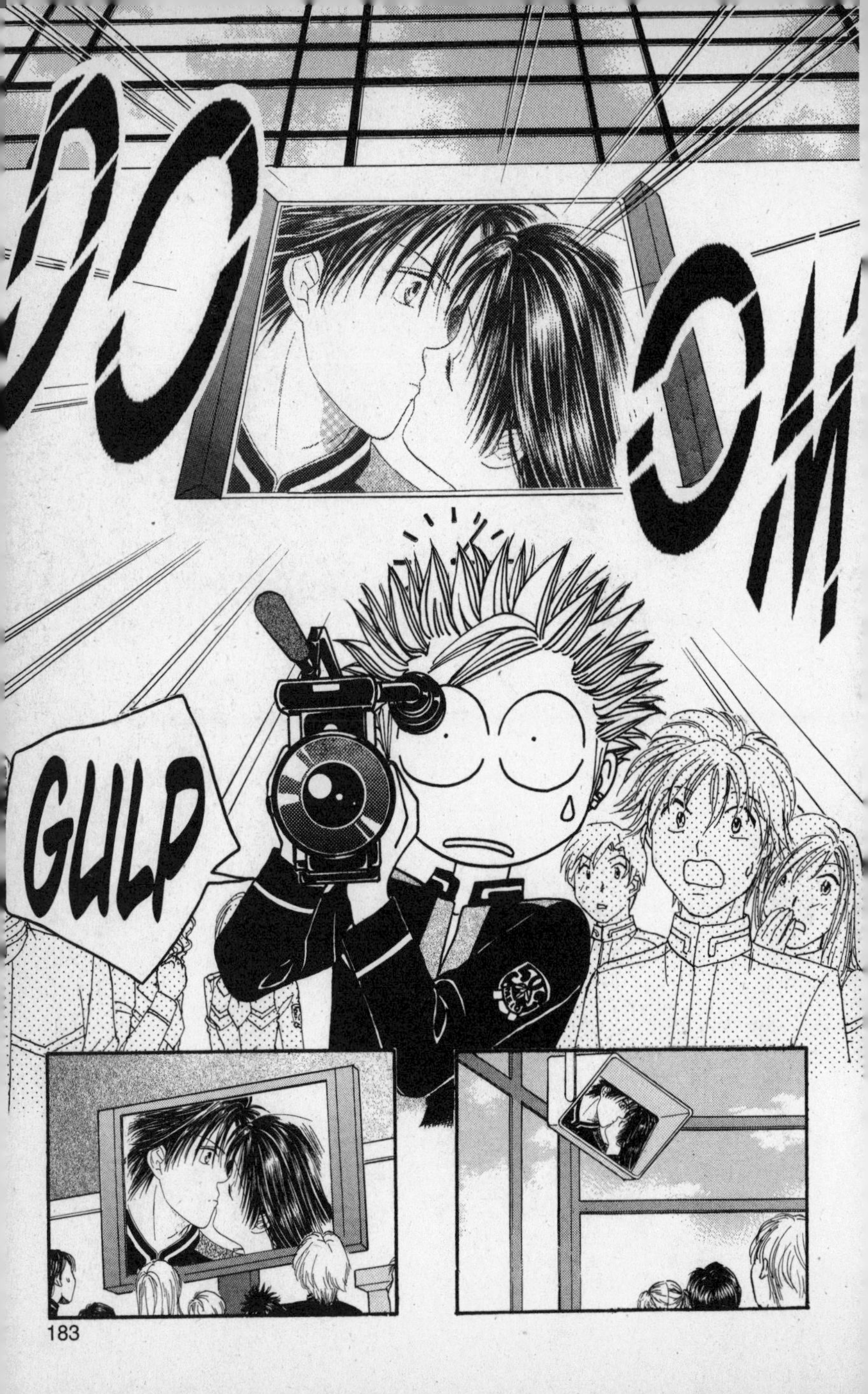
DOOM!!
GULP

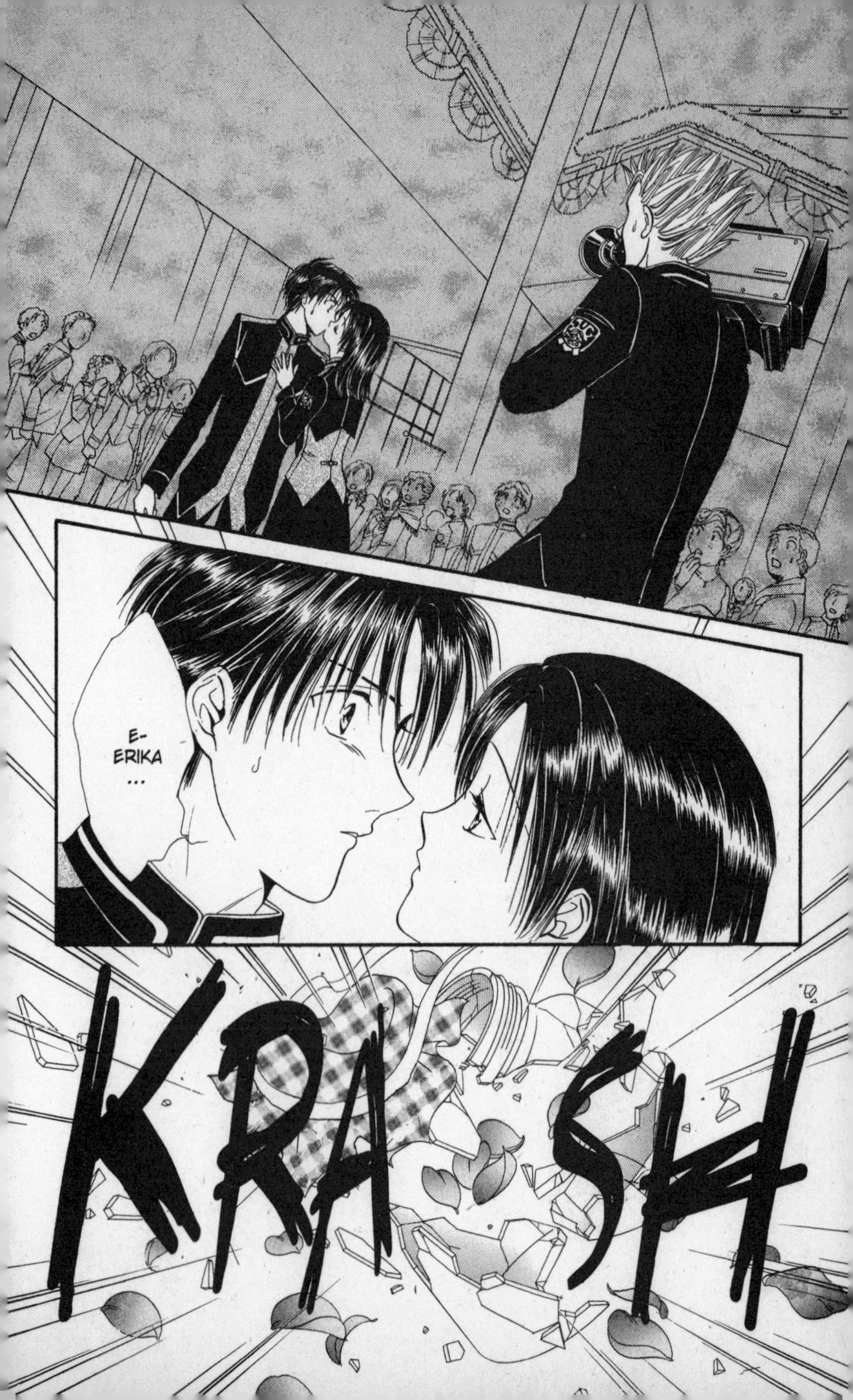
E-ERIKA...
KRASH

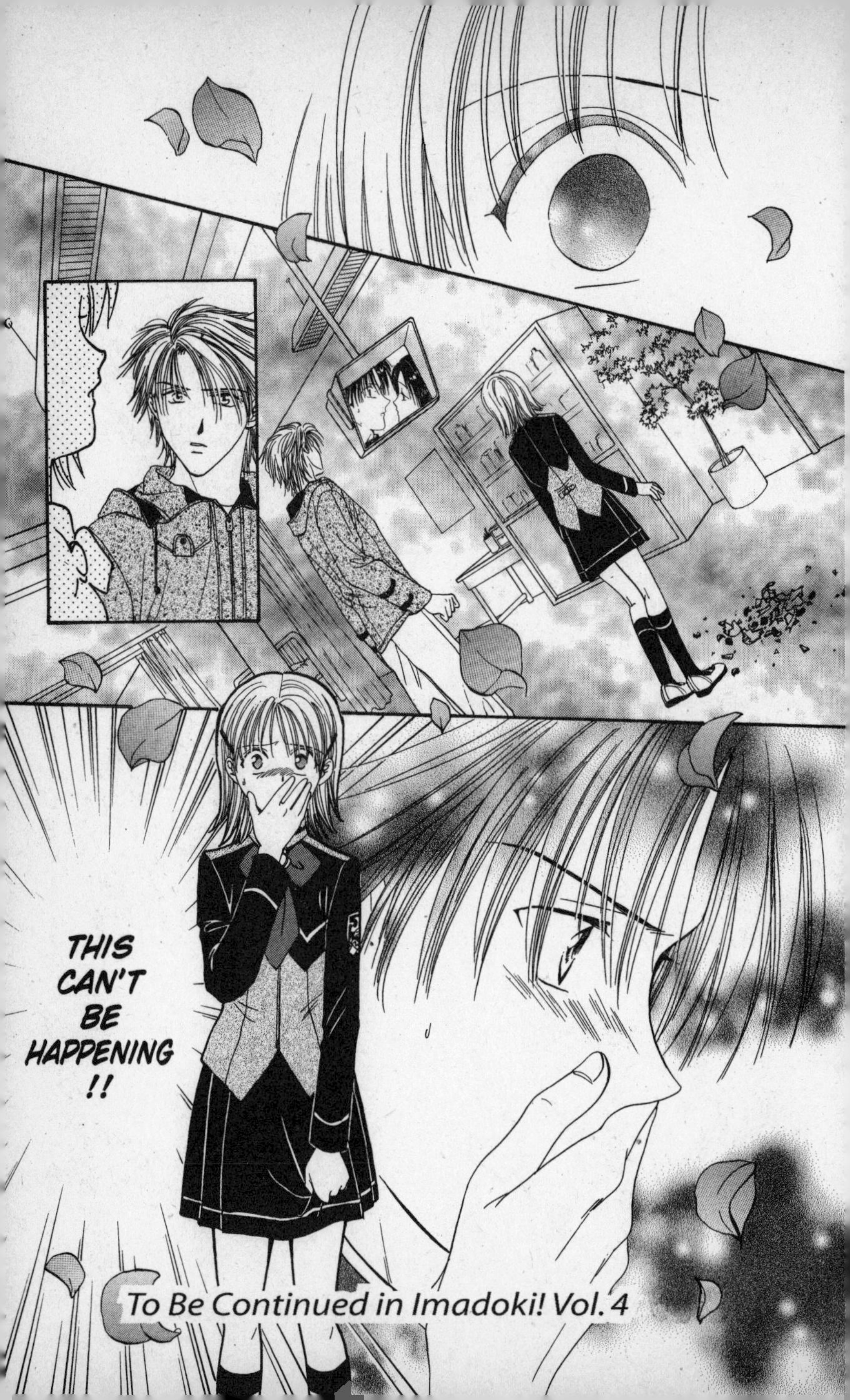
THIS CAN'T BE HAPPENING !!
To Be Continued in Imadoki! Vol. 4

EDITOR'S RECOMMENDATIONS

If you enjoyed this volume of  then here's some more manga you might be interested in.

© 1997 Yuu
Watase/Shogakukan, Inc.

Ceres: Celestial Legend

From the acclaimed author of *Imadoki!* and *Fushigi Yûgi* comes this darkly romantic story of love, betrayal and revenge. On her 16th birthday, Aya's world is turned upside-down after her family tries to kill her to protect a terrifying secret. Her struggle to survive pits her against nearly everyone she loves, including her beloved twin brother Aki.

© 1996 SAITO
CHIHO/IKUHARA KUNIHIKO &
BE-PAPAS/Shogakukan, Inc.

Revolutionary Girl Utena

As a little girl, Utena was once saved by a beautiful prince and she's dreamed of finding him ever since. Now all grown up, she's vowed to follow him, even if it means becoming a prince just like him! Drawn to the elite Ohtori Private Academy, Utena is forced to duel for the hand of the mysterious Rose Bride in her search for the true identity of her elusive savior.

© 2001 Miki
Aihara/Shogakukan, Inc.

Hot Gimmick

Sixteen-year-old Hatsumi Narita lives with her family in an apartment complex ruled over by the wealthy and much-feared Mrs. Tachibana. When the Tachibanas' domineering son, Ryoki, stumbles onto a Narita family secret, he agrees to keep it to himself—but only if Hatsumi becomes his "slave"!! Will her childhood crush, Azusa, be able to save her from Ryoki's creepy clutches?

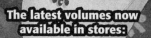

COMPLETE OUR SURVEY AND LET
US KNOW WHAT YOU THINK!

☐ Please do NOT send me information about VIZ products, news and events, special offers, or other information.

☐ Please do NOT send me information from VIZ's trusted business partners.

Name: _____

Address: _____

City: _____ **State:** _____ **Zip:** _____

E-mail: _____

☐ Male ☐ Female **Date of Birth** (mm/dd/yyyy): ___/___/_____ (Under 13? Parental consent required)

What race/ethnicity do you consider yourself? (please check one)

☐ Asian/Pacific Islander ☐ Black/African American ☐ Hispanic/Latino

☐ Native American/Alaskan Native ☐ White/Caucasian ☐ Other: _____

What VIZ product did you purchase? (check all that apply and indicate title purchased)

☐ DVD/VHS _____

☐ Graphic Novel _____

☐ Magazines _____

☐ Merchandise _____

Reason for purchase: (check all that apply)

☐ Special offer ☐ Favorite title ☐ Gift

☐ Recommendation ☐ Other _____

Where did you make your purchase? (please check one)

☐ Comic store ☐ Bookstore ☐ Mass/Grocery Store

☐ Newsstand ☐ Video/Video Game Store ☐ Other: _____

☐ Online (site: _____)

What other VIZ properties have you purchased/own? _____

_____

How many anime and/or manga titles have you purchased in the last year? How many were VIZ titles? **(please check one from each column)**

ANIME	MANGA	VIZ
☐ None	☐ None	☐ None
☐ 1-4	☐ 1-4	☐ 1-4
☐ 5-10	☐ 5-10	☐ 5-10
☐ 11+	☐ 11+	☐ 11+

I find the pricing of VIZ products to be: **(please check one)**

☐ Cheap ☐ Reasonable ☐ Expensive

What genre of manga and anime would you like to see from VIZ? **(please check two)**

☐ Adventure ☐ Comic Strip ☐ Science Fiction ☐ Fighting

☐ Horror ☐ Romance ☐ Fantasy ☐ Sports

What do you think of VIZ's new look?

☐ Love It ☐ It's OK ☐ Hate It ☐ Didn't Notice ☐ No Opinion

Which do you prefer? **(please check one)**

☐ Reading right-to-left

☐ Reading left-to-right

Which do you prefer? **(please check one)**

☐ Sound effects in English

☐ Sound effects in Japanese with English captions

☐ Sound effects in Japanese only with a glossary at the back

THANK YOU! Please send the completed form to:

VIZ Survey
42 Catharine St.
Poughkeepsie, NY 12601

All information provided will be used for internal purposes only. We promise not to sell or otherwise divulge your information.

♥ Tanpopo Yamazaki, a freshman at Meio High School. Her goal is to enjoy her school life.

♥ Koki Kugyo, also a freshman at Meio. Koki comes from a very wealthy family.

♥ Aoi Kyogoku, computer geek, classmate of Tanpopo and Koki.

♥ Tsukiko Saionji, vixen. Aspires to be Mrs. Koki Kugyo.

The Story So Far:

Tanpopo is a new student at the elite Meio High School. From rural Hokkaido, she feels hopelessly out of place among the school's snooty students, but that doesn't dampen her cheerful nature. The first boy she meets at her new school, Koki Kugyo, seems nice at first, then mean to her, but Tanpopo's personality eventually wins him over. Even Tsukiko Saionji, Tanpopo's tormentor, and Aoi Kyogoku, who despises the power of Koki's family, soon become her close friends. On a visit to Koki's house, Tanpopo learns that Koki's older brother disappeared two years before, and that his former fiancée, Erika Yanahara, is now engaged to Koki and living with him. At school, Tanpopo and Koki petition the student council to approve their Planting Club. Council chairman Ogata is willing to do so only if Tanpopo can get fellow student Arisa Uchimura to stop chasing after him. Tanpopo quickly agrees and goes looking for Arisa, which leads to a dangerous encounter at Arisa's favorite club. When Koki comes to her rescue, Tanpopo realizes that her feelings for him go beyond friendship!